*White Philanthropy*

# WHITE
# PHILANTHROPY

## Carnegie Corporation's
## *An American Dilemma*
## and the Making of a
## White World Order

MARIBEL MOREY

The University of North Carolina Press  *Chapel Hill*

*This book was published with the assistance of the*
*Authors Fund of the University of North Carolina Press.*

Set in Arno Pro by Westchester Publishing Services
Manufactured in the United States of America

The University of North Carolina Press has been a member of the
Green Press Initiative since 2003.

Library of Congress Cataloging-in-Publication Data
Names: Morey, Maribel, author.
Title: White philanthropy : Carnegie Corporation's An American dilemma
    and the making of a white world order / Maribel Morey.
Description: Chapel Hill : University of North Carolina Press, [2021] |
    Includes bibliographical references and index.
Identifiers: LCCN 2021003503 | ISBN 9781469664736 (cloth) |
    ISBN 9781469664743 (paperback) | ISBN 9781469664750 (ebook)
Subjects: LCSH: Keppel, Frederick P. (Frederick Paul), 1875–1943. |
    Myrdal, Gunnar, 1898–1987. American dilemma. | Carnegie Corporation of New York. |
    White nationalism—United States—History—20th century. | White nationalism—
    Africa—History—20th century. | African Americans—Social conditions—20th century. |
    Africans—Social conditions—20th century. | Imperialism—History—20th century. |
    United States—Race relations—Political aspects.
Classification: LCC E184.A1 M667 2021 | DDC 305.800973/0904—dc23
    LC record available at https://lccn.loc.gov/2021003503

*This book is dedicated to the memory of
W. E. B. Du Bois (1868–1963)
and to the hope that future generations,
including my daughter, Frankie,
will continue the fight for a world
free of domination.*

Although the Negro problem is a moral issue both to Negroes and to whites in America, we shall in this book have to give *primary* attention to what goes on in the minds of white Americans. . . . It is thus the white majority group that naturally determines the Negro's "place."

Americans also recognize that America has to take world leadership. The coming difficult decades will be America's turn in the endless sequence of main actors on the world stage. America then will have the major responsibility for the manner in which humanity approaches the long era during which the white peoples will have to adjust to shrinkage while the colored are bound to expand in numbers, in level of industrial civilization and in political power. For perhaps several decades, the whites will still hold the lead, and America will be the most powerful white nation.

—Gunnar Myrdal, *An American Dilemma: The Negro Problem and Modern Democracy* (New York: Harper & Brothers, 1944), xlvii, 1019.

# Contents

# Introduction

Gunnar Myrdal's *An American Dilemma: The Negro Problem and Modern Democracy* (1944) is, according to U.S. sociologist Aldon D. Morris, "the most famous and influential study of race every produced."[1] Indeed, as fellow U.S. sociologist Stephen Steinberg points out, "Monumental is the modifier most commonly attached to Gunnar Myrdal's study, *An American Dilemma*."[2] Supporting the significance of Myrdal's book, political scientist Naomi Murakawa writes that it has been "the touchstone book of racial politics." Historian Daryl Michael Scott concurs that *An American Dilemma* was "the era's most important study of black life" in the United States.[3]

Historian Thomas J. Sugrue has similarly noted the continued influence of *An American Dilemma* in U.S. life. For example, referring to former president Barack Obama's Martin Luther King Day speech in 2008, Sugrue comments that "Obama's high-minded words echo those of Swedish economist Gunnar Myrdal, whose 1944 book *An American Dilemma* still defines the basic dynamics of racial politics in America."[4]

Commissioned and financed by Carnegie Corporation of New York, a philanthropic organization founded by Gilded Age tycoon Andrew Carnegie in 1911, *An American Dilemma* totals over 1,500 pages across two volumes. It outlines the many facets of white Americans' discrimination against Black Americans in employment, housing, voting, policing, and court practices, and more publicly visible forms of anti-Black violence and intimidation such as lynchings.

Throughout the two volumes of *An American Dilemma*, Gunnar Myrdal argues that anti-Black discriminatory policies and behavior run counter to Americans' national egalitarian ideals, which he refers to as the "American Creed."[5] The author subsequently encourages his white American readers to meet such ideals. Assuming that white Americans' non-discriminatory treatment of Black Americans meant opening up the way for Black Americans to achieve "white levels" in all aspects of life in the United States—from "land, credit, jobs" and treatment "in law courts, by the police, and by other public services" to the "use of public facilities such as schools, churches, and means of conveyance," "personal relations," and the legal right to marry and have "sexual intercourse" with white people—Myrdal stresses that white Americans could make use of an increasingly strong and centralized national government in the United States to expedite Black Americans' assimilation into white U.S. life; prioritizing first the forms of anti-Black public policies to which white Americans were least committed.[6] He argues that doing so will help white Americans prove to themselves and to the world that they are a particularly egalitarian people.[7] Myrdal furthermore encourages Black Americans to accept assimilation as equality, underscoring that "it is to the advantage of American Negroes as individuals and as a group to become assimilated into American culture, to acquire the traits held in esteem by the dominant white Americans."[8]

Gunnar Myrdal's analysis of anti-Black discrimination as a moral problem in the hearts and minds of white Americans, to be solved by urging these dominant white Americans to mobilize the national government to assimilate Black Americans into dominant white U.S. life, has resonated with many Americans. Over sixty-five glowing reviews of the work were published in U.S. newspapers and magazines when it appeared in 1944. In that first year, the lengthy study went through four editions. Shorter summaries were also published, reviewed in newspapers, and sold to the U.S. public.[9] In 1944, the *Amsterdam Star-News* awarded *An American Dilemma* the runner-up book of the year, and the *Virginian Pilot* determined that it was the best study of U.S. life. The following year, the *Saturday Review of Literature* gave it the Anisfield-Wolf Award for the best book on "race relations."[10] The *New York Post* described Myrdal's study as "outstanding" and "the most illuminating study on the Negro in this country that has ever been made."[11]

During the summer of 1948, a group of Americans coming together as the "Committee of 100" coordinated a dinner in New York City to honor Myrdal, "as an expression of the gratitude of Americans for the great contribution he has made toward the solution of the tragic racial division in our land through his brilliant study 'An American Dilemma.'"[12] The Committee intended the dinner to serve as a fundraising event for the NAACP Legal Defense and Educational Fund; urging fellow "friends and admirers of Dr. Myrdal" attending the dinner "to provide a gift" to the organization.[13] Former first lady Eleanor Roosevelt, who had agreed to cooperate with Myrdal's team of researchers years earlier, was a speaker at the event. She was joined by other contributors to Myrdal's study, NAACP executive secretary Walter White, as well as Roy Wilkins, who had replaced W. E. B. Du Bois as editor of the NAACP's official journal *The Crisis*.

Beyond the general U.S. public, *An American Dilemma* both reflected and penetrated social scientific scholarship on race in the United States.[14] Historian Lee D. Baker writes, for example, that "*An American Dilemma* effectively reshaped the discussion of race and culture in the United States for the next fifteen years. It became a guide for an array of social policies, a standard text in university curricula, and a dominant reference in nearly every forum on race relations."[15]

Likewise, historian Alice O'Connor notes that in the 1940s U.S. social scientists "crystallized the elements of an emerging liberal orthodoxy on race," an orthodoxy "drawn together in a sweeping synthesis in Gunnar Myrdal's *An American Dilemma* (1944)."[16] "This new synthesis," she explains, "defined 'the race problem' within a black/white paradigm, traced the roots of racial inequality to a wide range of social and cultural disadvantages rooted in white prejudice, and embraced integration and racial assimilation as desirable social goals."[17]

Moving beyond the project's intellectual context to its future impact in the social sciences, historian Leah Gordon argues that *An American Dilemma* "exemplified and aided a shift in research on the race issue in much social scientific, as well as popular and social policy, discourse."[18] For example, Gordon argues that Myrdal's study encouraged U.S. social scientists during the next two decades to focus on the white psyche, or rather, on white prejudice when analyzing racial injustice in the United States.[19]

In the 1940s and well into the 1960s, *An American Dilemma* dominated discussions of Black Americans in the United States not only among social scientists but also among policymakers. For this latter group, Myrdal's study helped frame and justify the U.S. federal government's reengagement in shaping a national policy program on Black Americans, a role from which the federal government generally had shied away since the end of the Reconstruction Era in the 1870s. In 1946, for example, U.S. president Harry S. Truman convened by executive order a committee "to make recommendations with respect to adoption or establishment by legislation or otherwise of more adequate means and procedures for protection of civil rights of the people of the United States."[20] Written most immediately in response to white Americans' fatal violence against Black veterans returning from service during the Second World War, historian Kenneth Mack writes that the report produced by Truman's Committee on Civil Rights "was guided . . . by a Myrdalian framework that by now had become second nature to its members."[21] In its report, the president's committee not only explained how white Americans' discrimination against Black Americans was an affront to U.S. ideals, but also emphasized the central role that the federal government could play in bringing about more equitable treatment for Black Americans in various aspects of U.S. life. Much like Myrdal, the committee members listed the numerous ways that

Black Americans experienced white Americans' unequal and discriminatory treatment. In 1954, the Supreme Court also made explicit mention of *An American Dilemma* in its school desegregation case, *Brown v. Board of Education.* Years before, Supreme Court Justice Felix Frankfurter had told a U.S. journalist that "Myrdal's book was 'indispensable' for understanding the race problem."[22]

And yet, even as *An American Dilemma* was celebrated by many Americans, it also had its critics. Predictably, vocal proponents of white supremacy and Black subordination balked at Gunnar Myrdal's suggestion that white Americans should expedite Black Americans' assimilation into white U.S. life. In his book *Take Your Choice: Separation or Mongrelization* (1947), for example, Mississippi senator Theodore G. Bilbo argued: "Our democracy, our Nation, our people are in danger of destruction by the kind of doctrine presented by Dr. Myrdal. Such proposed solution of the race problem as would permit amalgamation of the races would bring with it no hope of the future—only utter desolation—for a Nation of mongrels."[23]

Indeed, after the Supreme Court cited *An American Dilemma* in *Brown v. Board of Education,* such criticisms of Myrdal's book grew louder. Thus, for example, another Mississippi senator, James Eastland, denounced both Carnegie Corporation and Gunnar Myrdal as communist fellow travelers, arguing that "Myrdal shows that his book was the work of several so-called social experts furnished him by the Carnegie Foundation [sic], of Alger Hiss fame."[24] Against the backdrop of the Cold War, describing Myrdal and Carnegie Corporation in the same breath as Alger Hiss, a former government official who had been embroiled in allegations of Soviet espionage, in addition to having served as president of the Carnegie Endowment for International Peace, was tantamount to accusing *An American Dilemma*'s author and funder of being un-American, and thus, uninvited influences on U.S. life.

But it was not simply adamant and vocal advocates of white supremacy who found fault with *An American Dilemma.* There were also those who were more staunch foes of white supremacy than Gunnar Myrdal and who viewed the book as further justifying white rule in the United States. In this vein, for example, U.S. writer Ralph Ellison expressed his ambiguity about *An American Dilemma.* In a review he wrote in 1944, though left unpublished for two decades, Ellison explained that "the Negro must, while joining in the chorus of 'Yeas' which the book deservedly evoked, utter a lusty and simultaneous 'Nay.'"[25] This is because while the study confirmed Black Americans' humanity to white Americans and explained how Black subjugation was a result of anti-Black discrimination (rather than as many white people had liked to believe, any biological inferiority among Black people), Ellison reasoned that Myrdal reconfirmed for white Americans the cultural inferiority of Black people. And Myrdal did this, Ellison noted, by suggesting in *An American Dilemma* that the path towards greater racial equality in the United States would require Black Americans to assimilate into white American life, and in the process, to acquiesce to white Americans' denigration of Blackness and privileging of whiteness.[26] To this point, Myrdal noted in *An American Dilemma* his "observation that peculiarities in the Negro community may be characterized as social pathology."[27]

In response to Myrdal's expectation in *An American Dilemma* that Black Americans should be willing to adopt all white U.S. cultural norms, if given the opportunity by white Americans, Ellison commented: "It does not occur to Myrdal that many of the Negro cultural manifestations which he considers merely reflective [of Black Americans' exclusion from white culture] might also embody [Black Americans'] *rejection* of what he considers [white Americans'] 'higher values.'" Ellison lamented Myrdal's assumption in *An American Dilemma* that Black Americans' path toward better treatment from white Americans should leave unchallenged—and in fact, acquiesce to—white Americans' belief in their own cultural superiority.

Other early critics of *An American Dilemma* such as U.S. scholars Oliver C. Cox, Herbert Aptheker, Doxey Wilkerson, and Charles V. Hamilton and Trinidadian scholars and activists C. L. R. James and Stokely Carmichael saw in *An American Dilemma* an effort to help leading white Anglo-Americans re-justify their dominance as an imperial power.[28] For example, in *Caste, Class and Race: A Study in Social Dynamics* (1948), Cox referred to the emphasis on U.S. democracy in *An American Dilemma*'s title and retorted: "We shall not discuss the concept from which the book derives its title, for it seems quite obvious that none of the great imperialist democracies either can or intends to practice its democratic ideals among its subject peoples."[29] To Cox, Myrdal's view that white Americans would rectify their policies and behavior once shown the gap between their democratic ideals and their discriminatory treatment of Black people was as naïve as expecting white imperial powers in Africa to do the same after being shown comparable data about the inconsistencies between their democratic ideals and their discriminatory practices and behavior towards Black Africans. In a similar way, Stokely Carmichael and Charles V. Hamilton argued in *Black Power: The Politics of Liberation in America* (1967) that "there is no 'American dilemma' because black people in this country form a colony, and it is not in the interest of the colonial power to liberate them."[30]

These and other critics of *An American Dilemma* such as Samuel DuBois Cook and Harold Cruse noted that white Americans have not necessarily felt, as Myrdal suggested in *An American Dilemma*, their discrimination of Black Americans as a moral problem.[31] And even when some did, Cruse argued in 1967 that the "relationships between groups in America, and on the international plane, are actuated by the power principle, not by morality and compassion for the underdog classes."[32] Or, as Jerome Green wrote two years later, "guilt feelings had never once in history induced the 'haves' to share their loot with the 'have-nots.'"[33] Moreover, even if some white Americans eventually would feel some guilt in their complicity in white supremacy and anti-Black discrimination and yearn to take action to rectify this collusion, Ralph Ellison reminded Americans that expectations for equality along the lines that Myrdal advocated reinforced white supremacy and Black subjugation by assuming white cultural norms, and relatedly, the devaluation of Blackness.

While never publicly critical of *An American Dilemma*, renowned scholar W. E. B. Du Bois was privately sympathetic to critiques of Myrdal's work as further justification for white Anglo-American domination. Du Bois's biographer David Levering Lewis writes: "If he never publicly questioned the Myrdalian concept of moral tension and its muting of economics, there is ample evidence that, privately, he concurred with the sharp criticisms of *An American Dilemma* made by Marxist scholars such as Herbert Aptheker, Oliver Cox, and Doxey Wilkerson, who largely dismissed Myrdal's *American Creed* as the opiate of the white liberals."[34]

From such a critical perspective, shared by Du Bois and others, Gunnar Myrdal's *An American Dilemma* served to help leading white Anglo-Americans in the United States reconfirm their false belief in their moral superiority in the world, the cultural superiority of whiteness over Blackness, and to define the terms and speed of Black Americans' assimilation into white U.S. life.

*White Philanthropy: Carnegie Corporation's* An American Dilemma *and the Making of a White World Order* amplifies the significance of these critics' perspectives on *An American Dilemma*. It confirms with historical evidence their claims that *An American Dilemma* was an exercise in white Anglo-American domination, an effort to help solidify rather than to challenge white rule within and beyond the United States.

More specifically, this book illustrates how Gunnar Myrdal's study never was commissioned, funded, or written with the goal of challenging white supremacy and Black subordination. Rather, it was commissioned and funded by Carnegie Corporation president Frederick P. Keppel and researched and written by Gunnar Myrdal precisely with the idea of helping white Americans rejustify their domination over Black Americans in the United States. This was part of a longer-term effort by Keppel to finance cooperative studies in the social sciences in order to help white policymakers in the Anglo-American world maintain domination over Black people; an effort quite in sync with his organization's mandate, established by Andrew Carnegie, to prioritize the needs and interests of white people across the Anglo-American world.

In addition, *White Philanthropy* illustrates how Keppel's decision to commission and fund the study of Black Americans that became *An American Dilemma* was also rooted in a particular anxiety that Keppel shared with his network of white Anglo-American advisers and colleagues in the 1920s and 1930s: that white policymakers in colonial Africa and the United States needed to respond more effectively to perceived threats posed by Black people, whether those threats came in the form of rising Black consciousness or particular societal ills such as crime and "untidiness" that these white men associated especially with Black people.[35] Otherwise, as Keppel and his network of colleagues and advisers reasoned, these perceived threats would escalate, and white people such as themselves would need to respond with violence, leaving the existing white Anglo-American world order ever more fragile.

The Swedish author of *An American Dilemma*, Gunnar Myrdal, was not directly part of this network of white Americans and Britons eager to solidify white domination over Black people in the 1920s and 1930s as means of staving off national, regional, and international conflict along the color line. Nonetheless, Keppel selected Myrdal because—while Myrdal was not exactly the British colonial officer with administrative experience whom Keppel initially imagined choosing for the U.S. study—he was a white European expert on "crime and disorders" with national public policymaking experience who, as Keppel came to appreciate during the search, would be well received by his network of advisers and colleagues in the United States.[36] Throughout the search, Keppel in fact remained consistent in his view that the central purpose of the U.S. study was to help guide white policymakers across governments in the United States better govern and control Black Americans, much as the ongoing African survey (based in London and also financed by Carnegie Corporation at the time) was set to help white policymakers across imperial governments in Africa better govern and control Black Africans.

Indeed, in *An American Dilemma*, Gunnar Myrdal maintained that white people in the United States—particularly those with most political power such as northerners and New Dealers—were his main audience for the study. And while writing *An American Dilemma* during the Second World War, Myrdal furthermore became especially invested in helping white Americans justify their continued domination both within and beyond the United States in ways that further complemented the intentions of President Keppel—and

Carnegie Corporation more broadly—that the organization's funding practices should help solidify white Anglo-American domination across oceans.

The opening chapters of this book present new and original research on Andrew Carnegie's vision for international order and show how it assumed the subordination of colonized groups across the Anglo-American world. These chapters illustrate how Carnegie's vision of international peace related to his advocacy of vocational and industrial education for Black people and other colonized people across the British Empire. They furthermore show how, once Carnegie passed away in 1919, his personal assistant James Bertram translated for fellow board members at Carnegie Corporation his former employer's expectations to privilege the needs and interests of white Anglo-Americans as key for maintaining international order along the color line. That is to say that Andrew Carnegie's expectations for international peace assumed white Anglo-American supremacy and the subjection of colonized people across the Anglo-American world including Black Americans in the United States.

These chapters demonstrate how, upon assuming the presidency of the corporation in 1923, Frederick Keppel incorporated into the corporation's mandate his own anxieties in the 1920s about the explosive nature of rising Black consciousness across the Atlantic and his affinity for using the developing social sciences as a tool for strengthening white Anglo-American rule. Thus, Keppel's decision to finance *An American Dilemma* (1944)—and before it, *The Poor White Problem in South Africa* (1932) and *An African Survey: A Study of Problems Arising in Africa South of the Sahara* (1938)—reflected both Carnegie Corporation's longstanding practice of privileging the needs of white people in the Anglo-American world and Keppel's own developing vision that cooperative studies in the social sciences could help guide white policymakers in the Anglo-American world in their efforts to remain dominant.

These two earlier studies were important antecedents to *An American Dilemma*. Regarding *The Poor White Problem in South Africa*, regularly described as *The Poor White Study*, historian Saul Dubow remarks that it helped "establish sociology as a discipline and the social survey as a basic methodological tool" and "firmed up links between official policy-makers, universities, and voluntary welfare organizations linked to the Dutch Reformed Church."[37] Discussing science and development throughout British Africa in the 1920s and 1930s, historian Helen Tilley describes the *African Survey* as "the most important intelligence-gathering project of the interwar period."[38]

In pushing forward this argument about the colonial African roots of *An American Dilemma*—and more specifically, about its very purpose of helping white policymakers further solidify white Anglo-American domination against perceived threats posed by Black people—this book further amplifies the significance of works by intellectuals and scholars such as Ralph Ellison, Oliver C. Cox, C. L. R. James, Harold Cruse, John H. Bracey, Samuel DuBois Cook, and more recently Nikhil Pal Singh, who have assumed that the funders and author of *An American Dilemma* largely were in sync with the project's goals, and that the book's basic goal—even as it presented itself as a means for greater equality for Black Americans—was to rejustify white domination within and beyond the United States.[39] To this critical reading of *An American Dilemma*, *White Philanthropy* contributes detailed historical evidence.

In so doing, this book aims to challenge the way that scholars of the U.S. civil rights movement, the U.S. social sciences, and U.S. philanthropy tend to talk about the significance and purpose of *An American Dilemma* in the United States. Civil rights scholars, for example, have generally understood *An American Dilemma* as the quintessential study both reflecting and inspiring racial liberalism in the United States—a way of talking about racial equality in the United States privileging the importance of changing the minds and hearts of white Americans and subsequently mobilizing the U.S. federal government to assimilate Black Americans into dominant white Anglo-American life.[40] From this perspective, and generally overlooking the inherent inequity in a definition of racial equality calling for the erasure of Blackness and privileging of whiteness, civil rights historians have tended to laud *An American Dilemma* as part of a "Second Reconstruction" period when white Americans once again believed in the value of mobilizing the federal government to enact policies favoring racial egalitarian goals. For their part, historians of the U.S. social sciences long have analyzed the ways that *An American Dilemma* both reflected and ushered in an era when greater numbers of social scientists analyzed white prejudice and, in the process, focused on individual psyches rather than structural change as means for addressing racial inequality.[41]

By contrast, scholars of U.S. philanthropy have predictably placed greater emphasis on the role of Carnegie Corporation in the making of *An American Dilemma*. In doing so, they have assumed—as Keppel tried to convince readers in his foreword to *An American Dilemma*—that fellow board member and former secretary of war Newton D. Baker, rather than Keppel himself, was the innovator of the study. Further underestimating Keppel's vision as a foundation leader, they have suggested that he made grant decisions largely by "hunch, coincidence, opportunity, friendship, and a wish to help than by clear, specific, consistently applied 'scientific' goals or principles."[42] In failing to see either the Carnegie Corporation president's role as innovator of *An American Dilemma* or his broader transatlantic purpose for the project, these scholars also have overlooked the significance of Keppel's and Myrdal's ongoing dialogue about the study and how the final manuscript largely met Keppel's expectations for a national blueprint to help white policymakers further fortify and justify white rule over Black people in the United States.[43]

This book disrupts these scholarly conversations about *An American Dilemma* by showing that they are based on a misunderstanding of both the purpose and the significance of Myrdal's 1944 study in the United States and what precisely the text's funder and author intended it to achieve. This is because, as I argue, *An American Dilemma* should be remembered as a project with great dialogue and intent between its funder and author, and a project whose author largely delivered on the funder's intentions. Again, Carnegie Corporation of New York in the 1920s and 1930s—both as an institution rooted in Andrew Carnegie's vision for international peace and under the leadership of President Frederick Keppel—was intent on helping white policymakers solidify a white Anglo-American world order. *An American Dilemma* was commissioned and financed by the corporation as part of this global project, and Myrdal delivered on these intentions, with Keppel and Myrdal only disagreeing on the relative importance of the white South for achieving Myrdal's national policy program.

In presenting this colonial African history to *An American Dilemma*, *White Philanthropy* furthermore introduces to scholars of African Studies, transnational studies, global history, world systems, imperial history, African Diaspora studies, and international politics—who long have analyzed the making of a white Anglo-American world order and Black resistance to the making of global white supremacy—how *An American Dilemma* was linked to *The Poor White Problem in South Africa* and *An African Survey* as part of Carnegie Corporation's plan in the first half of the twentieth century to further solidify white Anglo-American rule and Black subjection across the Atlantic.[44]

And yet, as much as I intend to contribute to scholarly conversations on *An American Dilemma*, I have not written this book simply for this purpose. I also have written it to disrupt contemporary public discussions about racial equality and white supremacy in the United States today. Because we Americans need to acknowledge that our national conversations about racial equality—still so shaped by *An American Dilemma*—continue to be intrinsically connected to a project among white funders, policymakers, and their advisers in the social sciences and education during the early twentieth century to create a world order led by white Anglo-Americans. I thus propose that when we Americans talk about ways to create a future free of racial domination within and beyond the United States, we should realize which intellectual sources on racial equality—such as *An American Dilemma*—are tying us down to continued white domination and nonwhite subjugation. For a more egalitarian future in the intrinsically connected national and international levels, let us find inspiration—not in such texts such as *An American Dilemma*, which are only thinly disguised efforts to continue white Anglo-American rule—but rather in those individuals described in the following pages who resisted the making of this white world order.

Considering that nationally celebrated Black critics and scholars such as Ralph Ellison and Oliver C. Cox discerned white supremacist roots of *An American Dilemma* early on, there is of course the question of why this colonial African history of *An American Dilemma* has not yet been told—why it has taken over seventy-five years to uncover and write it. For starters, it is fair to say that leading white Americans long have dismissed Black critics, Black scholars, and Marxist scholars of any racialized identities as producers of authoritative knowledge on white supremacy and Black subjection.[45] In this spirit, Ellison's and Cox's criticisms of *An American Dilemma* would prove little challenge to white Americans' embrace and celebration of *An American Dilemma*.

Even more, many mid- to late-twentieth-century white Americans, though keenly interested in detailing the making *An American Dilemma*, desperately wanted to distinguish Black Americans' subjugation in the United States from discussions of racial discrimination and violence in Europe during the Second World War and in Africa during the Cold War. This is because white Americans desperately wanted to present a public image of themselves on the global stage suggesting that they, in contrast to other dominant white groups in Nazi Germany, British Africa, or South Africa, for example, zealously cherished egalitarian ideals and thus would work to correct their violent and discriminatory treatment of fellow Black citizens. This is to say that white Americans reading *An American Dilemma* in the second half of the twentieth century would have had little personal incentive to investigate—or encourage the investigation through institutional and financial support—the colonial African roots of *An American Dilemma*.

Gunnar Myrdal himself encouraged this sense of U.S. exceptionalism in *An American Dilemma*. Granted, he did acknowledge *An African Survey* and its author, Malcolm Hailey, in the depths of *An American Dilemma* and illustrated how his own policy proposals for Black Americans in the United States complemented Hailey's own for Black Africans in colonial Africa. However, Myrdal's general thesis in *An American Dilemma* was that white Americans were an exceptionally egalitarian people, who, once made aware of their discriminatory treatment of Black Americans, would mobilize to correct these policies and behavior. In this way, Myrdal's complementary presentation of white Americans provided white U.S. readers with exactly the desired distance from international racial politics during the Second World War and the Cold War.

Adding to this favorable image of a uniquely U.S. ethos, both Keppel and Myrdal endeavored to frame the institutional and intellectual roots of *An American Dilemma* within an exclusively U.S. context. In the same foreword to *An American Dilemma* where Keppel celebrated Myrdal's book alongside *The Poor White Study* and *An African Survey*, for example, the recently retired foundation president deflected the project's colonial African roots by providing a relatively detailed story on how the study had originated with then-deceased board member Newton Baker.[46]

As Frederick Keppel described him, Newton Baker was the "son of a Confederate officer" who as secretary of war during the First World War had "faced the special problems which the presence of the Negro element in our population inevitably creates in time of national crisis."[47] With these national experiences, Keppel presented Baker as someone who "knew so much more than the rest of us on the Board about these questions, and his mind had been so deeply concerned with them, that we readily agreed when he told us that more knowledge and better organized and interrelated knowledge was essential before the Corporation could intelligently distribute its own funds."[48] Placing Gunnar Myrdal's analysis of Black Americans squarely within a U.S. context, Keppel wrote that the director had been selected because, as a Swede, he had little prior context and experience with minority groups.[49] From this perspective, Myrdal was a blank slate whose analysis in *An American Dilemma* reflected exclusively his observations in the United States.

This origin story, which *White Philanthropy* shows to be a half-truth at best, obscures the study's much more complex institutional and intellectual roots as well as its links to global conversations on imperial, colonial, and national planning. Some of the holes in Keppel's chosen narrative, though, were clear to those closest to the work. Keppel's assistant, Charles Dollard, who remained Gunnar Myrdal's main contact at the foundation throughout the span of his work in the United States, corrected an oral historian in 1966 who assumed that *An American Dilemma* had been the idea of Baker:

> I think that's folklore. Keppel tells that story in his introduction to the Myrdal book, about Newton Baker, who was his great hero. As far as I'm concerned, the idea for the study of the Negro in America was Frederick Keppel's. Characteristically, he was trying to [attribute] it to somebody

else. Also, there may have been a little attempt, there, to get, by implication, the backing of one of the strongest trustees we'd ever had who was by then, by the way, out of the picture. I don't mean to imply that Keppel wasn't absolutely sure of himself on the Myrdal study, but this helped a little bit.[50]

As Dollard suggested, Keppel made a strategic choice in adopting this origin story for *An American Dilemma*. Not only had Baker passed away by the time Keppel started sharing this origins narrative, thus making it easier for Keppel's genesis story to remain uncontested, but Baker was a lauded public servant with deep southern roots—a point that Keppel found important to stress in the foreword to *An American Dilemma*. Considering white southerners to be a crucial demographic for any viable national public policy program on Black Americans, Keppel seemed to have reasoned that Baker's imprimatur on the study could only help its reception among white southerners and the general U.S. public.

Dollard was not the only one who questioned the Baker genesis story. Serving as an informal adviser to Keppel in the 1930s, U.S. sociologist Donald Young recalled, "At the time there was a little friendly gossip about it. Most of us believed that the idea had probably been fed to Mr. Baker, that undoubtedly Mr. Baker had said that, but whether the initiative came from him was a matter of grave doubt. We had seen Mr. Keppel attribute things to other people at earlier times, and also Mr. Keppel had the kind of enthusiasm that could only come from a father, not from a step-father."[51]

While Frederick Keppel was uniquely invested in his genesis story for *An American Dilemma* with Newton Baker at its center, Gunnar Myrdal himself, years later when penning the preface to the twentieth anniversary edition of *An American Dilemma*, both acknowledged his close association with Keppel during the span of the project and stated that Keppel "was the major force in planning and pushing this undertaking even before I was engaged to carry it out."[52] In the 1960s, Myrdal thus further corroborated Young and Dollard's sense that Keppel had been personally and deeply invested in the corporation's study of Black Americans.

That said, Myrdal left unchallenged Keppel's suggestion—in his use of Newton Baker as supposed originator of the organization's study of Black Americans—that the U.S. study had exclusively U.S. origins. To this point, when Myrdal described the origins story to *An American Dilemma* over the years, he consistently promoted the foundation president's image of a Swede inexperienced with minority groups in the global North or colonized people in the global South, or as Keppel noted in the foreword, "someone who could approach his task with a fresh mind, uninfluenced by traditional attitudes or by earlier conclusions."[53] In this introductory section of *An American Dilemma*, Myrdal quoted Keppel's letter to him years earlier noting that the study should be "undertaken in a wholly objective and dispassionate way as a social phenomenon" and went on to describe his arrival in the United States in the fall of 1938, his endless list of research collaborators across the country and the various research memoranda he collected and read, along with the allocation of tasks among himself and his two writing collaborators, Arnold Rose and Richard Sterner, in producing the final manuscript.[54] As Myrdal likely reasoned, Keppel's image of him as an outsider whose analysis and conclusions on Black Americans resulted simply from his sojourn in the United States could only facilitate white Americans' reception of his work as particularly U.S.-centric and reliable. For scholars curious to research the intellectual and institutional roots of *An American Dilemma*, the book's foreword and preface authored by the project's funder and grantee, whether in the original or subsequent editions, hardly would suggest that the study had any roots outside of the United States.

Moving beyond *An American Dilemma*'s foreword and preface, *White Philanthropy* digs into archival material on Carnegie Corporation, Gunnar Myrdal, and their networks of peers to present the global genesis of this influential work in the United States. *White Philanthropy* shows that Keppel played a much more central role in conceiving and developing *An American Dilemma* than has previously been assumed. This realization opens the door to uncover the history of how *An American Dilemma* fit with Carnegie Corporation's prior work in colonial Africa. It also details how Gunnar Myrdal's experiences in 1930s and 1940s United States and Sweden complemented Keppel's and his advisers' contemporaneous conversations on the social sciences and the importance of white Anglo-American rule for national, regional, and international order.

This history of how *An American Dilemma* was intended to be—and became under the direction of Gunnar Myrdal—an effort to further solidify white Anglo-American domination at the national and international levels, begins with its main protagonist, Frederick Keppel, and the organization he inherited when he became its president in 1923. The following chapters illustrate how Myrdal's *An American Dilemma* succeeded in meeting the expectations of a foundation president who—reflecting his organization's vision for global white Anglo-American supremacy and his own anxieties about the potential for successful Black protest to challenge white Anglo-American rule—

believed that the social sciences could help white Anglo-American policymakers rejustify, recalibrate, and reinforce white domination over Black people both in colonial Africa and in the United States.

This story of the genesis of *An American Dilemma*, then, is less about racial equality in the United States, as many Americans would like to remember the study, and more—as other Americans long have speculated—about strengthening white Anglo-American control on both sides of the Atlantic.

CHAPTER 1

# Sufficiently White
## Carnegie Corporation's International Reach

Frederick P. Keppel became president of Carnegie Corporation in 1923 and
remained in that position until his retirement in 1941. During these years,
Keppel steered the organization to fund Gunnar Myrdal's *An American Dilemma* (1944) as well as its two predecessor studies, *The Poor White Problem
in South Africa* (1932) and Lord Malcolm Hailey's *An African Survey* (1938):
cooperative studies in the social sciences intended by their funder and authors
to help guide white policymakers address perceived problems in managing
white supremacy and Black subordination in the Anglo-American world.

And yet, the idea to reinforce a white Anglo-American world order was not
simply the result of Keppel's singular preference or of his advisers' influence
on him. Rather, as this and the next chapter show, it was an approach to international order along the color line encouraged by Keppel's board of trustees
at Carnegie Corporation, where lifetime trustee James Bertram served as translator of Andrew Carnegie's intentions as a philanthropist on the world stage.

In describing the organization that Keppel inherited in 1923, this chapter
considers Andrew Carnegie's allegiance to an English-speaking world, or, as
Bertram put it, to "communities of whites" in the British Empire, and more
broadly, throughout the Anglo-American world.[1] This preference for privileging the needs and interests of white Anglo-Americans would form the institutional backdrop to Keppel's subsequent decision to fund social scientific
research on white and Black people as a means of helping white policymakers
reinforce white Anglo-American supremacy across the Atlantic.

## 1. Frederick Keppel Becomes President of
## Carnegie Corporation

Up until 1923, when Frederick Keppel became president of Carnegie Corporation, the organization had gone through two interim presidents and one elected
president, each of whom stayed in the position no longer than a year. Keppel
was thus the first president of the foundation since Andrew Carnegie's passing in 1919 who remained in the role long enough to learn the personalities of

his board members, to determine what he would like to convince them to do, and ultimately to see grantmaking initiatives develop.[2]

The son of two Irish immigrants, Frederick Keppel was born in Long Island and graduated from Columbia College in 1898. Upon graduation, Keppel stayed on at Columbia University, first as assistant secretary, then as secretary, and ultimately as dean of the college. During the First World War, he left for Washington, D.C., in order to assist secretary of war Newton D. Baker.

After the war, Keppel and his wife, Helen Tracey Brown, niece of J. P. Morgan, and their five sons settled in Paris, where Keppel headed the Foreign Relations Department of the American Red Cross and became the first commissioner for the United States at the International Chamber of Commerce.[3]

Upon their return to the United States some three years later, the Keppels resettled in the New York area. While Keppel had assumed that he would return to Columbia College, as historian Michael Rosenthal notes, Columbia University's president at the time, Nicholas Butler, "saw Keppel's administrative talents, popularity, and success (he rose quickly in Washington to the newly created post of third assistant secretary of war) as a threat to his own control at Columbia."[4] Thus prevented from returning to the university, Keppel worked instead at the Russell Sage Foundation's New York City Regional Plan Initiative.

A year later, Carnegie Corporation's board invited Keppel to become president of the organization.[5] These men likely found this former Columbia College administrator, with roots in New York City, to be a reliable candidate who might stay in the organization long enough to lead it and shape its grantmaking initiatives.

Faced with an unmatched opportunity to head a prominent philanthropic organization, Keppel realized soon after his appointment that his new role did not come without some limitations. For one thing, the corporation had already earmarked funds for projects in the United States for some years to come. Thus, during Frederick Keppel's first year as president, the corporation paid out $12.95 million of the funds allocated for projects in the United States; and of this total, $12.35 million was based upon grants voted by the corporation in previous years.[6]

In other words, previous commitments decided upon by Carnegie Corporation's board of trustees before Keppel's appointment left him with little if any room for new initiatives in the United States during his early years as president. Some three years later in 1926, the corporation created even greater restrictions in its U.S. fund by reducing the list of unpaid obligations and adding nearly $1.6 million of this account as protection against capital depreciation. "As a result," Keppel reasoned in his 1931 annual report, "perhaps the widest opportunities open to the Corporation during the period have been found in the administration of the so-called Special Fund, applicable, according to the terms of Mr. Carnegie's supplementary gift, 'in Canada and the British Colonies.'"[7] Indeed, during his first years as president of Carnegie Corporation, Keppel turned much of his attention abroad.

For funding beyond the United States and specifically in Canada and the British colonies, the organization maintained a $10 million fund, which trustees casually termed the "Special Fund." Even though it was a relatively small sum compared to the $125 million that Andrew Carnegie had given to the organization during his lifetime and that went mainly toward its work in the United States, the Special Fund presented Keppel with an opportunity to develop grant programs of his own, and he embraced the opportunity to engage in a network of contacts and grantmaking possibilities beyond the United States.[8]

Keppel's decision to look abroad had some precedent at the organization. In his annual report for 1921, the corporation's former president, James Angell, had recommended that it consider financing projects in a more targeted way in other parts of the world. Angell wrote: "We now receive occasional requests for aid from Australia, South Africa, and elsewhere, but we are in no position to pass intelligently on these requests; much less have we taken the initiative, as I am disposed to think we should."[9] Reflecting long-standing ambiguity in the corporation's mandate abroad, Angell included the British dominions of Australia and South Africa in his view of its potential work abroad, even though the organization's charter specified that it only was empowered "to hold and administer any funds given to it for use in Canada or the British colonies for the same purposes . . . as those to which it is by law authorized to apply its funds in the United States."[10]

Keppel subsequently sought to determine the geographic scope of the corporation's charter, which referred only to the "United States, Canada, and the British colonies," not British dominions such as Australia and South Africa. In doing so, Keppel relied at times on the foundation's lawyers at Root, Clark, Buckner & Rowland in New York City, and at other times on the advice of James Bertram, Andrew Carnegie's personal secretary, who had been appointed lifetime trustee and secretary of the corporation by the Gilded Age tycoon.[11]

Bertram and the organization's lawyers had distinct means of reasoning through the geographic expanse of the corporation's charter. And this distinction was particularly clear in moments when Bertram and the lawyers offered overlapping advice, for example, as they did in their respective analyses of whether Carnegie Corporation could fund projects in the Philippines.

For Carnegie Corporation's lawyers, the heart of this query was whether the U.S. territory of the Philippines could be considered part of the United States, and thus within the geographic scope of Carnegie Corporation's charter. Confronted with this question, the lawyers argued that the corporation could not finance grants in the Philippines because the United States had never intended to incorporate the islands into its political body, "except in a matter involving international affairs."[12] To arrive at this conclusion, the organization's lawyers cited the Treaty of Paris, U.S. Senate resolutions, Congressional acts, U.S. Supreme Court decisions, and law journal articles. What mattered to these lawyers was the wording of Carnegie Corporation's charter— its mention of the "United States"—along with the U.S. legal community's consensus on the scope of the geographic expanse of the United States.

Like Bertram, the lawyers would agree that the Philippines existed outside the geographic scope of the corporation, but they would reason through this logic in drastically different ways. Rather than depending on legal documents or the U.S. legal community's general consensus on the geographic meaning of the United States, Canada or the British colonies, for example, Bertram would analyze the corporation's charter by thinking through his personal conversations with Andrew Carnegie and particularly Carnegie's philanthropic intentions in the Anglo-American world.

Turning to Bertram's developing relationship with Andrew Carnegie during the steel titan's lifetime, this next section shows how this former personal secretary of Andrew Carnegie interpreted the philanthropist's intentions for fellow Carnegie Corporation trustees and how, as corporation secretary and trustee, Bertram evolved to become a leading voice within the organization's board and particularly in shaping its grantmaking practices in colonial Africa during Keppel's tenure as president of Carnegie Corporation. It begins, however, not with Bertram, but with Andrew Carnegie himself.

## 2. Andrew Carnegie's Vision of Philanthropy in the "English-Speaking" World

Born in Dunfermline, Scotland in 1835, Andrew Carnegie was the son of a moderately successful linen weaver, whose craft began to lose value in response to general manufacturing trends, though specifically too as Scottish manufacturers and merchants raced to lower product prices in light of a decreasing export market during The Panic of 1837. By the 1840s, historian David Nasaw writes that Carnegie's mother, Margaret Carnegie, had "taken over the role as chief family breadwinner" by working for her brother, a cobbler, and then by setting up her own food shop at the family's cottage.[13] Though without a stable source of income, the family decided to follow relatives who had settled in the United States.

Arriving in Pittsburgh at the age of twelve, Andrew soon secured employment at the Anchor Cotton Mills, owned by a fellow Scotsman.[14] Working at a local telegraph office some two years later, Carnegie caught the attention of the superintendent of the Western Division of the Pennsylvania Railroad, who then hired him to be his personal telegrapher and private secretary. Becoming a protégé of this railroad executive, Carnegie learned both about the railroad industry and how to invest his salary.

At the age of twenty-nine, Carnegie resigned from his salaried position at the railroad company and dedicated his attention to various investments, including the Pullman Palace Company and the Pacific & Atlantic Telegraph Company.[15] With a relatively significant accumulation of wealth by his early thirties, Carnegie moved with his aging mother to New York City.

In the 1870s, and while residing in New York City, Carnegie would turn his attention increasingly to the steel industry in Pittsburgh, and increasingly over time too, he would rely on a fellow industrialist, Henry Clay Frick, to oversee his operations in Pittsburgh. In 1881, Frick had entered Carnegie's business orbit when Carnegie's associates at Carnegie Brothers & Company in Pittsburgh had found themselves with the need to secure "a steady, expandable, and relatively inexpensive supply of high-grade coke for their new blast furnaces."[16] They then reached out to Henry Clay Frick, owner of Frick Coke Company. During the next decade, the men continued to work together. By the early 1890s, Frick had convinced Carnegie to further consolidate Carnegie companies into a new company, Carnegie Steel, and to make him chairman.

Starting in the 1890s, Carnegie would rely on Frick, who managed Pittsburgh-based Carnegie Steel alongside his own Frick Coke Company, to be his eyes and ears in the local community. It was Frick, for example, who would famously keep Carnegie abreast of contract negotiations and strikes in Carnegie mills, such as the famous Homestead Strike in the summer of 1892.

By the last years of the century, however, the two men's relationship became increasingly strained and Carnegie subsequently called for Frick's removal as the executive head of Carnegie Steel. As part of the settlement, Frick Coke Company and Carnegie Steel merged and became Carnegie Company in April 1900, with Charles Schwab as president and chief executive officer.[17] Less than a year later, Schwab informed Carnegie that J. Pierpont Morgan was eager to buy Carnegie's shares of the company. Without negotiations, Morgan accepted Carnegie's asking price of $480 million, the equivalent of approximately $15 billion in today's currency.[18]

Sixty-five years old at the time, Andrew Carnegie already was well known in the United States and Great Britain as an advocate of philanthropy, particularly after the 1889 publication of his essay "Wealth" (also titled "Gospel of Wealth" in varying editions).[19] Now that he was formally retired, and with an unprecedented amount of wealth in his hands, Carnegie became ever more devoted to philanthropic giving. Over the years, he also became a proponent of "international peace."[20] Both causes came to reflect Carnegie's developing vision for the role of an industrialist such as himself in U.S. and British societies, as well as the place of these two empires on the world stage.

Nicknamed "the Star Spangled Scotsman" by English novelist William Black, Andrew Carnegie was recognized in England for pontificating about the values of the United States; a country that, from Carnegie's perspective, had helped him not only to amass a fortune, but also to transform him into a notable and important Scotsman in Britain. [21] Andrew Carnegie biographer David Nasaw notes that Carnegie routinely shared his "unsolicited views on matters of domestic and international affairs with John Morley, William Gladstone, Lord Salisbury, Lord Rosebery, Joseph Chamberlain, Arthur Balfour, and James Bryce in Britain, and with whoever happened to be in the White House or leading up the State Department."[22] These individuals were not always eager to hear Carnegie's thoughts and recommendations, but they nonetheless corresponded and met with him.[23] For his part, Carnegie found value in advising these men because he was committed to and invested in the future of the U.S. and British empires. In a similar spirit, Carnegie loudly proclaimed the virtue of philanthropy both to Americans and Britons.

Over a decade before he formally retired, Carnegie had produced his first article on the topic of philanthropy, "Wealth," published in the *North American Review* in 1889, which readers usually read alongside a subsequent essay he published in the same journal some months later, titled "The Best Fields of Philanthropy."[24] Geared towards audiences in the United States and Britain, Carnegie began "Wealth" by describing the values of industrialization and concentrated wealth in industrializing societies such as the United States and Great Britain.

Ironically for a child from Dunfermline, Scotland, who had witnessed how his family and neighbors had found it difficult to survive as industrialization coupled with a financial crisis had made their artisanal skills much less lucrative, Carnegie argued in "Wealth" that there was not a prior, idealized world for the working classes that existed before factory work. Rather, he claimed that factory work had created better and more affordable products that workers could themselves acquire. As he wrote, "To-day the world obtains commodities of excellent quality at prices which even the generation preceding this would have deemed incredible."[25] All in all, Carnegie reasoned in "Wealth" that both capital and labor benefited from industrialization. Though as he admitted, too, industrialization was leading to greater wealth inequalities between capital and labor, and that this was a problem that the wealthy needed to address. And by the wealthy, Carnegie explained that he meant individuals with "fortunes . . . not moderate sums saved by many years of effort, the returns from which are required for the comfortable maintenance and education of families."[26] Stressing the critical importance of addressing wealth inequality as means for preventing societal instability, Carnegie wrote in "Wealth": "The problem of our age is the proper administration of wealth, so that the ties of brotherhood may still bind together the rich and poor in harmonious relationship."[27]

Though rather than turning over the task of wealth distribution to state actors, as some contemporaries whom Carnegie criticized in the piece were proposing, he stressed that individuals with fortunes should take on the responsibility, "becoming the mere agent and trustee for his poorer brethren, bringing to their service his superior wisdom, experience, and ability to administer, doing for them better than they would or could do for themselves."[28] As Carnegie suggested in "Wealth," harmony between capital and labor could be achieved in a profit-maximizing society and without disrupting capital's vast accumulation of wealth. What was needed, Carnegie stressed, was for titans of industry to agree to surrender funds beyond those necessary for supporting their families' comfortable maintenance and education; a personal standard that he left to fellow tycoons to determine themselves.

With this general introduction to "Wealth," Carnegie then presented readers with various avenues for redistributing the so-called "surplus wealth" in the hands of leading industrialists. As a first option, Carnegie mentioned leaving it to descendants, but he saw this as the most "injudicious" of options, not only because doing so would strip descendants of ambition, but also, as Carnegie argued, because descendants long had proven unworthy of managing these estates and lands. Carnegie thus suggested that the wealthy should abandon this means of disposing excess wealth, in the best interests not just of their children but of the state's as well.[29]

A second alternative, "leaving wealth at death for public uses," was likewise dismissed by Carnegie, who thought that the person who accumulated the wealth is the one who is best placed to redistribute it: "It is well to remember that it requires the exercise of not less ability than that which acquired the wealth to use it so as to be really beneficial to the community."[30] In this vein, Carnegie proposed his third and preferred option: for "the rich man to attend to the administration of wealth during his life."[31]

If he could convince fellow industry tycoons to give away their excess wealth during their lifetimes, Andrew Carnegie imagined that he would be playing his part in creating a "reign of harmony" among capital and labor in industrializing societies on either side of the Atlantic. From his point of view, "We shall have an ideal state, in which the surplus wealth of the few will become, in the best sense, the property of the many, because administered for the common good, and this wealth, passing through the hands of the few, can be made a much more potent force for the elevation of our race than if it had been distributed in small sums to the people themselves."[32] As later sections in this chapter underscore, Carnegie indeed intended to focus his attention as a philanthropist on his "race," which he determined to be fellow white people throughout the Anglo-American world.

Believing that he had internalized the interests of both capital and labor by living the life of a worker and later of an industrialist, Carnegie stressed in "Wealth" that the working classes would prefer his proposed mode of wealth redistribution rather than higher individual salaries. "Even the poorest can be made to see this, and to agree that great sums gathered by some of their fellow citizens and spent for public purposes, from which the masses reap the principal benefit, are more valuable to them than if scattered among them through the course of many years in trifling amounts."[33] From Carnegie's perspective, the poor and working class would prefer gaining access to libraries and parks in their towns, for example, over increased wages.

At the conclusion of "Wealth," Carnegie turned his attention once again to his wealthy peers and offered them some guidelines on how to go about redistributing their surplus wealth. In this vein, he took pains to criticize charitable giving at the time, which he argued largely created habits of dependency among the poor.[34] Assuming industrialists wanted to bestow a positive work ethic (which Carnegie associated with the wealthy) among the working class (which Carnegie argued included "the slothful, the drunken, the unworthy"), he suggested that the "main consideration should be to help those who will help themselves; to provide part of the means by which those who desire to improve may do so; to give those who desire to rise the aids by which they may rise; to assist, but rarely or never to do all."[35] And this, Carnegie explained, distinguished his gospel of wealth—his vision for philanthropy—from charity in industrializing societies. Contrary to charitable giving, he argued, philanthropic giving would redistribute wealth back to the community without stunting the very individualism and competition that helped people help themselves. In this way, he suggested that philanthropists should return their surplus wealth "to the mass of their fellows in the forms best calculated to do them lasting good" by financing parks, recreation centers, art, and public institutions all of which would help "body and mind," "give pleasure and improve the public taste," and "improve the general condition of the people."[36] With these public goods accessible to them, and likely imagining or reimagining his needs as a boy in Dunfermline and Pittsburgh, Carnegie thus argued that the poor and working class would have the necessary positive surroundings, inspirations, and resources in their local environments to educate themselves on ways to improve their status in society. In a follow-up piece published just a few months later in the *North American Review*, "The Best Fields for Philanthropy," Carnegie also offered specific examples of philanthropy: funding public parks, universities, libraries, hospitals, medical colleges, laboratories, city halls, swimming baths, and church buildings.

Republished in Britain, the essays garnered a strong response there.[37] As Carnegie recognized, the "mother-land" was even more concerned than the United States about the "contrast between the classes and the masses, between rich and poor."[38] Among such early readers were the Welsh Methodist Minister Hugh Price Hughes and Catholic Cardinal Edward Manning who, alongside British Prime Minister William Gladstone, published reviews of Carnegie's two essays in subsequent issues of the *North American Review*. Hughes and Manning provided the strongest criticism, arguing that wealth inequality was an unnatural and unwelcome social phenomenon whose solution required working-class mobilization or comprehensive social reform rather than simply the voluntary giving by the elite rich. Despite offering the sharpest rebuttal, Hughes ultimately welcomed Andrew Carnegie's suggestions for greater philanthropy among the wealthy as a useful, if only temporary, approach to wealth inequality. In contrast to the two religious leaders, Gladstone agreed with Carnegie's argument in favor of philanthropy, although Gladstone did criticize Carnegie's dismissal of familial inheritance, which, for Gladstone, was an important, valuable form of national tradition. These three men's reactionary essays provide some context to the immediate reception enjoyed by Andrew Carnegie's two essays. While Carnegie's 1889 essays would become a founding text in modern U.S. philanthropy, they indeed met with some swift pushback early on.[39] And Carnegie replied.

In response to the three reviewers, Carnegie wrote an eighteen-page rebuttal, which he published in *Nineteenth Century*. And here, Carnegie responded to any and all criticisms of his essay, including Gladstone's minor injection that he, unlike Carnegie, valued hereditary wealth. Carnegie was invested in the reception of "Wealth," not only in the United States but in Great Britain as well.

Twelve years after publishing his two accompanying essays in the *North American Review*, and ten years after writing his response to the reviewers, Andrew Carnegie became a full-time philanthropist with the absolute mission of promulgating the value of his definition of philanthropy across the United States and Great Britain. Indeed, Carnegie's philanthropic decisions at the time reflected his commitments to both geographic regions. Within months of selling his shares of the Carnegie Steel Company in 1901, for example, he made three significant gifts: two in the United States and one in Scotland. He transferred $5 million in U.S. Steel gold bonds to the managers of the Carnegie Company in Pittsburgh (J. P. Morgan had since consolidated Carnegie Steel Company into U.S. Steel), with $1 million earmarked for libraries in the area, and the remaining funds to finance a Carnegie Relief Fund to aid particularly capable and deserving Carnegie Steel Company employees who had been injured or killed in service, or simply "after long and creditable service, need[ed] such help in their old age."[40] He also gave the New York City public library system nearly $5 million. In Scotland, he established the Carnegie Trust for the Universities of Scotland with a nearly $10 million bequest, in order to provide Scottish students with loans to attend university.[41]

A year later, in 1902, Carnegie founded a center in the United States to encourage research in the scientific fields, the Carnegie Institution of Washington, with a comparable initial gift of $10 million, though "later augmented by $12 million."[42] The following year, he acquired a rambling family estate in Dunfermline, Scotland, and with a $2.5 million endowment founded the Carnegie Dunfermline Trust to create a park that could bring some "sweetness and light" to the lives of industrial workers in Dunfermline.[43]

In 1904, a mining accident near Pittsburgh resulted in the death of 179 miners, many of whom were teenage boys. In response, the steel tycoon decided to endow $5 million for what became the Carnegie Hero Fund Commission, which was to be responsible for recognizing persons in "peaceful vocations" who act to "preserve or rescue their fellows."[44] In 1908, Carnegie established a similar hero fund in Great Britain with an endowment of $10 million, as well as others in France, Belgium, Denmark, Italy, the Netherlands, Norway, Sweden, and Switzerland, though none of the latter enjoyed the level of wealth of their counterpart funds in the United States and Great Britain.[45]

During these years, Carnegie also had his attention on teacher pensions. In 1905, for example, he established the Carnegie Foundation for the Advancement of Teaching with a gift of $10 million, which he increased by $5 million in 1908 and an additional $1.25 million five years later. The purpose of the foundation was to "provide retiring pensions for the teachers of universities, colleges, and technical schools in our country, Canada, and Newfoundland . . . without regard to race, sex, creed or color."[46] The organization's board of directors would find it nearly impossible to finance all university professors' pensions, so Carnegie empowered it to define the institutions that would be eligible for Carnegie pensions. In judging the relative merits of universities across the country, the foundation played a critical role as an accrediting agency in the United States during the first half of the twentieth century, at least until the National Commission on Accreditation was organized.[47]

During the final decade of his life, Carnegie established three more foundations, two in the United States and another in the United Kingdom: the Carnegie Endowment for International Peace in 1910, Carnegie Corporation of New York in 1911, and the Carnegie United Kingdom Trust in 1913. Of these, the one that stood apart—quite apart—from the rest was Carnegie Corporation of New York in terms of its wealth, scope, and management. A year before founding the organization in 1911, a seventy-five-year-old Andrew Carnegie had realized that he personally would be unable to dispose of his wealth before he died, so his lawyer, Elihu Root, had suggested that he endow a trust during his lifetime. Between 1911 and 1912, the steel magnate endowed the corporation with $125 million, making it the wealthiest foundation in the world at the time. And compared to the other foundations that Carnegie established, Carnegie Corporation was established with a rather broad mandate: "to promote the advancement and diffusion of knowledge and understanding among the people of the United States."[48] During the first half of the twentieth century, its only rival in wealth and expansive mission was the Rockefeller Foundation.[49]

Carnegie Corporation also was distinct from other Carnegie foundations in its management style. For one thing, Carnegie himself led the corporation. As Nasaw notes, "Carnegie named himself the corporation's first president, arranged for all trustee meetings and business to be transacted from [his home at] Ninety-first Street [in Manhattan], and appointed his bookkeeper, Robert Franks, as treasurer, and James Bertram as secretary."[50] Carnegie's lawyer, Elihu Root, became the corporation's vice president, and presidents of Carnegie's U.S. foundations populated the other seats on the eight-member board. He also treated it as an extension of his private office until his death in 1919. Considering his personal history of making gifts throughout the United States and Great Britain, Carnegie sought to expand the geographic scope of the corporation's charter. Approved by New York State in 1917, the new charter allowed the organization to "hold and administer any funds given to it for use in Canada or the British colonies for the same purposes in Canada or the British colonies as those to which it is by law authorized to apply its funds in the United States."[51]

Although the charter introduced two new geographic regions, the trustees of Carnegie Corporation called the $10 million allocated for funding outside the United States by different names that suggested various geographic jurisdictions. Thus, in addition to the "Canada and the British Colonies" fund, they spoke of the "fund provided by Mr. Carnegie for all of the English-speaking commonwealths."[52] Reflecting their conflation between Canada and the British colonies and the "English-speaking commonwealths," Andrew Carnegie and his trustees at Carnegie Corporation made grants in areas of the British Empire beyond strictly "Canada and the British Colonies," such as the British dominions of South Africa, Australia, and New Zealand.

During these years, James Bertram had become a loyal and constant presence in Andrew Carnegie's life. By then, the two men had shared symbiotic daily routines for two decades, after first meeting during one of the Carnegie family's lengthy sojourns in Europe some twenty years earlier. They had met in 1897, when Andrew Carnegie, his wife, Louise, and daughter, Margaret, were spending the winter in Cannes, France, Carnegie found himself in need of a personal secretary. A trusted Edinburgh contact informed him that Bertram had just returned to Scotland after a severe fever required him to leave South Africa where he had been working for the previous seven years, developing into a stage manager in South Africa's railway industry and then as secretary in its mining industry.[53]

Born in Corstorphine, Scotland, some fifteen miles from Andrew Carnegie's own hometown of Dunfermline, James Bertram was only twenty-four years old when he started working for the sixty-two-year-old Scottish-American steel titan who was then becoming ever more committed to philanthropy. Serving as personal secretary to Carnegie throughout the rest of the steel titan's life, Bertram subsequently assumed the role of secretary and lifetime trustee at Carnegie Corporation.[54]

Bertram's proximity to Andrew Carnegie was rather unique. Bertram arguably had more knowledge about Carnegie's vision for philanthropy than even

Carnegie's wife or daughter, both of whom later sat on Carnegie Corporation's board. During the 1890s and early 1900s, Bertram and Carnegie had enjoyed a daily routine of gathering in the morning. They read business reports, and Carnegie dictated letters, though with time, these business reports were replaced by donation requests.[55] And far from simply being part of Carnegie's daily routine in New York City, Bertram traveled with him and his family during their annual treks across the Atlantic.[56] Next to Carnegie for significant moments in the philanthropist's life, Bertram was there when Carnegie published "Wealth" and so too when he sold his shares of Carnegie Steel Company.[57]

Bertram's title as Andrew Carnegie's personal secretary would remain the same over the years, but, in practice, he became the manager of the industrialist's philanthropy. Bertram sifted through and decided the merits of the numerous requests that reached Andrew Carnegie's desk. As Nasaw writes: "Carnegie trusted Bertram to make the decisions, though from time to time he would question a particular application to make sure Bertram was paying attention."[58]

Later at Carnegie Corporation, Bertram would continue to enjoy a significant role in shaping the philanthropy of the then-deceased Andrew Carnegie. Granted that with Andrew Carnegie's passing, Bertram's role as sole manager of Carnegie's private philanthropy would be diluted by the presence of new individuals serving on the staff and board of Carnegie Corporation, but Bertram would maintain his influence by repeatedly determining whether the organization's trustees and staff, such as Keppel, were financing projects that Andrew Carnegie himself would have condoned.

## 3. James Bertram Interprets Carnegie's Intentions as Philanthropist

Upon assuming the presidency of Carnegie Corporation in 1923, Frederick Keppel learned that James Bertram was willing to challenge fellow trustees on Andrew Carnegie's vision for the foundation, even in the presence of Carnegie's widow, Louise Carnegie, who had joined the board in 1919, after Carnegie's death.[59]

During the first month of his presidency, for example, Keppel witnessed a rather dramatic moment when Bertram decided to vote against the entire board, which had decided to dedicate $3 million of the Special Fund for Canada and the British colonies toward unifying universities in the Maritime Provinces of Canada and Newfoundland. In response, Bertram argued that the "six years' income of the fund provided by Mr. Carnegie for all of the English-speaking commonwealths, or to use the language of the Trust, 'Canada and the British colonies,'" was disproportionately large for the comparatively small community of "whites" in the English-speaking world who actually lived in the Maritime Provinces of Canada.[60] The other trustees overpowered his single vote, but Bertram was unafraid of voting against the entire board, and shaming these individuals for financing projects that he thought went counter to Andrew Carnegie's intentions.

Regarding Andrew Carnegie's expectations for Carnegie Corporation, Keppel would soon learn that Bertram was particularly forceful about the philanthropist's intentions to assist primarily white people in the Anglo-American world. At various moments during Keppel's presidency, Bertram spoke of the "English-speaking commonwealths" and explained that this was the broad area that Andrew Carnegie had intended to help when he chartered Carnegie Corporation.[61] Bertram also specified that the populations whom Carnegie had intended to target and help in the "English-speaking commonwealths" were white.[62] In 1923, Bertram had tabulated these populations, noting that only over a million white people lived in the Maritime Provinces of Canada, while over seven million existed in the rest of Canada and over five million in Australia, with smaller populations in New Zealand and the Union of South Africa.[63]

There was a difference, Bertram explained to Keppel, between the technical language of Carnegie Corporation's charter, which specified the United States, Canada, and the British colonies as its geographic domain, and Andrew Carnegie's intentions as a philanthropist. As Bertram put it, Carnegie's reference to the "British colonies" was inclusive of some territories of the British Empire with the official status of "dominion" and exclusive of some with the formal status of "colony."[64] By "British colony," Bertram explained, Carnegie had meant "communities of whites"; a point Bertram stressed was clear in Carnegie's own grantmaking practices in the British Empire even if Carnegie never quite wrote down his policy on paper.[65] For purposes of interpreting the charter's language, then, Bertram suggested to Keppel that the British Empire's own distinctions between colonies, protectorates, and dominions were insufficient. Leaning instead on a dictionary definition of "colony," Bertram explained that Carnegie had meant to aid "settlements made by emigrants and with populations composed of emigrants or descendants of emigrants."[66]

While Bertram combined this dictionary definition of colony with his own interpretation of Carnegie's intentions to help communities of white people throughout the British Empire, Bertram could alternatively have reasoned that Carnegie had intended that the entirety of the current and past territories of the British Empire be within the corporation's geographic reach, given that every part of the empire had *some* population of white Europeans. However, the mere presence of white people did not satisfy Bertram's idea of Carnegie's vision. In determining whether a region of the British Empire comprised "communities of whites," Bertram analyzed which parts of the empire could ever be dominated by white people. In this vein, he explained to Keppel that India, the Philippines, and West Africa, for example, could never be white communities, and thus, that no "Carnegie money is likely to be spent" there.[67]

In his publications, Andrew Carnegie did not routinely use the word "white" as Bertram did with Keppel when describing the philanthropist's main agenda in the Anglo-American world. Rather, Carnegie preferred categorizing white Americans and Englishmen as the "English-speaking people" or part of the "Teutonic race."[68] But the effect was the same. White Anglo-Americans indeed were the community of people whom Carnegie sought to aid with the establishment of philanthropic foundations in the United States and Great Britain, and so too the people he sought to unite under his vision for global peace.[69]

Elaborating on his vision for international order in *Triumphant Democracy* (1893), for example, Andrew Carnegie had suggested the possibility of a British-American Union that could help establish further stability and peace at the global level. For him, there was absolute commonality among the citizens of Great Britain and the United States, whom he described as members of the "English-speaking race"—as a people with combined cultural and biological traits.[70] He wrote: "In race—and there is a great deal in race—the American remains three-fourths purely British. The mixture of the German, which constitutes substantially all of the remainder, though not strictly British, is yet Germanic. The Briton of to-day is himself composed in large measure of the Germanic element, and German, Briton, and American are all of the Teutonic race."[71]

Illustrating the biological similarities among white people in the United States and Great Britain, Carnegie also gave thought to the other parts of the British Empire that could be included in this imagined "British-American Union."[72] In this vein, he suggested that "Australasia," meaning populations in Australia and New Zealand, could unite on equal terms with the rest of the "Teutonic race."[73] By contrast, he argued, India could not be part of such a union because no "branch of the race now clear of any share in these [responsibilities in India] would willingly consent to become a partner in them."[74] In other words, Carnegie imagined that Australasia fit with his racialized view of the British-American world in ways that India did not. Ultimately, Carnegie argued in *Triumphant Democracy* that India would "be placed upon the road to independence, and the British-American Union would guide it to this as well as the present Union of the United Kingdom."[75]

Beyond seeing commonalities among white Anglo-Americans, Carnegie also emphasized in *Triumphant Democracy* the value of unifying all these people and regions, reasoning that a bound white English-speaking world—a "British-American Union"—could further international peace by serving as the world's arbiters.

To note, Andrew Carnegie was not unique among contemporaries in his ideas for an international English-speaking community or in assuming that such leadership would be white or that its further unification was essential for international order. As historian Duncan Bell observes, Carnegie was reflecting an ongoing and significant debate in the late nineteenth century about the potential unity between the United Kingdom and its settler colonies (precisely those regions Carnegie emphasized such as Australia, New Zealand, and the United States).[76] Bell furthermore underscores how these conversations on a "Greater Britain" in the late nineteenth century assumed a project of uniting white Anglo-Americans, with contemporaries communicating a shared international whiteness in both cultural and biological terms: "Greater Britain was underpinned, so it was thought, by a common race, where race was defined primarily by the beliefs, traditions, institutions, and behavioral characteristics associated with being 'English' (or British of 'Anglo-Saxon'). These were, in general, mutable and shaped by history rather than nature—although the space opened up by this mutability was (usually) implicitly delimited by the boundaries of 'whiteness.'"[77] Much like other advocates of a united "Greater Britain" on the world stage, Carnegie imagined bringing together white English-speaking people as world leaders and thus as safeguards of global order.

And so, while Carnegie shied away from using the explicit term "white" in his discussions of an Anglo-American union at the global level, it is fair to say that Bertram offered a relatively accurate translation of Carnegie's intention when he said that it was to unify white English-speaking regions of the world. Cherry-picking regions of the British Empire to include in his vision for a British-American Union, Carnegie had shown particular affinity for regions of the Anglo-American world such as the United States, Canada, Britain,

New Zealand, and Australia. Bertram added two more: South Africa and East Africa, both of which, he claimed, Andrew Carnegie would have supported as philanthropist.

As president of Carnegie Corporation, Frederick Keppel made his first grant in colonial Africa in 1925 and specifically chose Kenya, a British territory in East Africa that Bertram deemed sufficiently white, or rather, adequately populated by a governing body of white people. During the next two years, Keppel and Bertram would plan an exploratory trip to British Africa as the organization considered an expansion of its commitments on the continent. In the spirit of Bertram's reading of Carnegie's intentions in the Anglo-American world, the two men would limit their tour to East and southern Africa to the exclusion of West Africa.

During the next decade and up until his death in 1934, Bertram would play a leading role in defining Carnegie Corporation's geographic scope in colonial Africa, and as the next chapter shows, its substantive grantmaking practices in these regions of British Africa that Bertram deemed likely to remain under white rule. Bertram's influence, however, cannot simply be explained by noting his privileged position as a former personal secretary of Andrew Carnegie. This is because two other Carnegie Corporation trustees—John Poynton and Robert A. Franks—also previously had served as Andrew Carnegie's personal secretary and financial agent. And like Bertram, Poynton and Franks later assumed staff and lifetime trustee roles at Carnegie Corporation.

So Keppel's reliance on Bertram to define the geographic scope of the corporation's work in the British colonies cannot simply be explained by Bertram's personal relationship with Carnegie. Neither was it simply because Bertram had spent years living in South Africa, or because he sat on Carnegie Corporation's board. It also had to do with Bertram's firsthand experience leading Carnegie's personal philanthropic giving and, equally so, his own outsized and dominating personality. To this latter point, Keppel's assistant, James Russell, later remembered that Keppel took the corporation secretary on his first tour of West and southern Africa because he felt "that Bertram wouldn't approve of [a grantmaking program in Africa] unless he was asked to go. Bertram was a very difficult person."[78] James Bertram's outsized influence on the board—and his insistence that it was Andrew Carnegie's philanthropic intention to prioritize white people in the Anglo-American world—remained an internal, rather than a publicized matter, at Carnegie Corporation during the 1920s and 1930s.

To this point, in a 1927 report to fellow Carnegie Corporation board members on their exploratory trip to Africa, Bertram and Keppel would be rather sincere about the organization's geographic constraints, as they understood them to be. Explaining to fellow trustees why they had excluded West Africa from their tour of the continent, Keppel and Bertram underscored that the "white population is too small [in West Africa] to offer any opportunities to the Corporation."[79]

Beyond internal correspondence, though, Carnegie Corporation leaders at the time would shy away from sharing publicly their working definition of "British colonies," though they did seem to discuss it informally at times with trusted nonstaff and trustees. In 1927, for example, when Keppel met with the London-based missionary J. H. Oldham, Oldham confirmed that the "probable interest of Mr. Carnegie himself would have been in white settlers, rather than blacks."[80] Considering Keppel's increasingly close relationship with Oldham during the 1920s, as the next chapters illustrate, Keppel likely had shared with him Bertram's reading of Carnegie's intentions to privilege the needs of white people in Africa, with Oldham confirming to Keppel the likely validity of Bertram's analysis of this famous public figure's intentions in the British empire.

Such moments of openness from Keppel—with people beyond staff and trustees at Carnegie Corporation—about the corporation's explicit mandate to prioritize white communities in the Anglo-American world would be rare. For the most part, Keppel would shy away from doing so. Instead and throughout his presidency, Keppel would offer varying public explanations for the organization's geographic foci outside of the United States and would remain coy about its explicit emphasis on white communities.

In 1934, James Bertram would pass away. Seven years later, Keppel would retire as president of Carnegie Corporation, and just a year after that, he too would pass away. The deaths of these two men would mark the end of an era at Carnegie Corporation, an era that subsequent staff and board members would bring to a more formal conclusion by formally amending the organization's charter to exclude lifetime trusteeships. Furthermore, and showing greater anxiety about the two coexisting means of interpreting Carnegie Corporation's geographic reach, the organization of the later 1940s also would update its charter to reflect what its staff and board members long had been doing already under Bertram's guidance.[81] In 1948, for example, Carnegie Corporation amended its charter to include the British dominions along with the British colonies within the organization's geographic reach. In 1961, the corporation went even a step further to include past British protectorates, protected states, settlements, or trust territories.[82]

Focusing on Carnegie Corporation of the 1920s, this next chapter illustrates how President Keppel made a cautious first grant in colonial Africa, in part by relying further on James Bertram's reading of Andrew Carnegie's hierarchy of funding priorities within "communities of whites" in the Anglo-American world.[83]

## CHAPTER 2

# Paying for Our Well-Meant Attempts to Govern Subject Races

## *A Cautious Turn to Africa*

In a 1931 letter to Carnegie Corporation president Frederick Keppel, Carnegie Corporation trustee James Bertram reinforced the priorities of Andrew Carnegie, and by extension, the organization throughout the Anglo-American world: "Any money which Mr. Carnegie gave to the Colonies was given for the reason that they were communities of whites. . . . The reason that I personally was interested in having the sphere of action of Carnegie Corporation extended to Kenya and the other high tableland country of East Africa and to South Africa is that they are, or at least are potentially, white communities. Although the Corporation has provided money which will be spent on the natives the subventions are in aid of the education problems of white communities."[1] In this letter to Keppel, Bertram explained that his support for Carnegie Corporation's 1925 decision to allocate $37,500 for "cooperation with the British Government in educational developments in Kenya Colony" was in line with Andrew Carnegie's intentions to assist "white communities" in the British Empire.[2] Bertram reasoned that he had condoned funding education for Black people in Kenya because, once again channeling Andrew Carnegie's intentions as a philanthropist, the organization had been addressing an educational problem of a white community in the Anglo-American world: the problem of how to educate Black people under white rule.

Focusing on Carnegie Corporation's first grant in colonial Africa under Keppel's leadership, this chapter argues that Keppel took a careful initial step in developing and expanding the corporation's funding agenda in Africa. In his first grant in colonial Africa, Keppel not only relied on Bertram's reading of Andrew Carnegie's intentions as a funder in "white communities" in the British Empire, but he decided to fund a model of education for Black people that was well supported and advocated by his peers at the Rockefeller organizations and the Phelps Stokes Fund.[3]

As subsequent chapters illustrate, Keppel would become personally invested in solidifying white governance over Black people across the Atlantic and would take greater risks as a foundation leader to impose more of his personality onto the organization's funding program in Africa. And yet, even as Keppel would expand upon his first grant in Kenya and be willing to bring into his leadership of Carnegie Corporation's work in British Africa more of his personal preference for the social sciences as tools for white governance, he would continue to heed Bertram's geographic and substantive restrictions. In this vein, and quite astutely for someone who aimed to remain president of Carnegie Corporation for some time, Keppel would continue to express funding preferences in colonial Africa that sat well with Bertram's emphasis both on funding in areas of the Anglo-American world that Bertram considered sufficiently white and on projects and institutions privileging the needs of white people in these geographic regions.

With an eye towards underscoring the cautionary nature of Keppel's first grant in colonial Africa, this chapter begins by reflecting on Andrew Carnegie's 1907 lecture, "Negro in America." This first section provides context for James Bertram's depiction of Andrew Carnegie's intentions for financing a particular model of education for Black Americans and Bertram's confidence that Carnegie also would have supported its application among Black Africans in "white communities" of the British Empire.

## 1. Andrew Carnegie's "Negro in America" (1907)

In 1907, Andrew Carnegie delivered a lecture at the Philosophical Institute in Edinburgh, Scotland, where he indicated his reasons for funding a particular model of education for Black Americans and its relevance across the Anglo-American world. This was a perspective, again, that James Bertram later would mobilize to steer Carnegie Corporation's funding practices in colonial Africa.[4]

Speaking on the "Negro in America," Carnegie contrasted white people of the "English-speaking race" with "subject races" and explained to his Scottish audience the global relevance of his experience financing education for Black people in the United States.[5] In his view, his preferred educational model for Black Americans—one promoting training in industrial and agricultural practices that would leave unchallenged white domination and Black subordination in cultural, social, and economic life—could be exported across the Anglo-American world and applied to other "subject races," as a means of maintaining white dominance and furthering white people's economic and political interests across these regions.

Believing that he had selected a topic that should interest any Anglo-American audience whether in New York, Boston, Edinburgh, London, or Cardiff, Carnegie told his Edinburgh audience that the education of "subject races," from Black Americans to Egyptians, Indians, and Filipinos, was critically important for all white Britons because the form of education that white Britons chose for "subject races" long had had—and would continue to have—critical consequences for white Anglo-Americans' continued ability to dominate them.[6] As Carnegie stressed: "Education is moral dynamite which invariably explodes into rebellion. This is one of the penalties that we of the English-speaking race have to pay for our well-meant attempts to govern what are called subject races. In teaching our history, we supply them with the most deadly explosives, sure some day to burst and rend the teacher."[7]

In particular, Carnegie feared that the teaching of wars, revolutions, and Anglo-American ideals of liberty—education that was presumably appropriate for white people—would backfire and lead "subject races" throughout the Anglo-American world to demand equality with white people. "Intelligence forces equal rights," Carnegie elaborated, "hence the unrest in Egypt, India, the Philippines, and other countries under foreign tutelage is, in one sense, a wholesome sign as proving that the awakening masses are stirred to action and demand recognition as fellow-citizens, thus showing that our teaching, and especially our example, have had their inevitable and, let us never forget, their salutary effect."[8]

Like a mother who was proud of her children, Carnegie noted that "the English-speaking race" could be pleased with its role in empowering some subject races toward independence across the Anglo-American world. At the same time, he contrasted this image of educated and revolutionary Egyptians, Indians, and Filipinos with Black Americans, whom he described as "a respectable, educated, intelligent race of colored citizens, increasing in numbers, possest of all civil rights, and who in turn will by honest labor remain notably the chief factor in giving the world among other things its indispensable supply of cotton."[9]

As Andrew Carnegie explained in this 1907 lecture, there was nothing inherently unique to Black Americans that led them to be less revolutionary than Egyptians, Indians, and Filipinos. On the contrary, Carnegie reasoned that white Anglo-Americans' varying approaches to these various groups' education was the critical difference. White Americans' bar on educating Black slaves, Carnegie reasoned, had helped leading white Americans maintain this system of enslavement. To this point, Carnegie noted that "ignorance is the only foundation upon which dominion over others can rest."[10]

After the abolition of slavery in the United States, Carnegie relayed to his audience in Scotland that white Americans then had promoted a model of education among Black Americans encouraging them to find satisfaction and pride as a subjugated group, rather than in enflaming a plea for equal rights with white people. Making particular mention of two prominent U.S. schools promoting agricultural and industrial education for Black Americans—Booker T. Washington's Tuskegee Institute and Samuel Armstrong's Hampton Institute, discussed further in this chapter—Carnegie said that this preferred educational model for Black Americans served to elevate this "subject race" gradually from slavery to full citizenship with white Americans. In the meantime, and underscoring the interests of white Anglo-Americans such as himself, Carnegie explained that this educational model prepared Black Americans to continue providing a product which Carnegie reasoned was central for the economies of the southern United States, the United States as a whole, and the world: cotton.[11]

Admitting that some Black Americans harbored particular intellectual talents and merited higher forms of education, Carnegie noted that "like other races that have risen, our own included, the negro is capable of producing at intervals the exceptional man who stimulates his fellows."[12] Those gifted few should have places in all professions, Carnegie allowed, though the majority of Black Americans should continue to provide the labor that they had provided the southern United States before the Civil War.[13] Relatedly, Carnegie explained that the educational model for Black Americans advocated by the Tuskegee and Hampton Institutes had played a significant role in helping white and Black Americans "dwell in peace" in the country.[14]

Celebrating the educational model that supposedly had shaped Black Americans into honest laborers uninterested in challenging white domination, Carnegie suggested in this 1907 speech that white Americans' leading model of education for Black Americans could play a similar role in pacifying the egalitarian aspirations of other colonized groups in the Anglo-American world and in transforming these subjugated groups into reliable labor for the white "English-speaking race."[15]

As James Bertram later would relay to Frederick Keppel, and as this public lecture suggests, Andrew Carnegie helped fund education for Black Americans largely as a means of furthering the economic and political interests of white people in the Anglo-American world. Because while Carnegie did verbalize concern for improving the lives of Black Americans, he never intended to challenge the economic or political interests of white Anglo-Americans. Rather, by funding education for Black Americans, as Bertram stressed and Carnegie underscored to his audience in Edinburgh, Scotland, in 1907, he had aimed to provide white Anglo-Americans with a means of averting the revolutionary potential of "subject races." And for Carnegie, applying the Tuskegee educational model for "subject races" across the Anglo-American world was key towards these ends. Much as Bertram condoned in Carnegie Corporation's efforts to expand this grantmaking practice to colonial Africa, Andrew Carnegie's 1907 essay indeed suggests that the philanthropist had been eager to export this educational model outside the United States, as a further effort to solidify white Anglo-Americans' international domination.

This next section provides greater frame of reference to the dominance in the United States of the educational model for Black Americans that Andrew Carnegie celebrated in the 1907 lecture. After all, as this chapter argues, Keppel took a cautious first step in establishing a grantmaking program in British Africa, both by honoring Bertram's reading of Carnegie's intentions as a philanthropist in the Anglo-American world and by complementing a contemporaneous trend among his philanthropic peers to export this educational model from the United States to British Africa. It begins with a general overview of this educational model's development in the United States.[16]

## 2. Elite U.S. Philanthropy's Funding of Education for Black Americans

With the abolition of slavery after the U.S. Civil War (1861–1865), Black Americans in the southern United States began to reconstruct their lives as free people, which included the freedom to learn how to read and write. As historian Tera Hunter writes: "Sheer survival and the reconstruction of family, despite all the difficulties, were the highest priorities of ex-slaves in the postwar period. But the desire for literacy and education was closely related to their strategies for achieving economic self-sufficiency, political autonomy, and personal enrichment."[17] Newly free families sacrificed parts of their own earnings to build schoolhouses, provide books and supplies, and pay teachers' salaries. Without the support of their states, which increasingly were providing schooling for all white Americans, Black southerners found themselves paying for their own schooling and, at times too, leaning on the support of northern missionaries and the U.S. federal government.[18]

In contrast to many Black families emphasizing classical education as means for greater political and economic empowerment, wealthy white northerners with interest in supporting education for Black southerners largely sympathized with the efforts of former Union Army general and founder of the Hampton Institute in Virginia, Samuel Armstrong, and especially that of his student and future principal of Tuskegee Institute, Booker T. Washington.[19] While these latter schools continued to underscore the importance of a strong foundation in elementary education, at least in public Washington stressed to potential white funders that this particular model of education first-and-foremost would emphasize the training of Black southerners for jobs that would not challenge white supremacy and anti-Black subordination in the region and would thus favor the economic and political interests of white people.[20] As historian Emma L. Thornbrough writes: "The views expressed by Washington on education and the position of Negroes in American society and politics were so much in harmony with the views expressed by the white philanthropists who supported Tuskegee and other public men of the day that their speeches and writings frequently sound like paraphrases of each other."[21]

Illustrating the developing symbiosis between the rising dominance of the Hampton-Tuskegee educational model for Black Americans in the southern United Statues and white northern philanthropists' developing interest in funding this particular model of Black education, George Peabody established the Peabody Education Fund in 1867, a year before Samuel Armstrong founded Hampton Institute: "Convinced that education was instrumental to reconciling the North and South during the Reconstruction period, this New England merchant and banker chartered the fund to encourage 'intellectual, moral and industrial education' in the South and Southwest by stabilizing the public education system and fostering the growth of common schools."[22] Within ten years of operating the Peabody Education Fund, Peabody met Armstrong and was sufficiently impressed by Armstrong to accept the invitation to join the Hampton board of trustees.[23]

Following Armstrong's lead, the Peabody Fund specialized in funding country schools that offered vocational and agricultural education to Black southerners and teacher training for these schools. The Peabody Fund supported Armstrong's Hampton Institute alongside the Tuskegee Normal and Industrial Institute, which Washington, a former slave and Hampton graduate, founded in Alabama in 1881. Much like the Hampton Institute, Booker T. Washington's Tuskegee Institute trained Black teachers and officially taught practical skills that would help Black students succeed at farming and in other manual trades in the South such as construction and domestic work. Unlike Hampton's faculty and staff, however, most of the faculty and staff at Tuskegee were Black. In an effort to advance this form of manual education for Black Americans, the Peabody Fund worked hand in hand with yet another philanthropic organization, the John F. Slater Fund, established by a textile manufacturer from Connecticut in 1882.[24]

In the 1860s and 1870s, Black schools controlled by missionary societies and Black religious organizations generally had been "indifferent or opposed to the Tuskegee model of industrial training," while those funded by this network of white northern philanthropists tended to argue that this pedagogy for Black students comfortably served the interests of both former Black slaves and white leaders in the South.[25] During the next decades, this latter educational model funded by key white philanthropists only gained momentum in the southern United States, though, as this chapter later explains, its meteoric rise also met with public criticism, particularly from Black scholars such as W. E. B. Du Bois and Carter Woodson.

A turning point in this history of competing models for Black education in the South was Booker T. Washington's address at the 1895 Atlanta Exposition. With this speech—and this national platform—he gained the attention and allegiance of even more leading white northern industrialists, including Andrew Carnegie. Faced with an audience of Black Americans and prominent whites Americans from the North and South, Washington began the speech by noting how vocational and agricultural education for Black southerners "would cement the friendship of the races and bring about hearty cooperation between them."[26]

When Washington delivered his address in Atlanta, Georgia, it had been nearly two decades since white northern Republicans had withdrawn federal troops from the region.[27] And since then, southern states such as Georgia had been passing laws demarcating a subordinate status for Black people and a superior one for whites. Just four years prior to Washington's lecture in Atlanta, for example, Georgia's legislature had passed a law allowing the city to delineate the color line "in public conveyances 'as much as practicable.'"[28] A year after Washington's speech, the U.S. Supreme Court condoned such laws with its decision in *Plessy v. Ferguson*, holding that state-imposed laws calling for the segregation of white and Black people were not necessarily discriminatory, and thus, did not violate the Fourteenth Amendment's Equal Protection Clause of the U.S. Constitution.

Speaking from the southern United States in 1895, Washington proposed the Tuskegee model of education for Black Americans as a public policy recommendation reflecting a compromise between three groups of Americans: southern whites, northern whites, and Black Americans. Likely because he was speaking in front of a white southern audience gaining both ever more dominance in the region and support from white northerners, he first addressed the fears and anxieties of southern whites. In particular, he acknowledged white southerners' distress that education would empower Black Americans to expect equality with white Americans.

Washington took it upon himself to explain to southern whites, who had outlawed literacy and education to Black people during slavery, how and why any form of Black education was necessary. He first noted that Black people had been misguided in their efforts to achieve the same accomplishments as white people after the Civil War: "Ignorant and inexperienced, it is not strange that in the first years of our new life we began at the top instead of at the bottom; that a seat in Congress or the state legislature was more sought than real estate or industrial skill; that the political convention or stump speaking had more attractions than starting a dairy farm or truck garden."[29] Placating white Americans' anxieties that education for Black Americans would disrupt white supremacy, he echoed many white southerners' perspectives that Black Americans would need to work their way toward proving their equality. And he noted that Black Americans could begin to do so by showing white people that they found dignity in their manual work.

Illustrating his common thinking with his white southern audience, Washington then explained that the Tuskegee model not only would help Black Americans find pride in manual labor, but also help the southern U.S. economy advance after the catastrophe of the Civil War. Washington declared to his southern white audience: "One-third of the population of the South is of the Negro race. No enterprise seeking the material, civil, or moral welfare of this section can disregard this element of our population and reach the highest success."[30] While acknowledging that white southerners remained hesitant to support Black Americans' education, Washington noted that agricultural and industrial education was necessary for the region's economic rehabilitation and growth after the Civil War.

Washington foresaw his white audience's misgivings about Black education and emphasized that the Tuskegee model of education would not encourage Black Americans to think of themselves as equals to white Americans in the South; but rather, it would train them to accept entry-level work in southern agriculture and industry.[31] Even more, he stressed that this was entry-level work that would not upset the color line that southern whites were establishing at the time, pointing out: "In all things that are purely social we can be as separate as the fingers, yet, one as the hand in all things essential to mutual progress."[32]

Washington further clarified that the Tuskegee model of education not only played into the interests of southern whites, but also those of northern white industrialists. Just three years prior to Washington's Atlanta address, for example, the deadly Homestead Strike had taken place in one of Andrew Carnegie's steel plants near Pittsburgh, Pennsylvania, leaving several steelworkers and members of the Carnegie Steel Company police force dead and hundreds others in both groups injured. Historian Nell Painter explains that:

"Most Americans, shocked at the bloodshed and the passion displayed by the workers, blamed the Carnegie management for provocation through wage cuts and the fortification of the mill."[33] The Pennsylvania Governor had sent 8,000 militiamen to maintain order, but the chaos continued. That summer, there was an attempted assassination of the plant manager, Henry Clay Frick; and in the early fall, numerous striking workers were indicted on 167 counts of murder, rioting, and conspiracy.[34] All were found not guilty, but they had remained in jail awaiting trial for a month. While the Carnegie Steel Company succeeded in bringing an end to the strike, it was a signal that there would be equally tense labor struggles in the future.

Alluding to the fact that many strikers in this infamous strike had been white and some strikebreakers Black, Booker T. Washington further noted in his Atlanta address that northern industrialists should support the Tuskegee model of education for Black Americans because it would help strengthen a laboring class that was loyal to them. To this point, he called northern industrialists: "Cast down your bucket among these people who have, without strikes and labour wars, tilled your fields, cleared your forests, builded your railroads and cities, and brought forth treasures from the bowels of the earth, and helped make possible this magnificent representation of the progress of the South."[35] To white northerners in the audience, Washington thus stressed that Black Americans were loyal laborers who would simply serve to maximize white Americans' profits with their continued hard work. And for these reasons, Washington urged northern industrialists, precisely such as Carnegie and his northern peers in philanthropy, to support and help fund the Tuskegee Institute and complementary groups in its orbit.

At the same time, Washington also spelled out why Black Americans should support this particular form of education. He argued that their future was in the South among southern whites, and that they should make the best of it: "To those of my race who depend on bettering their condition in a foreign land or who underestimate the importance of cultivating friendly relations with the Southern white man, who is their next-door neighbor, I would say: 'Cast down your bucket where you are'—cast it down in making friends in every manly way of the people of all races by whom we are surrounded."[36] Washington urged Black Americans to accept that they belonged in the South, that they were southerners, and that they could achieve freedom by learning "that there is as much dignity in tilling a field as in writing a poem."[37]

Before Washington's speech, northern white philanthropists such as George Peabody, John Slater, and John D. Rockefeller already had been funding the Hampton-Tuskegee educational model for Black Americans.[38] In 1901, for example, the Rockefellers wrote directly to Washington and asked how they could help in expanding the work of the Tuskegee Institute throughout the South; within a few months, John D. Rockefeller Jr. himself was on a train south to visit Hampton in Virginia and Tuskegee in Alabama. "After visits to Hampton and Tuskegee Institutes and from many discussions with the school campaigners, Rockefeller, Jr., became sufficiently impressed with the Southern education movement to approach his father about establishing a new foundation to reinforce the reformers' efforts."[39] Two years later, the Rockefellers founded the General Education Board (GEB). Though the organization was initially to be called the "Negro Education Board," advisors close to the Rockefellers suggested that a more neutral name would not alienate white southerners as much.[40] In 1903, the Rockefellers incorporated the General Education Board with the general mission of promoting education in the United States irrespective of race, sex, or creed.[41]

After his 1895 Atlanta speech, and in these last years of the nineteenth century, Washington also heralded Andrew Carnegie's philanthropic support and greater commitment from the Rockefellers. Since Washington in 1895 had appealed to northern industrialists by underscoring ways that the Tuskegee educational model encouraged Black Americans to be and remain docile laborers loyal to capital, it is little surprise that he attracted the attention of even more northern white industrialists, including Carnegie who only three years prior had experienced a violent labor dispute in one of his steel plants. Even more, Washington's 1895 speech only further clarified for northern industrialists such as Carnegie how helping to fund a particular model of Black education could serve the political and economic interests of white northerners like himself and his peers who were eager to see a stronger southern—and by extension, national—economy.

In 1903, Carnegie made a substantial contribution of $600,000 to the Tuskegee Institute—a gesture further inspired by Washington's visit to New York City that year.[42] In a letter to a Tuskegee trustee published in the *New York Times*, Carnegie wrote: "I am satisfied that the serious race problem of the South is to be solved wisely only through Mr. Washington's policy of education—which he seems to have been specially born—a slave among slaves—to establish and in his own day greatly to advance. Glad am I to be able to assist this good work in which you and others so zealously labor."[43]

While enthusiastic about Washington's Tuskegee Institute, Carnegie never created an organization inspired by it such as the Rockefellers' GEB; nor did he play a leading role in financing Black schools. In the early 1910s, Andrew Carnegie—and by extension, Carnegie Corporation, which inherited its founder's funding practices in Black education—was rather on the periphery of this network of philanthropic organizations dedicated to funding Black education within and beyond the United States, further underscoring how Keppel's decision to fund the Tuskegee educational model in Kenya in 1925 was not simply a reflection of his own organization's priorities but, more broadly, of his peers in U.S. philanthropy.[44]

In the early decades of the twentieth century, after Washington's 1895 speech, the GEB was the wealthiest philanthropy dedicated to funding education for Black Americans, and it gained the cooperation of other philanthropic organizations invested in this field, such as the older Slater and Peabody Funds and the newer Jeanes and Phelps Stokes Funds.[45] The Jeanes Fund, or the "Negro Rural School Fund," was established in 1907 by Anna T. Jeanes, a Philadelphia Quaker, who directed that the income from her estate, valued at about $1 million, be used to assist rural schools for Black Americans.[46] Three years later, the GEB also gained the cooperation of the Slater Fund and the support of the Peabody Education Fund's various state agents overseeing education in the South.[47]

In 1911, the Phelps Stokes Fund joined this network of foundations, and it would play a sizeable role as advocate of the Tuskegee educational model for Black Americans and Africans alike. Founded by the estate of the deceased Caroline Phelps Stokes, the fund began with the complementary goals of improving housing and education for Black Americans, Native Americans, and "deserving white students, through industrial schools, the founding of scholarships, and the erection or endowment of school buildings or chapels."[48] Within a year after its founding, though, Caroline Phelps Stokes' nephew Anson Phelps Stokes steered the organization to focus more heavily on education than on housing. Writing to Booker T. Washington, Stokes asked him to imagine the best use of five to ten thousand dollars. In response, Washington wrote that "such a sum could be instrumental in accomplishing what he had long regarded as a necessity: distinguishing the worthy from the unworthy small denominational Negro schools."[49] Stokes took this suggestion to the organization's trustees, and the following year, the fund's board of trustees recorded: "The trustees, believing that such a report of existing conditions would prove invaluable to southern educators and legislators, to philanthropists interested in Negro education, to the principals and trustees of schools for colored youth, and to various educational boards, adopted the recommendations and asked the Commissioner of Education if he would accept the cooperation of the Phelps-Stokes Fund in making such a study on condition that the expenses of the agents should be paid by the fund."[50] As the trustees reasoned, such a report on schools for Black southerners would help educators, legislators, philanthropists, educational boards, principals, and trustees of schools assess the quality of high schools, colleges, and universities for Black Americans, and in the process, help steer public and private funding accordingly.

In 1912, Anson Phelps Stokes began a search for the best director of the study. Stokes had his sights particularly on the thirty-nine year-old Thomas Jesse Jones, who was a specialist in community education at the U.S. federal government's Bureau of Education. In his correspondence with Washington, Stokes explained that "the mere fact that Dr. Jones is at present connected with the Bureau of Education and that they would in all probability allow him to continue to occupy his office there, would be an important consideration."[51] It would be a study with the full sanction and prestige of the U.S. federal government behind it.[52]

During the next decades, Jones's survey of Black education—first in the United States and then in British Africa—would help this first generation of trustees and philanthropic staff at Carnegie Corporation confirm that their support of the Tuskegee educational model for Black Americans—and likewise Black Africans—was not only in line with their founder's intentions in the Anglo-American world, but also a sound funding decision supported by their philanthropic peers in the United States.

## 3. Thomas Jesse Jones's *Negro Education* (1917)

In the summer of 1917, the U.S. Government Printing Office delivered Thomas Jesse Jones's two-volume survey: *Negro Education: A Study of the Private and Higher Schools for Colored People in the United States.* The survey opened with a letter from the U.S. Commissioner of Education, P. P. Claxton, and an introduction by Stokes outlining the purpose of the study.[53] Jones commenced his work by discussing the importance of education for the inclusion of Black Americans in U.S. democratic life.[54]

Within the first page of his report, Jones mentioned Booker T. Washington—who had passed away two years earlier—and echoed this former Tuskegee principal's arguments for a particular model of education for Black Americans. Like Washington, Jones expressed that Black Americans' education would need to incorporate the interests of northern whites, southern whites, and Black Americans alike: "Democracy's plan for the solution of the race problem in the Southland is not primarily in the philanthropies and wisdom of northern people; nor is it in the desires and struggles of the colored people;

nor yet in the first-hand knowledge and daily contracts of the southern white people."[55] As Jones explained, white northerners, white southerners, and Black Americans needed to work together to create a comprehensive educational policy for Black Americans.

With white Americans' interests in mind, Jones reaffirmed the value of the Tuskegee model of education for Black Americans. In *Negro Education*, he explained that Black Americans' education should focus on providing them with skills adapted for the expectations and needs of rural communities in the South. Such an educational model, Jones argued, would help Black Americans learn the "sound habits of hand and head" that would help them become self-sustaining and, equally important, a well-trained and efficient labor force for white southerners. With a nod to white people in the North, and echoing the claims of Washington in his 1895 Atlanta Exposition address and Andrew Carnegie in "Negro in America" (1907), Jones stressed that educated Black labor would help strengthen the southern, and by extension the national, economies.[56]

Providing a "suggested program of educational development" for Black Americans from the elementary to college and professional levels, Jones argued in *Negro Education* that public school authorities needed to meet their obligations to educate Black Americans at the elementary level, with specific emphasis on their responsibility to increase literacy among this group of Americans: "So long as the elementary school facilities are insufficient, every kind of education above the elementary grades is seriously handicapped and the wellbeing of the community is endangered."[57] Beyond the attainment of literacy at the elementary level, Jones released his pressure on public school authorities and entertained the possibility of public and private options for Black Americans' higher learning.

With respect to secondary schools, he considered their main purpose to be training teachers for elementary education and believed that private philanthropists and public school authorities could continue working together in achieving this end.[58] Moreover, Jones argued that agricultural and mechanical schools could help expose Black students to useful knowledge about "gardening, small farming, and the simple industries required in farming communities."[59] Those educated in these trades, he explained, could go on and apply their knowledge on farms, for example, or teach other adults. Presumably those who had received secondary school education would teach similar subjects, but to children in elementary schools.

The highest level of education in Jones's educational program for Black Americans included college and professional education. Much as in the other two levels, Jones argued that this form of education should reflect the needs of the pupil and the community. Since a segregated society required Black doctors, teachers, and religious leaders, he stressed that Black colleges should provide for their training.[60]

After outlining this comprehensive policy for Black Americans' education, *Negro Education* offered an extensive survey of private elementary schools and public and private education above the elementary level in the South (with a final chapter on some select Black institutions in the North). In this second volume of the two-volume study, Jones presented a chapter on each southern state, with each individual chapter including a summary and assessment of the public and private educational facilities that he and his team of investigators had visited between 1913 and 1915.

### 4. Jones, U.S. Philanthropy, and the Tuskegee Model

Within two years after the publication of *Negro Education*—and in a move that only would increase Jones's influence among foundation leaders—Jones ceased working for the U.S. federal government and became the Phelps Stokes Fund's education director.[61]

Just months prior to the publication of *Negro Education*, the U.S. Senate had passed a resolution requesting the U.S. Department of the Interior's Bureau of Education to disclose any funds it received from private organizations such as the Carnegie and Rockefeller philanthropies. Given their Gilded Age capitalist founders, long viewed by many Americans as industry titans undermining the abilities of the U.S. working classes to thrive, legislators distrusted these groups' intentions in helping the U.S. public. On March 3, 1917, the U.S. Congress provided that "no Government official or employee shall receive any salary in connection with his services as such an official or employee from any source other than the Government of the United States, except as may be contributed out of the treasury of any State, county, or municipality."[62] No longer could philanthropies directly pay the salaries of sitting government employees such as Thomas Jesse Jones.

The U.S. commissioner of education experienced some level of worry about this development, and so too did Jones, who admitted to Anson Phelps Stokes that "there is too, the possibility that it may be well for us to withdraw from the bureau before some erratic Congressman has had an opportunity to suggest that we should withdraw."[63] Before Congress took any further steps to curtail philanthropy-government collaboration, Jones accepted a position at the Phelps Stokes Fund.

Under Jones's leadership, a network of philanthropic organizations including the Phelps Stokes Fund, the GEB, Carnegie Corporation, and smaller auxiliary philanthropic organizations such as the Rosenwald, Slater, and Jeans Funds coordinated with each other and with U.S. state and local officials in furthering a model of industrial and agricultural education for Black Americans well into the 1930s.[64]

In this way, this first generation of professional foundation staff members in the United States could reason that their continued support of this model of education for Black Americans was not simply a continuation of their founders' funding practices, but was also based on modern empirical research provided by Jones. That said, Jones's research not only had its supporters but also its vocal critics, including W. E. B. Du Bois and Carter G. Woodson.[65]

Historian and editor of the NAACP's *The Crisis*, Du Bois reviewed Jones's report in the magazine's February 1918 issue.[66] Showcasing his disapproval of the project, Du Bois wrote that fellow Black people and "persons who know the problem of educating the American Negro will regard the Jones' report, despite its many praiseworthy features, as a dangerous and in many respects unfortunate publication."[67] As Du Bois detailed, this was because Jones's study further cemented the already-dominant insistence "on manual training, industrial education, and agricultural training" among Black Americans in the region.[68] More specifically, Du Bois wrote:

> This is an unfortunate and dangerous proposal for the simple reason that the great dominating philanthropic agency, the General Education Board, long ago surrendered to the white South by practically saying that the educational needs of the white South must be attended to before any attention should be paid to the education of Negroes: that the Negro must be trained according to the will of the white South and not as the Negro desires to be trained. It is this board that is spending more money today in helping Negroes learn how to can vegetables than in helping them to go through college.[69]

Under such a policy carried out by leading U.S. philanthropies, Du Bois predicted that Black Americans would have few options in traditional, liberal arts, and civic-minded education. Even when a few Black Americans could amass the funds to establish such schools, Du Bois also noted that a teacher financed by these foundations was probably not far away trying to change its curriculum.[70] In fact, Du Bois rightly foresaw that Jones's recommendations would lead to further entrenchment of white philanthropists' theory that a particular type of vocational and agricultural education for Black Americans was key to improving the condition of Black Americans in the South, and even more importantly to them, to improving the economic strength of the region and country.

Much like Du Bois, Black historian Carter Woodson perceived that the 1917 study was a menacing tool that could potentially undermine the proper education of Black Americans in the South. Woodson also acknowledged that some Americans had received the report with open arms. In "1917 assembled in Washington the outstanding Negro educators to discuss the two-volume report," Woodson recalled. "Some of the educators assembled who had given their approval took pride in defending it as a great achievement."[71] Referring to the conference that Commissioner of Education Claxton had organized in D.C. months after the publication of *Negro Education*, Woodson reflected nearly two decades later in 1936 the significance of Jones's project and its impact among powerful Americans shaping Black Americans' education: "The worst of all the results of his biased report was that the system of education which it endorsed produced a mis-educated class of Negroes who are the greatest liability of the race."[72]

Woodson wrote these reflections on Thomas Jesse Jones's *Negro Education* nearly two decades after its publication, and in the context of protesting Du Bois's decision in the 1930s to collaborate with elite white foundations—and particularly the foundation funding Jones—in organizing and planning an "Encyclopedia for the Negro." In his open letter addressed to the network of northern philanthropies considering collaboration with the Phelps Stokes Fund and Du Bois, Woodson would make public his disappointment in Du Bois's decision to collaborate with a foundation they both long had criticized for its corrosive role in the lives of Black Americans. In writing such an open letter, Woodson viewed himself as being consistent in his stance against the Phelps Stoke Fund. By contrast, he argued that Du Bois—whom he outed in this open letter for once calling Jones "that evil genius of the Negro race"—had compromised his integrity as a Black scholar in "the hope of a few dollars."[73]

As Du Bois once imagined and Woodson continued to press well into the 1930s, Jones's report on Black education in the United States strengthened the perception of white philanthropists and of their organizations' staff and trustees that the Hampton-Tuskegee model of education for Black Americans was worth supporting. Building upon his open letter to northern philanthropies in 1936 and just weeks after Jones's passing in January 1950, historian Woodson wrote in the *Journal of Negro History*: "Jones's judgment led most Negroes to consider him an evil in the life of the Negro; but he was nevertheless, catapulted into fame among the capitalists and government officials supporting the education of Negroes. They made Jones the almoner of the despised race with the title of Educational Director of the Phelps Stokes Fund which he served from 1913 to 1946. When he said do not give here and do not help yonder the 'philanthropic' element heeded his biddings."[74]

During the 1910s and well into the next two decades, this first generation of white U.S. philanthropic trustees and staff members found in the recommendations of Jones's *Negro Education* legitimation for their founders' funding patterns in Black education. As Du Bois and Woodson watched on in the 1920s and 1930s, Jones and his educational model for Black Americans gained greater traction in the United States and across the Atlantic.

## 5. Jones and Carnegie Corporation's 1925 Grant to Kenya

In 1919, Jones and the Phelps Stokes Fund's trustees brainstormed their next steps. Having served abroad during the First World War and "in connection with Y.M.C.A. education work among negro troops,"[75] Jones drew from his experience when he wrote to the Phelps Stokes Fund trustees that "consciousness of the international responsibility of America is the deepest and most abiding impression that comes to the American who has any contact with the leaders of thought and action in Europe during these thrilling days of reconstruction."[76] Jones thus advised that the Phelps Stokes Fund should extend its purview beyond the United States. To this end, Jones referred to the London-based secretary of the International Missionary Council (IMC), J. H. Oldham, who had reviewed Jones's *Negro Education* in the pages of the *International Review of Missions* and had suggested the utility of the Jones Report for British Africa.[77] Jones added in his letter to the fund trustees: "The implication of these appreciative words is that the fund should become a center of information on Christian education in mission fields, that we should help mission boards and colonial boards of education to understand the methods so successful in the education of the Negroes in our southern states."[78]

Following Jones's lead, the Phelps Stokes Fund in the 1920s began to collaborate with missionary societies and the British Colonial Office in much the same way it had in the 1910s with the U.S. Bureau of Education in Washington, D.C.: by producing surveys of educational facilities for Black people authored by Thomas Jesse Jones.[79]

Jones's first African survey, *Education in Africa: A Study of West, South, and Equatorial Africa by the African Education Commission, under the Auspices of the Phelps-Stokes Fund and Foreign Mission Societies of North America and Europe* (1922), presented the findings that he and his team of missionary and education experts had collected while traveling throughout West and southern Africa in 1920. With the principal mission of assessing the effects that European models of education were having on African communities, the research team analyzed "how education could be more adequately related to the physical and cultural conditions of African life."[80] Aside from Jones, the commission included several Europeans and one Black African, Dr. J. E. Kwegyir Aggrey of the British Gold Coast. At times called the "Father of African Education" or the "Booker T. Washington of Africa," Aggrey was then a faculty member at Livingstone College in North Carolina and had met Thomas Jesse Jones a decade earlier during a YMCA event in Virginia.[81] "Aggrey was chosen because he was an outspoken supporter of the Tuskegee philosophy of education," writes historian Sylvia M. Jacobs, and because he had the "reputation as a person who could work with both blacks and whites."[82]

In *Education in Africa*, Jones addressed an audience of white Europeans skeptical of Black Africans' humanity and of the value of educating them. He was speaking, that is, not so much to white missionaries, who had long had supported efforts to educate Black Africans, but members of the British Colonial Office and white settlers throughout Africa. Accordingly, he argued that schooling would help Black Africans advance from their supposed lower stage of civilization toward the presumably higher stage of white civilization. To this point, Jones stressed: "their folk-lore, their handicrafts, their Native music, their forms of government, their linguistic powers, all are substantial evidences of their capacity to respond to the wise approaches of civilization so that they may share in the development of the African continent."[83] Here, he also drew on his work in the United States, writing that the "future possibilities of the African Natives may be somewhat forecast by the success of Negroes in other parts of the world, notably in America, where the descendants of the Africans are living in such large numbers."[84] Jones argued that, like other human beings around the world, Black Africans were capable of evolving into a higher "rank of civilization."[85] Though he also noted that this would take time because Black Africans were so much less advanced than the "most advanced race."[86] Jones underscored in *Education in Africa* that white Europeans and white Americans in Africa were having a positive influence on Africans. Far from thinking that white people were an unwelcomed element in Africa, Jones explained that the presence of white missionaries, colonial governments, and settlers had brought greater gains than losses to native Black Africans.

That said, Jones also suggested that white people should amend Black Africans' education to reflect the needs and interests of white missions, governments, commercial concerns, and Black Africans alike.[87] To make this point, Jones made explicit mention of the late Booker T. Washington and how Washington's model of education for Black Americans could serve as an example in Africa: "Booker Washington's life and work personify the methods, the principles, and the ideals necessary for those who would work for and with Africans. Most of all must the Africans themselves be guided and inspired by these ideals if they would participate in the salvation of their great continent."[88] Whether in Africa or the United States, Jones proposed that the Tuskegee model of education could serve the educational interests of Black people and the financial and political interests of white people.

Reflecting on Jones's views, scholar Edward H. Berman writes: "Education for the African masses—as for the Negro masses—was to be simple, utilitarian, and rooted to a strong agricultural bias. For the native leadership there would be, first, training for teachers and religious workers; second, instruction for those who would specialize in agriculture and industry; and third, training for those who would enter the professions of medicine, theology, engineering, and law."[89] Even for elite Africans, Berman continued, "there would be a strong emphasis on agricultural and simple industrial subjects, hygiene and sanitation, gardening and rural economics before the professional training commenced."[90]

In 1922, the *New York Times* reviewed *Education in Africa* and called Jones an "entirely impartial" researcher "setting forth the future of the African races."[91] It also celebrated Jones's efforts to export the Tuskegee model of education to Africa and apply it to Africans: "What Dr. Jones has done is to bring to bear upon Africa the ideals and experience associated with the great colleges of Hampton and Tuskegee."[92]

But there were also critics. In correspondence with Oldham, for example, former East African medical officer Norman Leys shared his impressions of Jones whom he presumably already had met in London. Leys wrote to Oldham:

> I pressed Jesse Jones to tell me whether he thought American negroes as a whole different in nature and capacity from the Europeans they live among and whether he expected from them a different kind of future. He admitted that he did. I told him that explained everything, to me, of his differences with du Bois and others. If a stable boy is going to be a king some day he has no less need to learn how to sweep the stable well. But stable sweeping should be taught as training for kingly duties. Jones in effect says it isn't wise, it isn't sensible, to teach a negro child what

European children are taught because as men they will have a different status. That is not relatively but absolutely contrary to Matt. XXV 40 & 45, and St. Paul's directions to Philemon.[93]

A Christian Socialist, Leys believed that all Christians were obligated to subscribe to the inherent equality among all human beings. Though Leys did not advocate for white Europeans to leave Africa, he did emphasize that they had an obligation to educate Black Africans as they would fellow white people.[94]

Clearly aware that Oldham admired Jones, Norman Leys tried to illustrate in his letter to Oldham the differences between Jones's approach to Black education and Du Bois's own, which Leys thought better mirrored the Bible's lessons for white people's treatment of Black people.[95] Leys thus reasoned to Oldham that Jones's educational policy revealed the latter's belief that Black people across the Atlantic should be prepared for an inferior status in white societies. Leys also noted to his British colleague that Jones seemed unaware that his educational policy went contrary to the Christian teachings of treating the poorest brethren as one would treat Christ himself.[96]

On his end, Oldham largely perceived Leys to be an idealist and himself and Jones to be realists on best practices in colonial African administration. Considering that Leys had lived in colonial Africa for sixteen years whereas Oldham then had never visited the continent and Jones had merely spent a year there, Oldham's perception of himself and Jones as realists and Leys as idealist is puzzling. Regardless, Oldham remained confident in Jones's proposed educational model for Black Africans and brought it to the attention of the British Colonial Office. In 1923, in anticipation of the imperial education conference scheduled for the summer of 1925, Oldham wrote to under-secretary of state for the colonies, William Ormsby-Gore, and requested an opportunity to discuss education in Africa.[97] Within weeks, Jones was back in London for a conference with the British Colonial Office and key governors on educational policy.[98]

The attendees of this meeting decided to form a "Permanent Advisory Committee on Native Education in Tropical Africa," which would be located in London.[99] Ormsby-Gore subsequently argued in the House of Commons that it was vital for the British government to concern itself with Africans' education and to arrive at a coherent educational policy in the process. Here, he pointed to Jones's *Education in Africa* as a guide: "We were led to this largely as the result of a most extraordinary and interesting report issued by Dr. Thomas Jesse Jones, who has traveled not only through British colonies but through French Africa, Belgian Congo and Portuguese colonies. He has made a most helpful contribution to the subject of African education from the point of view of the native. It is hoped that Dr. Jones may pay a similar visit to the East African colonies."[100] Accordingly, the British Colonial Office invited him to conduct a second survey.

Like the first study, *Education in East Africa* (1925) was financed by the Phelps Stokes Fund. And, as in the first study, Jones cast the potential for Africa in positive terms, writing that "it is inevitable that the honest observer shall present Africa as a Continent of Great Opportunities and Greater Responsibilities."[101] Unlike his first two studies, however, in which Jones verbalized some effort to consider the interests of Black people along with those of various groups of white people, *Education in East Africa* (1925) did not consider the voices, interests, and aspirations of Black Africans. Insofar as Jones expressed concern for Black Africans, he did so in the broadest terms, mentioning that government, missions, and settlers could all agree that "the conditions and needs of the community must be vital considerations in all efforts for improvement" of education."[102]

Before the publication of Jones's second survey, the British government hosted a dinner in his honor. At the dinner, Jones spoke on behalf of the Phelps Stokes Fund and reciprocated the admiration he had been receiving among leading British officials: "We are all greatly delighted by the dinner to be given by 'His Britannic Majesty's Government to meet the Chairman of the Phelps-Stokes Education Commission to Africa.' I spent last night at Mr Oldham's and conferred with him at length as to my address in response to the toasts being given by Major Ormsby-Gore and Sir Michael Sadler."[103] Ormsby-Gore was, of course, the under-secretary of state for the colonies. Sadler was an academic and former head of a commission who had surveyed education in India.[104]

Within months of the publication of *Education in East Africa* (1925), the Permanent Advisory Committee on Native Education in Tropical Africa, which included Ormsby-Gore, Sadler, Oldham, and several other representatives from the British government and missionary circles, produced its first white paper, entitled *Educational Policy in British Tropical Africa*.[105] Writing in the *International Review of Missions* that year, Oldham celebrated the Secretary of State's decision to issue this report outlining the native educational policy proposed by Jones.[106] The British government had yet to allocate funds to implement the policy; however, with this white paper, it expressed formal approval of it. In the United States, the *New York Times* published a review of Jones's second African survey in which it once again described Jones as the quintessential objective observer: "Dr. Jones displays a remarkably sound judgment. About his opinions, there is nothing of mere emotion."[107] During the 1910s and 1920s, many leading white Anglo-Americans in journalism, as well as government and philanthropy, would determine Jones's prescriptions for Black Americans' and Black Africans' education to be reasonable and sound.

## 6. Building on Carnegie Corporation's 1925 Grant to Kenya

In the spring of 1925, Thomas Jesse Jones met with Carnegie Corporation president Frederick Keppel at the corporation's offices in New York City. Encouraging the organization to extend education grants in colonial Africa—the corporation had made the grant to Kenya earlier that year—Jones noted to Keppel that his reports on African education were then available.[108] Based on these conversations, Keppel already had read Jones's second report on East Africa, a report further confirming for this relatively new president of Carnegie Corporation that his first grant in British Africa conformed not only to Bertram's vision of the organization's geographic and substantive scope abroad, but also to prevailing recommendations among his peers in philanthropy.

During the next decade, Carnegie Corporation would collaborate with Jones and the Phelps Stokes Fund in advocating segregated agricultural and industrial education for Black people in the United States and throughout British Africa. In this vein, for example, the organization funded five "Jeanes schools" for teacher training in Kenya, Southern Rhodesia, Northern Rhodesia, and possibly too Nyasaland. Modeled after U.S. schools financed by the Jeanes Fund, these "Jeanes schools" were training schools for teachers who would go on to educate African students in the industrial and agricultural trades promoted by the Tuskegee model.[109] Years later, Keppel concluded that "in British Africa, nothing has proved more interesting than the development of Jeanes Schools for the natives as a factor in racial and cultural adjustments."[110]

In 1925, after this first cautious step in launching a funding practice in colonial Africa that would sit well with his board's vision of Andrew Carnegie's intentions as a philanthropist and complement too other peer organizations' funding practices in the field, Keppel became intrigued by other funding opportunities on the continent. Some months after his meeting with Jones, Keppel met with another fellow Phelps Stokes adviser, J. H. Oldham. Much to the chagrin of Jones and the Phelps Stokes Fund more broadly, Oldham would encourage Keppel to fund research in the social sciences.[111] Even more, and as the next chapters illustrate, Oldham soon would overshadow Jones as Keppel's principal adviser on Africa.

In fact, and in leaning on Oldham, Keppel would move beyond the work of his U.S. philanthropic peers (and Andrew Carnegie's own explicit recommendation that the Tuskegee educational model was the panacea for strengthening white Anglo-American domination and the subservience of "subject races" throughout the Anglo-American world) in favor of also financing social science research as a critical tool for achieving complementary ends.

James Bertram would condone Keppel's decision, though he would continue to stress to Keppel that Andrew Carnegie had intended to finance projects *within* and *for* white communities. Against the backdrop of institutional imperatives to privilege the needs of white communities in the Anglo-American world, Keppel would fund cooperative studies *within* and *for* white communities in colonial Africa and then the United States. And in the process, he would further develop a perspective of his own on the critical value of the social sciences for solidifying international order after the First World War: a vision of world order that presumed the value of fortifying white Anglo-American leadership and Black subjection across oceans.

## CHAPTER 3

# From Education to the Social Sciences

*Finding New Tools to Tame the "Growth of a
Racial Consciousness among Black Peoples"*

After Carnegie Corporation made its education grant to Kenya in 1925, Frederick Keppel received a ten-page plea from J. H. Oldham to finance "scientific
research" in British Africa, an appeal Oldham also had made to Keppel's colleagues at the Rockefeller organizations during his trip to New York City that
fall of 1925.[1]

In 1925, Oldham was still an adviser to the Phelps Stokes Fund, which was
still actively promoting the two surveys of education in Africa authored by
Thomas Jesse Jones, whose assent as an authoritative adviser on education
for Black people in the United States and throughout Africa W. E. B. Du Bois
and Carter Woodson had been watching with horror since the 1910s.

Shifting focus from education to "scientific research," Oldham made this
pitch to U.S. philanthropies, not as an agent of the Phelps Stokes Fund, but
largely in his capacity as adviser and liaison to the British Colonial Office,
which was then interested in crafting scientifically informed public policies in
British Africa. As far as what this particular network of white men in London
and New York City would mean when they discussed "scientific research"
and its leading purpose in British Africa, they generally would express it as a
need for the meticulous collection of data on white and Black people by white
government administers or scholars in the developing social sciences for the
purposes of guiding white policymakers' work.

Aware that he was making his request to individuals sitting an ocean away
from London and British Africa, Oldham explained why these philanthropic
organizations in the United States should invest in funding such scientific research across the Atlantic. Oldham reasoned that scientific research (at least
the type of "scientific research" he had in mind in British Africa) could help
pacify the "growth of a racial consciousness among black peoples [which] is
likely to result in the American Negro problem coming to be regarded on
both sides as only one element in a world problem of the relations between
the white and black races."[2]

As this chapter illustrates, Oldham's message found a receptive audience at
Carnegie Corporation, if not at the Rockefeller organizations. Keppel not

only circulated Oldham's memorandum among his board, but relied on its contents to justify developing a grant program in British Africa. Indeed, Oldham had such a tremendous impact at the corporation that he would eclipse Thomas Jesse Jones as Keppel's leading consultant on British Africa during the next two decades. Future corporation secretary Florence Anderson would acknowledge decades later that Oldham was Keppel's "chief adviser with regard to people and grants in the African colonies from at least 1925 to 1936."[3] While Keppel would continue to lean on other experts on colonial Africa including Jones, Oldham would become Keppel's go-to consultant on anything beyond African education in British Africa, particularly related to funding scientific research.

This chapter focuses on this moment at Carnegie Corporation when Oldham's memorandum played a critical role in guiding the organization to expand upon its 1925 education grant to Kenya and to fund scientific research on the continent. Making sense of the document's impact at Carnegie Corporation and Oldham's subsequent meteoric rise as Keppel's main adviser on Africa, the chapter argues that Oldham gained this influence at the corporation precisely because Keppel appreciated Oldham's perspective on the radical implications of rising racial consciousness among Black people and on the potential for scientific research to temper this threat and further solidify white Anglo-American domination on the global stage.

This first section begins with an analysis of Oldham's general fear of Black unity and why Keppel took it seriously in 1925.

## 1. J. H. Oldham's Fear of Black Unity and Why Carnegie Corporation Took It Seriously

In the fall of 1925, Oldham gathered with the Rockefellers' Laura Spelman Rockefeller Memorial officials over the span of three days, and then met with Keppel at Carnegie Corporation. At the time, the Laura Spelman Rockefeller Memorial was displaying an inclination for financing the social sciences in the United States and Europe, while Carnegie Corporation's grant to Kenya earlier that year would have suggested to any observer such as Oldham that the organization had some interest in financing projects in colonial Africa. Since Oldham intended to advocate the value of funding scientific research in colonial Africa, he likely reasoned that one or both of these two philanthropic organizations in New York City might be receptive to his appeal.

Sharing with Keppel a summary of his earlier discussions at the memorial, Oldham begins his memorandum by describing Africa as a "new continent" whose partition by European powers had brought problems that both Europeans and Americans should find important to address and solve.[4] Of all possible tensions developing from Europeans' presence in Africa that could impact white Americans across the Atlantic, Oldham stressed the dangers of rising racial consciousness among Black people.[5] Considering that white Americans had "within their borders nearly a tenth of the African race," Oldham calculated that his audience should become invested in minimizing any Black solidarity across the Atlantic.[6]

Writing these words in 1925, J. H. Oldham was then living during a decade described by political scientist Robert Vitalis as one "marked by new theorizing on imperialism, the challenge to white supremacy, and the prospects of race war."[7] Indeed, scholars long have chronicled the making of transatlantic whiteness and global white supremacy from the late nineteenth and early twentieth centuries.[8] For example, in connection with W. E. B. Du Bois's comment in 1910 that the "world in a sudden, emotional conversation has discovered that is it white and by that token, wonderful!" Marilyn Lake and Henry Reynolds have detailed that as "Du Bois and contemporaries on the other side of the colour line saw clearly, the emergence of the 'new religion' of whiteness was a transnational phenomenon and all the more powerful for that, inspiring in turn the formation of international movements of resistance, such as the pan-African and pan-Asian alliances that threatened to bring about the very challenge to their world dominion that white men feared."[9]

Oldham indeed was a participant in this violent struggle to retain and strengthen white rule and Black subjection across the Atlantic in the early twentieth century. And like many of his white contemporaries, he was fearful about the radical potential of pan-African alliances. While Oldham and colleagues in London and New York and throughout British Africa were trying to justify white domination of, and violence toward, Black people and other "subject races," critics of this making of a white world order were becoming stronger in voice and numbers.[10]

Particularly threatening to white Anglo-American men such as Oldham, and especially in the 1920s when he wrote the memorandum, were Black nationalists and internationalists, especially Jamaican-born Marcus Garvey, whose Universal Negro Improvement Association (UNIA), with headquarters in New York, had become the "dominant black nationalist organization in the United States and worldwide in the immediate post–World War I era."[11] As historian Keisha Blain notes, "from 1919 to 1924, the organization attracted millions of followers in more than forty countries around the world."[12] Garvey, like other Black internationalists, intended to free Black people from white domination across oceans, and in the process, directly challenge white supremacy.[13]

Across the world in the early 1920s, the UNIA became a significant mass movement advocating unity among people of the African diaspora. In 1920, for example, a crowd of 25,000 people in New York City's Madison Square Garden elected Garvey the "provisional president of Africa."[14] Four years later, in the same venue, Garvey said that what "was needed was a cadre of dedicated 'American and West Indian Negroes' who would 'build up Africa in the interests of our race.'"[15] In this way, Black nationalists and internationalists such as Garvey necessarily intended to challenge directly the white rule that Oldham and his colleagues, including those at Carnegie Corporation from Andrew Carnegie and James Bertram to Frederick Keppel, long had considered critical for national and international order.

Predictably, Garvey's popularity met with opposition among many white Americans. In 1925, for example, the U.S. government imprisoned Garvey on charges of using the mail to defraud the public; and by December 1927, the United States had deported him back to Jamaica. Though the UNIA continued to exist as a mass movement in the United States, it lost momentum by the end of the decade.[16] And yet, in 1925, when Oldham shared with Keppel his own anxieties about a rising pan-African consciousness, Garvey's movement was growing in popularity. In fact, Blain and Adam Ewing trace the continued popularity of Garveyism well into the 1930s, and through the work of other public leaders and activists such as Mittie Maude Lena Gordon, Ethel Waddell, Celia Jane Allen, Ethel Collins, Amy Jacques Garvey, Amy Ashwood Garvey, Maymie Leona Turpeau De Mena, and other local organizers throughout the world from the United States and Kenya to the West Indies.[17]

When Oldham wrote—and Keppel read—his memorandum in 1925, it was the growing popularity of Garvey and the UNIA that likely first came to mind when they discussed the threat of a rising racial consciousness among Black people. Specifically to Keppel, for example, Garvey had gained his attention and the attention of his government colleagues some years earlier during the First World War through the War Department's Military Intelligence Branch (MIB)—also referred to as the Military Intelligence Division—which monitored activities in Black communities.[18] As historian Mark Ellis explains, secretary of war Newton Baker (who later became a member of Carnegie Corporation's board) approved the creation of MIB upon the United States' active engagement in the First World War. While MIB initially focused on monitoring "enemy agents," "anti-war activities of American left-wing radicalism," and "ethnic groups ill-disposed toward the Allied cause, such as German Americans,

Irish Americans, and Indian nationalists seeking the overthrow of British Rule," Ellis explains that it also soon "became convinced that black disloyalty represented further real threat to national security."[19]

U.S. Major Ralph Van Deman, who had proposed the idea of the MIB to Baker, subsequently argued that there was a real danger of a violent "black rebellion" in the United States.[20] Deman thus reasoned with colleagues that Black Americans might choose to address white supremacy and Black subjection through violence, rather than by appealing to white people such as themselves, "providing only that the time was propitious and the colored population was able to carry out their plans."[21] Hence, the MIB mobilized to spy on and infiltrate Black communities throughout the United States.

While the findings of the MIB were sent to Baker, it was specifically "Third Assistant Secretary of War Frederick P. Keppel, to whom racial matters were often referred."[22] Thus Keppel read vast quantities of communications related to "Negro Subversion," ranging from analyses of "radical organizations and activities in the black community that had a potential impact on the military; discrimination against blacks, military and civilian, including incidents leading to race riots; and treatment of and performance by blacks in the army."[23] The reports expressed a general anxiety about Black Americans' allegiance to the white U.S. government and its allies during the war. And in this vein, they signaled out Marcus Garvey as a threat to the war effort.[24] As noted in the archival records of the War Department's Military Intelligence Division, "One subject covered from late in World War I and throughout most of the interwar period was Marcus Garvey and his Universal Negro Improvement Association and African Community League."[25]

In 1925, Garvey thus likely remained for both Oldham and Keppel a most prominent example of a rising racial consciousness among Black people. Though by then, it likely was not simply Garvey who represented the rising racial consciousness among Black people that Oldham, Keppel, and their colleagues feared. Other pan-African movements at the time, while not reaching the mass popularity of the UNIA, signaled the broad appeal among Black people for resisting white rule on both sides of the Atlantic. Such individuals included Cyril Briggs, founder, in 1919, of the African Blood Brotherhood; Amy Ashwood Garvey, founder of the UNIA's newspaper, the *Negro World*, and most visibly for Keppel and his colleagues, W. E. B. Du Bois.[26]

Du Bois was then reviving pan-African congresses intended to bring together an elite cadre of Black people to resist white rule and plan for Black freedom at an international level. A graduate of Fisk and Harvard Universities, he had helped found the National Association for the Advancement of Colored

People (NAACP) in 1909 and subsequently had led the association's magazine, *The Crisis*. Working toward greater unity among Black Americans and Black Africans, Du Bois argued some years earlier that a small percentage of Black Americans were called to serve the masses of Black people across the Atlantic: "We as American Negroes, are resolved to strive in every honorable way for the realization of the best and highest aims, for the development of strong manhood and pure womanhood, for the rearing of a race ideal in America and in Africa to the glory of God and the uplifting of the Negro people."[27] With the intention of uniting and empowering Black people across oceans, and under the leadership of Black Americans such as himself, Du Bois organized a pan-African congress in Paris in 1919, to be followed by four more between 1919 and 1927.[28]

Just as Du Bois convened the 1919 congress, Keppel then was living in Paris and serving as director of Red Cross Foreign Operations.[29] In his professional capacity at the Red Cross in Paris, where he also participated in the international settlement meeting after the First World War—the 1919 Paris Peace Conference—it is not beyond reason that Keppel would have known about the two simultaneous, though separate, meetings taking place in the city respectively among white and Black leaders. If so, his developing perspective since the First World War that stable white domination and rising Black unity could not long coexist could have been heightened. It was in such a moment in his life, living in Paris after the First World War and engaging in discussions on the future of international order, that Keppel likely became that much more convinced—as Oldham would stress to him in the 1925 memorandum and he would endorse by broadcasting the document amongst his board—that rising Black consciousness was not simply a national problem as he and colleagues at the U.S. War Department had analyzed it, but a transatlantic threat to international order.

To this point, and further underscoring reasons for Carnegie Corporation president Keppel's captivated reception of J. H. Oldham's memorandum in 1925, sociologist Frank Füredi notes that Keppel's network of white Anglo-American colleagues and advisers, many of whom, like Keppel, served in the First World War, had perceived the conflict in Europe as a "'civil war' between white nations," and "in the minds of contemporary observers this was the death blow to the notion of white solidarity."[30]

After the First World War, elite white Americans and Britons such as Keppel and his colleagues in government and philanthropy had become generally anxious about the future of international politics, with many of them reasoning in the 1920s that the existing international order "seemed precariously unstable and the manifestation of racial consciousness was now seen as a direct challenge to the international status quo."[31] Fearing that "because of the universality of white racism, the world of colour would somehow respond in kind and unite against the common enemy," such white Anglo-Americans became preoccupied with how "to prevent an explosion of racial grievances in Africa and Asia, which was now expected."[32]

Continuing to gather against the backdrop of these white Anglo-Americans' rising anxieties about pan-African unity, the pan-African congresses subsequently convened in London, Brussels, Paris, and Lisbon. By 1927, the gathering was attracting a much larger group of 208 delegates from eleven countries. Its agenda was likewise broad and included "the history of Africa and the West Indies; the economic development and political division of Africa; education, art, and literature in Africa; and an exhibition arranged by Du Bois of fifty-two charts on the African diaspora."[33] In the final years of the 1920s and particularly with the onset of the Great Depression, Du Bois's pan-African congresses lost funding support and momentum. But in 1925, when Oldham shared his memorandum with Keppel, these congresses were yet another example for Keppel and his colleagues and advisers that a rising racial consciousness among Black people existed and posed a threat to white supremacy at the global level.

Beyond these congresses, Du Bois, in personal correspondence and publications, continued in the 1920s and 1930s to try to build ties across the pan-African diaspora and to speak critically of the making of the very white global order that Carnegie Corporation and its advisers were trying to solidify. To this point, Du Bois would write in a personal letter in 1934 that he long had "chafed over the unfair way in which the Carnegie [Corporation] and other funds have acted with regard to visitors to South Africa."[34]

Specifically, Du Bois found "intolerable that they should confine American students to white men, and allow neither the South African natives nor American Negroes to come in contact with each other."[35] A keen observer of elite philanthropies' work over the years, Du Bois knew that the corporation under Keppel's leadership in the 1920s and 1930s was dedicated to bridging white, rather than Black, people across the Atlantic, including in its grants program in colonial Africa.[36] Du Bois would even use himself to test the theory in the 1930s, then requesting from Keppel the opportunity to visit the British dominion of South Africa.[37] In 1939, Keppel ultimately ended the conversation with Du Bois by stressing that he had "just heard from our friends in South Africa, and to my disappointment they seem to be in doubt as to the desirability of your making a visit to the Union [of South Africa] just now."[38]

Emphasizing just how much he valued his network of white advisers, Keppel furthermore explained to Du Bois that "we have done pretty well in the past fifteen years by seeking and following [their] advice and I hesitate to break away from the policy."[39] As Du Bois readily knew by watching Carnegie Corporation funding practices and personally corresponding with Keppel over the years, this foundation and its president long had been invested in promoting white solidarity—and dissuading comparable Black unity—across the Atlantic.

Much like Keppel, whose anxieties about rising Black solidarity arguably had roots since the 1910s, Oldham also had maintained for some years an anxiety about rising racial consciousness among Black people. Four years before his 1925 conference with U.S. foundation leaders in New York City, for example, Oldham had traveled from London to the Tuskegee Institute in Alabama. After a week there, Oldham had taken note of rising African unity among Black African teachers and so too among Black African students throughout the United States. In this vein, he had celebrated the Tuskegee educational model and its impact on Black Americans, but had written back home with caution about the manifestations of pan-African nationalism that he witnessed among some Africans in the United States.

In correspondence with Lionel Curtis—a key founder of the Royal Institute of International Affairs (Chatham House) in London, one of the "post-Versailles internationalist think tanks" alongside the Council on Foreign Relations in New York—Oldham juxtaposed Black Americans educated fully under the Tuskegee educational model with Black African students who only studied or were taught for some fleeting years under this pedagogy.[40] Oldham noted to Curtis that Black Americans and Black Africans alike existed under white domination respectively in the United States and Africa, but observed that Black Americans lacked "any kind of sourness of disposition," showed "restraint and balance of judgment" and "a cheerful optimism."[41]

Bringing a global perspective to his analysis of white Anglo-American rule, Oldham explained in correspondence to Curtis that the Tuskegee educational model could play a central role in aiding white colonial officers to better subjugate people throughout the empire, if only by educating them to accept their own subordination and white Europeans' superiority. Referring to growing Indian nationalism, for example, Oldham further reasoned that the "Indian situation would be much more hopeful than it is if Indians possessed a larger measure of [Black Americans'] gifts."[42]

To Oldham's mention of British India, Mohandas Gandhi had been leading a nonviolent nationalist movement, and although India did not gain independence until 1947, it was clear to many British observers in the 1920s such

as Oldham that this "jewel of the British Empire" was heading that way. Historian John Cell observes that already by 1915, the then commissioner of New
Delhi, Malcolm Hailey (the same Hailey who would lead Carnegie Corporation's African survey) "was ready to concede that the intelligentsia were authen-
tic spokesmen for an insurgent force that was sweeping the Eastern world."[43]
Born in western India and then studying and becoming a barrister in London,
Gandhi was one of these highly educated Indians whom Hailey and Oldham
cautiously watched and feared as critical threats to white domination.

In correspondence with Curtis, Oldham calculated that Black Americans
had gained a certain non-confrontational disposition after being educated
under the Tuskegee model that allowed for an unchallenged white supremacy in the United States. If Europeans had exported this educational model to
India some years or decades earlier, Oldham reasoned that they could have
better managed and subjugated Indians into accepting British supremacy and
Indian inferiority.

Oldham furthermore explained to Curtis that he perceived similarities between the Indian nationalists whom he vilified and some Black Africans whom
he met in the United States. These included a man from Rhodesia who had
studied in the northern United States before taking a teaching position at the
Tuskegee Institute. In particular, Oldham told Curtis, this individual had relayed to him that he planned to return to Rhodesia in order to help his fellow
people. Oldham summed up: the man "is thoroughly loyal and has the Tuskegee outlook. But as I talked with him I touched exactly the same things that
one knows so well in one's Indian friends. It may be long in coming but sooner
or later we shall have the same situation in Africa that we are facing in
India."[44] Oldham feared that like Indians, Black Africans such as the Tuskegee professor soon would mobilize and unite to lay claim to independence
from the British Empire, casting some doubts for Oldham as to whether this
model of education could be the panacea towards helping white Anglo-
Americans maintain their domination over Black people, let alone many other
"subject races" in the Anglo-American world.

While Oldham excluded the professor's name in his correspondence with
Curtis, historian Kenneth James King notes that it was Tuskegee's African
history professor, Simbini Mamba Nkomo, whose own personal transformation in the 1910s and early 1920s offers a glimpse of the developing racial consciousness that Oldham perceived and so feared among Black people.[45]

Described at varying times as Zimbabwean, South African, and Mozambi-
can, Nkomo attended Greenville College in Illinois. Some years earlier, in 1917,
and while finishing school there, Nkomo had produced a pamphlet with the

intention of appealing to white philanthropists for assistance in financing a school which he intended to open after graduation and which he vaguely described would serve "African boys and girls" in his "native land" in Africa.[46] In this pamphlet, Nkomo mobilized white people's point of view on Africa and Black people generally in order to appeal to their sensibilities, including their presumed disinterest in specifying geographic regions within the continent or ethnic groups among Africans. Though by the time he met with Oldham four years later, Nkomo seemed to have abandoned past efforts to appeal to white people such as Oldham and white people's own hopes for Black people: a perspective that Nkomo's 1917 pamphlet suggests he knew quite well.

In this earlier pamphlet, for example, Nkomo had presented to white U.S. readers an image of Africa as a backward continent populated by "jungles," "hut[s]," witch doctor[s]," and an "ignorant African boy" such as himself.[47] By contrast, and again appealing to white readers keen to imagine the positive effects of Europeans' presence in Africa, Nkomo had depicted in a positive light white missionaries proclaiming "Jesus, the Saviour of the world" and attributed to them and their God his decision to pursue higher education.[48] At the end of this promotional document, Nkomo had comforted his targeted white readers who might be hesitant to help a Black man seek higher education by emphasizing that he intended only to expand upon white missionaries' work among Black Africans.

To this point, Nkomo had explained to these white American readers that upon returning to Africa after pursuing schooling in the United States, he planned to "teach the African boys and girls the things of God and His power to save them through the blood of Jesus Christ, his only begotten Son."[49] Beyond the gospel, Nkomo had comforted his white readers by stressing that he expected to teach them "something about scientific farming, because there is so much land that is not tilled properly."[50] Playing into white philanthropists' image of white and Black people in Africa and assuaging their fears of educating Black Africans, Nkomo then had hoped to convince white Americans to support his plans to launch a schoolhouse for "African boys and girls."

However, by the time Nkomo was a faculty member at Tuskegee Institute in Alabama and meeting with Oldham in 1921, he seemed less willing to appease white people's derogatory image of Black people or to alleviate white people's fears of educated Black people such as himself. Between the publication of this 1917 pamphlet and his meeting with Oldham, that is, Nkomo experienced some transformation in his views on white rule and Black subordination or, at least, on his willingness to publicly excuse these twin forms of domination and subjection. To this point, Nkomo founded and became executive secretary of the African Student Union (ASU) of America, and in 1919 he coordinated an African Student Conference in Chicago, which attracted fifty Africans and eight hundred others.[51] When Oldham met Nkomo two years later at the Tuskegee Institute, he was meeting with a man who had become increasingly sympathetic to a pan-African identity uniting Africans throughout the continent and the diaspora.

Moreover, Nkomo's promotion of racial pride went beyond his work at the ASU to his classroom at the Tuskegee Institute, a school that—at least publicly—bought into its founder's and funders' expectations for white rule and Black subordination. And yet, beyond the watchful eye of white funders, the Tuskegee Institute maintained some space for nurturing racial consciousness among Black students, as well as a sense of pan-African internationalism which Nkomo "regarded as the foundation of true progress for Africans."[52] For example, Nkomo told the school's president, Robert Moton, "'I am sure that I have tried to do all I could for the students who were in my history classes. In all my class work I have laid great deal of stress of *the National spirit* or the Spirit of racial *selfvaluation* which is the foundation of true progress along all lines.'"[53]

For Nkomo at least, racial pride among Black people—irrespective of national or tribal origins—was an important step toward freedom from white domination and violence in the United States and Africa. However, Nkomo's powerful sense of self-purpose would stop short four years later, in 1925, the same year that Oldham met with Keppel and shared his evolving anxieties about Black nationalism in Africa. "Suddenly and tragically Nkomo died in 1925," historian Kenneth King writes, "bringing to an end for a time this particular coalition of African and American Negro youth in a common cause. His presence at Tuskegee had been a great attraction for several Africans, who all, not insignificantly, left as soon as he did."[54]

Four years earlier, when Oldham visited the Tuskegee Institute, though, Sambini Mamba Nkomo was still teaching at the school. In conversation with Nkomo, Oldham furthermore had learned that African students in the United States had formed an African students association, of which the Tuskegee professor was founder and executive secretary. As Oldham recounted to Curtis, all of these men had "an African consciousness: their loyalty and interest is not Liberian or Rhodesian or Gold Coast, but African."[55] With a rising African consciousness among African students in the United States, Oldham concluded in his correspondence with Curtis that Black Africans stood a chance of challenging white rule on the continent. He reasoned to his friend in London: "The number of educated Africans at present is small, but they hold their own with the European just as the Indian can do." It was time, Old-ham told Curtis, for their network of white men to plan ahead in Africa, so that "when (at however distant a time) we reach the stage which we have now reached in India and Egypt we shall have a situation more easily to deal with."[56] And by dealing with the situation, Oldham imagined neutralizing Black Afri-cans' internationalist claims and preserving white European rule across oceans.

It was in his 1925 memorandum to Carnegie Corporation that Oldham ad-dressed how to do so. Explaining that the "difficulties of the situation in Africa are due in part to the fact that the powerful new forces at work in the conti-nent have not yet been brought sufficiently under intelligent control," Old-ham proposed that a "well-considered experiment" in scientific research could help achieve "a better understanding of the real nature of these forces and thereby greater ability to master them."[57] Clearly anxious about white people's declining abilities to maintain domination in colonial Africa, Oldham stressed the importance of scientific research as a tool for social control, a clarion call that President Keppel answered.

Focusing on Oldham's networks in 1920s London, this next section provides further context to his recommendation in 1925 that greater data collection in colonial Africa could help white policymakers strengthen their dominance in the face of rising pan-Africanism.

## 2. Intellectual Context for J. H. Oldham's Support of Thorough Data Collection in British Africa

Since the 1910s, Oldham had served as secretary of the International Mission-ary Council and founding editor of the *International Review of Missions*. It was in the latter position that Oldham had reviewed Jones's *Negro Education* (1917) and suggested to readers of the *International Review of Missions* that Jones's recommended form of education for Black Americans could apply for subju-gated groups throughout the British Empire.

As secretary of the International Missionary Council, Oldham was in rou-tine contact with the British Colonial Office with whom he regularly negoti-ated the interests of missionaries throughout the British Empire. Among Colonial Office politicians, Oldham subsequently enjoyed a reputation as a "man of reason and moderation."[58] Gaining the trust of leading policymakers in London, Oldham was able to introduce Jones to British government offi-cials. In the process, Oldham not only brought Jones to the attention of the British government, but helped establish his own reputation as an adviser to the British government on African education. In this role, for example, under-secretary of state for the colonies William Ormsby-Gore asked Old-ham in 1923 to lead a committee on African education, though it was formally chaired by the under-secretary and included several leading members of the British government. The resulting report, *Education Policy in British Tropical Africa* (1925), which was published two years later, largely echoed the recom-mendations of Jones's two African surveys.[59]

During the 1910s and 1920s, Oldham was cultivating a network of leading British policymakers, U.S. foundation leaders, and education advisers on Af-rica. As liaison to these various groups, Oldham also would become a formal advocate of further scientific research in colonial Africa. In 1925, the same year as the publication of *Education Policy in British Tropical Africa* and some months before Oldham traveled to meet with U.S. foundation leaders in New York City, the report of a royal commission on labor and land practices in East Af-rica, chaired by Orsmby-Gore, was published.[60] Historian George Bennett notes that, precisely after the publication of the Ormsby-Gore report on East Africa, there was a general feeling in the British government that further re-search was needed on colonial Africa.[61]

As an adviser with developing connections with U.S. foundations, the Co-lonial Office turned to Oldham and encouraged him to seek funds for such scientific investigations in British Africa and particularly East Africa, where the Royal Commission had conducted its own report.[62] As Oldham noted in his memorandum to U.S. philanthropic managers later that fall in 1925, the "recent Report of the Parliamentary Commission to East Africa strongly ad-vocated increased provision for scientific research."[63]

Justifying his appeal to philanthropic organizations in the U.S. rather than the British government, Oldham reasoned in the 1925 memorandum that fund-ing from London was going to be insufficient for social science needs in Af-rica.[64] In light of the Royal Commission's recommendations, Oldham explained to his potential U.S. funders that only "a small percentage of the proposed im-perial loan for the development of transport in East Africa will be earmarked for scientific research."[65] Turning to the British colonial governments in Africa, Oldham also confessed that the East African governments confronted much more serious and dire problems such as plant, animal, and human diseases that would overwhelm and likely exhaust any available sums for research.[66] Acting as an agent of the British Colonial Office, Oldham thus suggested to the Rockefeller and Carnegie groups that non-governmental funding sources from the United States could help finance this work in British Africa, in ways that the British imperial and colonial governments could not.

In appealing to U.S. foundations, Oldham indeed was following direct orders from the British government. However, Oldham also personally believed in the value and importance of social research. In a book published a year earlier, *Christianity and the Race Problem* (1924), for example, Oldham had advocated the need for further social investigations of indigenous communities in the British Empire.[67] Like the Colonial Office, Oldham believed (as he also expressed in his memorandum to U.S. philanthropic leaders in 1925) that collecting data, or rather conducting fieldwork, was an important key to maintaining white governance in Africa.[68] Beyond methodology, Oldham and his network of contacts in the British government also maintained a certain public policy goal for this research in Africa: They expected that fieldwork would help white policymakers and administrators develop solutions to perceived problems in white rule and Black subjection and, in the process, help white policymakers stabilize their domination in Africa.

In 1925, the Laura Spelman Rockefeller Memorial listened patiently to Oldham, but the organization remained rather steadfast in insisting that it had no particular interest in developing a grantmaking program on the continent.[69] A year later, the memorial indeed made a one-time grant of $35,000 to the Phelps Stokes Fund for education work in Africa, though under the condition that the Rockefellers' name not be made public in connection with this funding project.[70] At the time, the Rockefeller organizations wanted to avoid the public perception that they were interested in establishing grantmaking programs in colonial Africa, whether in education or the social sciences.

During the next decade, the Rockefeller organizations would go on to finance scientific research on British Africa, though again not directly in response to Oldham's requests for greater scientific research on the continent. Rather, the Rockefeller funds would support work on British Africa, though based in London and as part of their efforts to strengthen the social science fields in Europe. For example, just as the Rockefeller organizations reorganized in 1929 with the Rockefeller Foundation absorbing the smaller Laura Spelman Rockefeller Memorial's funding practices in the social sciences, the Rockefeller Foundation joined Carnegie Corporation in financing the International Institute of African Languages and Cultures (IIALC) in London, which Oldham had founded in 1926.

Ultimately, the Rockefeller groups would eclipse Carnegie Corporation in their support of London-based research centers such as the London School of Economics and the IIALC, and yet they never would match Carnegie Corporation's interest in funding social scientific research in Africa. Repeatedly, the Rockefeller groups would stress that they maintained little interest in expanding their commitment to the social sciences beyond the United States and Europe, with any support they offered in the realm of research on Africa stemming from their commitment to research in these two geographic regions. By contrast, when Oldham traveled to meet with U.S. foundation leaders in New York City during the fall of 1925, he found a particularly welcoming audience with Carnegie Corporation president Frederick Keppel.

In 1925, Keppel was sufficiently impressed by Oldham's memorandum to circulate it among his trustees.[71] And far from unusual, this would prove to be a characteristic move by Keppel during important junctures in his tenure at Carnegie Corporation, whether in 1925 when he found himself inspired by Oldham's memorandum or in the mid-1930s when he intended to commission a U.S. analogue to Lord Hailey's *African Survey* (1938), which the corporation was then financing in the 1930s through Chatham House in London. To this point, as later chapters explain, U.S. sociologist Donald Young remembered a similar experience with Keppel when he decided to fund the study that would become the U.S. version of Hailey's study: *An American Dilemma*. Young recounted:

> I did write this long letter reiterating what I had said over there [at Keppel's office], and got a very very warm note from Mr. Keppel, both for the conversation and the letter, but particularly for the letter, which he was having duplicated and sent to the trustees in support of the proposal. I remember taking it in to [SSRC director] Mr. Crane and saying, "Is this in support of that proposal as Mr. Keppel had it?" Crane read it over and said, "No." But it could be so read, as a matter of fact. Sometimes when you put things in writing you don't say quite what you meant, but maybe it was better that way.[72]

Much as with Young's letter over a decade later, President Keppel shared, in 1925, Oldham's memorandum with fellow board members as means of justifying a new grantmaking idea and deflecting his own role in promoting it.

That is, when Keppel wanted to shift the direction of board decisions at Carnegie Corporation towards new funding practices—and as fellow board member Henry James once remarked, "Keppel loved to try something new"—he preferred doing so by deflecting attention away from himself and toward an expert adviser.[73] Such an adviser, whose knowledge Keppel reasoned that the board would respect, would elaborate what he himself wanted to accomplish at the organization. And there are several reasons to believe that Keppel, at a personal level, found appealing Oldham's call for scientific research in colonial Africa. For starters, Keppel's war service in the U.S. Department of War likely gave him sympathy for policymakers—whether in Washington D.C. or London—who were trying to create informed public policy decisions and were thus eager for data on their targeted populations. Not least, the U.S. War Department had collected field research on Black Americans as means of pacifying Black unity against white rule in the United States, and Keppel had been at the center of this knowledge-gathering. And before the First World War, Keppel had been Columbia College dean for years and, thus, had been in a prime position to appreciate the developing social science fields in a leading university.

Soon after Oldham's visit, and with the approval of the corporation's board, Keppel coordinated plans to travel to British Africa with an eye to expanding the organization's presence on the continent. Though first, Carnegie Corporation would send a U.S. adviser to survey the people and institutions in Africa that Keppel should visit.

## 3. Carnegie Corporation Tours British Africa

In one of the first concrete steps he took in acting on Oldham's advice, Keppel sent former Columbia University colleague James Earl Russell to East and southern Africa the following year on a reconnaissance trip. Russell had recently retired from his post as dean of the university's Teachers College. Unsurprisingly, then, Russell contacted and met with several alumni from Teachers College including white South African alumni Charles T. Loram and Ernst Malherbe.[74]

As far as the geographic scope of the trip, Oldham had argued in conversation with Carnegie and Rockefeller officials a year earlier that greatest attention should be placed on East Africa, largely channeling the British Government's agenda at the time and particularly the recommendations of the Royal Commission on East Africa.[75] Carnegie Corporation indeed sent Russell to East Africa, though also South Africa: two regions of British Africa that Bertram furthermore had considered sufficiently white to merit Carnegie Corporation's support.

Between East and southern Africa, Russell, Keppel, and Bertram would place greater emphasis on southern Africa and likely for several reasons. For starters, Russell connected with Teachers College alumni in South Africa during the reconnaissance trip. And once Bertram and Keppel retraced Russell's steps the following year, it also would become relevant that Bertram had lived in South Africa for several years before becoming Andrew Carnegie's secretary in 1897.[76] So while the corporation, in theory, was equally interested in East and southern Africa as sufficiently white regions of British Africa, the organization shared several personal bonds to South Africa that made this region especially appealing for the organization's leadership in the 1920s.

Underscoring the significance of these personal relationships, the two Teachers College alumni in South Africa with whom James Russell met would play instrumental roles in developing the corporation's newfound interest in funding research in the social sciences on the continent. Considered an expert in Africans' education among this developing network of white Anglo-Americans and South Africans, Charles T. Loram had been part of the Phelps Stokes Fund network in colonial Africa for some years. In 1917, for example, Loram's dissertation on *The Education of the South African Native* came to global attention after Oldham reviewed it alongside Jones's report of Black education in the United States.[77] And when Oldham and Jones coordinated the Phelps Stokes Fund's first African report, South African prime minister Jan Smuts had sent Loram, his chief inspector of "native education" in Natal and member of the Union Native Affairs Commission, to accompany Jones.[78]

While funding scientific research in South Africa, Carnegie Corporation would soon learn that nurturing unity among white people was an ambitious project. For example, the dominion of South Africa had a long history of animosities between English-speaking white South Africans and Afrikaners. While Keppel would have had reason to be naïve on this point, his travel companion would not. After all, Bertram had spent years in southern Africa, which would have made him vividly aware of this strain among white people in the region. However, Bertram's own subsequent surprise at the rising political strength of Afrikaner nationalism in the late 1920s seems to suggest that he either assumed the ultimate dominance of Britons in a British dominion or that Afrikaners, from their own reasoning and particularly after the peace agreement ending the South African War (1899–1902), would find it expedient to merge with British South Africans in shared white leadership of the British dominion.

To Bertram's particular chagrin in the late 1920s, he would learn that this latter group of white South Africans was gaining greater political power and that their vision for white rule was increasingly hostile, rather than conciliatory, with a broader Anglo-American world.

This level of hostility among Afrikaners and colonists of British descent in southern Africa enjoyed a relatively long history. However, for some years before Keppel and Bertram's African tour following James Russell's own, the British dominion of South Africa had been governed by Afrikaners intent on reconciling hostilities between and among white people in the region. To this point, Jan Smuts, the former South African prime minister who had sent Charles Loram to join Jones on the Phelps Stokes Fund's first African report, was an Afrikaner nationalist who had fought against the British during the South African War. Unlike his successor and fellow Afrikaner J. B. M. Hertzog, though, Jan Smuts had been eager to build ties among these two communities of white people in South Africa. In fact, even as the South African government became increasingly hostile to a broader Anglo-American world in the late 1920s, Smuts would remain a key player in this network of Anglo-American philanthropists, their advisers, and colleagues in government. Smuts's own biography offers glimpses into his ambivalent role as a white Afrikaner nationalist in South Africa and collaborator with an international network of white Anglo-Americans intent on solidifying white Anglo-American rule. To this point, Smuts was born in 1870 to an Afrikaner family in the British Cape Colony, and reflecting some affinity for Britain, he studied at Cambridge and Christ's College in England, returning to the British colony in 1895. However within some years, Smuts grew increasingly critical of British dominance in the region and during the South African War served in opposition to the British.

Ending with a peace treaty, the South African War concluded with a unification of southern Africa's English-speaking colonies, Natal and the Cape, with Afrikaner republics, the Orange Free State and the Transvaal. Together, in 1910, these regions of southern Africa formed the Union of South Africa, a self-governing dominion within the British Empire.[79]

With the recently warring region transforming into a dominion of the British Empire, historian Leonard Thompson writes that Alfred Milner, appointed high commissioner of South Africa and governor of the Cape Colony, "planned to rule the former republics autocratically, without popular participation, until he had denationalized the Afrikaners and swamped them with British settlers. When that was done, and not before then, it would be safe and expedient to introduce representative institutions."[80]

That said, Milner was trying to suppress a rather sizeable population with political will in the region. Afrikaners not only represented over half of the white population of southern Africa, but opposition to British rule within this group remained strong. To this point, and reflecting continued and sizeable rejection to British domination in the newly established British dominion, white South Africans did not elect British leaders to steer the new Union of South Africa. Rather, they elected former Afrikaner generals of the South African War Louis Botha and Jan Smuts.

Just three years earlier, Botha and Smuts had come to power in the Afrikaner-dominated region of the Transvaal. By then, they had realized that their war-time Afrikaner nationalism needed to develop into a more conciliatory policy toward all white people in the region, including Britons. In this way, they could secure as many votes as possible within a voting population that was half British and half Afrikaner. Louis Botha and Jan Smuts thus "described their policy as one of 'conciliation,' which involved reconciling the differences among Afrikaners and between Afrikaners and British Transvaalers."[81]

Becoming leaders of the Union of South Africa in 1910, Prime Minister Louis Botha and Deputy Prime Minister Jan Smuts continued their strategy of conciliation among the two groups of white people in South Africa. This conciliation plan not only aimed to unite white people within the Union, but also to further suppress Black South Africans in the process. For example, historian Grace Davie notes that leading Black South Africans "felt betrayed when the white power-sharing settlement that ended the war dictated that African franchise rights would not extend beyond the Cape, where, starting in 1853, some property-owning African men had been able to access the ballot."[82] Not only were white South Africans stripping Black South Africans of the right to vote, but also of the right to own land: And these were rights that Black Africans had exercised in some parts of southern Africa before unification. The Natives Land Act of 1910, for example, "limited the territory that Africans could legally own to a mere 7.5 percent of the total territory of the country."[83]

In response to these restrictions, African National Congress (ANC) leader Sol Plaatje argued for the repeal of the Act, and subsequently journeyed to London as part of an ANC delegation to appeal their grievances to the British government. But as Davie notes, "The Colonial Office refused to study the matter and deemed South Africa's native policies a domestic affair."[84] Back in South Africa, leading white South Africans expected to further cement their unity as two groups of white people equally invested in white rule and Black subjection in the region. And far as the threat of Black political power in the region, Davie writes that white people in South Africa "could rely on coordinated state-sponsored violence to uphold the pillars of racial and economic power."[85]

After Louis Botha passed away in 1919, Prime Minister Jan Smuts continued their shared policy of prioritizing the unity of white South Africans.[86] Though when Carnegie Corporation adviser Russell traveled through South Africa in the mid-1920s, Smuts was no longer prime minister.[87] The policy advocated by Smuts of coordinating with British settlers in South Africa and more broadly, the British Empire had comforted British officials, but it had been far from unanimously shared among fellow Afrikaners in the region. Among the latter group, this policy became exceptionally controversial during the First World War when, as historian Leonard Thompson notes, "Botha and his colleagues accepted the fact that South Africa, like the other self governing British dominions, was automatically involved, since it was not a sovereign state."[88] And so, while Botha and Smuts might have been sympathetic to white Anglo-Americans' calls for greater unity among the United Kingdom and its settler colonies such as South Africa, they quickly would find that they were not in the majority among Afrikaners at the time, who, most immediately inspired by the First World War, sought leadership more critical of, and independent from, British settlers in South Africa and the British Empire generally.

Beyond Smuts's longstanding cooperation with the British government, Afrikaners found yet another prominent reason to criticize his leadership in the 1920s: they were disenchanted with his support of industry at the expense of white South African workers. Building a coalition with the Labour Party, National Party leader J. B. M. Hertzog defeated Jan Smuts in 1924.[89] Against the backdrop of an economic recession lasting several years, exacerbating white South Africans' anxieties about poverty amongst their racial group— and most recently an armed workers' strike in 1922 ending in martial law and several hundred deaths under Smuts's leadership—both the Labour and National Parties criticized the Smuts government "for promoting 'big financial' interests and jeopardizing the future of South Africans 'as a civilized people.'"[90] Noting the white population's unemployment rates, the two winning parties stressed the existing problem of poverty among white South Africans. They argued that white rule in the union would be threatened without protecting "civilized labor" for the "civilized races" against primarily Black South Africans.[91]

This was not a new concern. The "Pact Government" of the National and Labour Parties in the early 1920s mobilized a long-standing anxiety over white poverty in South Africa. Since the turn of the century, historian Judith Tayler writes, the "presence of white pauperism was viewed as a reproach in terms of the dominant Christian value system. It was also a source of discomfort and distaste to the middle classes wherever physical proximity was unavoidable and above all it was perceived as a 'weak link' which enfeebled the white population and threatened its perceived mission as a civilizing agent."[92] For several decades at least, Afrikaners and English-speaking South Africans had been sensitive to the existence of poverty among whites, seeing it as a threat to their claims of racial superiority over Africans.

In the latter years of the 1920s, Hertzog's National Party in South Africa would gain such popularity that it would no longer need to build a coalition with the Labour Party in order to win the general election of 1929. In this way, Carnegie Corporation secretary James Bertram and president Frederick Keppel would watch warily in the late 1920s as an increasingly powerful National Party in South Africa embraced rhetoric increasingly hostile to the British. As yet another affront to Carnegie Corporation's own vision of white Anglo-American rule, the party's campaign rhetoric was publicly hostile (rather than simply publicly patronizing) to Black South Africans.

Before then, however, in the mid-1920s when Carnegie Corporation first was developing a grant program in British Africa, Keppel and Bertram visited a South Africa where the National Party's pro-Afrikaner and anti-British rhetoric, though present, was tempered by its coalition with a Labour Party peopled with English-speaking white South Africans. Together in the mid-1920s, a South African government led jointly by the National and Labour Parties revealed a shared concern for white unity in South Africa, a concern that resonated with both Bertram and Keppel. After all, the two men were in South Africa as part of the corporation's general efforts to support the interests of white Anglo-Americans across the white Anglo-American world, including British settlers in Africa.

Among those in South Africa at the time who acutely reflected this heightened concern for bridging divides among white Afrikaners and British settlers, and were interested in collaborating with white Anglo-Americans toward such efforts, was former Teacher's College student Ernst Malherbe, with whom Russell met during his trip through the region. A "tenth-generation Afrikaner and the son of a Dutch Reformed minister," Malherbe had studied at Columbia's Teachers College during the 1920s.[93] When Malherbe met with Russell in South Africa, Malherbe was then teaching at Cape Town's Faculty of Education and enjoying the critical success of his recently published Columbia dissertation on education policies in South Africa, *Education in South Africa: 1652–1922* (1925).[94]

Like fellow South African Charles Loram, who served as adviser to the Phelps Stokes Fund, Ernest Malherbe had found much to learn in white Americans' experiences with education. But unlike Loram, who was particularly interested in shaping Black Africans' education, Malherbe imagined creating a general, national education research bureau.[95] In particular, historian Brahm David Fleisch writes that one model Malherbe "had in mind was the United States Bureau of Educational Research, which collected and published educational statistics and initiated original research."[96] More specifically,

Ernst Malherbe aimed to have a centralized national bureau on education in South Africa that collected empirical data on its population; analyzed problems in education empirically; and, from this empirical data and analyses, offered policy solutions to solve the problems. Fleisch writes: "What South Africa needed, Malherbe believed, was a genuinely 'scientific' approach to social policy making."[97] To reach this goal, Malherbe imagined that he would need the aid of Americans who presumably had expertise and money for such endeavors.

Russell alerted these white South Africans that Carnegie Corporation's president would be visiting the following year to discuss further funding opportunities in the region.

## 4. The Corporation Decides to Fund Research in British Africa

In November of 1926, Carnegie Corporation's trustees approved Keppel's proposed trip to retrace Russell's journey in colonial Africa and gauge opportunities for effective use of the Special Fund on the continent: the $10 million fund at Carnegie Corporation applicable in Canada and the British Colonies. They resolved to send Bertram as well.[98]

Years later, Keppel's assistant, John Russell (son of James Russell) remembered that Keppel "felt that Bertram wouldn't approve of [a grant program in Africa] unless he was asked to go. Bertram was a very difficult person."[99] By asking Bertram to accompany him on this trip, Keppel likely tried to ensure the allegiance of a leading board member who was not only reluctant to embrace new ideas, but whose interpretation of Andrew Carnegie's philanthropic intentions in the Anglo-American world—and specifically his intentions for funding initiatives on or for white and Black people in the Anglo-American world—carried weight on the corporation's board. It also helped that Bertram had lived in South Africa and spoke Zulu and thus could facilitate the trip.[100]

Aware of Keppel and Bertram's forthcoming tour, Phelps Stokes Fund education director Thomas Jesse Jones wrote to Loram. By then, Jones was aware that Russell had met with Loram and thus too that Loram was likely to meet with Bertram and Keppel the following year. Defending his education-focused agenda, Jones cautioned Loram about the importance of his interactions with Carnegie Corporation leaders. Jones relayed:

> The important consideration for you at the present time seems to me to be your approach to President Keppel and Mr. Bertram, who must be won to a constructive program in Africa. I have some fear that Dr. Keppel

may be won to the research approach and also that he may turn his interest to the needs of the whites in South Africa. As you know, I believe both in research and certainly in the education of the whites. My concern is that these two interests shall not exclude the practical approach as explained in our Jeanes school program.[101]

While Carnegie Corporation did not publicly state the geographic and substantive priorities in its grantmaking, it seems from Jones's letter that he was relatively aware of Bertram's insistence that Andrew Carnegie would have condoned only financing projects in white communities in Africa that would benefit whites. Jones also seemed aware of Oldham's influence on Keppel, and the subsequent possibility that the corporation increasingly would become interested in funding scientific research on the continent. Spelling out for Loram the vital role that he could play in Keppel and Bertram's tour throughout Africa, Jones stressed how Loram could help steer these two foundation leaders away from the temptation of focusing so singularly on white people and on funding research.

From June to September of 1927, Keppel and Bertram visited the British colony of Kenya and the British protectorates of Uganda, Tanganyika, and Zanzibar; Southern and Northern Rhodesia, which were, respectively, a British colony and a protectorate; and the Union of South Africa, a British dominion. Loram indeed had prioritized the visit by using his vacation time to travel with the two U.S. men over the span of several weeks.[102] However, Keppel and Bertram ultimately agreed with Russell's assessment that Malherbe—whom Keppel also had met years earlier at Columbia—was a particularly useful contact with a worthy project idea.[103] During the trip, Keppel heard Malherbe suggest that Carnegie Corporation should fund a scientific study of white poverty in South Africa.[104] In a *Cape Times* piece published before Keppel's trip to Africa, Malherbe had explained this idea in some detail, writing: "'We shall never solve the Poor White problem adequately until we get thorough and first-hand knowledge of the causes underlying this malady.... Only when we have made a correct diagnosis and are certain of the causes can we remedy them.... The results must be published so as to be accessible to the whole of the public.'"[105]

Upon their return to their New York offices in 1927, Bertram and Keppel shared a report of their trip with fellow trustees at Carnegie Corporation. Referring once again to Bertram's own geographic limitations for the foundation, they reasoned that the British colonial governments in West Africa, with the help of the Phelps Stokes Fund, were already providing support for Black education in the region, and that its "white population [was] too small to offer any opportunities to the Corporation."[106] In East and southern Africa, Keppel and Bertram explained in the report that they had visited 124 institutions and met with 439 government and education leaders to discuss the corporation's potential work in Africa.[107]

As Jones had feared, Keppel and Bertram arrived at a list of grantmaking recommendations that included "scientific research."[108] To this point, Keppel and Bertram suggested to fellow trustees a five-year limit in the corporation's involvement in Africa, with "scientific research" listed as the first of seven foci for potential funding on the continent.[109] This first category was followed by "library service," "native education and culture," "other non-Europeans," "art and archaeology," "adult education," and "visits to and from Africa."[110]

Under scientific research, Keppel and Bertram recommended supporting the South African government's Research Grant Board, which the two men deemed was "both competent and willing to work with the corporation."[111] Established in 1918, Fleisch writes that the aim of the Board was to encourage research in South Africa, though it "was only partly successful as it was confined to distributing research grants to individuals, but was not permitted to initiate research projects itself," a role that Carnegie Corporation then could play on its behalf.[112]

In the following months, Carnegie Corporation would confirm its intentions to work with the South African Research Grant Board and would decide to organize projects through it. However, it would not fund the board directly. Instead, the corporation would empower a group of local trustees to manage and disperse funds on its behalf in South Africa, and so too, to decide on projects worthy of Carnegie support in the region. Loram, while unsuccessful in preventing the organization's growing interest in financing scientific research in British Africa, would continue to remain a trusted adviser of Carnegie Corporation; and to this point, he would serve as one of the organization's three trustees in the region.[113]

As a second line item under the general category of "scientific research," Keppel and Bertram suggested "A Co-operative Research" on poor white people in South Africa. Explaining the problem of white supremacy and Black subordination, the two men wrote to fellow Carnegie Corporation trustees: "There are now more than 120,000 of the small total of Europeans who have sunk below the economic level of the more advanced natives and who present a problem of the utmost gravity, which neither sociology, nor economics, nor public health, nor psychology and education can deal with alone."[114] By reaching a level of poverty below that of some Black Africans, the two men noted, poor white South Africans had destabilized white rule in the region. And this problem merited the corporation's attention. As sociologist Frank Füredi underscores: "Keppel's enthusiasm for the poor white study was motivated by his concern with the maintenance of existing racial boundaries."[115]

In their 1927 report to Carnegie Corporation's board, Keppel and Bertram also proposed another study, which they listed under the category of "native education and culture." Specifically, they argued the importance of analyzing Black Africans' minds with a view toward creating tests "suitable to the Bantu mentality, and in one of the more widely distributed tribal languages." In this way, they imagined that schools and governments could more easily and scientifically determine the most qualified applicants, without relying completely on missionary recommendations or "on the good opinion of some native commissioner or other official."[116] This would be research on Black Africans to be used by white colonial administrators in their efforts to better govern on the continent.

Almost immediately after the trustees in New York City approved this 1927 grantmaking plan in colonial Africa, President Keppel telegrammed J. H. Oldham the news.[117] Oldham was, and would remain, a hovering presence in the corporation's fund for Canada and the British colonies throughout the span of Keppel's presidency. During the next months, and in actualizing one of their recommendations, the corporation selected Richard A. C. Oliver, a white U.S. psychologist, to develop elementary educational material "in one of the native languages."[118] In the process of selecting a region of British Africa to conduct this work, the corporation followed Oldham's suggestion to locate it at the same school in Kenya that had received the corporation's support some two years earlier.[119] Oliver arrived in Kenya in March of 1930 and, in 1932, published his *General Intelligence Test for Africans: Manual of Directions*. A year later, he submitted to the corporation his final report on educational research in East Africa.[120] Before arriving in Kenya in 1930, though, Oliver spent six months in London where he conducted preparatory research work. During his time in London and at Keppel's urging, the psychologist met with Oldham several times. It is difficult to overstate the many times that Oldham and Keppel corresponded, and the extent to which Keppel would continue to lean on Oldham for advice in his use of the corporation's fund for Canada and the British colonies throughout the duration of his tenure at the foundation.[121]

All that said, throughout the 1920s and 1930s, Carnegie Corporation would remain a loyal advocate of the Tuskegee educational model for Black people and of Jones's surveys of Black education, specifically. In fact, President Keppel

and Secretary Bertram further celebrated Jones's work in their seven recommendations to the board in 1927, observing: "Without question the most
important single step in the advancement of the African native has been the
adaptation, under the leadership of Dr. Thomas Jesse Jones and Dr. J. H. Dil-
lard of the Phelps-Stokes Commission, of the principle of supervision for rural education which has been so successful in our own negro schools."[122]
Indeed, throughout these two decades, the foundation remained enthusiastic
about the role that it was playing alongside peers in U.S. philanthropy in helping to export this educational model across the Atlantic.

And yet, inspired by J. H. Oldham and the general intellectual trend toward
scientific research at the British Colonial Office and among white policymakers in British Africa, Carnegie Corporation's trustees and staff would respond
to calls for greater support of scientific research as yet another important tool
for white rule on the continent. Led by Keppel, Carnegie Corporation would
be moving beyond its peers' preferred universal cure at the time for securing
white domination and Black subjection across the Atlantic: the Tuskegee educational model for Black people.

Within the corporation's general turn to scientific research in British Africa, the next chapters show that Keppel would introduce his personal affinity
for *cooperative* research studies and finance two such studies with the explicit
goal of helping white policymakers fortify white domination in colonial Africa.
The first of these investigations, which this chapter already has introduced,
would be *The Poor White Problem in South Africa* (1932), followed by Malcolm
Hailey's *African Survey* (1938), for which Oldham would play an even larger
role as its principal coordinator between Carnegie Corporation in New York
City and colonial officers and researchers at Chatham House in London.
This second study in colonial Africa furthermore would motivate Keppel to
commission and fund a national study of Black Americans that he expected
to be a U.S. analogue to the African survey, both in its research structure and
in its public policy intent to aid white policymakers across governments—
whether across imperial governments or states in the United States—better
coordinate their public policies on Black people and, in the process, strengthen
white unity, solidarity, and domination across governments.

## CHAPTER 4

# Building White Solidarity in South Africa

In dialogue with fellow trustees at Carnegie Corporation and in correspondence with his South African adviser Charles Loram, Carnegie Corporation president Frederick Keppel stressed that the investigation into white poverty in the British dominion of South Africa should take on the research structure of "co-operative research." Reflecting on its novelty among the people he met in Africa, Keppel described it as a "kind of co-operative enterprise" never "undertaken in Africa, though there is keen interest in what has recently been taking place in the United States."[1]

As this chapter illustrates, Keppel was then adding to the study of white poverty in South Africa his own personal preference for a model of collaborative research which was being popularized by the U.S. Social Science Research Council at the time: a model bringing together social scientists across disciplines both to research, from their respective disciplinary lenses, a given social problem of interest to policymakers and to author their own segments of the collective project. Focusing on the evolution and reception of the first cooperative study in the social sciences that Keppel financed at Carnegie Corporation as an explicit tool for strengthening the domination of white people and subordination of Black people, this chapter illustrates the developments of the study's research structure and public policy aspirations and of South African politics during the late 1920s and early 1930s.

The chapter argues that Keppel was invested in guiding the research structure of *The Poor White Problem in South Africa* (1932), routinely described as *The Poor White Study*, and that the study met with his approval and expectations for a cooperative study in the social sciences authored by a team of researchers offering policy recommendations that would help guide white policymakers to further secure their domination over Black people.

While pleased with the progress of *The Poor White Problem in South Africa*, this chapter concludes by explaining that Keppel, at the urgency of Bertram, would encourage the board by 1930 to look beyond South Africa for a new set of advisers in the British Empire. Keppel and Bertram then would be acting in response to the shifting political landscape in South Africa at the time, and particularly to the rising dominance of an Afrikaner-led National Party that was decreasingly interested in allying with white English-speaking South Africans and increasingly vocal in its anti-Black rhetoric. Because above all, as Bertram consistently stressed to Keppel, this U.S. foundation chartered to work in the "United States, Canada, and the British colonies" was motivated to fund projects in South Africa as a region intrinsically tied to, not distinct from, the British Empire. And for Bertram, too, his preferred model of white domination, which he associated with the intentions of Andrew Carnegie, not only privileged the interests of white Anglo-Americans but also expressed some concern for Black people, however patronizing and insincere, and most visibly through its support of the Tuskegee educational model.

This chapter on President Keppel's first collaborative study in the social sciences as instrument for white domination and Black subjection begins by discussing how he tried to further obfuscate his own—and Carnegie Corporation's—central role in the project by soliciting an invitation for the study from the Dutch Reformed Church.

## 1. Keppel Finds Inspiration in "Co-Operative Research" in the United States

Upon returning from their tour of East and southern Africa in 1927, Keppel and Bertram indicated to fellow trustees the importance of obscuring the central role played by Carnegie Corporation in drafting the idea for a study of white poverty in South Africa. "An invitation to the Corporation from some non-political body to support the study is essential," they reasoned, "and we have had intimations that such an invitation would be forthcoming from the Dutch Reformed Church, the best possible agency; for most of the poor whites are of Dutch stock, and practically all are Dutch (or rather Afrikaans) speaking and under the wing of this Church, which is now expending considerable sums for poor-relief among them."[2] With approval from his board, Keppel asked contacts in South Africa to approach the Dutch Reformed Church and recommend that it make a formal request to the corporation to finance a study of white poverty.[3]

The Dutch Reformed Church in South Africa was an organization for and by Afrikaners which long had been tackling poverty in the region.[4] By asking the Church to formally request the project, Keppel and Bertram took steps to assure that the white South African public would understand this cooperative study of white poverty in South Africa to be a project requested from within South Africa and specifically within the Afrikaner community, who dominated the class of "poor whites." As they surely had been warned by advisers in South Africa, such an invitation from the Dutch Reformed Church would

help the project receive a positive reception among Afrikaners, who were critical as research subjects for this particular study and who remained a sizeable
voting group in the region. Fulfilling these intentions, a formal letter of invitation from the Church arrived in New York City on December 1927.[5] Carnegie
Corporation was thereafter prepared to finance a study of white poverty in
South Africa.[6]

Though behind the formal request of the Dutch Reformed Church was
Keppel, who was keen to export to South Africa a collaborative research
model being popularized at the Social Science Research Council (SSRC) in
the United States. Granted, South African adviser to Carnegie Corporation,
Ernst Malherbe indeed had offered some initial thoughts on the relative scope
of the project, elaborating on five strands of possible analysis: economic, psychological, educational, health, and sociological. However, Malherbe had left
relatively open the precise structure of such a study. He did not define the
number of people he imagined would participate and come together to tackle
the five strands of analyses: whether one, a few, or many. Assuming a team of
researchers, Malherbe equally left undefined whether its division of labor
would be determined by methodological approaches, sub-topics, or geographic
regions within South Africa. In a similar spirit, Malherbe also left undefined
whether the researchers would publish their own contributions, or whether
such a team of researchers would provide a main researcher with memoranda that this team leader then would incorporate into their own published
synthesis.

Adding depth to Malherbe's five recommended strands of analysis, Keppel
subsequently suggested to fellow Carnegie Corporation board members a research structure that would bring together a team of researchers trained in
these various fields who would author their own findings.[7] Emphasizing the
relative novelty of this research model in South Africa, Keppel repeatedly admitted to fellow board members that "this kind of co-operative enterprise is
untried in South Africa," though existing in the United States.[8] In the United
States, these methods were being developed and popularized at the Social
Science Research Council (SSRC), an organization that had captured Keppel's
interest for a few years.

Established four years earlier in 1923 by U.S. political scientist Charles E.
Merriam, the SSRC was based in New York City. The SSRC was formed as a
national body intent to help U.S. social researchers plan and integrate their
work; and building upon its organizational purpose, it brought together economists, sociologists, political scientists, demographers, psychologists, anthropologists, and historians from their respective professional organizations.[9]

While the "SSRC institutionalized a pattern of independent cooperation among the social science disciplines," historian Dorothy Ross writes, "the research projects funded and devised by the SSRC were not generally interdisciplinary in conceptualization. What brought disciplines together was their joint concern to promote their own fields."[10]

Throughout its first years in existence, the SSRC's ambitions would expand. The council not only would intend to bring together social scientists across disciplines in the United States but to relate their social analyses to contemporary national public policy discussions. That said, some of the SSRC's members would remain anxious that the social sciences (by contrast to the natural sciences whose level of "objectivity" social scientists tended to idealize) were in their infancy and, thus, too "subjective" and insufficiently "objective" to guide public policymaking.[11] That said, an early and principal funder of the SSRC was the Laura Spelman Rockefeller Memorial, and the memorial encouraged the council to keep in mind an audience of public policymakers.

In 1922, the memorial's director Beardsley Ruml had explained to his board the value of funding the social sciences, noting that it was "becoming more and more clearly recognised that unless means are found of meeting the complex social problems that are so rapidly developing, our increasing control of physical forces may prove increasingly destructive of human values."[12] In the early 1920s, Ruml thus suggested to the memorial's trustees that the organization should fund, both in the United States and throughout Europe, academic centers and university departments in sociology, ethnology, anthropology, psychology, economics, history, political science, and biology. In doing so, Ruml expected that the memorial could help researchers in the social sciences further develop their fields and, in the process, help policymakers in both regions address "the complex social problems" of the day.[13]

Placing particular emphasis on the SSRC, the memorial allocated one fifth of its appropriations to the organization from 1924 onward, covering ninety-two percent of the $4.2 million the SSRC spent in its first decade. In return, the SSRC elaborated a model of cooperative research in sync with the memorial's priorities: by bringing together teams of social scientists to analyze, from their varying specialties, a common social problem with contemporary relevance.[14] In this model of collaborative research, as illustrated in the SSRC's committee structures and output at the time, each participating researcher would author their own segments of the collective project.

When Keppel and Beltham traveled through East and southern Africa in 1927, the SSRC was only four years old. Though already by then, Keppel's colleagues at the memorial were funding the social sciences in the United States and throughout Europe, and most prominently the SSRC.[15] So within the network of philanthropic managers in New York City of which Keppel and Bertram were a part, the SSRC was a known and highly respected entity, which helps explain Keppel's own confidence that its research model was worthy of emulating and exporting to South Africa.

Beyond this general context, Keppel had a firsthand relationship to the SSRC. The summer prior to his tour of Africa, for example, he had met with SSRC founder Charles Merriam and had suggested to him a potential research topic for the new organization. And far from temporary, Keppel's interest in the SSRC only increased during the next years. In 1930, he would deliver a lecture at the SSRC's 1930 summer conference.[16] More broadly, Keppel would continue to attend these yearly SSRC meetings in Hanover, New Hampshire, attracting other philanthropic leaders, university researchers, research institute staff, and federal government officials.[17] For the SSRC, Keppel also would author a chapter for *Recent Social Trends* (1933), a comprehensive survey of societal currents and phenomena in the United States during the 1920s that had been commissioned by U.S. president Herbert Hoover in 1929, funded by the Rockefeller Foundation, and coordinated by the SSRC.[18] When Keppel and Bertram shared with fellow Carnegie Corporation trustees a report of their trip throughout East and southern Africa and included mention of "cooperative research," Keppel had not yet participated in *Recent Social Trends*. However, Keppel already had become enamored of the organization.

With the SSRC in mind, Keppel built upon Malherbe's recommendation and suggested to Carnegie Corporation's trustees a cooperative research study in the social sciences bringing together scholars of varying methodological trainings, each to be responsible for authoring their own contributions in the collective project. Soon after securing from Carnegie Corporation's board funding for a study on poverty among white South Africans, President Keppel's South African advisers vocalized once again their lack of experience with such collaborative studies in the social sciences. Quite anxiously, they repeatedly asked Keppel for guidance in meeting his methodological expectations for the project.

## 2. A U.S. Research Model in South Africa

In April 1928, South African adviser Charles Loram relayed to Keppel that he and the corporation's growing network of South African advisers had discussed the need for a "trained sociological investigator," a topic that had been

broached with Keppel, "who had left South Africa with the intentions of recommending to us a person familiar with group investigation as a kind of coordinator of studies."[19]

While the South African advisers waited to hear from Keppel, they provided further structure to the channels of funding and accountability for the
study on white poverty.[20] These advisers, (interchangeably termed South African "trustees" of Carnegie Corporation) had been tasked by Carnegie Corporation in New York City with allocating funds to the Research Grant Board.[21]
The advisers further specified that the Research Grant Board then would coordinate with the Dutch Reformed Church in bringing together a "Board of
Control over the investigation." This Board of Control would include representatives of the church and the Research Grant Board along with an Executive Committee, headed by South African Senator F.S. Malan and education
expert Charles Loram, a Phelps Stokes Fund adviser and trusted adviser of
Carnegie Corporation in South Africa. As Carnegie Corporation staff later
recollected, this Board of Control then "appointed a Commission of Investigation (often referred to as the 'Carnegie Commission'), each commissioner
assuming full responsibility for a definite part of the work."[22] The Board of
Control appointed five principal investigators and two assistants. In total then,
there were over twenty advisers and researchers in South Africa involved in
coordinating the study on poverty among white South Africans.[23]

As the Board of Control stressed to Keppel early on in their gatherings,
none of the individuals involved in the project had experience coordinating
group investigations. Nor did the British dominion have a professionally
trained sociologist "with knowledge and experience of the technique of sociological investigation as leading ultimately to remedial action."[24] Without a
professionally trained sociologist or a researcher with experience coordinating collaborative research projects with public policy goals, and reflecting the
developing methodologies of the U.S. social sciences, the South African advisers reasoned that they were at an extreme disadvantage to meet their funder's
expectations for the project.

While Keppel searched for such a sociologist from abroad, the South African advisers appointed Dutch Reformed Church minister J. R. Albertyn head
of the sociology volume, in spite of the fact that Albertyn had no training in
sociology or experience in field research, as Loram repeatedly told Carnegie
Corporation. Although the minister's presence on the team of investigators
would help the study's reception in South Africa, Loram noted, Albertyn represented the study's weakest link in the most crucial role of the project.[25]

As a solution, Loram furthermore underscored to Keppel the importance of sending a sociologist from abroad who could advise the South African team on research methodologies in the social sciences, and hopefully too, in organizing the research team. If Keppel could send such a researcher, Loram noted in conversation with fellow South African advisers that "both Dr. Keppel's object and that of the writer would be achieved."[26] Throughout the next years, Loram remained adamant that the South African team needed guidance in these collaborative methods in the social sciences and in the specific investigative tools of sociologists.

To fellow trustees in New York City, Keppel relayed little knowledge of the anxieties shared by their South African advisers.[27] However, throughout the span of the project and in correspondence with Loram and other South African advisers, Keppel indeed remained aware of their worries. In December 1927, for example, Keppel wrote to the president of the Rockefellers' General Education Board in New York City asking for a "young man who would act as general organizing secretary of the job" in South Africa.[28] The reply, however, was that it would "not be easy to find the man you have in mind. One appreciates at once that he must embody a combination of qualities of personality, knowledge and particularly of wisdom."[29] On writing to economist William Beveridge at the London School of Economics, Keppel received a recommendation for J. H. Driberg, a lecturer in ethnology at the school who had worked as an administrative official in the Ugandan government. In addition, Driberg spoke eight African languages, though he had only a slight reading knowledge of Dutch, and even less of Afrikaans.[30] Consequently, the South African Board of Controls voted against Driberg, reasoning his "experience had not been quite in the direction desired in the present study."[31]

The problem, however, was elsewhere. As Keppel soon learned, he was simply making the mistake of recommending British candidates for the task in South Africa. A white South African of British descent, Loram did not personally share his fellow South African advisers' aversion to British collaboration. In fact, he found himself at odds with the Board of Controller's and investigators' exclusion of white Britons throughout the process of coordinating Carnegie Corporation's study of white people in poverty. As Loram wrote to Keppel after the first meeting of the study, "the Dutch section is opposed to any person from Britain taking part in the study. They say that they themselves are not racially minded but that they have to think of the mass of the people. That is nonsense," Loram acknowledged, and tried to placate the anti-British sentiment among Afrikaner members of this Carnegie Commission.[32] He could do little more, though, than keep Carnegie Corporation abreast of the project's development.

In this vein, Loram alerted Keppel to the various tendencies of the researchers and advisers on the project, ranging from those such as himself who were "mildly pro British" to others who were "anti British," "mildly anti-British," and "non anti-British."[33] And when it came to the much-needed professionally trained sociologist who could guide the investigators on methodology and then coordinate their work, Loram explicitly advised Keppel in 1928: "If you can send us a man especially if he is a non-Britisher everybody will be pleased."[34] Complying with Loram's rather straightforward recommendation, Keppel subsequently presented the names of U.S. sociologists, with Carnegie Corporation subsequently sending two U.S. sociologists to assist the South African group: Kenyon L. Butterfield and Charles W. Coulter.[35]

Over the next years, Keppel would find it more difficult to miss—as he seemed to have done even in light of Loram's repeated reminders—that there were relatively strong and growing animosities among white Afrikaners in South Africa toward white British people and the British Empire more broadly. And yet, quite distinct from this increasingly bubbling anti-British sentiment in South Africa during the late 1920s and early 1930s, the published report produced by the South African Carnegie Commission continued to underscore the need for greater unity among the two groups of white South Africans, and with a roadmap on how to achieve it. Unsurprisingly in this way, *The Poor White Problem in South Africa: Report of the Carnegie Commission* (1932) met with Keppel's praise, even as the Afrikaner-led government in South Africa mobilized the study for its own ends.[36]

## 3. *The Poor White Problem in South Africa* (1932)

In 1932, *The Poor White Problem in South Africa: Report of the Carnegie Commission* came out in print. Each of its five volumes was authored by different members of the Carnegie Commission and each covered separate disciplinary approaches to the "poor white problem," while also including the group's "joint findings and recommendations."[37] In this way, the structure of the South African report approximated the structure of the SSRC's developing study in the United States, *Recent Social Trends* (1933), for which President Keppel was writing a chapter.[38] To this point, *Recent Social Trends* included an introductory "review of findings" by the research committee, followed by contributions authored by the separate investigators in the research team. While *Recent Social*

*Trends* included these separate contributions as distinct chapters in a single volume, *The Poor White Study* included them as five separate volumes, each preceded by the group's "joint findings and recommendations."

In *The Poor White Problem in South Africa*, the investigators took pains to define the object of their study: "poor whites." Since many of these rural white people were Dutch-speaking, the researchers were largely investigating communities of Afrikaners, although they preferred not to place repeated emphasis on this point. Choosing to keep some distance from rising Afrikaner nationalism, at least in the public report, the investigators furthermore described this community largely by their poverty status and largely rural locations, without engaging in discussions of Afrikaners' nationalist claims to the region or competing British imperial fervor. As Malherbe wrote, in his own volume on education, "*Statistically speaking we call a Poor White an impoverished white person of rural origin.*"[39]

Beyond Ernst Malherbe's education volume, the other four volumes also included an introductory section defining the term "poor white." All five volumes also shared with readers their methods of investigation, field research methods not coincidentally promoted at the SSRC and more generally by U.S. social scientists at the time. In fact, it was in the introduction to his volume that Malherbe explained some of the novelty in South Africa of a cooperative research structure in the social sciences modeled after the developing social science fields in the United States.[40] Thus, he noted, whereas data-gathering commissions in the dominion held "formal 'sittings' at certain centres in the country to which people were invited to give evidence in a more or less formal way," his and his team's "methods were much more informal."[41] Malherbe continued: "We wanted as far as possible to study the poor whites in their natural habitats—on the farms, in the cities, on the diggings, on relief works, road parties, and in the poor white settlements under the Church and the State Departments of Labour, Lands and Forestry."[42] Much like the Carnegie Commission in South Africa, departments of sociology in the United States such as the University of Chicago's sociology department at the time promoted field research methods embracing "a combination of different research methods to build up a multifaceted picture of the problem under investigation."

Malherbe furthermore explained how he and his colleagues on the Carnegie Commission had engaged in this fieldwork collaboratively. In essence, they traveled together over a span of a year and covered approximately 30,000 miles mostly by car to visit and interview "287 poor white adults, 235 farmers, shopkeepers, attorneys police and magistrates."[43] The team took turns asking questions, chiming in when it was a topic of particular concern to their own assigned topic in *The Poor White Problem in South Africa.*[44] Relaying their methods of interviewing families in their homes, Malherbe wrote: "We generally went in groups of two or three and sometimes singly. Each of us made his own notes as we went along and generally wrote them up more fully as soon as possible later on. Though each investigator took turns in guiding the conversation into that channel in which he was most interested so as to get the facts which concerned his side of the investigation."[45] Beyond these group trips to visit rural white people, the researchers also conducted their own individual research. For example, Malherbe noted that he visited over 200 schools, tested over 15,000 students in 170 schools, and interviewed "25 inspectors of schools, 36 ministers of religion, 16 school board secretaries, 12 medical doctors, 26 superintendents of hostels, and 256 teachers."[46]

Like Marie Elizabeth Rothmann, who collaborated on the sociological report and wrote its section on mothers and daughters, and R. W. Wilcocks, who authored the psychological report, Malherbe emphasized the researchers' habit of writing down notes during and after interviews. Scholar Susanne M. Klausen notes that, even if the study was Malherbe's brainchild, it was Rothmann who did more fieldwork than anyone on the team: she "clocked more hours, covered more territory, and visited more families and communities than any of the men on the *Poor White Study* research team."[47] The sole female researcher on the team, political scientist Tiffany Willoughby-Herard writes that Rothman was "a founding theorist of Afrikaner Nationalism" who published several books and articles on "key aspects of Afrikaner Nationalism— especially with regard to the role of women in the domestic sphere and all arenas of feminized labor."[48]

The length of these investigators' individual volumes varied, though most spanned approximately two hundred pages. At 154 pages, the shortest volume was the fourth one, which focused on health and was authored by W. A. Murray, senior assistant health officer at the Union Department of Public Health in Pretoria, South Africa. The longest, at 364 pages, was Malherbe's own education report.

In the Carnegie Commission's "joint findings and recommendations," the investigators articulated the policy importance of their research topic. In this vein, they explained the value of analyzing Afrikaners in poverty: "Even where poor white families live in a predominantly native environment, cases of their 'going kaffir' are undoubtedly quite the exception. But long-continued contact with the inferior coloured races has in some respects had deleterious social effects on the European."[49] The investigators stressed that the very purpose of analyzing poverty among white people was to unite white people across class (and thus, too, ethnic) lines and thus secure white racial dominance over Black Africans in the region. From the researchers' perspective, any weakness in white people's superiority was a threat to white rule in the region, and poverty among white people was one such peril that needed to be remedied.

In their analysis, the South African investigators stressed that white people in poverty and the general population of white Europeans in the British dominion shared the same intelligence and, thus, the same propensity to benefit from education.[50] In stating this, the researchers were challenging general assumptions among the British settler population that Afrikaners' poverty was caused by some biological determinism toward lower intelligence. And they were doing so by complementing leading social science scholarship at the time, such as in the United States and Europe, which challenged biological determination in wealth and intelligence among white people.[51] This literature increasingly was showing that wealth and intelligence among white people across class and ethnic lines were caused by environment, rather than biology.

Adding to this literature at the time and challenging prejudicial images of poor Afrikaners as a biologically inferior group, the South African investigators explained that these Dutch settlers had experienced "economic and social decline" because, compared with the British settlers who arrived later in the Cape, the Dutch had been "severed from European progress and development for many generations, and lived chiefly under the simple conditions of a pioneer subsistence economy, with hardly any difference between rich and poor."[52] Lest British settlers fear that they too would degenerate in a similar way, the researchers quickly noted that the regional educational system had been far inferior in the past and that this helped explain why the Dutch community was unable to adapt to "modern economic conditions" in South Africa under British rule.[53] In other words, white readers of these "joint findings and recommendations" could find some solace that education for white South Africans had improved over time, thus helping white people such as themselves avoid the same fate as many Dutch settlers.

After celebrating the utility of a proper educational system to keep white South Africans out of poverty and highlighting the intellectual potential of poor white people to reap the benefits of white people's improved educational options in South Africa, the Carnegie Commission then took a step back to explain further how and why poverty continued to exist among white South Africans. The commission noted, for example, that poor white people in South Africa indeed had absorbed and appropriated certain "psychological traits" in the past century that contributed to their own status: "The manner of life of the rural population and their simple economic tradition caused a type of mentality, i.e., certain psychological traits, to develop among the people, by which (even if for no other reasons) they were handicapped in the adjustment (or effective adjustment) to the new demands of modern conditions."[54]

In other words, the researchers argued that while Afrikaners shared the same intellectual potential as British settlers, they had over time acquired certain psychological traits that impeded their access to the higher economic status enjoyed by many white Britons in the region. Among these characteristics, the authors listed a "certain roving spirit" among those who deserted farm life and became unskilled laborers, while those on farms clung to farm life even though it could not support them and their families.[55] Isolated, the authors argued, white people in poverty also had no sense of "business management" and lacked "industrious habits."[56] Injecting the impact of Black Africans upon poor white people's psychology, the researchers noted that the former's relatively cheap labor caused the latter to associate manual labor with Black Africans and thus to object to "manual labour, as such, or to working for wages."[57]

*The Poor White Problem in South Africa*, though heavily focused on white people in poverty with passing references to Black people, was a study invested in fortifying white supremacy and Black subjection. The South African team, for example, revealed this commitment both in their analysis of why poverty among white people, rather than poverty amongst all white and Black South Africans, was particularly *problematic* and in their policy solutions to poverty among white South Africans. The team explained, for example, that the "term 'poor white' could hardly have come into common usage except in a country inhabited by an inferior non-European population as well as by Europeans."[58] Throughout their "joint findings," the researchers assumed that Black Africans perpetually would and should have inferior status to white South Africans. To this point, the investigators took for granted that white workers in poverty, even while psychologically hampered from lifting themselves out of poverty, would always prove to be superior to Black African laborers. "Practical experience seems to show that even with unskilled work the average poor white is a better labourer than the average native if the European is placed under sympathetic supervision and is given an incentive to improve his performance."[59] Given the opportunity to illustrate all of their talents, and thus provided an opportunity to sever from the negative psychological traits they had attained in poverty, the authors argued that white workers consistently would prove superior to Black coworkers.[60]

Beginning its investigations in a South Africa under a Pact Government comprised of a "coalition of the Afrikaner republican National Party, with mostly rural support, and the socialist (but pro-British) Labour Party, with support concentrated in the white working-class towns," the Carnegie Commission's report was published three years into a South African government led by the National Party, which won the 1929 election with sufficient votes to release it from its alliance with the Labour Party.[61] Both the Labour and National Parties, as noted earlier, espoused the value of white supremacy and Black subordination in the region. By comparison, though, the National Party was more vocally strident in its Afrikaner nationalism, anti-British rhetoric, and its intentions to indefinitely oppress and subjugate Black Africans.[62]

It was against this changing political landscape that the Carnegie Commission members drafted their policy recommendations for addressing white South African's poverty in the region. In dialogue with the Pact Government's own prior efforts to privilege the needs of white people in the region by passing protective labor legislation, for example, the investigators reasoned that such long-term legislation would have the counterproductive role of impairing white people's ability to compete with Black Africans. It would do so presumably by encouraging the defeatist and dependent psychological traits that poor white people had developed over the years. Such legislation, they furthermore argued, also would exacerbate competition among white and Black laborers in other sections of the labor market untouched by these legislative acts. Compared to the defeated Pact Government, the authors of *The Poor White Problem in South Africa* believed that white people would thrive best without long-term protective labor legislation. Given the proper education and training, they argued, white South Africans would prove superior to Black South Africans, and thus, generally overpower Black South Africans in the labor market.

And yet, expressing some anxieties about white South Africans' actual ability to dominate the labor market without any protective legislation, the commission acknowledged that some short-term laws reserving work for white South Africans—at the expense of Black South Africans—might be appropriate, though only as a "measure of transition for a period during which the poor white is given the opportunity to adapt himself to new conditions in South Africa."[63] Looking for ways to improve the chances for white South Africans to dominate the labor market without long-term protective labor legislation, the commission adopted the perspective of employers who might favor Black South Africans demanding lower pay. The commission thus emphasized that all labor wages—both Black and white—should be fixed at a "reasonable 'white' wage."[64] Assuming all laborers demanded the same salary, the investigators reasoned that employers consistently would choose the white person over their Black peer: "Practical experience seems to show that even with unskilled work the average poor white is a better labourer than the average native if the European is placed under sympathetic supervision and is given an incentive to improve his performance."[65] The report left unanswered how and why this necessarily would be the case, or how South African workers would enforce this pay equalization without passing permanent protective legislation, which the researchers generally resisted in their analysis.

While the South African investigators were ambiguous about the role the South African government should play in policing labor practices, they were more direct in advocating more permanent state support for housing in cities and the countryside, along with legislation to transform supposedly restless young white men into efficient and successful farmers and laborers.[66] Among those rural white people who could move to cities, the investigators recommended overruling trade and apprenticeship regulations that barred these largely unskilled workers from working in factories and so too advocated further training to adapt these rural white people for modern industrial labor.[67]

Moving beyond white adults to white children, the investigators also recommended compulsory education, not only to teach children how to read (and thus feel less isolated in rural life), but also to prepare them to secure work in the vocational and industrial trades. In this way, the researchers explained that this new generation of white children would be better prepared than their parents for a changing labor market in South Africa.[68] It is also worth noting that investigators expected that the jobs these children would come to take would keep them above the status of Black South Africans. In this critical way, this education recommendation for white South Africans differed from the Tuskegee educational model that—while also promoting industrial and vocational training—aimed to train Black people for jobs that would leave unchallenged white supremacy and Black subjection.

Thinking about the correlation between nutrition, intelligence, and the physical growth of children, the team recommended that food access and quality be improved in schools and at home among white families in poverty.[69] As a final note, the investigators recommended further scientific studies on white people in poverty in South Africa and, in particular, suggested that a "state bureau of social welfare be created."[70]

Applying this final recommendation of the Carnegie Commission in South Africa to its own grantmaking practices, Carnegie Corporation helped fund Malherbe's efforts to create an "expanded 'National Bureau of Research in

Education and Social Work'" in South Africa. Financed jointly by the South African government and the corporation, South Africa's Bureau for Educational and Social Research would become "the centre of the development of this new relationship between social science and policy in South Africa."[71] Though more immediately in the mid-1930s and reflecting on the immediate impact of *The Poor White Problem in South Africa*, Malherbe later remembered: "The Carnegie Poor White Investigation proved to be a pioneer effort in social research which had considerable significance for social work in South Africa."[72] South Africans within and beyond the fields of the social sciences found relevance in its pages.

Following the publication of *The Poor White Problem in South Africa*, the reigning National Party convened in 1934 a Volkskongress (People's Congress) to consider the Carnegie Commission's findings.[73] Bringing together white South African leaders and representatives from the Dutch Reformed Church and the government, the People's Congress analyzed strategies to alleviate poverty among white South Africans and its consequences.[74] It subsequently resolved to "conquer poor-whitism before it conquered the nation" and organized a Continuation Committee to accomplish this goal throughout the dominion.[75]

Committed to white supremacy, though one particularly defined and dominated by Afrikaners, the South African National Party preferred to bypass the project's unifying mission among all white South Africans in favor of glorifying the marginalization and impoverishment of a segment of Afrikaners under British rule. In this way, Afrikaner nationalists used the Carnegie Corporation–funded study to illustrate how they could lift Afrikaners out of poverty and thus build an Afrikaner nation across class lines in South Africa.[76]

If Carnegie Corporation had intended *The Poor White Problem in South Africa* to be a vehicle for cementing white supremacy and Black subordination in the region, it had not expected to produce a study that would be used in order to marginalize—even if only rhetorically—the interests of white South Africans of British descent. Rather, the organization's principal goal, reflecting its own understanding of Andrew Carnegie's intentions for Carnegie Corporation, was to privilege the interests of white Anglo-Americans such as British settlers in South Africa, arguably, over the interests of Afrikaners.

Perhaps because Bertram, even more than Keppel, was vested in keeping the organization loyal to Carnegie's philanthropic intentions in the Anglo-American world, it was Bertram rather than Keppel who would vocalize most concern about South Africa's shifting political climate. Meeting with U.S. sociologist Charles Coulter upon his return from South Africa to the United States in 1930, for example, Bertram relayed to Keppel that the U.S. sociologist "confirmed [his] fears by admitting categorically that the [Carnegie] Commission [in South Africa] was not and could not be expected to be independent inasmuch as they are all directly or indirectly in the pay of the present Nationalist Government."[77] Already, even before the Carnegie Commission published its report, Bertram had been suspicious of the region's political climate and its impact on the corporation's investments there.

That same year, Bertram's general sentiment was further clarified when, for example, Keppel mentioned the idea of inviting South African Labour Party leader and former member of the Pact Government, Thomas Boydell, to tour the United States on one of the organization's visitor grants.[78] Responding to Keppel's suggestion, Bertram vocalized his complaint that the National Party in South Africa not only was presumably anti-British but also quite resistant to the work on behalf of Black Africans to which Carnegie Corporation was committed. Bertram associated Boydell, though a member of the Labour Party, with the National Party's anti-African sentiments.[79] Discounting the value of inviting Boydell to the United States, Bertram wrote to Keppel: "While you say 'we may not wholly agree with his general policy with regard to the Natives' unless I am mistaken he has been as a member of the Nationalist Government definitely against all that we stand for in the amelioration of the lot of the Natives."[80] For Bertram, white British rule was a superior form of white governance to the one advocated by the National Party in South Africa because it took at least some tepid interest in the lives of Black people by supporting, in common with Carnegie Corporation, the Tuskegee model of education for Black people.[81]

By contrast, Keppel would maintain a relatively unshaken belief in the value of the corporation's work in South Africa, writing in the preface to Gunnar Myrdal's *An American Dilemma* (1944) that the "volumes on the Poor Whites of South Africa, published in 1932 represent[ed] a relatively modest enterprise, but they have largely changed the thinking of the South Africans upon a social question of great importance to them."[82] From his perspective, the project had been successful in creating a base of white domination and Black subjection in South Africa and, in the process, immunizing the region from destabilization. Beyond his own foreword to *An American Dilemma*, Keppel communicated his continued pride in the South African study in some personal notes from his 1939 trip to London, noting that Henry Clay, economist of the Bank of England, had said to him that "both the Poor White Study and the Hailey reports were of the first importance among the contributions to South Africa."[83]

While Keppel would remain generally unstartled by the South African National Party's ascendancy in the 1930s or by its reception of *The Poor White Study*, Bertram indeed was taken aback by South Africa's changing political landscape in the late 1920s. Partly because of Bertram's discomfort with the National Party's reign, Carnegie Corporation subsequently would look elsewhere for advice on its grantmaking practices in the British colonies. That said, and rather than delving into an explanation of South Africa's evolving political landscape, Keppel and Bertram would choose to justify the move to fellow trustees at Carnegie Corporation by emphasizing the logistical difficulties in coordinating through South Africa the organization's grantmaking practices throughout British Africa.

## 4. Carnegie Corporation Questions the South African Government's Model of White Rule

At the corporation's February 1929 board meeting, Keppel shared his and Bertram's logic for looking beyond South Africa for advisers on the organization's use of funds in the British Empire. Specifically, Keppel stressed the logistical challenges in dispersing funds among British territories in Africa, noting that it was "next to impossible to secure coordination of research and other activities as between the Union of South Africa on the one hand, and Southern Rhodesia, Northern Rhodesia, Nyasaland Protectorate, Kenya Colony, Uganda Protectorate and Tanganyika mandated territory on the other."[84] Though largely a public justification, there was truth to Keppel's statement to the board. For example, just a year earlier, in 1928, Keppel had recounted to a British colonial administrator in Kenya that the Research Grant Board was helping the corporation develop a research program in South Africa, but that "your friends in the Colonial Office, however, would not let us build up any relationship between that Board and the work in the colonies and protectorates."[85]

Adding to Keppel and Bertram's frustrations about the corporation's ability to coordinate its grantmaking programs in Africa through its South African advisers, J. H. Oldham had advised Keppel in 1927 to wait before financing further projects in East Africa.[86] Oldham was a member of the British government's Commission on Closer Union of the Dependences in Eastern and Central Africa, and the committee then was analyzing white settlers' wishes for greater unity and self-government in this region of British Africa.[87] If white settlers were successful in unification, Oldham had warned Keppel, the political landscape would be shifting relatively significantly in East Africa.

Acquiescing to Keppel and Bertram's criticisms of the organization's reliance on South Africa for developing its grantmaking program across the continent, Carnegie Corporation's trustees subsequently suggested that Keppel convene with colonial officers in London "for the purpose of obtaining at the center of the British Empire such information as might be available regarding the administration of this Special Fund."[88] By 1930, Carnegie Corporation looked to London, rather than South Africa, for guidance on the best use of the organization's funds in the British Empire. And yet, even as the organization shifted to London, the next chapter shows that Carnegie Corporation's interest in the British Empire would remain on Africa and that Keppel also would retain an investment in funding cooperative studies in the social sciences as means of helping white policymakers to further reinforce white domination on the continent.

Focusing on Carnegie Corporation's turn to London in the early 1930s, this next chapter describes the genesis of the African survey that inspired Keppel to commission an analogous cooperative study in the United States: analogous both in its research structure and public policy goals. The African survey, like the U.S. study, would be headed by one principal investigator and would aim to stabilize white supremacy and Black subjection—not by explicitly creating a blueprint for greater unity among white people within a particular region of the British Empire, as *The Poor White Study* offered, but rather—by offering white policymakers across governments means of sharing knowledge and synchronizing their policies on Black people.

CHAPTER 5

# Uniting White People across Empires in Africa

Following Carnegie Corporation's shifting attention to London, this chapter focuses on the second cooperative study in the social sciences that Frederick Keppel financed as means to help guide white policymakers fortify white supremacy over Black people: the London-based study of imperial Africa which became Malcolm Hailey's *African Survey* (1938). The chapter argues that *An African Survey* (1938)—much like *The Poor White Problem in South Africa* (1932) and *An American Dilemma* (1944)—reflected Keppel's evolving interest in funding cooperative studies in the social sciences as means of helping white policymakers strengthen white domination over Black people and yet, too, the particular anxieties and preferences of his shifting network of white advisers in London.

Coming together in London in 1931, Carnegie Corporation's new advisers on the British Empire would synthesize their expectations for research and their anxieties about fragile white governance in British Africa to suggest a study that would be distinct in research structure from the *The Poor White Problem in South Africa*. In structure, *An African Survey* would prove to be much more vertical. Rather than bringing together a team of equally visible researchers authoring their own separate reports, such as those on *The Poor White Problem in South Africa*, this London-based project would be headed by a single colonial officer who would be aided by a team of largely anonymous researchers and be solely responsible for delivering a final manuscript synthesizing his analysis of the collected data.

The two studies' geographic scopes also would prove distinct. Compared to *The Poor White Problem in South Africa*, for example, *An African Survey* would span beyond a single region of the British Empire in Africa to cover various imperial holdings across the continent. This also reflected an ideological difference between the two projects. Though both the architects and authors of *An African Survey* and the South African-based study remained intent on helping white policymakers solidify white supremacy and Black subordination in colonial Africa by providing data on white and Black people to a principal audience of white policymakers, the African study reflected its architects' particular belief that communicating and harmonizing public policies on Black people across imperial governments was critical toward this end. In other words, Keppel's new network of colonial advisers in London imagined that consistency in policymaking across "white administrations" in Africa, including the "English, French, Belgian, Portuguese" territories, was essential for the preservation of continued white governance on the continent, including British control.[1]

Furthermore, distinct from Carnegie Corporation's South African advisers, the corporation's London advisers would conclude that their study of Africa should convey some concern for the welfare of Black Africans. In this way, the architects and researchers on this cross-imperial African study would prove to be more in sync with Bertram's—and by extension Carnegie Corporation's—preferred model of white supremacy and Black subjection than their South African counterparts had been. Such a preferred model of white supremacy privileged the needs and interests of white Anglo-Americans and, relatedly, vocalized a patronizing concern to help Black people under white domination to demonstrate their inherent equality to white people in ways that would complement continued white rule.

In describing the developing research structure and public policy goals of the project that would become Lord (Malcolm) Hailey's *African Survey* (1938), this chapter provides greater detail on how Keppel's inclination for funding cooperative research as a response to his and colleagues' anxieties about the threat of rising Black consciousness to white Anglo-American domination at the international level evolved in conversation with varying communities of white advisers and researchers on either side of the Atlantic during the 1920s and 1930s.

## 1. Carnegie Corporation President Keppel Reaches Out to J. H. Oldham

In May of 1931, Keppel met with his new set of advisers in London, heeding the call from fellow Carnegie Corporation trustees to travel to Europe "for the purpose of obtaining at the center of the British Empire such information as might be available regarding the administration of this Special Fund."[2] As noted in prior chapters, Carnegie Corporation referred to its allocated funds for Canada and the British colonies as its "Special Fund."

This time, Bertram did not accompany Keppel. Two other corporation trustees, Henry James and Henry Suzzallo, traveled with him instead. Even so, Bertram remained a guiding force in Keppel's discussions in London, especially concerning the geographic and substantive scope of Carnegie Corporation's mandate abroad. For example, when Keppel inquired whether there might be a way to include West Africa in that category of "British colonies," Bertram reconfirmed the corporation's mandate to assist colonies in any part of the Anglo-American world "that . . . are, or at least are potentially, white communities."[3] As Bertram furthermore explained to Keppel, "India can never be a white community, nor can the Philippine Islands, nor can West Africa."[4] Consequently, when in London, Keppel told his new advisers that the organization did not fund projects in West Africa or India, though it did and would in South Africa.[5]

Beyond Bertram, other trustees at Carnegie Corporation also offered some advice to Keppel in advance of his 1931 trip to London, though more to the substantive types of grants that the foundation president should privilege in conversation with advisers. Urging Keppel to stay away from supporting proposals that would "scatter rather than to concentrate" the organization's "potentialities in carrying out the provisions of the Charter," they suggested that he should try to discover "movements and organizations which are of moment and value in the cause of diffusing knowledge and understanding among the people of the United States, Canada and the British Colonies."[6] In other words, a leading group of trustees at Carnegie Corporation notified Keppel with some of their expectations for the type of grantmaking ideas that he would deliver to them in New York City after his trip to London: he was to think boldly about potential grant proposals and, as Bertram underscored, to remain mindful that the organization's mandate was principally to aid white communities in the Anglo-American world.

Keppel also sought the counsel of J. H. Oldham in selecting potential advisers in London.[7] With his ongoing interest in colonial Africa, the London-based missionary had become head of the International Institute of African Languages and Cultures, as well as a member of the British Colonial Office's Native Education Commission and of Chatham House's Africa group. With Oldham as Keppel's main contact for convening a group of advisers in London, the foundation president took a decisive step towards assuring that his new set of advisers would continue Carnegie Corporation's interest in British Africa.

In 1931, and at Keppel's request, Oldham would bring together a group of men at the Royal Institute of International Affairs, also known as Chatham House.

## 2. Carnegie Corporation's Chatham House Advisers

Founded in 1920 and receiving its royal charter in 1926, Chatham House was established as the sister organization of the Council on Foreign Relations in

New York City. Based on the "idea of an Anglo-American institute of international relations," these two organizations would "help their members to guide official thinking" after the First World War.[8] Chatham House and its sister organization in New York City emphasized cooperation among Anglo-Americans. To this point, political scientist Inderjeet Parmar notes that the "Anglo-American tendency within Chatham House is clearly highlighted in any examination of its study group proceedings and meetings."[9]

During his trip to London in 1931, Keppel would meet with various contacts beyond Chatham House, though he later recalled that "the most important feature of the visit was the informal conference held at Chatham House."[10] With Oldham's help, Carnegie Corporation assembled a group which it would call its "Chatham House advisers" to provide information on the various intellectual trends and needs of colonial administrators and researchers at the time. At Chatham House, Carnegie Corporation leaders and their advisers would meet formally for a full day ever other year between 1931 and 1939, and while the roster of advisers shifted over the years, six individuals consistently attended these gatherings: London School of Economics director William Beveridge; then–Rhodes Trust secretary Philip Kerr; Chatham House founder Lionel Curtis; assistant under-secretary of state at the Colonial Office George J. F. Tomlinson; and, former Colonial Office secretary William Ormsby-Gore (whose East African report, as noted earlier in this book, formed the basis for Oldham's call to Keppel some years back for greater philanthropic support of scientific research in British Africa).[11]

Keppel also met routinely with Chatham House's general-director, Ivison Macadam. Much like Ormsby-Gore, Macadam was an ever-present and reliable adviser to the corporation during the 1930s.[12] And though Oldham only attended the first two gatherings in 1931 and 1933, he remained a close contact to Carnegie Corporation throughout the years, and would meet with Macadam, Kerr, and Curtis to coordinate the corporation's London-based African survey.[13]

In 1931, this group of Chatham House advisers would express to Keppel a particular interest in scientific research in British Africa. Specifically, they would suggest to Keppel that a cross-imperial survey of equatorial and southern Africa would be of great service to administrators and policymakers in the continent's various imperial powers.

Granted, by suggesting a study across European imperial powers in Africa, these advisers could have been appealing to a U.S. foundation president's particular interest in financing social scientific research in Africa. And they would have reason to do so, since Keppel indeed was there to gain information on potentially significant projects that these advisers would find useful and worthy of Carnegie Corporation funding. And Oldham, who had brought together this team of men in London, knew full well that Keppel had become interested in financing scientific research—and specifically cooperative studies—in British Africa. Assuming Oldham had made Keppel's general inclination known to these men in London, some of them could have reasoned that it would not hurt to appease a funder's grant interests. And if Keppel had exposed his organization's search for a significant grant idea, these London-based advisers would have had reason to build upon Keppel's unique preference for cooperative research in British Africa and scale up the size and scope of the proposed project.

And yet, this would not be an accurate description of the dynamics at this 1931 London meeting largely because these men meeting at Chatham House sincerely—and for some time—had been advocating the value of conducting further scientific research in colonial Africa.

Some years earlier, after all, Oldham and the British Colonial Office, particularly William Orsmby-Gore's East African Report of 1925, had advised further scientific investigations in Africa and especially as means of helping white policymakers and administrators better solidify white domination and Black subjection on the continent. Before and since then, Chatham House had sponsored an "Africa Group," calling for greater scientific research on the continent. Two members of this group, Oldham and former governor-general of Nigeria Frederick Lugard, then established the International Institute of African Languages and Cultures (IIALC), which, with the help of anthropologist Bronislaw Malinowski, made "applied anthropology" in colonial Africa its focus.[14] Concomitantly at Oxford University and inspired by former South African prime minister Jan Smuts's 1929 Rhodes Lectures, which emphasized the importance of comprehensive research into so-called "Africa problems," Philip Kerr and Lionel Curtis established an African Institute, which also advocated for further research.[15]

So rather than simply parroting a U.S. funder's preference for financing further research in Africa, Carnegie Corporation's new set of advisers in London quite sincerely found value in planning such work. Further to this point, these Chatham House advisers' grant idea for a study of Africa did not completely reflect a clear and detailed study of Keppel's interests and the mandate of Carnegie Corporation. For starters, their proposal went beyond the scope of the British Empire—arguably the span of Carnegie Corporation's geographic jurisdiction outside the United States—to include other imperial powers in Africa. Even more, the group proposed a study anchored by a single author, while Carnegie Corporation's previous cooperative study in British Africa—*The Poor White Problem in South Africa*—was penned by a group of researchers, each responsible for authoring their own strand of the collective project. Further unlike *The Poor White Problem in South Africa*, the African study's proposed means for stabilizing white governance in Africa called for cross-imperial harmonization of public policies.

Later that summer of 1931, Keppel returned to New York City eager to explain to fellow Carnegie Corporation trustees that their new set of advisers in London had showed genuine interest both in Africa and in coordinating cooperative research in the social sciences. In his personal notes from the trip, which he had drafted during his days in London, Keppel wrote that former British prime minister Baldwin had suggested Africa as "obviously [the] most important place" in the British Empire, a region "which had always been his nightmare."[16] Various Chatham House advisers also conveyed to Keppel their sense of the urgency of the matter. Philip Kerr, for one, believed that such a "work in Africa would do much to minimize chances of war."[17] Although he did not go into detail about how and why he expected war to erupt in Africa, he did suggest to Keppel that a deadly conflict in Africa could be avoided if imperial governments rid themselves of inconsistencies in their governance on the continent. If these imperial powers together collected knowledge on Africa and Black Africans, Kerr reasoned, they would have a chance to further cement their domination on the Africa continent.[18] For his part, Frederick Lugard told Keppel "not to take too long a time" in deciding on the relative merits of the proposal.[19]

While in London, Keppel also spoke by telephone with a former member of the research committee of the British Colonial Office and current secretary of the Universities Bureau of the British Empire, Sir Frank Heath, who "approved the general interest in Africa" and noted that one of the "biggest problems [was] the divergence of ideas between East Africa and the Union."[20] Such a survey, Heath suggested, could help close the existing gap between imperial and white-settler governments' policies in Africa. This was a divide existing in East Africa, as Oldham had stressed to Keppel for some time, and in the Union of South Africa under an increasingly Afrikaner nationalist government.

In the formal report to his board, Keppel echoed his personal notes, noting to Carnegie Corporation trustees that the "preponderant emphasis of the suggestions and discussions rested upon the African field."[21] Highlighting the former British prime minister's support for the project, Keppel wrote that "Mr. Baldwin . . . said quite explicitly that in his own ruminations on the Imperial situation, Africa constantly emerges as the most difficult, and in some ways the most portentous, area."[22] And, as a whole, Keppel reported, the Chatham House advisers believed that "the most important contribution which could be made at the present time would be the financing of a broad study of equatorial and southern Africa, to be conducted under the direction of some man of outstanding distinction."[23] Carnegie Corporation's board of trustees subsequently approved a grant of $75,000 to support such a project over the span of a two-year period.[24] Within a few years, though, this budget for the African survey would increase to $115,000.[25]

Chatham House founder Lionel Curtis, who had corresponded with Old-ham a decade earlier about the latter's trip to Tuskegee Institute, summarized for Keppel later that summer of 1931 the importance and value of such a survey of Africa, which the U.S. foundation had just agreed to support. As Curtis noted, no government alone could perform the survey. Africa, Curtis explained, was "broken up into a number of territories none of which [was] financially able to undertake a thorough and comprehensive study of the native peoples."[26] In other words, Curtis reasoned that a U.S. foundation such as Carnegie Corporation would not be overstepping the terrain of the European imperial and colonial governments in Africa, but rather would be doing for these white policymakers what they themselves could not achieve alone.

Moreover, in Curtis's view, such a project would not simply serve to stave off a war on the continent, as his Chatham House colleague Philip Kerr stressed, but would also help the "helpless" and "childlike" natives of Africa.[27] To this point, Curtis wrote to Keppel: "This continent is now exposed to the impact of Western civilization, which will ruin the life of its childlike peoples unless it is controlled. In order to control it we must study not only the ideas, institutions, customs and languages, but the effects which an economic revolution is having upon them in all its aspects."[28] While Curtis and Kerr disagreed on their characterization of Black Africans, they reached the similar conclusion that continued white governance was needed on the African continent. Even more, these men agreed that further research of policies across empires in Africa would serve as a useful means of social control on the continent.[29] In response, Keppel noted to Curtis that he was very glad to get his letter, "which sets forth much better than I could have done without its help, the need of a general African Study."[30]

Keppel, in other words, was not taken aback by the language that Curtis used to describe Black Africans as a particularly "childlike" people nor in the purpose Curtis and the rest of the Chatham House advisers attached to the survey.[31] And this is because—as Keppel's actions, silences, word choices, and reliance on certain trusted and dear advisers over these years would suggest—he was much more invested in helping white policymakers fortify white domination than in verbalizing empathy for Black people in general.

During the next meeting with Keppel at Chatham House in the summer of 1933, and while this group of advisers continued its search for an appropriate director to head the African survey, Kerr and Baldwin took the opportunity to further elaborate on the group's anxieties and hopes for the project.[32] Communicating their fears of Black solidarity against white supremacy in Africa, both men underscored the continued value of the project, even as the search for its director dragged on. They explained to Keppel that the British Empire was governing in a region of the world where, unlike the United States, Black people were a majority. Their concern was that Black people's dominant population numbers in British Africa made it particularly difficult for white Britons to ensure white supremacy in the region. Even more, they stressed that "further aggravation of the problem is due to the fact that the blacks, e.g., the large and vigorous aggregation of Bantu tribes, are in contact, not with one, but with several white administrations—English, French, Belgian, Portuguese— each of whom pursues a racial policy different from the other and with little reference to what the others are doing."[33] By bringing into harmony these various imperial white regimes in Africa, these Chatham House advisers underscored to Keppel that the white minority might have a better chance of maintaining dominance on the continent, a form of domination that they reasoned was easier for white Americans to achieve as a majority of the population in the United States.

With these anxieties in mind, Carnegie Corporation's London advisers expected that a survey of African policies and African people would prove to be as useful to white policymakers in Africa as census data in India was proving to be for its British administrators and policymakers. Considering that this network of British colonial agents in London, including Oldham, had been anxious about British Africa's future precisely because they felt that the British Empire was losing control over India in the face of Indian nationalism, it is not obvious why they would seek tools from this severing part of the Empire in order to guide their retention of another region. And yet, this is precisely what they recommended. In this vein, Keppel mentioned in his notes about the meeting that "Mr. Lionel Curtis dwelt upon the fact that Africa lacks a body of information essential to public administration, such as has been provided and has been the foundation of the work of Indian administration."[34] For this network of white men, the purpose of a survey of Africa or India was clear: to help white administrators and policymakers gather data on a vast region as means for helping to maintain British control.

Taking a step back from Carnegie Corporation's early conferences at Chatham House, this next section begins with the origins story for *An African Survey* provided by Lord Lothian (Philip Kerr) in the book's foreword. Pushing back against attributing the book's genesis simply to Jan Smuts—as Kerr did in *An African Survey* and many scholars since then have echoed—the following sections describe these Chatham House advisers' various debates in the 1920s about the appropriate structure of social research and the best means and definition of white governance in British Africa. These layered tensions and varying visions for data collection in Africa found their way into the structure, purpose, and institutional home of Carnegie Corporation's London-based African survey.

## 3. These Chatham House Advisers' Rationale for an African Survey

Malcom Hailey's *An African Survey*, much like Gunnar Myrdal's *An American Dilemma* years later, begins with a foreword detailing an overly simplistic origins story. Written by Kerr, the foreword to *An African Survey* begins with particular mention of Jan Smuts's Rhodes Lectures at Oxford University, noting that as a result of Smuts's call for a survey of Africa, a committee "was formed to carry the project into execution," leading to the survey.[35]

In 1929, former South African prime minister Jan Smuts indeed had traveled to England to deliver the Rhodes Lectures at Oxford, and after the second of three lectures, historian Helen Tilley explains that "a veritable who's who of Britain's imperial and academic elite" attended these talks as part of a two-day gathering of private discussions on colonial Africa.[36] Most historians echo Kerr's forward, arguing that Hailey's *An African Survey* (1938) originated with Smuts's 1929 presentations at Oxford.

Though as this chapter explains, Smuts was simply part of the story—not the whole story—of how *An African Survey* came to be.[37] A central character in this genesis story, previously overlooked by historians, was the survey's funder: Keppel himself, who was developing a verified interest in funding cooperative studies as means for strengthening white governance over Black people.

Returning to Smuts's 1929 lectures, it was here that the former South African prime minister elaborated on his call for greater scientific research on the continent. Suggesting that Oxford University itself could be the center of such work, Smuts argued that the university could establish a "'General Staff' to think out African problems as one co-ordinated whole."[38]

Inspired by this idea for a center of African studies at Oxford, Smuts and the conveners at the 1929 Rhodes Lectures reflected on the possibility that such an institute could organize a survey of imperial policies across Africa. As Kerr later explained in his foreword to *An African Survey*, Smuts pointed out in 1929 that "Africa was developing under the control of a number of European powers, that different and often conflicting principles were being applied by them in the administrative, social, educational, and legal fields, and that nowhere was there any survey of what was taking place in Africa as a whole."[39] By December of that year, Jan Smuts and Philip Kerr traveled to New York City to meet with U.S. foundations and inquire about securing funding for such a center at Oxford University.[40]

By then, Smuts was rather familiar with this network of U.S. philanthropies. He knew the Phelps Stokes Fund through Thomas Jesse Jones's surveys of African education. In his capacity as then-South African prime minister, Smuts had sent along Charles Loram to assist Jones in his first education survey in Africa. Kerr, by comparison, was less familiar with U.S. foundation officials. Though in a striking echo to Oldham's 1925 memorandum, Kerr stressed to U.S. contacts that Black populations across the Atlantic posed a common threat to white policymakers in the United States and colonial Africa.

In preparation for their trip to New York City later that year, in 1929, Kerr wrote to his colleague Frank Aydelotte, who was serving as U.S. secretary to the Rhodes Trustees. Relating the importance of this project to a U.S. audience, Kerr argued to Aydelotte that the "relations between Africa and the United States [are] clearly going to become more and more important because of the negro populations, and it occurs to me that Smuts, who is a very persuasive fellow, might interest the appropriate foundations and so pave the way for the early commencement of at any rate the African end of the institute."[41] In December, Frederick Keppel confirmed with Charles Loram, the Phelps Stokes adviser based in South Africa, that Smuts indeed had been in New York City and that the corporation, along with the Phelps Stokes Fund's Thomas Jesse Jones, had helped coordinate his meetings with U.S. foundation leaders.[42] Building upon discussions at Oxford earlier that year, Kerr and Smuts sought support for an Institute of Government at Oxford which, again in the spirit of Smuts's 1929 Rhodes lectures, would maintain a strong focus on Africa. And indeed, among the Institute's various projects, the two men suggested that a survey of imperial policies in Africa would be quite useful.

However, the African survey that was ultimately funded by Carnegie Corporation and based from Chatham House did not directly evolve from Smuts's and Kerr's ideas for an African study in 1929. For example, in 1929, Smuts and Kerr barely discussed who—if any single individual or a group—should direct the project or how the researchers would be organized. Even more, what Smuts once might have imagined as a tool for white governance in Africa (a form of white governance, that according to Smuts, could remain rather uninterested in Black Africans' own concerns) would evolve into a project quite invested in detailing a plan for African development. This evolution, to be clear, occurred as Carnegie Corporation's Chatham House advisers convened and brought to these discussions their own expectations for research and governance in Africa. Reflecting various expectations for scientific research and white rule on the continent, Carnegie Corporation's Chatham House advisers in the 1930s arrived at a relatively unique research structure and public policy goals for an African survey.

## 4. These Advisers' Preferred Research Structure and Public Policy Goals for an African Survey

In the 1920s, various individuals in the British Empire beyond Jan Smuts were calling for further scientific investigations in Africa. In conversation and memorandum with U.S. foundations in 1925, as noted earlier, Oldham had argued that there was a need for greater scientific research of the continent. And as Oldham stressed to U.S. foundations, this was not simply his own recommendation, but one supported and urged by the British Colonial Office.[43]

That same year and reflecting this general sentiment among imperial policymakers in London, Oldham had taken part in an "African group" at Chatham House which gathered for the "disinterested study of African affairs." However, he and fellow participant and former governor-general of Nigeria and author of *The Dual Mandate in British Tropical Africa* (1922), Lord (Frederick) Lugard became "'dissatisf[ied] with the prevailing order of things' in colonial administration, and particularly with the 'negative policy of drift' they perceived concerning the 'burning problems in Africa at the time.'"[44] In response, Oldham and Lugard subsequently established the International Institute of African Languages and Cultures (IIALC) in 1926. Based in London, and with the support of anthropologists, missionaries, colonial officials, and linguists across Europe, the two men set off to create a research center that would "'bring scientific knowledge and research to the solution of the practical problems which presented themselves in' any effort to administer 'primitive races.'"[45]

Within Chatham House, Lionel Curtis was a former assistant colonial secretary in South Africa who later served as a member of Robert Cecil's League of Nations section at the Paris Peace Conference. Curtis had founded Chatham House with a group of fellow U.S. and British delegates to the 1919 peace conference in Paris. The value of scientific research in the British Empire, and specifically British Africa, was not lost on him. In fact, Curtis had established Chatham House with the explicit purpose of studying international problems as means of preventing future wars, and in this spirit, Chatham House would make it a priority to support scientific research within the British Empire.[46]

Lionel Curtis's interest in scientific research at the imperial level dated back, at least, to his days in South Africa just after the South African War when high commissioner Alfred Milner had recruited young Oxford graduates such as Curtis to fill administrative positions in the newly acquired colonies of the Transvaal and the Orange River colonies. These young men would be called "Milner's Kindergartners."[47] Unlike their mentor Alfred Milner or South African leader J. B. M. Hertzog—though like Jan Smuts and P. W. Botha in the early years of the Union—Milner's Kindergarteners were sympathetic toward greater unification among all white people in southern Africa and hoped one day to foster harmony amongst white people across the African continent and throughout colonial empires. In this spirit, Milner's Kindergartners would welcome Smuts, an Afrikaner statesman, into their British imperial network in England and ask him to deliver the 1929 Rhodes Lectures at their alma mater, Oxford University.

Other members of Milner's Kindergarten with whom Keppel met at Chatham House in 1931 and throughout the rest of the decade included Philip Kerr (Lord Lothian) and Leopold Amery (Lord Amery).[48] At least since 1910, historian Helen Tilley notes that these men "had been actively campaigning to promote more systematic studies of the empire's constituent parts."[49] Considering the general worldview of Milner's Kindergartners, such research presumably would assist white people across the British Empire better manage white supremacy and Black subordination and, in the process too, help these various communities of white people across the Empire to find commonality, and perhaps greater union amongst each other.

In their effort to share knowledge across the British Empire, Milner's Kindergarteners had founded the *Round Table* in 1909, a British journal serving as a reservoir of imperial information. The journal, as well as Chatham House, were part of the broader effort of their "Round Table Movement" to strengthen ties among white people within and beyond the British Empire, including the United States.[50] Based in London, historian Paul Rich writes that this network of men, Milner's Kindergartners, "managed to exert considerable influence on British political debate despite its relatively marginal position inside the establishment and the absence of strong institutional support."[51]

Beyond members of Milner's Kindergarten, others with whom Keppel met at Chatham House during the 1930s had joined the *Round Table* since its founding. They included Ivison Macadam, who served as director-general of Chatham House, along with Reginald Coupland, who had succeeded Curtis as Beit lecturer in colonial history at Oxford.[52] In 1920, Coupland was then elected Beit professor and professorial fellow of All Souls College, Oxford University, where he taught history classes for colonial service candidates.[53] The following year, Coupland was joined at All Souls College by fellow Milner's Kindergartner Lionel Curtis, who had been elected to a fellowship at the College.[54] Fellow Kindergartener Philip Kerr, who also had served as editor of the *Round Table* and would remain one of Keppel's faithful advisers at Chatham House, alongside Curtis, Macadam, Amery, and Coupland, became secretary of the Rhodes Trust at Oxford University in 1925.[55] To say the least, Milner's Kindergarteners and their fellow travelers were a growing presence at Oxford University in the 1920s. This is all to say that when former South African prime minister Jan Smuts delivered the Rhodes Lectures at Oxford in 1929, he entered a network of Milner's Kindergarteners that throughout the previous decade had cemented an interest in promoting greater scientific knowledge across the Empire and a greater physical presence at Oxford. This group also extended its reach and influence to Chatham House in London.

That said, these various members of Carnegie Corporation's Chatham House advisers in the 1930s perceived different policy goals when they advocated further knowledge production in the British Empire, and specifically on British Africa. Members of Milner's Kindergarten, for example, yearned to play their part in uniting white people within the British Empire, from white settler communities to the British Colonial Office, and beyond to regions of the Anglo-American world they perceived to be allies of the British Empire.[56] This cross-imperial interest had been born from their own experiences living in South Africa just after the South African War when men such as Afrikaner statesman Jan Smuts made efforts to unify white people of British and Dutch descent in the region.

On this point, Oldham differed from Milner's Kindergarteners. While the former group of men expanded upon their experiences in South Africa to promote an inclusive image of white people across the British Empire and the Anglo-American world, Oldham harbored greater animosity toward some white settler communities in colonial Africa. Particularly in response to involuntary labor laws in Kenya in the early 1920s, for example, Oldham had grown dissatisfied with the role of white settler communities on the continent.[57] And so, while both Oldham and members of Milner's Kindergarten saw value in nurturing further unity among white people in the Anglo-American world, Oldham held reservations about white settler communities in British Africa, if not about imperial governments.

Oldham and Milner's Kindergarten also differed in their reception of one particular individual: former South African prime minister Jan Smuts. While Milner's Kindergarteners viewed this white Afrikaner leader as the very embodiment of their efforts to bridge white people within the British Empire, Oldham was repulsed by Smuts' discussions of Black Africans. This is because, absolutely more than Smuts and Milner's Kindergarteners, Oldham viewed himself to be a friend of Black people and to be playing a part toward white people's eventual equal treatment of Black people. In this vision of himself, Oldham repeatedly placed white settler governments such as Kenya and South Africa as principal nemeses for his idealized vision of white governance. He privileged instead a model of a white world order uniting white Anglo-Americans, particularly rooted in building networks between London and New York City, and espousing some semblance for ameliorating the lives of Black people.

Embracing these expectations in white governance, Oldham had found particularly off-putting Smuts's 1929 Rhodes Lectures, even as others in his London networks celebrated the talks. In a published response to these lectures, Oldham stressed: "We have to make up our minds whether we are to regard the peoples of Africa primarily as instruments of our own advantage or as ends in themselves."[58] From Oldham's perspective, a legitimate version of white governance in Africa included, not only an effort to unite white people, but also some publicly stated concern for Black Africans, even if only patronizing and self-serving for white people.[59]

Thus, these Chatham House advisers had differing expectations for white rule in colonial Africa and so too for the policy goals of amassing greater knowledge on the continent. In this spirit, and even as they would argue in unison to Keppel that there was absolute value for greater scientific investigations in colonial Africa, they would disagree on the tone and emphasis that such research should take on Black Africans. Like Milner's Kindergarteners, Oldham was invested in building bridges among certain groups of white people in the Anglo-American world; more than the former, he also found it crucial to mobilize scientific research toward ultimately—even if only some day in the distant future, and still under white domination—improving the living conditions of Black people. In policy circles in 1930s London, including the

British Colonial Office, it was Oldham's perspective that represented the middle ground, the perceived reasonable approach to white rule in British Africa.

Referring to this developing perspective in elite Anglo-American circles in the 1920s and 1930s as "the new racial pragmatism," sociologist Frank Füredi notes: "The elimination of displays of racial arrogance was consistently promoted by racial pragmatists" such as Oldham. "Indeed this was the hallmark of what was considered to be enlightened opinion in the interwar period. Racial arrogance was accused of inciting many of the revolts against white domination."[60] Committed to solidifying white domination, Oldham and like-minded colleagues at Chatham House viewed individuals such as Smuts, publicly displaying "racial arrogance" against Black Africans, as yet another potential threat to a white world order.

And so, while Carnegie Corporation indeed financed an African survey much as Smuts and his sympathetic audience of Milner's Kindergartners at Oxford University had been advocating for some years, the study that evolved through Carnegie Corporation's London meetings distinguished itself from the expectations of these Oxford contacts. For starters, Carnegie Corporation took the advice of some of its key advisers at Chatham House who shared Oldham's perspective on white governance to distance the project from Oxford University. In this vein, for example, the corporation did not follow Philip Kerr's initial suggestion that the proposed study could be organized from the Oxford Rhodes Institute.[61] Instead, the corporation heeded the recommendation of a former member of the research committee of the Colonial Office and current secretary of the Universities Bureau of the British Empire, Frank Heath, that the survey "should be by an independent body, i.e., not from Oxford alone." Over correspondence later that summer, in 1931, Keppel and Lionel Curtis concurred that Chatham House should be the survey's home.[62] As yet another effort to distinguish the African survey from Smuts and his fellow travelers at Oxford University, Carnegie Corporation's Chatham House advisers in London decided to search for a director who, rather than simply and singularly trying to unify white people across imperial powers in Africa, would also display some public concern for Black Africans.

Continuing this analysis on the evolving structure and public policy purpose for the African survey, this next section explains why Keppel would condone his Chatham House advisers' preference for a single individual both to lead the research team and to author the study's single report. It also explains in greater detail these advisers' ongoing debates on the sort of individual who should conduct such scientific research, specifically whether a colonial administrator or an anthropologist.

## 5. At Chatham House, Keppel Accepts Cooperative Research Led by a Single Director

In 1931, Keppel had reason to find attractive his London advisers' suggestion that a single director should head the survey of Africa. In his own 1931 "Report of the President" of Carnegie Corporation, he noted that philanthropies were moving beyond "lavish grants for general research programs and surveys, and in favor of more specific enterprises which individuals of recognized ability will not administer, but will themselves conduct."[63] Regarding such an individual, Keppel reasoned that "for its own sake society should find some better way than exists at present to recognize and support the highly gifted individual who fits into no predetermined category and who has ambitions other than the making of money (for the business world, even in these days, finds ways of giving the exceptional man his chance)."[64]

Particularly in 1931, then, Keppel had reason to heed his London advisers' suggestion that a single director, with relatively authoritarian control over the content and direction of the project, should lead the team of researchers on a cooperative study. As far as the exceptional individual to direct the study, Keppel and his London advisers would look for a statesman whose political reputation was "beyond reproach in government circles; any doubts on this front might jeopardize the project's ability to gain access to sensitive information and secure the trust of colonial officials."[65] In their ongoing debates on who was best situated to provide colonial governments with scientific knowledge, Keppel's advisers in Chatham House would side with adversaries of anthropologist Bronislaw Malinowski who privileged colonial administrators over university-trained scholars.

As further context for this London-based debate, and by the time of these Chatham House meetings, Oldham had recruited anthropologist Bronislaw Malinowski from the London School of Economics to help him and Frederick Lugard lead the IIALC. Considered to be "probably the most influential British figure in the emerging race relations lobby in the interwar period" and increasingly a darling of U.S. foundations, Oldham had been able to recruit for the IIALC support from the Rockefeller Foundation which, in the process of the Rockefeller organizations' consolidation in 1929, had adopted the Laura Spelman Rockefeller Memorial's interest in supporting the social sciences in the United States and throughout Europe.[66]

Subsequently, Oldham and Lugard had created a five-year plan for the Institute that placed "applied anthropology" as its focus.[67] Placing particular emphasis on the value of university-trained anthropologists as providers of scientific knowledge on British Africa, the IIALC in the 1930s distinguished itself both from Oxford, whose intellectual growth in anthropology was stagnate during these years, and the British Colonial Office, which was suspicious of anthropologists as sources of practical knowledge in Africa.[68]

In a 1929 article titled "Practical Anthropology," which Bronislaw Malinowski had shared with U.S. foundation leaders, the British anthropologist argued that the IIALC was well situated to provide colonial administrators with the "practical application of scientific knowledge."[69] Through Oldham and Lugard, the Institute had entry into the British Colonial Office, and through Malinowski, it had access to the "knowledge of theoretically trained specialists" at the London School of Economics.[70] In particular, Malinowski argued against the norm at the time for colonial administrators, rather than anthropologists, to provide the Colonial Office and settler governments in Africa with its scientific knowledge of the continent. Malinowski also responded to colonial governments' own suspicions of anthropologists.

For the most part, historians Adam Kuper and Wendy James note that British and colonial governments in the 1920s and 1930s agreed with anthropologists such as Malinowski that "anyone working in the colonies would be better prepared if he knew something about the peoples with whom he would be dealing. But it was difficult to persuade the British government that the anthropologists had anything very specific to offer."[71] Many in the British government perceived anthropologists to be potentially subversive figures and too keen on "minute detail of anthropological observations," which were of little use to the "practical men" of the colonies carrying out their jobs as colonial administrators.[72] In response to such conversations in the British Empire on the relative usefulness of anthropologists for colonial management, Malinowski stressed that the anthropologist—rather than practical men in service—would be familiar enough with scientific analysis to produce proper scientific knowledge on Africa and its people.[73] Historian Wendy James notes that Malinowski's 1929 article "marked the beginning of a debate on the question of the usefulness of anthropology, and a long series of defensive articles by anthropologists which continued well after the war."[74]

Bronislaw Malinowski was—beyond Milner's Kindergarteners, Oldham, and Lord Lugard—yet another significant player in early 1930s London advocating the need for further scientific research in British Africa. And yet, in the search for a director to lead the African survey, Carnegie Corporation's Chatham House advisers would not heed Malinowski's suggestions. Rather, they would—and reflecting the inclinations of imperial officials—prefer a colonial administrator to head the project.

This is not to say, however, that the voice of the IIALC and specifically of Oldham was completely muted in the Chatham House group's search for a director. In a perspective shared by Oldham and the British Colonial Office at the time, the corporation's advisers in London looked for a colonial statesman whose expectations for white domination in Africa incorporated some public sympathy for Black Africans (again, even if simply patronizing and largely symbolic). Reflecting the ultimate policy goals of such a perspective, these advisers expected the director to agree that self-government in Africa would be the eventual—though far-off—goal of white rule on the continent. To this point, historian Helen Tilley recounts that the committee agreed that the director "would need to demonstrate what they called the 'necessary balance' between 'sympathy for the under dog,' Africans, and 'understand[ing] of] the white man's point of view as settler in Africa.'"[75] Reflecting this competing vision for sustainable white governance in colonial Africa coming to the fore in London, Carnegie Corporation's Chatham House advisers agreed to find a director who would display some concern, rather than simply indifference, for Black Africans. This was a perspective of white rule supported at the time—not principally by Milner's Kindergarten and fellow travelers such as Jan Smuts, but rather—by Oldham and colleagues at the British Colonial Office.[76]

As far as candidates fitting this description, Keppel and his London advisers considered individuals such as Richard Feetham, judge-president of the Natal provincial division in South Africa; Sir Arthur Salter, formerly of the League of Nations secretariat who had returned to London from Geneva the previous year; and Patrick Duncan, a prominent South African politician who was then chairing the special court of the Bechuanaland protectorate and also administering Carnegie Corporation's funds in South Africa.[77] Sharing his frustrations Curtis wrote to Keppel in the summer of 1932: "Men of the caliber and training to produce such a report are few and far between.... The fact that a man is unemployed and free is usually evidence that he is not up to the standard for which we are looking."[78]

While Keppel and his Chatham House advisers were experiencing frustrations in finalizing a director for the African survey, it is worth noting too that they were considering candidates from South Africa. Some years earlier, James Bertram at Carnegie Corporation had decided that rising Afrikaner nationalism in South Africa undermined his preferred vision of white governance, and Keppel subsequently had heeded his guidance by redirecting the organization's focus to London. To make sense of these candidates' consideration, it is worth noting that both Duncan and Feetham were two members of "Milner's Kindergarten" who had remained in South Africa. For President Keppel's advisers in London, both men with roots in South Africa were simply members of their own close-knit imperial network of Milner's Kindergartners. And in this way, these London advisers seemed to take for granted that these South African candidates would be like-minded in their vision for a white Anglo-American world order. Thinking of Duncan and Feetham simply as an extension of the very men with whom he was meeting in London, Keppel seemed rather receptive to them as potential directors of the proposed survey. [79] Plus, it had been Bertram, not Keppel, who had felt particularly offended by the South African National Party's vocal anti-British sentiments and heightened demonization of Black Africans.

However, fellow corporation trustee Henry James, who had traveled with Keppel to London, showed greater reservations. As he put it, "experiments, if any, should clearly be started outside the Union, partly to avoid the Dutch problem."[80] By the "Dutch problem," James likely meant the South African government's increasing hostility toward white South Africans of British descent, as well as their public demonization of Black Africans, which ran counter to the corporation's expectations at the time for white Anglo-American rule.

Alerted to such further complications, Keppel wrote to Chatham House's Ivison Macadam stressing that "in order to avoid possible embarrassments later, we should be afforded an opportunity in advance of any negotiations on your part with a given individual, to tell you unofficially what we would later say officially about him."[81] What was becoming clear to James, if not immediately to Keppel, was that this region of the British Empire—and potentially any politician or civil servant with any proximity to the South African National Government—could deviate from Carnegie Corporation's developing norms for a sustainable white world order, which was sensitive to the needs and interests of white Anglo-Americans as a first priority and shy about publicly expressing a general disregard for Black people.

Subsequently, Keppel and his Chatham House advisers looked to British India and considered the vice-chancellor of the University of Durham, William Sinclair Marris, and the finance minister of the government of India, Sir George Schuster. These searches fizzled. However, by the summer of 1933, they finally had a director: Sir Malcolm Hailey, who was soon to retire from his post as governor of the United Provinces in India.[82]

By 1933, the research model for the African survey was developing within this particular London context and proving to be quite distinct from Carnegie Corporation's prior cooperative study in South Africa as well as Jan Smuts's original expectations for a study of Africa. Not only was it more vertical in structure than *The Poor White Problem in South Africa* (1932), with a lead director responsible for the project's final report, but its intent in white governance in colonial Africa—quite contrary to the expectations of this South African study and Smuts's own—would include some public sympathy (even if only in a patronizing way) toward Black Africans. Even more, and unlike *The Poor White Problem in South Africa*, its means for stabilizing white domination in Africa would go beyond consolidating white supremacy and Black subordination in one region of British Africa. Rather, reflecting Smuts's and other Chatham House advisers' visions for an African survey spanning across vast geographic space, the London-based project intended to achieve this goal by helping white policymakers across imperial powers in Africa learn from their common administrative experiences on the continent and ultimately help them coordinate their policies on the continent.

## 6. Malcolm Hailey's *African Survey* (1938)

In 1933, Lionel Curtis affirmed to Keppel that his "old friend" Malcolm Hailey would be available to take on the role. And yet, two more years would pass before Hailey could retire from the India Office.[83] In the meantime, Keppel's advisers hired Hilda Matheson, former political secretary to British Member of Parliament Nancy Astor and later director of talks at the BBC, to serve as secretary of the survey. Considering the amount of work and leadership that Matheson assumed over the survey at the time, historian John Cell notes that "executive manager would have been a more appropriate job description."[84] Before Hailey could even leave India and conduct any sort of fieldwork in Africa, which he began in July of 1935, Hilda Matheson in London coordinated several preparatory studies. These included a social and economic analysis of the continent from W. M. MacMillan, a survey of native administration from Margery Perham, and reports from anthropologist Diedrich Westermann, biologist E. B. Worthington, and economist Charlotte Leubuscher.[85]

From 1935 to 1936, Hailey toured South Africa and then Central and East Africa.[86] That January 1936, he returned to England and met with his staff at Chatham House and a month later returned "through Kenya before proceeding to the Congo, Nigeria, and the Gold Coast, reaching Senegal in June."[87] Informed by his "heavily classical Victorian education and then by his Indian career," Hailey's biographer writes that he "went about his work, methodically tackling piles of books, articles, reports, and (by then) Colonial Office files; writing longhand summaries of individual documents and synthetic memoranda on special subjects, some short, others ranging to ten pages or so."[88]

In the summer of 1936, Hailey was in London again and ready to start drafting his survey. Relatively quickly, though, he became overwhelmed with the task ahead of him and suffered a nervous breakdown. Cell notes that Philip Kerr found Malcolm Hailey in September of 1936 "in the depths of gloom. He feels he cannot do the Report. What has really happened is that he became so interested in the detail when he was in Africa that by the time he came home he had subconsciously intended to write a book which could only be done in five years."[89]

Hailey remained in this catatonic state for several months, finding it nearly impossible to write the manuscript, but he did commit to writing a chapter on "'Law and Justice,' a subject that had long interested him in India and the only one he did from scratch."[90] Meanwhile, other researchers stepped up to draft the other sections of the manuscript. London School of Economics's Lucy Mair submitted material for sections on "Land" and "Native Administration," while a former member of the Tanganyika service, John Keith, helped Hailey generally with chapter drafts.[91]

In December of 1936, Keppel received a letter from Philip Kerr updating him on Hailey's physical and mental state, and he agreed to extend the project's timeline. Keppel furthermore secured extra funds for the completion of the project, which was also requiring an increasing number of assistants.[92] By the following October, Hailey had been admitted to a clinic in Switzerland, and then, in January of 1938, he moved to the south of France to recuperate further.[93] By then, Cell notes, "the *Survey* committee decided to go ahead and have the whole report put into galleys on the assumption that by summer Hailey might be able to proofread, do a few revisions, and help with the conclusions."[94] Against this general current of despair, the British Colonial Office released Sir Frederick Pedler to assume the editorship of the survey, though it insisted that this secretary to the commission of higher education in East Africa and Sudan remain unnamed in the book's acknowledgments.[95] Together with Matheson, Keith, and others, Pedler analyzed the material collected by the research team. Hailey edited the final manuscript.[96]

In August of 1938—over seven years after Keppel and his Chatham House advisers had agreed to coordinate a survey of Africa—Philip Kerr wrote to Keppel to say that the study was "rapidly approaching completion." Malcolm Hailey was back to health and "working very hard on the proofs," though Kerr admitted that they owed it "to Miss Matheson that the Survey did not collapse when Hailey got ill last year."[97]

Years later, Gunnar Myrdal would enter a somewhat similar nervous state. Visiting the Swedish director in Hanover, New Hampshire, where he had settled to read material in the summer of 1941, Keppel's assistant Charles Dollard would note to the foundation president that Myrdal looked "much less fit than when" he had seen "him in New York and has obviously gone through a period of great depression and tension."[98] Explaining to Keppel why Myrdal was in such a state, Dollard then reasoned: "The basic difficulty is his separation from his wife," who was still in Sweden but who would travel through war-torn Europe to rejoin her husband some weeks later. Even more, Dollard noted, there were also "secondary worries about his competence to turn out a good book."[99]

Much like Hailey, Myrdal would freeze at the task of producing a sweeping presentation of white and Black people across a relatively vast geography, with the added expectation of providing policy recommendations to help fortify white governance over Black people. As with Hailey in the late 1930s, Keppel would remain patient with Myrdal in the early 1940s. At Myrdal's own insistence that his wife's presence would help him move beyond his depressive state, for example, Keppel coordinated with contacts in Washington, D.C., to secure his wife's safe passage from Sweden to the United States during the Second World War.[100]

In the end, Myrdal would remain in this nervous state only for a few months in the summer of 1941 and his spirits would lift once reunited with his wife Alva Myrdal in Princeton, New Jersey, where he settled to write *An American Dilemma* (1944). With the help of Alva Myrdal and two research assistants, Swedish statistician Richard Sterner and University of Chicago sociology graduate student Arnold Rose, Gunnar Myrdal set to work on the manuscript in September of 1941.[101] The Swedish director would fail to acknowledge Alva Myrdal and Richard Sterner for helping to craft specific parts of the book, though he did credit Rose in the preface to *An American Dilemma* for writing seven of the forty-five chapters and three of the ten appendices.[102]

Similar to Myrdal's study, the African survey was directed by a single individual whose research and writing were greatly facilitated by numerous researchers many of whom remained unacknowledged.

Published in 1938, *An African Survey* was a hefty volume of 1,662 pages (1,837 including the index).[103] Hailey and his team acknowledged in the book's introductory pages that they had limited their geographic scope to the areas in Africa "lying south of the Sahara" if only because they decided "to exclude those areas of the continent which have come under Mediterranean littoral influences."[104] Incorporating some "convenience" factors in shaping the geographic expanse of the survey, they furthermore noted that their geographic boundary ran "along the northern boundary of the territories included in the

French West and French Equatorial Africa, the Congo, Uganda, and Kenya; the Survey does not, in consequence, include Ethiopia and other Italian possessions, or the Anglo-Egyptian Sudan."[105] Excluding Zanzibar and Madagascar, the team shared that they had maintained a particular focus on "the mainland" of Africa south of the Sahara, and specifically on British, French, and Belgian territories.[106] Within the general geographic constraints they created, they wrote that "chief attention ha[d] been given to the Union of South Africa and the British, French, and Belgian colonies and mandated territories, partly because it is in these areas that the problems of development are most important, and partly owing to the lack of opportunity for more than a brief visit to the Portuguese possessions."[107]

Thus focusing on the Union of South Africa and the British, French, and Belgian colonies and mandated territories, Hailey and fellow researchers reported in *An African Survey* that they had amassed data on African populations; the development of African languages, population records, systems of government, law and justice, non-European immigrant communities, native administration, and systems of direct taxation.[108] In the nearly-2,000-page manuscript, Hailey also discussed labor problems, the state and the land disputes, agriculture production issues, challenges in forestry, water supply, soil erosion, health, education, the external aspect of African economic development, the internal aspect of African economic development, the use of cooperative societies, minerals and mines, transport, and communication.[109]

While not absolute in its survey of an entire continent, it was indeed an expansive collaborative project in data collection over vast geographic regions. In the spirit of this cooperative research, Hailey offered his thanks to the many who had "supplied substantial drafts for chapters or special memoranda, who read the chapters in draft or proof and supplied comments, and who gave assistance in other ways, such as the loan of material, or answers to queries."[110] In the list, Hailey included over two hundred individuals, though all of them, including Matheson, would be eclipsed in this vertical research structure with a single named author responsible for the final manuscript. As Hailey's biographer, John Cell writes, he "personally wrote only a fraction of the *African Survey*," and yet, he "himself soon came to be regarded as a principal spokesman for colonial reform and development" with his reputation as an Africanist "deliberately and systematically inflated."[111]

In an introductory section titled "The Approach to African Problems," Hailey noted that the purpose of collecting data on cross-imperial policies, land, and populations in Africa had been to "prove some service to the Pow ers which have possession of territories in Africa, and of some benefit to the African people."[112] More specifically, and acknowledging the ongoing war in Europe, Hailey explained that Germany was seeking to take back its colonies in Africa. To make sense of these conflicting European claims to land in Africa, Hailey first underscored to his target audience of white policymakers of the British, French, and Belgian territories that they would need to prove that their reasons for colonizing Africa were unique from Germans' own, noting that the "nature of the contribution which the European occupation will have made to the future of the African peoples" will become a critical means of justifying territorial claims.[113] Looking to assist these white policymakers at the imperial and colonial levels, Hailey emphasized the ways that his vast collection of data could help them both improve Africa and the lives of Black Africans, and in the process, rejustify their governance of these territories. With this general purpose and audience in mind, Hailey presented a list of problems that impeded Black Africans' welfare, to which he and his team had dedicated chapters. And ultimately, Hailey suggested the need for further research on these interconnected problems. Urging his white readers to continue the data-collection work of *An African Survey* as principal means for guiding their newfound responsibility to contribute to African development, Hailey wrote: "Africa presents itself as a living laboratory, in which the reward of study may prove to be not merely the satisfaction of an intellectual impulse, but an effective addition to the welfare of a people."[114]

## 7. The Reception of *An African Survey*

Even before the publication of *An African Survey* in 1938, Carnegie Corporation president Frederick Keppel had expressed his satisfaction with the scope and tone of the study. Meeting with his advisers in London, he noted in 1937 that "Lord Hailey had carried out a general study of Africa of which the Corporation was very proud."[115] Though the project was yet to be published, Hilda Matheson had shared with Keppel the introductory and concluding chapters, which, as Keppel explained to Kerr, allowed him to see the "statesmanlike quality of the book as a whole. We are very proud of our share in this enterprise and very grateful to you and your associates for making that share possible."[116]

During the 1930s, Keppel already had been receiving similar declarations of praise from advisers in London who had remained abreast of the African survey's evolution. At Chatham House, Ormsby-Gore admitted to Keppel that the "Hailey Report would be of real importance in history. The essential thing was that there should be machinery for following it up effectively."[117] Agreeing with Ormsby-Gore, Amery noted the importance of elaborating on Hailey's report and "converting it from paper into the minds of those who took part in the administration of the Colonial Empire."[118] Added to the group of Chatham House advisers by the mid-1930s, British economist Henry Clay told Keppel that "he thought that both the Poor White Study and the Hailey reports were of the first importance among the contributions to South Africa."[119] Magnifying his own admiration for Hailey and *An African Survey*, Keppel not only would receive admiring words from fellow white Britons but also a leading Black South African.

In 1939, Davidson Don Tengo (D. D. T.) Jabavu wrote to Keppel to thank the foundation for the "epoch-making book of Lord Hailey on African Research."[120] In response, Keppel found Jabavu's comments sufficiently relevant to forward to Malcolm Hailey. Here, the foundation president told the director of *An African Survey* that in "these trying times the enclosed may give you a moment's amusement and relaxation. It's from a man who is as black as the ace of spades, I suppose, about the most distinguished native in South Africa."[121] In this letter to Hailey, Keppel referred to Jabavu's racialized identity and his public reputation in South Africa in order to substantiate his claim that a reliable Black African had endorsed *An African Survey*, news, which, Keppel urged Hailey (and presumably too, himself), should provide "a moment's amusement and relaxation." As Jabavu's note suggested to Keppel, they were producing social scientific knowledge that could stabilize white governance with Black people's consent.

As far as Jabavu's identity, historian Grave Davie writes that he was "the first African graduate of the University of London, the first faculty member appointed to the South African Native College (University of Fort Hare), and an enthusiastic promoter of vocational training, like Booker T. Washington."[122] He was also the son John Tengo Jabavu, founder of South Africa's first Black periodical *Imvo Zabantsundu*.[123] Particularly after his father's death in 1921, the younger Jabavu had become politically active in South Africa, though by the late 1930s, when he wrote to Keppel, Jabavu was generally considered a persona non grata among many fellow Black South Africans.[124] Several years earlier, in 1936, Jabavu had helped convene an All African Convention (AAC) where delegates discussed South African Prime Minister Hertzog's proposed efforts to abolish Black South Africans' voting rights in the Cape in exchange for greater land access throughout the Union. Historian Catherine Higgs writes that: "At a meeting between Hertzog and AAC delegates in

February 1936, it appeared—perhaps with the aid of artfully manipulative newspaper reports—that the AAC privately supported the creation of a separate voting roll. Critics branded the AAC, and Jabavu especially, as sellouts."[125]

This is to say that, by the late 1930s when Jabavu wrote that letter to Keppel celebrating *An African Survey*, Jabavu had lost much public influence among Black South Africans, though, relatedly, at least some of Keppel's advisers, such as Jan Smuts, considered him to be "South Africa's most important African leader."[126] For such a network of white men, Jabavu's endorsement of *An African Survey* was encouraging.

To the question of why Jabavu might have found much to praise in *An African Survey*, it is fair to say that the study echoed Booker T. Washington's own proposed vision of white supremacy and Black subordination by suggesting a gradual movement towards white people's equal treatment of Black people: a gradual shift which assumed that Black people still needed to evolve to achieve white people's "better" standards. A conservative activist such as Jabavu likely found attractive that Hailey had proposed white people's better treatment of Black people without criticizing directly white domination in Africa. Even more, and considering the developing political context in South Africa under Prime Minister Hertzog, Jabavu likely found refreshing the extent to which Hailey showed any concern for Black Africans' welfare.

That same year, in 1939, and reflecting Keppel's consistent admiration for Hailey and the *African Survey*, the corporation president invited Hailey to visit his colleagues in New York City.[127] Clearly pleasing to Keppel, *An African Survey* quickly was becoming a main sourcebook on Africa among British colonial officers and administrators.[128] As Sir Frederick Pedler noted, it was "essential reading for all Government officers and academic and scientific workers who were concerned with Africa. There can be no doubt that it stimulated and influenced a great deal of action and further study."[129]

In 1939, the Royal Scottish Geographical Society awarded Hailey the Livingstone Medal for his work on the survey. Named after the late David Livingstone, the society's medal has served since 1901 to recognize "outstanding service of a humanitarian nature with a clear geographical dimension."[130] Beyond such recognitions, *An African Survey* also influenced policy in British Africa. It has been regarded, Cell writes, "as a significant landmark in helping to define and legitimize the field of African studies, as well as in the evolution of the Commonwealth."[131] In particular, *An African Survey* is associated with the passage of the Colonial Development and Welfare Act of 1940, which reflected Hailey's call for further scientific research in Africa and so too for development programs on the continent.[132] Throughout the next decades, the book would continue to enjoy a venerable status among British policy circles, with Cell noting: "as late as the 1990s the second edition was still being consulted as a standard reference work on the continent during the colonial era."[133]

To what extent, though, did *An African Survey* completely achieve the expectations, including the public policy expectations, of Keppel and his Chatham House advisers? Years earlier in 1931, after all, Keppel and his advisers had agreed on a particular research structure and purpose for an African survey. Back then, they had imagined a cooperative research study with a single director as head, and this vision stayed intact. Their general purpose for the project also remained intact in the book's final form, since Hailey both played his part in providing a cross-imperial analysis of African policies to link white administrators across empires and, without questioning continued white rule, showed some concern for Black Africans' subjugated positions under white domination.[134]

However, while Keppel and his Chatham House advisers had imagined that the project would cover French, British, Belgian, and Portuguese territories in Africa, Hailey and his team acknowledged in *An African Survey* that they had enjoyed a "lack of opportunity for more than a brief visit to the Portuguese possessions."[135] So at some level, the project's geographic scope was ultimately narrower than its funder and architects initially had expected. Even more, a significant development occurred between 1931 and 1938: The European powers had gone to war with each other, and Hailey thus found it critical to distinguish British, French, and Belgian claims to territories in Africa—if not Portuguese (and Italian) claims—from Germany's own. The war thus added a certain urgency to the project's public policy recommendations.

All that said, the project indeed remained cross-imperial as Keppel and his Chatham House advisers had intended. And yet, while not something much mentioned by Keppel or his advisers at Chatham House, it is telling that Hailey did not produce a source of knowledge equally available and accessible to these three imperial powers. After all, it was published in English without a simultaneous translation into French or Dutch: the dominant languages of the French and Belgian governments. Focusing on the lack of a French translation, for example, British economist Arnold Plant lamented in his review of the book in 1939: "Many of the people who make or administer policy in Africa read French more readily than English. It would be a thousand pities if the influence of this *Survey* were long delayed or narrowly restricted for want of a French translation."[136] Such a French translation never came, further underscoring how *An African Survey*'s cross-imperial collection of data was intended always to serve primarily the interests of the English-speaking world from which the project was born.

That said, *An African Survey* did ultimately encourage some contact between the imperial powers in Africa. As an example, British biologist E. Barton Worthington writes that "the scientific side [of *An African Survey*] developed later in a substantial way and can be seen as an important consequence of the Survey itself."[137] More specifically, Worthington mentions the "creation in 1950 of the Scientific Council for Africa South of the Sahara (CSA), with P. J. du Toit of South Africa and J. Millot of France as chairman and deputy chairman, and [himself] as secretary-general."[138] Beyond this inter-governmental research coordination, *An African Survey* indeed enjoyed broadest and longest-lasting appeal among English readers within the British Empire. Not only was the survey published in English, but it promoted a vision of white rule that was gaining prominence among key Anglo-Americans at the time.

To this point, and complementary to Carnegie Corporation's expectations for the project and its own preferred model of white rule, Hailey stressed that white governance was still necessary in Africa, and not simply or principally to maximize the economic interests of European powers, but increasingly now too in order to guide Africans towards "African development."[139] Because as Hailey assumed, "the pace and direction of [African civilization's] evolution will be influenced by the nature of the social and political institutions which the policy of the Colonial Powers leads them to establish, and of the facilities for development which they provide."[140]

*An African Survey* furthermore amplified the calls of several Chatham House advisers, including Oldham, Lord Lugard, and Lord Devonshire, for continued white governance in British Africa: a vision for white rule intended not only to benefit white people but to show some public concern for Black Africans' interests (even if only half-heartedly and patronizing in its continued insistence on white domination and white superiority). From this lens, *An African Survey* would help British policymakers to distinguish themselves from more hard-line contemporary white supremacists in Africa such as South Africans Jan Smuts and J. B. M. Hertzog who, by comparison, were more comfortable publicly dismissing the humanity of Black people.

However, at the end of the day, *An African Survey*—much like its admirers—shared much in common with Smuts, Hertzog, and other like-minded white policymakers in this Anglo-American network. And this is because this project intended to leave unchallenged continued white governance in British Africa. That is, *An African Survey* suggested that European administrators and policymakers in Africa should increase in degrees the concern they vocalized for Africans, though leaving in the hands of white Europeans the speed and extent of Africans' ultimate freedom from white domination.

In fact, historian Marc Matera writes that some Black intellectuals and activists in 1930s London working in what Cedric Robinson has coined the "Black Radical Tradition," acknowledged both the utility and limitations of the text: celebrating Hailey's criticisms of white imperialism in Africa for failing to improve the lives of Black Africans and, yet too, lamenting its continued support for white European governance in the region.[141] In this vein, for example, Black Trinidadian intellectual C. L. R. James wrote in his 1941 essay, "Imperialism in Africa," that *An African Survey* rightly suggests that "there is only one way to save the situation, and that is to raise the standard of living, culture, and productivity of the native Africans."[142] James seemingly admired Hailey's text for its advocacy of Black Africans, even as the author left relatively untouched the validity of continued white rule in Africa. Matera writes that Hailey's cross-imperial study furthermore played a positive role among African intellectuals in London at the time, by further encouraging them to "think in terms of the similarities between their circumstances" across Africa.[143] Though pointing to Hailey's failure to question white governance, Matera admits that Black intellectuals in 1930s London ultimately were "ambivalent about Hailey's work."[144]

By comparison, Black U.S. intellectual W. E. B. Du Bois was much more decisive in his public criticism of *An African Survey*. Compared to Black intellectuals in London (or Jabavu in South Africa), Du Bois then lived an ocean away in the United States and never had lived as a Black subject in colonial Africa. This psychological and geographic distance likely explains why Du Bois was more publicly critical of *An African Survey*. Describing *An African Survey*, Du Bois criticized Hailey's text as a "splendid effort but designed to present the English point of view forcibly and completely. Not a single charge against English Colonial Policy in Africa has been left without very careful answer and excuse. All unpleasant details are elaborately glossed over."[145] Du Bois pointed out that Hailey's *An African Survey* was not written for Black people or for their principal benefit. Rather, it was a project privileging the point of view and interests of white people.

Writing this critique of *An African Survey* in his general review of *An American Dilemma* some years later, Du Bois would take pains to distinguish—in public, if not in private correspondence where he was more up-front about his scruples with *An American Dilemma*—Myrdal's work from Hailey's own.[146] One could imagine that this U.S. study placed Du Bois in a similarly ambivalent position to Black African intellectuals reading *An African Survey*: torn

between celebrating and criticizing a project that both called for white policymakers to be more empathetic toward Black subjects and, yet too, aimed to
rejustify white domination. To this point, in his published review of *An American Dilemma*, Du Bois would underscore how Myrdal differentiated himself
both from Hailey and other contemporary scholars in the United States by
insisting "on regarding the Negro problem as basically a moral problem; [by
dismissing] the argument of unchangeable racial differences; of the mores and
subconscious impasse; of absolute psychological conditioning and ineradi-
cable ignorance."[147]

Building upon Du Bois's own private—if not public—reservations about
*An American Dilemma*, the following chapters show how Myrdal's project was
rooted in the making of *An African Survey*, and more deeply in Keppel's experience funding cooperative research studies on white and Black people intended to help white policymakers reinforce white domination over Black
people. These chapters thus underscore how *The Poor White Problem in South
Africa* (1932), *An African Survey* (1938), and *An American Dilemma* (1944) complemented Keppel's developing vision for white Anglo-American rule across
the Atlantic. This vision increasingly internalized Carnegie Corporation Secretary James Bertram's—and the Chatham House advisers'—preference for a
form of white rule that expressed publicly some concern for Black people,
even if only symbolically and as means for rejustifying white Anglo-American
domination over Black people.[148]

The next chapter details the steps that Keppel took to elaborate upon a
fellow board member's criticism of the foundation's funding practices for Black
Americans in the United States and, in the process, to import some of the research structure and public policy purpose of the African survey. Subsequent
chapters describe its evolution into Gunnar Myrdal's *An American Dilemma*.

## CHAPTER 6

# Importing Malcolm Hailey's African Survey
to the United States

In the 1930s, President Keppel would build upon fellow Carnegie Corporation board member Newton D. Baker's critique of the foundation's funding practices in Black education in the United States to import into the country key aspects of the research structure and public policy purpose of Malcolm Hailey's ongoing African survey, which the corporation was financing through Chatham House in London. In adapting for a U.S. audience his vision for a U.S. version of Hailey's project, Keppel remained loyal to the research structure and public policy intent of the London-based study while also taking into account a different ecosystem of scholars and policymakers in the United States.

In the spirit of the African survey, and with the help of the Social Science Research Council (SSRC) in the United States, Keppel planned a cooperative study of Black Americans to be led by a single white European director, who, though assisted by a team of researchers, alone would be responsible for authoring the final report. As far as the U.S. project's public policy purpose, Keppel hoped that his new director—like his predecessor across the Atlantic—would be able to help white policymakers across local and regional governments share information and coordinate their policies on Black people.

In the process of consulting some white U.S. social scientists who suggested that the search for a white European director should focus on European countries without imperial aspirations, Keppel ultimately compromised on his ideal for a European statesman precisely such as Hailey with colonial administrative experience to direct the project. Considering white Swedes to be proximate allies in the white Anglo-American world, much like white Afrikaners who served as Carnegie Corporation's advisers in South Africa, Keppel ultimately selected a Swedish public policymaker (as Keppel wrote in his notes) with experience in "crime and disorders" and with crafting and implementing, if not specifically public policies on colonized people, a successful national policy program in Sweden.[1] Since the public policy goal of a U.S. analogue to the African survey would be to help white policymakers across the United States coordinate their policies on Black Americans, this European statesman with national public policy experience became an attractive candidate to achieve in a U.S. context what Keppel and his Chatham House advisers then imagined Hailey was set to achieve among white policymakers across the Belgian, French, and British imperial powers in Africa.

Beginning with Baker's criticism of Carnegie Corporation's continued practice of funding the Tuskegee educational model for Black southerners, this chapter provides context for Baker's analysis of shifting needs in white Americans' governance of Black Americans over the previous decades. Noting personnel changes on Carnegie Corporation's board, the chapter explains how and why Keppel felt particularly empowered in the mid-1930s to build upon Baker's criticism and directly challenge a long-standing funding practice at the corporation established by Andrew Carnegie himself.

The chapter concludes by illustrating how President Keppel, with the general intent of importing into the United States the research structure and public policy goal of the African survey, adapted his search for a European colonial officer such as Malcolm Hailey and commissioned Gunnar Myrdal to direct Carnegie Corporation's third cooperative study in the social sciences intended to help white policymakers in the Anglo-American world address new and evolving perceived threats posed by Black people.[2]

## 1. A Carnegie Corporation Trustee Challenges the Corporation's Support of the Tuskegee Educational Model for Black Americans

At Carnegie Corporation's annual board meeting in 1935, trustee and former U.S. secretary of war Newton D. Baker stood up to challenge the foundation's long-standing funding practices for Black Americans. Decades later, Keppel's assistant, John Russell, would provide oral historians with some detailed context of that day.[3] Russell was the son of Keppel's neighbor and former colleague at Columbia University, James Russell, who had traveled to colonial Africa in 1926 to scout grantmaking opportunities for the corporation. John Russell would remember that after the board members voted "as usual for Negro education," Baker's interest was piqued.[4] At that moment, as Russell recounted, Newton Baker put down his pipe and asked board chair Nicholas Butler if he could interject.[5] This was, of course, the same Nicholas Butler who, as president of Columbia University, had obstructed Keppel's return to the university after the First World War. Butler had since become president of the Carnegie Endowment for International Peace, providing him with an *ex officio* seat on Carnegie Corporation's board.[6]

Standing to speak to fellow members of the board that October of 1935, Baker first noted that he was pleased to see Carnegie Corporation making grants to Black schools such as Fisk University and Hampton Institute, because he was a trustee in a number of such Black institutions. That said, Baker asked his colleagues on the board why the organization allocated money toward Black education, and particularly to these Black schools in the South. Russell remembered that Baker then asked: "Do you do this because of some conscience you may have? Or are you doing it to really improve Negro education?"[7] As Russell remembered, Baker had continued: "I'd be interested in why you do it, because if you are out to improve Negro education, it seems to me that you could do it better than this in some other way. I'm also inclined to believe that things are much better off in Hampton and at Fisk and at Tuskegee than they are in your own backyard. I don't know this for a fact about New York, but I do know it for Cleveland."[8]

According to Baker, Carnegie Corporation's main grant allocations for Black Americans were doing little, if anything at all, to address societal problems he associated with Black Americans in the United States. Referring to his own experience in Cleveland, Baker said, "If this problem of the Negro is what you are really after, it is a vast one and an enormous one and a dreadful one. From the material that we have gathered in our own city, it seems almost insurmountable."[9] Baker thus was asking fellow board members if they wanted to follow Carnegie Corporation's long-standing precedent of funding the Tuskegee model of agricultural and vocational education for Black Americans in the southern United States or if they actually wanted to do something to solve the societal problems he associated with Black people, which, as he noted, were worse in northern cities such as Cleveland.[10]

This was the same Newton Baker who, while secretary of war during the First World War, had approved the establishment of a Military Intelligence Bureau and after internalizing a colleague's warning about a potential "Black rebellion" during the War, had remained abreast of the MIB's vigilance over Black communities. It was his subordinate, Frederick Keppel, as noted earlier in this book, who had fielded these files on "Negro Subversion" during the war.[11] Years later, W. E. B. Du Bois would recount a relatively lengthy meeting he had with then secretary of war Newton Baker, who had stressed to him that the federal government "'was not trying by this war to settle the Negro problem'—to which Du Bois retorted, 'True, but you are trying to settle as much of it as interferes with winning the war.'"[12] Two decades later, former secretary of war Baker—and his former assistant Frederick Keppel—would try to solve the so-called "Negro problem" in the United States, not through the War Department in Washington, D.C., but through the elite private foundation in New York City that Keppel then led.

That October of 1935, Carnegie Corporation's board subsequently excluded from the following year's budget its long-standing grantmaking program in "Negro education," writing in its minutes that "at the suggestion of Mr. Baker the Executive Committee was asked to give consideration to the general question of *negro education and negro problems,* with special reference to conditions in the Northern States."[13] While the organization considered Baker's criticism of its funding practices in Black education, it halted its financing of projects focused on Black Americans.

Baker was not the first Carnegie Corporation trustee to question the organization's grantmaking practices in Black education. At least since 1930, Keppel had had doubts about the matter and had even approached fellow board member Henry James with his doubts. For his part, James had counseled Keppel not to recommend anything new in "any part of negro education."[14] From the archival records, it is unclear exactly what Keppel intended to recommend or veer away from in the organization's funding of Black schools. Though, as James counseled, any recommendation at the time to move away from Andrew Carnegie's explicit preference for financing the Tuskegee educational model for Black Americans in the United States would likely have met with resistance from the board.

In 1930, the corporation's board still included four individuals—James Bertram, John Poynton, Robert A. Franks, and Nicholas M. Butler—who had known Andrew Carnegie personally and, with the exception of Butler, had been appointed by Carnegie to serve lifetime terms (a practice that the organization subsequently discontinued).[15] Robert Franks had been Carnegie's financial agent, and John Poynton and James Bertram had been his personal secretaries. For years after Carnegie's death in 1919, these three men continued guiding the corporation's trustees according to Carnegie's intentions. For example, and as noted throughout previous chapters, Bertram led fellow trustees in shaping the organization's grantmaking practices in British Africa by reflecting on Carnegie's intentions in the Anglo-American world and specifically on the importance Carnegie placed on privileging the needs and interests of white Anglo-Americans in his philanthropy. But even as the Carnegie Corporation board had long acceded to Bertram's guidance, not all trustees gladly accepted this leadership. As one fellow board member recalled, Bertram had an "unfortunate habit of voting no on everything as a matter of constitutional principle."[16] Bertram, like Poynton and Franks, tended to reject fellow trustees' attempts to create new programs that deviated from Andrew Carnegie's own grantmaking precedents.

In 1930, there was also the problem of these three lifetime trustees' relationships with each other. Keppel's assistant, John Russell, remembered this dynamic quite clearly: "Franks and Bertram would fight. Poynton and Bertram and Franks would all fight."[17] The nature of their arguments is unclear. However, seeing that all three had been Andrew Carnegie's confidants, it is possible that they were vying for control of who among them could speak on behalf of the founder's wishes and thus define the future of Carnegie Corporation.

In the context of British Africa, Bertram dominated Franks and Poynton as the principal translator of Carnegie's intentions as a philanthropist. That, however, was not the case in the United States, where Carnegie himself had established funding practices, including supporting the Tuskegee educational model for Black Americans. For the organization to move away from this funding pattern in the United States, as compared to colonial Africa where Andrew Carnegie had not developed a comparable reputation as a philanthropist, would represent a direct challenge to Carnegie's grantmaking traditions. In 1930, as Henry James explained to Frederick Keppel, the organization was not prepared to do so.

Unlike the three lifetime trustees, Butler enjoyed a seat on the board only so long as he was president of the Carnegie Endowment, but like the lifetime trustees, Butler presented Keppel with some challenges in developing new grant programs at the organization. For starters, Butler was known among Carnegie Corporation trustees for his bullying.[18] After a seemingly notorious board meeting in 1929, the same trustee who commented on Bertram's voting style mentioned to Keppel that the "discussion between Butler and Bertram yesterday certainly emphasized in my mind one point, and that is that it is extraordinarily important for you and for the Corporation in the future to get on the board somebody we will like and with whom we can work, who won't let himself be bullied by Butler."[19] Among those that Butler tried to overpower was Keppel, who had been Columbia College dean during Butler's reign as Columbia University president.[20] Without mincing words, Keppel's assistant later remembered the two men's working dynamic at Carnegie Corporation: "Nicholas Murray Butler was awful. Keppel had been his dean [at] Columbia College, and Keppel and Butler didn't get along at all."[21]

Butler's biographer, Michael Rosenthal, wavers on the reasons for this tension, but roots them in the two men's overlapping years together at Columbia

University.[22] At the corporation, Butler "found it offensive to deal as an equal with someone he regarded . . . as a 'glorified office boy.'"[23] Not only did Butler look down on Keppel as a former subordinate at Columbia, but also because he disapproved of Keppel's particular leadership styles at Carnegie Corporation. As Butler himself said: "Of all the trusts, large or small, with which I have ever been associated, Carnegie Corporation is far and away the most incompetently managed." He later elaborated, "Everything they proposed and had been recently doing, was in flat contradiction of Mr. Carnegie's hopes, plans and ideals. I suggested that the name of the Corporation be changed to the 'Anti-Carnegie Corporation.'"[24]

Thus, in 1930, Keppel had three trustees on the board who would resist changes to Andrew Carnegie's grantmaking practices in the United States and a strained relationship with the board chair, Nicholas Butler, who was also resistant to any such changes.[25] However, the three lifetime board members passed away a few years later, between October 1934 and September 1935, a month shy of that year's annual board meeting.[26] And so, in October 1935, when Baker stood up to question the foundation's funding practice in Black education, he was speaking to a smaller group of trustees that included only one member—Nicholas Butler—who readily and routinely questioned Keppel's leadership and the corporation's allegiance to Andrew Carnegie's philanthropic intentions. Likely reasoning that the passing of Poynton, Franks, and Bertram left room to express doubts about the foundation's funding practice to a smaller and possibly more receptive audience, Baker stood up to speak that October of 1935. And seizing the opportunity to build upon Baker's criticism, Keppel sent his assistant, John Russell, to Cleveland to learn more about Baker's point of view.[27]

## 2. Northern U.S. Context for Newton Baker's Critique

Upon the recommendation of Newton Baker, John Russell visited the Cleveland Foundation in order to see a map of the so-called "problem of the Negro" in the city.[28] Founded in 1914 by banker and lawyer Frederick H. Goff, the Cleveland Foundation pooled the "charitable resources of Cleveland's philanthropists, living and dead, into a single, great, and permanent endowment for the betterment of the city" with a particular interest in the "mental, moral, and physical improvement of the inhabitants" of Cleveland.[29] Throughout its early existence, the Cleveland Foundation funded local surveys and social scientific studies of its city with the idea of improving the living conditions of its citizens.

In many ways, the Cleveland Foundation's city-wide surveys should be understood within the broader context of the social survey movement in the United States and Great Britain at the time. Again, these surveys focused on city-level analyses rather than the broader cross-imperial survey of Africa then advocated by Carnegie Corporation's Chatham House advisers.

Some precursors to the Cleveland Foundation's city-wide surveys included *The Hull House Maps and Papers* (1895) and W. E. B. Du Bois's *The Philadelphia Negro: A Social Study* (1899), along with Charles Booth's *Life and Labour of the People in London* (1889–1903) and Seebohm Rowntree's *Poverty: A Study of Town Life* (1901).[30] But as sociologist Martin Bulmer notes, scholars usually root the genesis of the city-level social survey movement in the United States with the publication of the six-volume *Pittsburgh Survey* (1909–1914), the first empirical study in the country to explicitly use the term "survey" in its title. Bulmer identifies five main characteristics of such studies: fieldwork; "comprehensive rather than partial coverage, within a local area, usually a city"; data about "individuals, families, and households rather than aggregate data"; efforts to produce "quantitative statements about the people and the area(s) studied"; and, "links to social action, social intervention, and social reform."[31] Ultimately, *The Pittsburgh Survey* would inspire other U.S. cities to commission comparable investigations; over the next twenty years, more than 2,5000 local communities would do so.[32]

During his visit to Cleveland that October of 1935, John Russell was particularly impressed by a city-wide map at the Cleveland Foundation showing how Black Americans lived in the areas of Cleveland that were densest, "where all the social problems were concentrated."[33] The map included overlays and was divided by precincts: "The first overlay was, say, real estate values. The next overlay was population say. The next was races. . . . And then they would bring down—pick anything you want, any of the social problems—homicide, venereal diseases, prostitution, unemployment, everything," Russell later recalled.[34] As he explained to Keppel, the map "was a spectacular demonstration of what happens when a slum-ghetto is allowed to develop and what happens when industry can no longer use its people."[35]

In a letter to Carnegie Corporation secretary Robert Lester a year earlier, in 1934, Newton Baker had elaborated on his analysis of unemployment and living conditions among Black Americans in northern cities such as Cleveland, noting how tensions could arise as "tidy" and "sanitary and hygienic" white Americans accustomed to urban life resisted the presence of "untidy" Black Americans whose habits "were better adapted to cabin life in the palmetto swamps."[36] Mobilizing a complimentary image of white people and derogatory image of Black people in Cleveland, Baker had suggested to Lester that any racial conflict among these two groups in northern states would be propelled by "tidy" white Americans acting out of a disdain for "untidy" Black Americans. Baker thus reasoned that white Americans would resist Black Americans' presence in the urban north, because they were orderly Americans resisting the presence of the disorderly. Baker recommended that to avoid such a conflict, foundations such as Carnegie Corporation should pay further attention to the societal problems in northern urban centers that he associated with "untidy" Black people.

Placing Baker's worries in a broader context, he indeed reflected the anxieties of Keppel and his advisers in South Africa and London's Chatham House since the 1920s that a racial conflict among white and Black people was imminent, including in the United States. Though rather than emphasizing rising Black consciousness as the main threat to "racial peace," as J. H. Oldham and colleagues did in the 1920s, Baker in the 1930s justified his anxieties by underscoring societal ills that he associated with Black people. However, like Keppel and his network of advisers on the British Empire since the 1920s, Baker emphasized white people's willingness to resort to violence towards Black people if—to use Baker's vocabulary—the "tidy, sanitary, and hygienic" world of white people was challenged by the "untidy, unsanitary, and unhygienic" world of Black people. From the shared perspectives of these white Anglo-American men, then, it was critically important to help fellow white people in the Anglo-American world find new ways to better manage, better control, and better dominate Black people.

In a letter to Keppel three months after making his remarks at Carnegie Corporation's 1935 annual board meeting, Baker underscored his central claim that the "Negro problem" had become a northern problem. Quoting from this letter, historian Ellen Condliffe Lagemann notes that "fearing that 'in the past like neglect of like problems has resulted in such tragic episodes as the Springfield and East St. Louis riots [of 1908 and 1917]' [Baker] wanted the situation investigated and publicized as a national urban rather than an exclusively Southern problem.'"[37] Expressed both in this letter and his previous correspondence with Carnegie Corporation along with his own remarks at the 1935 annual board meeting, Newton Baker associated Black Americans with urban congestion, violence, and lack of sanitation and hygiene in northern urban centers such Cleveland, New York City, as well as Springfield and East St. Louis.

Specifically to the "tragic episodes" in East St. Louis, Illinois, in 1917, historians and sociologists have offered various reasons why white mobs that summer "looted and torched black homes and businesses and assaulted African Americans in the small industrial city."[38]

One view, proposed by sociologist Elliott Rudwick, was that white residents of East St. Louis had opposed competition for industrial employment and housing from Black southerners, who were recent migrants.[39] Acknowledging Black Americans' presence in northern communities long before the Great Migration, Charles L. Lumpkins places these moments of white violence in a broader historical framework and argues that they had "much to do with white reaction to perceived threats to white racial entitlements by black community building and politics in [the] context of the historic African American quest for freedom and equality."[40] In other words, white Americans were not simply reacting to Black Americans as recent migrants to East St. Louis in 1917, but rather as a longer-existing community of residents who were challenging white supremacy and Black subjection in the region. In the 1930s, however, former Cleveland Mayor Newton Baker did not view white prejudice as a principal cause for tensions between white and Black people in the city. Rather, he tended to see these tensions as the result of delinquencies among Black people.[41]

Seizing on Baker's criticism of Carnegie Corporation's funding practice in Black education, but sidestepping Baker's suggestion to study Black Americans in certain discrete northern urban centers, Keppel reasoned that it was the proper time to push the corporation toward a new approach to Black Americans at the national level. As Baker helped Keppel to understand, the problems posed by Black Americans for white Americans such as himself and Keppel could not be solved simply by financing the Tuskegee educational model in the southern United States. Rather, the problems were more complex and, by the 1930s, also located in the northern region of the country.

Further helping Keppel's cause to redirect the organization's attention in its funding practices on Black Americans to focus not simply on the southern but also the northern United States, the trustees that October 1935 had gathered in the foundation's offices in midtown Manhattan, only a thirty-minute subway-ride away from Harlem. And that October, Carnegie Corporation trustees would have had reason to believe Baker's critique that the foundation's financing of the Tuskegee educational model in the southern states did little to address their evolving anxieties about Black Americans in the United States.

Scholar Anthony Platt notes that while public violence in Harlem in March 1935 was relatively brief and moderate, it "was regarded by many citizens of Harlem and by city officials as an alarming sign of widespread frustration and protest among the black citizens of New York."[42] These images of violent public protest, which had captured the attention of New Yorkers, likely only encouraged Carnegie Corporation board members to be that much more receptive to Baker's recommendation that the foundation's funding practices for Black Americans, so focused on education in the South, were outdated.[43]

Adding to President Keppel's sense of empowerment at the time, the corporation was appointing three new board members whom Keppel himself had recommended to replace the three recently deceased lifetime trustees. Appointed with term limits, they were Nicholas Kelley, Frederick Osborn, and Lotus D. Coffman. Kelley was a lawyer in New York City and son of U.S. settlement house researcher and reformer Florence Kelley. Also a New Yorker, Frederick Osborn was an independently wealthy white man who had become interested in empirical research and public welfare, and particularly with "the social issues surrounding population."[44] Just the previous year, he had coauthored a book titled *Dynamics of Population: Social and Biological Significance of Changing Birth Rates in the United States.*[45] Coffman, who was president of the University of Minnesota, was celebrated for overseeing innovative changes at the institution, such as creating a college for academically gifted students, a center for continuing education, an orientation program for incoming freshman, and, a two-year collegiate course; the student population doubled during his tenure.[46] Selected by Keppel himself and approved by the board, these three trustees had no personal relationships with the deceased Andrew Carnegie; nor did they entertain any hostilities toward one another. Keppel thus had yet another reason to appreciate Baker's view that this was an opportune moment for Keppel to suggest something bold in addressing the so-called problem of Black Americans in the northern United States.

However, before recommending a new grant idea to the board during the following year's annual board meeting, Keppel found it expedient to confirm that he indeed had Baker's blessing for elaborating upon his criticism of the foundation.[47] A month before Carnegie Corporation's next annual board meeting in October of 1936, Keppel traveled to Cleveland.[48] And there, as Keppel wrote in his notes, he and Baker discussed the "negro situation"[49] More specifically, Keppel noted that Baker was "rather attracted by [his] suggestion of a concentrated report. Said it would depend upon the man."[50] Empowered by

Baker and a new and younger board, Keppel slowly was injecting his developing idea for a national study on Black Americans modeled on Hailey's survey
of Africa.

At Carnegie Corporation's annual board meeting the following month,
the trustees replaced their old grantmaking category of "Negro education" in
favor of "the Negro." Toward this new and broader initiative, the trustees allocated $50,000, thus giving Keppel some initial funds to elaborate upon
Baker's criticism of the corporation's singular focus on Black education in the
South, and his urgency that the organization instead needed to address the
new "Negro problem" of violence, crime, poverty, and lack of sanitation and
hygiene in northern U.S. cities.

### 3. Through an International Lens, Keppel Reflects on Baker's Criticisms

Just weeks after this October 1936 board meeting, Keppel started expressing
his intentions for a study of Black Americans that would explicitly challenge
the Tuskegee model of education for Black Americans as the main recommendation of Carnegie Corporation—and by extension of other prominent
white Americans—for effectively governing Black Americans.

In November 1936, Keppel told Dutchman J. Th. Moll, who was then visiting New York City, that he wanted to move away altogether from Black education.[51] As this adviser later told another colleague: "Especially [Keppel]
wants to get away from the point of view that 'education' and 'school instruction' can be the panacea, a conception which still has a remarkable hold on most
people's mind, notwithstanding the disappointing results of the energy employed in this direction and of the big sums of money spent on schools, etc."[52]

That same month, Keppel met with J. H. Oldham at the corporation offices
in New York and confided more details about his intentions for the U.S. project and particularly "his idea for a man of the Hailey type for a study of negro
conditions in the United States."[53] As far as what he was looking for in a "Hailey
type," Keppel relayed to J. Th. Moll that there was something to be said "for a
man of governmental or administrative experience in dealing with alien races.
This makes the Corporation inclined to look for their man in England or
Holland or, perhaps, France."[54] In late 1936, Keppel envisioned commissioning someone to direct the U.S. study who had experience governing colonized groups. As Keppel would later crystallize, he meant someone precisely
such as Malcolm Hailey who had served as a colonial administrator in the
British Empire. As Keppel then was reasoning, this was a project that a white

administrator, with experience creating and applying public policies intended to control and dominate subject groups in the British Empire, could conduct by applying his knowledge and experience to Black Americans in the United States.

For this network of white Anglo-American men—from Andrew Carnegie to Frederick Keppel and J. H. Oldham—Black Americans were analogous to other colonized groups across the United States and British Empire that white policymakers needed to govern and control. In this way, Keppel and his network of advisers and peers in philanthropy felt relatively comfortable transferring funding practices across the Atlantic, such as the Tuskegee educational model for Black people, or in this case, a model for cooperative research in the social sciences.

With the idea for a research study headed by a British colonial administrator such as Hailey, Keppel also reached out to the Social Science Research Council. The SSRC, as noted earlier in this book, had been Keppel's initial source of inspiration for funding cooperative research studies as a response to his own and colleague's anxieties in the 1920s about rising Black consciousness. The first of these Carnegie Corporation–financed studies was *The Poor White Problem in South Africa* (1932) and, the second, Hailey's African survey, which would be published two years later in 1938. This third study would take place in the United States, with its institutional home at Carnegie Corporation and Keppel coordinating the work himself.

Although Keppel was quite adamant in his desire to replicate the African survey, there were more geographically proximate models that he could have looked to. For instance, some years earlier the Julius Rosenwald Fund had invited an official in the Dutch Colonial Service and social anthropologist in the University of Batavia, Bertram Schrieke, to "make a study of Negro life and education, especially in the Southern states, on the basis of [his] extensive but quite different experience with education and race relations in the Orient."[55] Arriving in the United States in September of 1934, Bertram Schrieke had spent a month reading in Chicago, then seven months traveling throughout the United States, and then ten months writing his report back in Chicago.[56] In the report, titled *Alien Americans: A Study of Race Relations* (1936), the Dutch anthropologist expanded his scope of analysis beyond Black Americans in the South to other minority groups in the United States such as Chinese and Japanese Americans in California. Though maintaining a particular focus on Black Americans, he had concluded that "ancient ideals and slogans, such as 'A free college education for everybody,' should be abandoned, whereas conscious endeavors should be made to form a free peasant class."[57]

Reflecting on this central policy recommendation in *Alien Americans*, fellow anthropologist Ethel John Lindgren writes that Schrieke appealed to "'a New South,' both 'white' and 'black,' to counter economic dependency and periodic decline, at the mercy of world price movements, by building up a sounder rural economy, attainable only through their co-operation."[58]

Keppel was not impressed by Schrieke's focus on Black southerners and on ever-more agricultural education for Black people as the answer to his and colleagues' anxieties about the evolving dangers posed by Black Americans and the frailty of a white Anglo-American world order. When a Dutch official passing by Keppel's New York City office mentioned Schrieke as a potential director of the study of Black Americans, Keppel responded that "he didn't want to start from [the] educational end."[59]

Another possible model for Keppel, as he shaped the structure of the study that would become *An American Dilemma*, was *Recent Social Trends in the United States: Report of the President's Research Committee on Social Trends* (1933), a cooperative research study at the national level that U.S. president Herbert Hoover had commissioned, the Rockefeller Foundation financed, and the Social Science Research Council (SSRC) coordinated.[60] Keppel himself had contributed a chapter on "The Arts in Social Life," but for the project he now had in mind he wanted a leading director who, like Malcolm Hailey, would solicit the aid of researchers while remaining singularly responsible for producing the final report.[61] In this way, the research structure of the proposed U.S. study distinguished itself not only from *Recent Social Trends*, for example, but also *The Poor White Problem in South Africa*.

In his own personal writings, Keppel never articulated how he went from listening to Newton Baker in the fall of 1935 to deciding a year later that this was the opportune time to redirect the foundation's grantmaking practices for Black Americans and towards financing a U.S. analogue to Hailey's survey. Considering Keppel's personality and decision-making processes, though, this was not so unusual. Robert Lester, who assumed the position of corporate secretary after James Bertram's passing, described to an oral historian decades later how Keppel "thought intuitively. . . . He never liked to fill in the interstices. He thought fast, and I never knew how he went from point to point. I won't say he never knew, but you rarely knew how he jumped from one point to another. In that way he was possibly the most exciting man I've ever been around."[62] That is to say that Keppel reasoned by associating ideas. In doing so, Lester suggested that Keppel related ideas and concepts that his colleagues did not necessarily associate and, perhaps to their frustration, Keppel did not vocalize how he arrived at his analyses.

To this point, while Keppel translated Hailey's project to a U.S. context, he did not tend to vocalize his reasoning with colleagues. And yet, there was a logic behind his thinking. When hearing and absorbing Newton Baker's criticism of the so-called "problem of the Negro" in various northern cities in the United States, it seems that Keppel came to think of the African survey because the problems vocalized by his Chatham House advisers on the eve of the African survey echoed in many ways the complaints that Baker expressed about local governance in cities such as New York City and Cleveland. For starters, the common observation and complaint among these white men in Keppel's network at the time was that Black people posed threats to white people, whether it was a rising Black consciousness (as Oldham had expressed in the 1920s) or societal ills they associated with Black people (as Baker underscored within a U.S. context in the 1930s). These white men shared the assumption that, if these perceived threats posed by Black people escalated, white people such as themselves rightfully would respond in violence, thus leading to further deadly conflict among white and Black people.

As we have seen, Keppel's advisers on the African survey had stressed that a main avenue toward avoiding such conflict among white and Black people in colonial Africa was to better reinforce white domination; to do that, they argued that it would help for the various imperial and colonial governments to share knowledge in public policymaking on the continent. By doing so, white governments would learn how to govern Black people *better*, to dominate Black people *better*, and thus to strengthen white domination on the continent.

A national study of Black Americans would have a similar rationale, of enabling white policymakers across governments—in this case, across U.S. domestic governments in the North and South rather than across colonial and imperial governments in Africa—learn from each other's experiences and, in the process, arrive at better and more synchronized public policies to contain the perceived threats increasingly posed by Black people in the North.

## 4. Carnegie Corporation Replicates the Research Structure of the African Survey in the United States

One of the very first U.S. academics with whom Keppel discussed his idea for a cooperative national study of Black Americans was Northwestern University anthropologist Melville Herskovits.[63] For a person intent on replicating the London-based study in the United States, speaking with a U.S. anthropologist known for studying Black culture in the United States and colonial

Africa probably seemed like a good place to start, especially since, as the next chapter will underscore, Keppel did not have in the United States (as he had at Chatham House at the time) a group of key public administrators keen to publicly sponsor and promote such a project. If not a public administrator, Keppel's years visiting Chatham House had taught him that an anthropologist would be the next-best option for advising him on shaping a U.S. analogue to the African survey.

Herskovits had come to his attention some months after Newton Baker had made his points at the 1935 annual board meeting through an application for financial support of Herskovits's research "into the scientific problems arising from the study of Negro cultures and physical types as found both in the New World, and in the areas of West Africa from which the New World Negroes were derived."[64] Keppel and Herskovits began a personal correspondence and met in person to discuss Herskovits's research and then Keppel's idea for a national study of Black Americans.[65] Herskovits soon pointed Keppel toward Black economist Abram Harris and white sociologist Donald Young as two potential advisers for the project.[66]

By recommending these two colleagues, Herskovits was already signaling to Keppel how a U.S. version of the African survey would evolve from its London-based analogue. Unlike the academe in Britain, that is, Herskovits suggested to Keppel that white anthropologists such as himself as well as Black and white economists and sociologists studied Black Americans. In the United States, Black Americans were earning doctorates in the social sciences, and particularly those with PhDs from Columbia and Harvard were commanding some attention and respect from their white peers. Many of these white academics, however, did not think of their Black colleagues as equals; on the contrary, they engaged in discriminatory practices by limiting the scope of Black scholars' work to race-based analyses, undermining their authority as sources of knowledge on white supremacy and Black subordination, and barring them from employment at elite universities. Many Black scholars such as Harris found employment at Black institutions such as Howard, Fisk, and Atlanta Universities, as well as more technical colleges such as Hampton and Tuskegee.

Further distinct from the academe in Britain where anthropologists commanded the study of Black people, Herskovits also signaled in his recommendations of Harris and Young that Black Americans were not simply the research subjects of anthropologists analyzing "primitive groups." Rather, they also were the subjects of study for sociologists and economists such as Harris and Young, who were analyzing inequalities among members of "a modern society."

In correspondence with Donald Young, Herskovits mentioned that he had recommended to Keppel both him and Abram Harris. Keppel "did not know of Abe at all," Herskovits reported, "but reacted promptly and very favorably to yours; apparently Keppel doesn't know you as a researcher in this field, and was delighted to learn that you might be available."[67] Subsequently Keppel reached out to Young, who was working at the SSRC in New York, and asked Young to describe how a study of Black Americans could be directed by a European director, assuming that such a European received generous funding.[68]

In January of 1937, Young sent Keppel a six-page letter, noting that "several weeks ago you asked me to mull over your thought that a socially effective interpretation of the Negro in American life could now be written by a European of keen and detached discernment if he were afforded ample financial and technical assistance."[69] In the six-page letter, Young went into relative detail on the range of data that the study should cover and, for example, the length of time for such a project.

Over the next months, Young would learn that Keppel went and shared the letter with his board, a decision that the sociologist found startling. As Young later told Carnegie Corporation's oral historian, he had not endorsed Keppel's idea for a study of Black Americans. Rather, Young stressed that he simply had outlined how Keppel should go about selecting a director and staff for a study that the foundation president already had in mind to organize.[70] Much as with J. H. Oldham's own memorandum over a decade earlier, Donald Young's letter would serve to help Keppel lean on an adviser to steer his board.

As Keppel continued planning the project, and in correspondence with Young and Herskovits, Keppel would explain that he was excluding U.S. candidates for the directorship of the study, because as Young paraphrased back to Keppel in January of 1937, the foundation president wanted a fresh perspective, "an improved approach to the study of American race relations difficult of successful exposition by a native of the United States."[71] At one level, Keppel was simply justifying to U.S. social scientists such as Young and Herskovits why he was not selecting them to direct the project. At another level also, Keppel was expressing to a U.S. audience of scholars his evolving justification for modeling this study of Black Americans on the African survey, which, as he understood it, should be directed by a European statesman. Young ultimately would complement the foundation president's decision to focus on European candidates, writing to Keppel, the "emotional involvements of Negro and white Americans handicaps established residents of the United States not only with respect to the attainment of that degree of objectivity requisite for a dispassionate account of the coloured minority but also mitigates against the acceptance of any such account as unbiased by fellow residents."[72]

To find such a person, Keppel turned to his Chatham House advisers, who would understand precisely the kind of study he was imagining and the kind of European director he sought. In London in the spring of 1937 for one of his bi-annual meetings with advisers there, Keppel sought out Chatham House general-director Ivison Macadam and "raised the question for the man to run the proposed negro study."[73] Keppel worked through various suggestions with Macadam. Ruling out William Rappard, former director of the Mandates Division of the League of Nations, which oversaw the administration of colonial territories lost by the Central Powers at the end of the war,[74] Keppel "wondered whether some early man at the League of the Layton type might be considered."[75] He was referring to Sir Walter Layton, former director of the economic and financial section of the league and current editor of *The Economist*.[76] They also discussed Philip Kerr (Lord Lothian), a central figure of Milner's Kindergarten and future British ambassador in Washington, D.C., who had been keeping Keppel abreast on the progress of Hailey's survey.[77]

In London that April of 1937, Keppel lunched with Canadian high commissioner to Britain and future governor-general of Canada Vincent Massey. As Keppel noted, Massey "was also interested in the plan for the negro study. He said what about Sir Arthur Salter—it is only a question of whether we can catch him."[78] Former head of the economic and financial section of the secretariat at the League of Nations, Salter was in high demand at Chatham House. Not only had he been an early candidate for the African survey (which he turned down), but he also was being suggested as a possible director of its U.S. analogue. Salter then was the Gladstone professor of political theory and institutions at Oxford University, and, as Kerr advised Keppel, was not likely up for the new project.[79]

Keppel continued his inquiries in London. He recorded in his notes that William Beveridge of the London School of Economics, who then had accepted the mastership of University College, Oxford, had told him that he was "interested and approving of proposed study of negro in the United States. Says there is a shortage of first-rate men in England but will try to make suggestions."[80] Several days later, Keppel again met with Kerr, and the two discussed Hailey's project in the same breath as the proposed U.S. project. Keppel noted that Kerr was very "enthusiastic about Hailey's job. Says that Hailey made an extraordinary impression upon everyone whom he met in Africa, and that Hailey 'on Africa' will be the standard book for a generation."[81] Equally so, Keppel jotted down that the two men spoke of the "negro study in the U.S. Lothian interested, doubts whether *Salter* is up to it, but will try to think of a name. Believes an Englishman or Scotsman could best do the job."[82] Already with Hailey in mind, Keppel wondered to himself on paper whether Kerr was "thinking of proposing Hailey."[83]

During the final days of his trip to London, Keppel kept seeking guidance for his suggested U.S. analogue to Hailey's project. Oldham, who already knew of Keppel's idea for a Hailey type to direct a study of Black Americans, advised him to reach out to Oxford lecturer in colonial history Reginald Coupland to ask him about Roy Forbes Harrod, a lecturer at Christ Church, Oxford. Meeting with Lionel Curtis and Hailey, Keppel also mentioned as a possibility Hilda Matheson, described by historian John Cell as the "executive manager" of Hailey's project.[84] In response, Malcolm Hailey seemed to agree that "administrative experience [was] better than academic."[85] Keppel wrote down these names in his developing list of potential personnel for the U.S. study.

At this point, and although Keppel had been seeking a "Hailey type," he began wondering what it would mean for him to commission such a person for the U.S. project. He certainly wanted someone who, like Hailey, could attract the collaboration and cooperation of white policymakers across governments and, ultimately too, secure their collaboration and admiration. Years earlier, Keppel had singled these out as qualities in a letter in which he had noted the value of having Hailey as director of the African survey: "The attitude both of the Minister for the Colonies and of General [Jan] Smuts [of South Africa] makes it clear that Hailey personally will have every co-operation both from the Colonial Office and in South Africa. He speaks good French, as I made it my business to find out, and this fact plus his reputation in India and his delightful personality will help him with the French and Belgian aspects of the problem."[86] But while the ability to navigate different networks of white policymakers across governments with varying cultural, social, and political norms was a requirement for the U.S. project, as it had been for the African survey, Keppel came to realize that a director for the U.S. study—if he indeed was to be received well by the SSRC and its peers in the academe and public policymaking circles—should originate from a nonimperial and nonfascist country in Europe. Here, Donald Young's advice proved especially valuable.

## 5. Keppel Adapts a "Hailey Type" to a U.S. Context

In response to Keppel's message that a European should direct the U.S. study on Black Americans, Donald Young had advised Keppel in January 1937—three months prior to Keppel's trip to Chatham House—that a European's sheer "lack of first-hand contact with American racial problems, however, may not be regarded as a guarantee of freedom from bias. Problems of adjustment in the relations of a majority population with minority peoples have fused practically every nation of the world, and are today prominent in many."[87] Young continued: "This is especially true in such colonial countries as Holland, England, France and Italy, and in others which include minority peoples of distinct racial or national origin within their borders, such as Germany and Hungary. The Scandinavian countries are perhaps the most free today of such influences."[88]

To understand Keppel's ultimate decision to heed this part of Young's advice in the search for a U.S. director, it is important to note that even as Keppel related to his Chatham House advisers and very much intended to commission someone from this network with experience governing subject groups in the British Empire, he also deeply wanted this U.S. study to be as successful in a U.S. context as an African survey was set to be in colonial Africa, and especially British Africa.

By the end of that summer of 1937, and with a new understanding of what he meant by a "Hailey type," Keppel jumped on the recommendation of former director of the Laura Spelman Rockefeller Memorial, Beardsley Ruml, to consider Karl Gunnar Myrdal, a Swedish economist-turned-population-expert and member of the Swedish parliament. As Keppel wrote approvingly in his list of potential candidates for the U.S. study, Myrdal had a "responsible position on [the] Social Board for Sweden" and "has worked on crime and disorders."[89]

As historian Walter Jackson notes, criminology was indeed an interest of Myrdal's, although at the time, Myrdal was not particularly known in Sweden or the United States as an expert on "crime and disorders," which makes Keppel's description of Myrdal here especially intriguing.[90] If anything, Keppel's notes suggest that his conversation with Ruml was rather honest. Assuming Keppel was up front with his longtime peer in elite philanthropy, Keppel likely explained to Ruml in confidence that they were looking for someone to conduct a study of Black Americans that would help white policymakers better manage and control, what they perceived to be, a national problem of delinquencies among Black Americans. This would help explain why Ruml then would emphasize Myrdal's work on "crime and disorders," and why Keppel would find this work important enough to underscore in his notes. Even more, and what likely pleased Keppel in conversation with Ruml, this candidate long had been vetted by Keppel's peers in philanthropy. During the 1930s, Gunnar Myrdal had become one of the Rockefeller organizations' most prized grantees in the social sciences in Europe. As part of this initiative, Gunnar and his wife, Alva Reimer Myrdal, both received Rockefeller fellowships to read in England and then travel throughout the United States touring departments in the social sciences during the 1929–1930 academic year.

After the First World War, the Laura Spelman Rockefeller Memorial had initiated this fellowship program with hopes of helping young European researchers gain exposure to the newly growing fields of the social sciences in the United States so that (with continued Rockefeller backing) they could strengthen the social sciences in their home countries. The idea behind the fellowship program was that European governments could avoid a second global war if social scientists aided them in containing social problems by crafting scientifically informed public policies.[91] Within this general initiative, and as discussed earlier in this book, the memorial (and then the Rockefeller Foundation which took over the memorial's social science program with the consolidation of the Rockefeller organizations in 1929) funded social science institutes and researchers across Europe.

After a yearlong sojourn in the United States and another year spent at the Graduate Institute for International Studies in Geneva, the Myrdals had returned to Stockholm in the early 1930s, where Gunnar became professor in political economics and financial science at Stockholm University.[92] He also became a member of the committee directing research at the Rockefeller-funded Institute for the Social Sciences, and Alva became director of the Institute for Social Pedagogy.[93]

During these years, the Myrdals became involved with the Social Democratic Party and advocated the importance of applying modern social research to public policy making. In this vein, Alva and Gunnar Myrdal wrote *Kris i befolkningsfrågan* (Crisis in the Population Question, 1934), for which Gunnar wrote the "demographic and economic aspects" and Alva the "treatment of social policy."[94] In *Kris*, the couple had engaged with the ongoing debate on fertility rates in Europe and argued that they had a policy answer to this problem in Sweden, a debate that had come to the fore in Sweden and neighboring European countries after the First World War.[95]

More specifically, several belligerent countries in Europe had become anxious that they would suffer steep population declines after the First World War since they had lost numerous young men during the war. They believed that these men's deaths would lead to a loss not only in the quantity, but also the quality of population and leave the nation at a disadvantage, with a smaller and weaker social corpus.[96] Some citizens perceived that this was disastrous for the nation's sense of identity, while others (who assumed that more workers meant a stronger economy) perceived the nation's compressed social body as a threat to the nation's economy.[97] Thus, in the 1920s, France, Germany, and Italy passed laws encouraging certain citizens to reproduce at higher rates.[98] To this point, and as part of these discussions on population quality and quantity in Europe following the First World War, the Third Reich in Germany notoriously urged white "Aryans" to reproduce at increasingly higher rates and discouraged the same behavior among citizens whom it viewed as biologically inferior, such as Jews. In order to limit the population numbers among the latter group of citizens, the Nazi government not only dissuaded procreation but committed mass murder against Jews and other perceived biologically inferior groups.[99]

Sweden had remained neutral during the First World War, though it too participated in these continental discussions of population quantity and quality in the 1920s and 1930s. Against such anxieties, the Myrdals proposed a policy program in *Kris* to encourage *all* modern Swedish couples to procreate. The publication of *Kris* brought Gunnar and Alva Myrdal considerable acclaim and influence. Some scholars have suggested that the "Social Democratic Party, as a political argument in favour of welfare policies, effectively used the public debate that was created in the wake of Myrdal's book."[100] That was indeed the case, when, in 1936, Gunnar Myrdal became a member of the Swedish Parliament and member of the Royal Population Commission, which was making his and Alva's policy recommendations in the 1934 book a reality. Alva meanwhile had become "chair of the Swedish Professional Women's Association . . . , secretary of the government commission on the right of married women to work outside the home, and an active member of the Social Democratic Women's Association."[101] At thirty-nine and thirty-five, respectively, Gunnar and Alva were creating solid professional lives for themselves in Stockholm. They also had three young children and a newly constructed home in the Stockholm suburbs. It was at that point that Carnegie Corporation of New York came along with an offer to tempt the Myrdals to move, at least temporarily, to New York City.

## 6. Keppel Communicates Expectations to Gunnar Myrdal

In his letter of invitation to Myrdal in August of 1937, Keppel described in greater detail the purpose of the study: "I have been discussing with some of the members of my Board of Trustees the desirability of financing a comprehensive study of the Negro in the United States to be undertaken in a wholly objective and dispassionate way as a social phenomenon."[102]

Summarizing for Myrdal his expectations for the project, Keppel injected words that he had not yet used routinely with his network of advisers across the Atlantic. Most prominently among these were "comprehensive study" and "social phenomenon." Though not particularly common in Keppel's correspondence with advisers in the United States, London, and throughout British Africa at the time, he used these terms in *The Arts in American Life* (1933), an extension of the chapter he completed for *Recent Social Trends* (1933).[103] There, Keppel and coauthor R. L. Duffus noted that they had analyzed the "arts as a social phenomenon in a given country over a limited period of time."[104] Given what they described in their chapter, Keppel and Duffus promised to provide readers an analysis of social changes in Americans' views, production, and consumption of art. By injecting this same vocabulary in his letter to Myrdal some four years later, Keppel likely hoped to communicate to Myrdal his expectation that the U.S. director would analyze national societal changes among Black Americans. As Newton Baker noted some years earlier, such changes included Black Americans' escalating migration from southern to northern United States and (at least from Baker's perspective) their increasing association with societal ills in northern urban communities.

As for Keppel's mention to Myrdal of a "comprehensive study"—this idea appeared in the foreword to *The Arts in American Life*, authored by the President's Committee on Research in Social Trends, which noted: "The usual practice of concentrating attention upon one social problem at a time often betrays us into overlooking . . . intricate relations. Even when we find what appears to be a satisfactory solution of a single problem, we are likely to produce new problems by putting that solution into practice. Hence the need of making a comprehensive survey of the many social changes which are proceeding simultaneously, with an eye to their reactions upon one another."[105] Such a portrayal of comprehensive surveys assumed the value of cohesive analysis bringing together various scholars' distinct analytic frames. With such an expansive vision for a comparable study of Black Americans, Keppel used language familiar to him to explain to Myrdal that he had in mind financing a comprehensive study, using interchangeably the terms "comprehensive" and "cooperative." However, unlike *Recent Social Trends* (and *The Poor White Problem in South Africa*)—and like Hailey's soon-to-be-published survey of Africa—Keppel explained that Myrdal would be singularly responsible for synthesizing this collective material and producing the final report.[106]

In the spirit of these cooperative surveys, Keppel intended for the study of Black Americans to solicit the assistance of teams of U.S. social scientists, to be organized through his source of inspiration for cooperative studies, the SSRC.

In his letter of invitation to Myrdal, Keppel noted that the SSRC would assist in staffing his team of researchers.[107] Indeed, the SSRC's cooperation in staffing and managing Myrdal's team of researchers would be key to Keppel, particularly since Keppel would be managing this U.S. study without the U.S. equivalent of his Chatham House advisers who had been overseeing the administrative details of Hailey's project.

That is to say that, compared with the African survey and even *The Poor White Problem in South Africa*, Keppel assumed much more direct responsibility for the U.S. survey. After personally leading the search for the director, he leased offices for Gunnar Myrdal at the Chrysler Building, located blocks from the foundation's offices in midtown Manhattan.[108] Years later, Myrdal would recount that Keppel "followed the study with intense interest. I know that it meant much to him."[109] Reflecting Keppel's personal investment in the study, and his fellow board members' trust in his vision, Myrdal's project would become one of the most expensive social scientific projects in U.S. history. Between 1938 and 1942, Carnegie Corporation's board allocated $280,000 to complete the project (which translates to a purchasing power of over $5 million today).[110]

In *An American Dilemma*, Gunnar Myrdal would reflect on the novelty of this research model, admitting that "the study has an unusual character as it was not initiated by an individual scholar or academic institution but sponsored by Carnegie Corporation itself and, in a sense, carried out within the Corporation. The general plan that a number of American experts should be asked to collaborate by preparing research monographs while the director himself should write a final report, was also developed by the Corporation."[111] Indeed, Keppel had imported into a U.S. context a rather novel research model for cooperative work in the social sciences: a model inspired and developed during his discussions with advisers at Chatham House in the 1930s.

Some months after receiving Carnegie Corporation's invitation to direct its national study of Black Americans, Myrdal met with the organization's board during a trip to the United States that he already had planned months earlier. That spring of 1938, Myrdal was delivering the Godkin lectures at Harvard University and several lectures to U.S. government agencies and their officials in Washington, D.C.[112] When Myrdal met with Carnegie Corporation's board, many Americans were celebrating him both as a leading economist and population planner in Sweden.

Compared to Keppel, who, a year earlier in private conversation with Ruml, had underscored Myrdal's work on "crime and disorders," Myrdal remembered that the board then was particularly interested to hear of his success in implementing a national policy initiative in Sweden. For the previous year, and against the backdrop of Myrdal's trip to the United States that spring, Keppel and his colleagues at Carnegie Corporation had come to better appreciate the scope of the Swedish scholar's national public policy experiences and how they fit well with, at least for Keppel, his own expectations that the U.S. director would take on a particularly national lens to help white governments across the northern and southern U.S. coordinate their policies on Black Americans.

Myrdal recounted: "What we discussed at that time, in which Freddie Keppel was tremendously interested in bringing forward, was what Alva and I had been doing, what I particularly had been doing, in problems of population and family in Sweden. That must have interested them."[113] As Myrdal recalled, the corporation's trustees found most relevant his and his wife's work confronting a societal problem at a national level in Sweden: the "population problem" of low fertility rates among Swedes in the 1930s. In fact, the organization was so moved by the couple's population work that, while Gunnar Myrdal directed the study on Black Americans, it commissioned Alva Myrdal to translate into English for a U.S. audience the couple's 1934 text, *Kris i befolkningsfrågan*. In 1941, Alva Myrdal published this adapted English-language translation as *Nation and Family: The Swedish Experiment in Democratic Family and Population Policy*.[114]

This next chapter explains the relative novelty in a U.S. context of Myrdal's study on Black Americans: a study whose research structure and public policy purpose had been shaped by a foundation president eager to finance a U.S. version of Malcolm Hailey's *African Survey*, published that year, in 1938, when Myrdal commenced work. As such, Carnegie Corporation's study of Black Americans would be a project whose funder intended for it to help white policymakers across governments in the North and South share information and, in the process, establish at a national level more sustainable ways of governing, and thus controlling the perceived threats posed by Black people.

## CHAPTER 7

# The Novelty of a "Hailey Type" Study in the United States

Within his first year as director of Carnegie Corporation's study on Black Americans, Gunnar Myrdal received advice from President Keppel to hold off on proposing policies until the conclusion of the 1940 U.S. national election, in which Franklin D. Roosevelt was running for an unprecedented third term to defeat Republican rival Wendell Willkie. Myrdal recorded that Keppel "stressed that the whole aspect of the social policy might have another outlook to me after I had seen the lining up of the different parties before the election and the election results, which would be a further reason for thinking over the matter."[1] Hoping that this study would produce recommendations that could help guide policymakers across the country to coordinate public policies on Black Americans, Keppel found it critical for Myrdal to wait and see the development of the national political horizon in the United States.

And yet as Keppel very well knew, white policymakers in the United States were actively hostile to the idea of coordinating public policies on Black Americans across governments in the United States. This contrasted with his network of white policymakers in the British Empire who had been eager to coordinate a survey of Africa as means for better coordinating policies across imperial powers in Africa. In the United States, and at least since the Civil War (1861–1865), ongoing national debates had centered on the ability of the federal government to dictate state-level policies on Black Americans, and hostility to coordination of policies at the national level was widespread especially among many white policymakers.

Reflecting this long-standing resistance to the national coordination of public policies on Black Americans, no U.S. policymaker had requested Carnegie Corporation to finance this national study. And demonstrating his own acknowledgment of the project's potentially contentious reception, Keppel made little effort to enlist a host institution in the United States to become the public face of this third cooperative study intended to guide white policymakers in better governing, controlling, and, relatedly, dominating Black people.

As this chapter argues, Keppel's study of Black Americans was quite novel in a U.S. context at the time, and not simply—as the prior chapter highlighted—because of its vertical research structure. The project was furthermore unconventional in the United States because U.S. policymakers (even when soliciting research on Black Americans) resisted any national policy response to Black Americans and, furthermore, because general funding for research on Black Americans had plummeted during the prior decade. Keppel was thus funding a project that, in 1930s and 1940s United States, was novel in research structure and policy goals, and he was financing it at a time when the country's ecosystem of funding for social scientific research on Black Americans was struggling.

Throughout the span of the project, Keppel would remain both vigilant and anxious about the suitability of his relatively expensive experiment to propel a national synchronization of public policies on Black Americans in the United States as means for both thwarting perceived threats posed by this group of colonized people in the Anglo-American world and, relatedly, for further fortifying white Anglo-American domination. Upon the completion of the project in 1942, for example, Keppel would tell Myrdal that: "I had risked my own reputation so definitely [with the U.S. study], that it has never been far from the front of my thoughts."[2]

By financing and planning such a novel and ambitious study in the United States, Keppel risked his own and his organization's reputation to a point that easily could have ended his career at Carnegie Corporation. His colleague Charles Dollard later recounted, the "Negro problem was a very unpopular problem in 1939."[3] Consequently, the project "never would have gone forward without Keppel, because, at any point, the trustees would have been glad to back out. They were scared stiff of it—a Swede investigating the color problem in America. It seemed to them an invitation to a nightmare."[4]

Perhaps because Keppel knew that this would be his final significant project as head of Carnegie Corporation, from which he retired in 1941, he was willing to wager big on a topic that had captivated him since his tenure as third assistant secretary of war during the First World War: the perceived threat posed by Black people on either side of the Atlantic to his and peers' vision of international peace and the role the social sciences could play in solidifying this white world order. And perhaps too because he had enjoyed few opportunities as president to make a relatively significant mark on the organization's grant-making practices in the United States, Keppel readily (though clearly, as he acknowledged to Myrdal, with some anxiety) embraced the opportunity to help white policymakers across governments in the United States achieve what he and his Chatham house advisers imagined that Hailey's *African Survey* (1938)—published the same year that Myrdal commenced work on its U.S. analogue—was set to achieve among imperial governments in Africa.[5]

Before delving further into the U.S. project, this chapter underscores the relative newness of Carnegie Corporation's study of Black Americans within the United States during the 1930s. It begins with an overview of U.S. approaches to the funding of the social sciences on Black Americans and public policymaking on Black Americans during the 1920s and 1930s.

## 1. Rockefeller Funding and the Social Sciences on Black Americans

In 1929, the Rockefeller Foundation's board dissolved the Laura Spelman Rockefeller Memorial (LSRM) and appointed former Harvard economist and dean of business administration at the University of Michigan Edmund E. Day to direct the social sciences program which the foundation inherited from the LSRM. At the same time, former LSRM director Beardsley Ruml was appointed director of the newly formed Spelman Fund and assigned the task of overseeing the funding of any final LSRM projects that the Rockefeller Foundation was not planning to absorb.

Among the many consequences of the Rockefeller organizations' consolidation between 1929 and 1930, social scientific research on Black Americans, or rather, on "race relations," dramatically decreased to a halt at the Social Science Research Council. For this network of white foundation officials and social scientists at the time, the study of "race relations" was synonymous with the study of Black Americans. Above all, these white men tended to equate Black Americans—rather than white Americans' continued insistence on white supremacy and Black subjection—as the central *problem* and *abnormality* causing strains between white and Black people. For them, the study of "race relations" and the study of societal ills they associated with Black Americans tended to be one and the same.[6]

During the consolidation of the Rockefeller organizations in 1930, and again conflating the study of "race relations" and Black Americans, the Rockefeller Foundation's managers squarely questioned whether they wanted "to include the negro in the social science program."[7] Just before then, LSRM's outgoing director Beardsley Ruml had reviewed the organization's field on Black Americans.

In his 1929 memorandum, Ruml reflected on the LSRM under his leadership, writing that the organization had funded social scientific studies of Black Americans along with organizations "working on a national basis for the improvement of the relations between white and colored races."[8] It also had financed Black universities such as Fisk, Howard, and Atlanta Universities "that would be strongly equipped in the social sciences and able to develop professional training in law, business, social work and public administration."[9] From Ruml's point of view, this multi-faceted approach of funding white and Black scholars' social scientific studies of Black Americans and "race relations" was playing its part to help white and Black Americans reach a more harmonious state of cohabitation in the United States.

While vocal in its embrace of the social sciences, the LSRM was building upon some precedent in the United States since the late nineteenth century of white philanthropic support for social scientific research on race. W. E. B. Du Bois's *Philadelphia Negro* (1899) was, for example, an early example of a white philanthropist supporting social scientific research on Black Americans in the United States.[10] This study had been financed by Susan Wharton, a Quaker philanthropist whose family was a principal benefactor at the University of Pennsylvania. Wharton requested in the 1890s an investigation of Black Philadelphians' living conditions.[11]

At the time, other Black scholars also published studies on Black Americans, particularly through the American Negro Academy. Founded by leading Black scholars and writers such as William H. Ferris, Paul Laurence Dunbar, W. E. B. Du Bois, W. S. Scarborough, and Kelly Miller, in order to promote literature, science and art, education, and culture among Black Americans, the Academy produced journal-length papers "on subjects related to the culture, history, religion, social rights, and social institutions of African-American people."[12] The American Negro Academy came to a close in 1924, however, just a year before the LSRM became interested in funding the social sciences in the United States

In 1925, the LSRM under Ruml's guidance had taken it upon itself to examine "the means of studying the Negro problem in its various phases." Early on in his position as director, Ruml had noted to the memorial's trustees that this so-called societal problem was discussed sometimes as "the Negro Problem, the Race Question, the Tide of Color, and so forth."[13] Stressing that it was best to move away from these general discussions, Ruml advocated focusing on the "problem of finding out whether and by what means bi-racial (or possibly polyracial) groups may live together harmoniously in a single unit."[14] Assuming many Americans acknowledged that Black Americans should be, whether immediately or sometime in the future, equal citizens of the United States, Ruml concluded that these studies should focus on finding out how white and Black Americans could coexist more peaceably and, one day, become equal citizens.[15]

In 1925, the memorial funded investigations into the status of the social sciences on Black Americans and these fields of study at Black universities.[16]

Relying on these studies, the memorial decided to assist in the development of research in psychology, anthropology, history, sociology, and economics and business law at Fisk University, a leading Black university in the United States where the memorial also partially funded the Department of Statistics and Records. Beyond university departments, the memorial also established "fellowships for professional training in the social sciences, in business, and in jurisprudence" among Black Americans.[17]

The memorial also funded specific studies of Black Americans carried out at several universities. At the University of Chicago, for example, support went to a "plan for community research studies . . . dealing with the negro in industry and negro employment."[18] At the University of North Carolina, the memorial funded "studies of music and of negro social background," as well as studies "in the development of negro business institutions, in the negro agricultural credit system, and in credit facilities for negro business" under the leadership of the white sociologist Howard Odum.[19]

Beyond university departments, the LSRM helped finance Black historian Carter G. Woodson's Association for the Study of Negro Life and History and both "for continuation of social and historical studies carried out under the direction of Dr. Woodson" and "studies along civic, social and industrial lines" conducted by Charles Johnson at the National Urban League in New York City.[20] For all these efforts, though, the LSRM stopped short of funding a national study with aspirations of coordinating public policies on Black Americans across the country.

Absorbing the memorial's funding practices in the social sciences after 1929, the Rockefeller Foundation then chose to divorce its support of the social sciences from its grantmaking practices on Black Americans. As Rockefeller Foundation officials reasoned, their sister organization, the General Education Board (GEB), should represent the Rockefellers' funding focus on Black people. Since its founding, the GEB had been a leader among its white philanthropic peers interested in maintaining a grants focus on Black Americans, and particularly by promoting the Tuskegee educational model of education for Black Americans.[21]

Appropriating the LSRM's grantmaking practices in the social sciences yet severing its focus on Black Americans, the Rockefeller Foundation subsequently decreased its funding of this field of investigation. As a grantee whose principal funder remained the Rockefeller organizations well into the 1940s—with the Rockefeller organizations providing "more than ninety percent" of its financing—the Social Science Research Council (SSRC) followed suit and decreased its own focus on Black Americans and "race relations."[22]

It was against this backdrop of decreasing research emphasis on Black Americans at the SSRC after 1929 that Keppel approached the organization with the idea for a cooperative study on Black Americans, requiring teams of social scientists.

## 2. The Social Science Research Council before and after the Rockefeller Organizations' Consolidation in 1929

As long as the Laura Spelman Rockefeller Memorial had existed, and particularly under Beardsley Ruml's leadership, the SSRC had an expressed interest in studying Black Americans. For example, the same year that Ruml established a program on the "Negro problem" at the memorial, the SSRC founded an "Advisory Committee on Problems Related to the Negro." Echoing Ruml's own emphasis that the "Negro problem" was really a "problem of finding out whether and by what means bi-racial (or possibly polyracial) groups may live together harmoniously in a single unit" to be addressed by white and Black American scholars alike, the SSRC renamed the committee a year later as the "Advisory Committee on Interracial Relations" and solicited the participation of both white and Black U.S. social scientists.[23]

The SSRC furthermore made its echo to the memorial's research priorities quite explicit by mentioning in a committee memo that the purpose of the group was to analyze "the social welfare of the negro in his relationship with the whites," or rather, "the negro-white relationship from the social point of view."[24] Even more specifically than Ruml's own program at the memorial, though, the council focused "on the status of research on problems of the Negro, to consider what types of studies should be made and how such studies might be correlated."[25] From 1925 to 1930, and with the support of the memorial, the council funded several social scientific studies on Black Americans by white and Black scholars alike with the general goal of increasing this body of scientific literature in the United States.

During these years, the SSRC's "Advisory Committee on Interracial Relations" also formed two subcommittees: one on tests for racial differences and another on governmental and political aspects of "interracial relations." These committees included, among others, scholars such as white anthropologist Melville Herskovits and Black zoologist Ernest Just.[26] From 1925 to 1930, this SSRC committee and its two subcommittees funded studies on Black Americans and appointed colleagues in the social sciences to direct them. Among the directors were Black social scientists such as Charles S. Johnson, Guion Johnson, E. Franklin Frazier, Carter G. Woodson, and Charles S. Johnson and white social scientists such as Franz Boas, Robert S. Woodworth, and Howard W. Odum.[27] These men oversaw studies and surveys titled *Problems of the Colored Race in the United States*; *Negro Culture on St. Helena Island*; *The Negro Family*; *Discovery and Collection of Historical Materials among Negroes*; *Racial and Social Differences in Mental Ability of Rural Negroes*; *Interracial Attitudes*; *Racial Differences, with Division of Anthropology and Psychology of the National Research Council*; and, the *Influence of Heredity and Environment*.[28] These eight surveys resulted in nine book manuscripts and four articles.[29]

However, just as the Rockefeller Foundation acquired the memorial's funding interest in the social sciences after 1929, the SSRC discontinued this "Advisory Committee on Interracial Relations" and its two subcommittees. As mentioned earlier, the Rockefeller Foundation, unlike the LSRM, found little interest in funding social scientific research on Black Americans.[30] Even more, this moment of reorganization within the Rockefeller group coincided with the SSRC Advisory Committee's decision to discontinue its collaboration with the National Research Council's "Negro Committee," a joint effort that the Columbia University anthropologist and National Research Council (NRC) member Franz Boas had perceived could be fruitful for both organizations two years earlier.[31] By 1930, the SSRC's Advisory Committee was "anxious to quit" and to separate from the NRC.[32] With the dissolution of this joint committee and with decreased interest from its principal funder in social scientific studies of Black Americans and "race relations," the SSRC in the 1930s steered its attention toward research studies of the Great Depression.[33] During that time, the Rockefeller Foundation continued to fund the SSRC, but the grantmaking programs of the foundation (like the SSRC's own research interests) in the social sciences had no specific focus on Black Americans or "race relations."

That said, the Rockefeller Foundation indirectly continued to finance some research on Black Americans and "race relations" in the United States by supporting departments of anthropology, sociology, history, economics, and psychology at the University of Chicago, Columbia University, the University of North Carolina, and other centers of research throughout the country. During these years, the foundation also pooled some resources, though significantly less than the memorial had, to support Carter Woodson's Association for the Study of Negro Life and History.[34]

In addition, some studies in the social sciences funded by the Rockefeller Foundation included sections on Black Americans. For example, one of the ten monographs included in *Recent Social Trends* (1933), which the SSRC coordinated and the Rockefeller Foundation funded, focused on an analysis of "races and ethnic groups in American life," authored by T. J. Woofter.[35] And Donald Young's *Research Memorandum on Minority Peoples in the Depression* (1937), which included an analysis of Black Americans alongside other minority groups in the United States, was one of thirteen studies funded by the SSRC's Committee on Studies in Social Aspects of the Depression to "stimulate the study of depression effects on various social institutions" in the 1930s.[36]

Beyond these passing opportunities for Rockefeller funding, there was little elite philanthropic support for researchers writing on Black Americans and "race relations" in the United States during the 1930s, before Keppel came along with the idea for a national study of Black Americans, to be coordinated by the SSRC and to incorporate teams of U.S. social scientists. Though during these years, just before Carnegie Corporation's project, there indeed had been one moment of fleeting hope that greater funding would flow into the social scientific study of Black Americans.

Specifically, in the mid-1930s, the Phelps Stokes Fund became interested in planning an "Encyclopedia of the Negro," which it expected would pull in support from these networks of U.S. scholars and elite philanthropies. However, neither the Carnegie nor Rockefeller groups ever came to its financial aid and the project subsequently stalled in the 1930s. Nevertheless, its genesis story also can help shed further light on the relative novelty of the research structure and public policy purpose of Carnegie Corporation's study of Black Americans, which was started just when the encyclopedia project came to an end.

## 3. Before Keppel's London Import, There Was W. E. B. Du Bois's Encyclopedia

Serving on the advisory board of the "Encyclopedia of the Negro," Donald Young and Melville Herskovits—who would become close advisers to Keppel on Carnegie Corporation's study of Black Americans—had been friendly colleagues since the early 1930s.[37] And in correspondence with each other later that decade, they discussed the tensions surrounding the encyclopedia project. Among such early participants of the project, an early and major point of contention was the fact that the Phelps Stokes Fund had not initially invited leading Black scholars W. E. B. Du Bois or Carter Woodson to join the project.[38] Du Bois ultimately would collaborate, while Woodson would become a leading critic of the project.

In an "Open Letter to the Afro-American on the Negro Encyclopedia," circulated in June 1936 among leading foundations and researchers involved in planning the encyclopedia, Woodson first admonished the central role played by Thomas Jesse Jones in shaping the editorial leadership and purpose of the project.[39] With Woodson underscoring that, over time, "it became more evident than ever that what they want is not an encyclopedia of the Negro but such portrayal of him as will suit [Anson Phelps] Stokes and [Thomas Jesse] Jones."[40] Woodson also criticized Du Bois for collaborating with Jones and the Phelps Stokes Fund, whom he and Du Bois long had criticized for their hurtful role in shaping Black education: "For disservice to the race by espionage, undermining, and hamstringing Du Bois himself referred to him a few years ago as 'that evil genius of the Negro race, Thomas Jesse Jones, a white man.' Now for the hope of a few dollars Du Bois dons a new uniform and supports their proposition. Poverty makes strange bed-fellows."[41]

In the 1930s, Du Bois indeed found himself willing to work alongside an organization he long had admonished, in order to bring about the encyclopedia project. Again, this was the same philanthropic organization for whom Thomas Jesse Jones still served as leading education adviser and that had financed Jones's *Negro Education* (1917), which Du Bois had criticized in the pages of *The Crisis*. But again, Du Bois was particularly committed to seeing through to publication an encyclopedia project on the African diaspora. From his end, Anson Phelps Stokes had reasoned with the GEB's Jackson Davis that Du Bois—whose role as editor-in-chief was unanimously supported by all Black colleagues planning the encyclopedia—would need to colead the project with "a white man of high standing and conservative reputation," leading them to pick the white sociologist Robert E. Park, who had served "for many years at Tuskegee helping Booker Washington."[42] And as far as Du Bois himself, Anson Phelps Stokes explained to Davis: "Ten years ago, or even five years ago, it would not have been possible to consider Dr. Du Bois for this position in spite of the fact that he is recognized as the outstanding Negro scholar. He had become such an aggressive protagonist that his name created a lack of sympathy in various conservative circles. This is, of course, all partially still true but all who have met him in the last year have been amazed at how much he has mellowed."[43]

Given the Phelps Stokes Fund's grantmaking practices in Black education, Du Bois probably knew that the organization's reasons for financing an encyclopedia on Black people were distinct from his or Woodson's likely reasons for dreaming of a pan-African encyclopedia. Because to know the Phelps Stokes Fund at the time meant knowing that the organization was particularly invested in analyzing and quantifying the benefits of the Tuskegee educational model for Black people, which the fund promoted and financed on both sides of the Atlantic. From this perspective, and as Woodson suggested, the Phelps Stokes Fund likely found interest in financing its "Encyclopedia of the Negro" as means of surveying Black achievement ever since the Tuskegee educational model had gained dominance among its networks of advisers and peers in philanthropy, government, and education. So rather than a pan-African encyclopedia likely hoped by Du Bois, considering his longstanding efforts to further fortify Black unity across the Atlantic—to be led by a team of Black scholars and intended both to cultivate pan-African pride and counter prejudicial assumptions about Black people's accomplishments and capabilities—this version of the encyclopedia on Black people shaped by the Phelps Stokes Fund would incorporate white scholars and maintain white peers as its main audience, with the project's focus on Black excellence furthermore serving as proof that the fund's own investment in Black people's education was meeting with success. Even as these white Anglo-American men in philanthropy intended to keep white supremacy intact when they funded the Tuskegee educational model for Black people, they also wanted to believe that their funding practices were leading Black Americans to prove in the long run their inherent equality with white Americans. In this version of the pan-African encyclopedia, Du Bois would thus work alongside a white coeditor, in dialogue with an advisory board of white and Black Americans and a team of Black and white contributors.

Without the necessary resources to execute a project of this scale, and eager to solicit the collaboration of its main intended audience of white philanthropic peers, the Phelps Stokes Fund sought the support of the Rockefeller organizations and Carnegie Corporation. This was ultimately a frustrating and fruitless process consuming the attention of Du Bois and the Phelps Stokes Fund during the greater part of the 1930s and overlapping with Carnegie Corporation's decision to finance its own national study of Black Americans.

During these years, board members at the GEB, the Rockefeller Foundation, and Carnegie Corporation would continue receiving news from staff members and colleagues that the Phelps Stokes Fund's project was bound to fail. Not only had the SSRC declined the invitation to appoint two representatives on the advisory board of the encyclopedia, but the representatives whom these philanthropic managers sent to the group's meetings continued to return with negative impressions of the project's development.[44] From what these philanthropic managers could gather, the team of Black and white scholars under the directorship of Du Bois and Park (later to be replaced by white sociologist Guy B. Johnson) was fraught with tensions and antagonism.[45]

Reflecting these long-standing interpersonal strains among the planners of the encyclopedia, and even before Woodson's press release, Donald Young

had complained to Melville Herskovits that he saw "no hope that the Encyclopedia can be turned into the sort of work in which you and I would be interested," and told him that he would not be attending the next meeting.[46] "If
I had any hope that you and I by our attendance at the meeting could exert 'a
restraining influence,' as you put it, I'd be there with bells on, but I do not
believe that a dozen of us could do more than make nuisances of ourselves
without swerving the leaders of the project a fraction of an inch from the
course they have planned. These are hard words, but I suspect that you rather
agree with me."[47] In response, Herskovits echoed Young's dissatisfaction, sharing that he too would miss the next meeting: "I think you're right at that, and
so I too am sending regrets. As a matter of fact I was thinking of the jaunt in
terms of that peculiar type of recreation obtained from fighting a lost cause."[48]

That is to say that Herskovits and Young would walk away from the "Encyclopedia of the Negro," even before Woodson's press release further aggravated
elite foundations' negative perceptions of the project. Far from alone, Young
and Herskovits would be joined by the Rockefeller and Carnegie organizations, which two years later formally declined the Phelps Stokes Fund's
request for support.

In November of 1938, soon after Carnegie Corporation's board had decided
against cosponsoring the Phelps Stokes Fund's encyclopedia project, Keppel
wrote to Anson Phelps Stokes to share the disappointing news. Keppel as-
sured Stokes "that the trouble in my Board did not rise from memories of Du
Bois as a firebrand, but from a general feeling that the idea of a specialized Negro
Encyclopedia at all was a mistake."[49] While the Phelps Stokes Fund saw value
in the encyclopedia project, its philanthropic peers at Carnegie Corporation
saw the study as a "mistake," because funding a study that could have the
effect—even indirectly—of increasing racial pride among Black people and
thus contributing to escalating Black consciousness was leaning into one of
Keppel's and his white Anglo-American advisers' most basic fears since the
1920s. Instead, Carnegie Corporation funding would go toward the corporation's own national study of Black Americans, which, in contrast to the "Encyclopedia of the Negro," was to consider Black people as a societal problem and
to offer white policymakers across governments in the United States with an
opportunity to understand the problem and its solutions at the national level.

In suggesting such a project, and as already stressed, Keppel was importing into the United States key elements of Malcolm Hailey's *African Survey*
(1938); as this next section illustrates, he also was building upon three inter-
twined intellectual trends in 1920s and 1930s New York City and Washington,
D.C. This included a tendency to view societal problems from a national per-

spective and to enlist a cooperative social science study in order to analyze these nationwide problems, most represented by *Recent Social Trends* (1933). It also reflected an increasing inclination among Americans at the time to try to find national public policy solutions to perceived societal problems. To this final point, U.S. president Franklin D. Roosevelt was strengthening the role of the U.S. federal government with his various social policy programs under the New Deal.

However, Keppel's colleagues in New York City philanthropic circles and D.C. policy networks tended to distinguish their analyses of Black Americans from these general national trends in policymaking. While they—like Carnegie Corporation—increasingly viewed Black Americans as a national rather than regional problem and included analyses of Black Americans in their cooperative study of national problems, they resisted suggesting any synchronization of public policies on "race relations" or Black Americans across local and regional governments. Instead, they preferred to leave public policy answers to the supposed problem of Black Americans and "race relations" at the city and state levels.

This contradictory stance of leaving public policy reforms regarding Black Americans to the local and state levels, while addressing many societal problems at the national level, is the subject of the next section.

## 4. U.S. Calls for National Policymaking on Black Americans

Since the U.S. Civil War (1861–1865) and particularly during U.S. participation in the First World War (1917–1918), historian Barry Karl notes that Americans had nurtured a growing sense of national unity and had taken part in a global trend to further centralize power in their national government.[50] And yet, even as the First World War and particularly the Great Depression led many of these Americans to acknowledge a national community and the need for national solutions to various social problems across the country, they also resisted further centralization in the federal government. As Karl and fellow historian Stanley N. Katz write, the "slow consciousness within the New Deal that federal responsibility would ultimately have to be the answer [to social reform] is a mark of the reluctance to admit the ending of an era" when nineteenth-century Americans long had "controlled social organization and social behaviour in states and local communities."[51] In other words, Americans in the first half of the twentieth century reluctantly and with some trepidation marched toward a greater national consciousness and greater reliance on the federal government to address "social problems."

In addressing such "social problems," historian Harvard Sitkoff explains that Franklin D. Roosevelt's administration during the New Deal—more than any other previous administration—became vocal about anti-Black discrimination in the United States and the need for a national approach to Black Americans' status.[52] And yet, it would be members of his administration—not Roosevelt himself—who increasingly would voice the need to address anti-Black discrimination at the national level, and they would do so mainly during Roosevelt's second term. Generally, though, and throughout his tenure as U.S. president, Roosevelt resisted calling for national legislative changes on anti-Black discrimination.

Justifying his decision, Roosevelt explained to Walter White, the executive secretary of the National Association for the Advancement of Colored People (NAACP), that white southerners in the U.S. Congress would have overpowered any effort he would have made to pass laws on Black Americans, writing that "I've got to get legislation passed by Congress to save America. The Southerners by reason of the seniority rule in Congress are chairmen or occupy strategic places on most of the Senate and House committees. If I come out for the antilynching bill now, they will block every bill I ask Congress to pass to keep America from collapsing. I just can't take that risk."[53] Historian David M. Kennedy notes that white southerners in Congress viewed any such attempt by the U.S. federal government to create public policies on Black Americans as reminiscent of a post-Civil War Reconstruction Era when the national government had interfered with the South's public policies on race.[54]

The Roosevelt administration confronted a U.S. Congress that was led by southern Democrats, who saw any attempt by the federal government to interfere in issues pertaining to Black Americans as reminiscent of the Reconstruction Era.[55] To this point, such white politicians resisted what was patently the least controversial policy critical of white supremacy and Black subjection in the United States: anti-lynching legislation. The proposed anti-lynching law simply had suggested that local officials would confront federal penalties if they failed to prevent the murder of Black residents, and that the federal government then also should step in if local authorities failed to prosecute the perpetrators.[56] The number of lynchings of Black Americans in the United States had decreased throughout the 1920s (from seventy-six in 1919, to seven in 1929). However, there continued to be gruesome torture and killings of Black Americans at the hands of white Americans during the 1930s.[57] Even if passed, the federal law would hardly have challenged white rule in the South. However, just by acknowledging and criticizing white supremacy, the proposed legislation became toxic in Washington, D.C. Its advocates confronted a wildly resistant Congress and failed to secure Roosevelt's endorsement.

But it was not just that "President Roosevelt found himself tightly constrained by the southern wing of his party," as Leah Wright Rigueur notes, but that the "programs and agencies of the New Deal were rife with discrimination; in this sense, the Republican and Democratic parties of this era did not display clear-cut differences in their civil rights policies."[58] Instead of President Roosevelt or the Democratic-led Congress, it was Eleanor Roosevelt and some sympathizers in his administration who increasingly expressed a need for a national approach to public policies on Black Americans, particularly after the election of 1936, when Americans voted Roosevelt back for a second term.

As far as the U.S. federal government's increasingly vocalized concern for Black Americans in Roosevelt's second term, scholars offer various reasons. Wright Rigueur notes that the 1936 election marked Black voters' turn from the Republican to the Democratic Party. Wright Rigueur writes: "On November 3, 1936, 71 percent of black voters cast their ballots for the Democratic incumbent Franklin Delano Roosevelt. That choice would mark the beginning of a radical realignment in American politics, a change so deep and lasting that in the present era, most find it hard to believe that a majority of the black electorate ever voted for Republican presidents."[59]

It was in this context that Eleanor Roosevelt "moved rapidly from a public position in favor of equal opportunity to one of endorsing specific civil rights measures. Boldly, she joined the campaign to abolish the poll tax and spoke in favor of a federal anti-lynching law. The more vehemently southern Democrats objected to her interference in racial issues, the more wholeheartedly she committed herself to the cause."[60] Moreover, as Harvard Sitkoff points out, Eleanor Roosevelt's public statements in favor of greater concern for racial inequality inspired others in the New Deal administration to "work for racial equality and justice."[61]

As part of this effort, Franklin D. Roosevelt's administration appointed the first Black federal judge and the first Black U.S. assistant attorney general, William Hastie and William Houston, respectively.[62] And even before the 1936 election, by mid-1935, approximately forty-five Black Americans had positions in cabinet departments and New Deal agencies.[63] Anointing themselves the "Federal Council on Negro Affairs," though more commonly called the "Black Cabinet or Black Brain Trust" by the press, these cabinet members would meet routinely in the D.C. home of the director of the Division of Negro Affairs of the National Youth Administration, Mary McLeod Bethune, to discuss the impact of relief efforts on Black Americans and so too the racial practices of the administration.[64]

After 1936, various individuals in the administration publicly expressed heightened concern for Black Americans' equal treatment across the country. In this vein, for example, Bethune's Division of Negro Affairs of the National Youth Administration sponsored a three-day "National Conference on Problems of the Negro and Negro Youth" in January of 1937; the attendants included Black Americans in the federal government, such as Bethune and representatives of the Departments of Agriculture, Commerce, Interior, and Labor, the Farm Credit Administration, the Public Works Administration, the Works Progress Administration, and the Civilian Conservation Corps. Among white Americans in attendance were First Lady Eleanor Roosevelt, the secretary of commerce, the director of emergency conservation work, the commissioner of education, an assistant secretary of the U.S. Treasury, and the secretary of agriculture.[65] This conference, sponsored by the U.S. federal government, concluded by requesting that the federal government, "as guardian and protector of all the people, take the lead and set the example by abolishing racial segregation in all of its departments, divisions, and branches; and that it refrain from lending its aid and support to the extension of segregation in the United States, the several States and Territories."[66] Quite explicitly, the conference participants embraced racial desegregation as a national imperative.

Thus, Carnegie Corporation shared different anxieties about Black people than those harbored by this network of Americans in Roosevelt's administration at the time, and thus different reasons for calling for a national approach to public policymaking on Black Americans. For example, Eleanor Roosevelt, Mary McLeod Bethune, and fellow travelers in the federal administration seemed to take a more domestic lens on white Americans' discriminatory treatment of Black Americans and particularly one focused on elevating the status of Black Americans to equal standing with white Americans. That motivation for a national policy on Black Americans was inspired presumably by far more egalitarian civil rights sentiments than those shared by Carnegie Corporation's leadership at the time. From their end, Carnegie Corporation's trustees were particularly concerned about the dissipating relevance of the Tuskegee educational model in the southern United States as the answer for addressing threats they perceived that Black Americans posed to national and international order. The organization thus financed a study intended to help white policymakers in the United States to better govern and better control Black Americans as a national problem, in ways that they reasoned the Tuskegee educational model was outdated.

For their different rationales, Carnegie Corporation and key figures in the U.S. federal government in the 1930s became convinced that Black Americans' status required a nationally coordinated public policy response. And yet, though arguably equally invested in shaping a national policy program on Black Americans, it would be Carnegie Corporation rather than the U.S. federal government that would take the public risk of financing a cooperative study to help guide such national coordination. Indeed, it was a risk for Keppel, because as much as 1930s Washington D.C. expressed peppered interest in crafting a national approach to public policymaking on Black Americans, U.S. public policymakers long had been accustomed to retaining a local or state— rather than a national—perspective on potential policy solutions to the supposed problem of Black Americans' very existence in the United States.

As this next section illustrates, and even as U.S. policymakers started to commission cooperative studies in the social sciences intended to shape public policymaking on Black Americans and "race relations," they would tend to focus their analyses on the city-level and continue looking to local or state, rather than national, governments for public policy solutions to societal problems they associated with Black Americans and "race relations."

## 5. Policymaking and the Social Sciences on Black Americans in the United States

In the decades preceding Carnegie Corporation president Keppel's decision to fund a U.S. version of the African survey, U.S. public policymakers had commissioned and financed studies of Black Americans and "race relations," though, if not at the national level, at the city-levels, and largely in response to fatal violence between groups of white and Black Americans on public streets, with particular urgency for coordinating a follow-up study when the violence was directed by Black Americans toward white Americans.

While still focusing at the city level, the one major exception of a government-funded study on Black Americans that did not grow directly out of public violence between white and Black Americans was *Black Metropolis: A Study of Negro Life in a Northern City* (1945), by Black sociologists St. Clair Drake and Horace R. Cayton.[67] Considered by fellow sociologist Robert Washington in 1997 to be one of the "the best sociological stud[ies] of any black community yet produced," the project began in 1936 as a series of investigations into juvenile delinquency in Chicago's South Side, financed by the Works Progress Administration.[68] And though the WPA's reasons for supporting this fieldwork remain unclear, it does suggest that these policymakers associated Black Americans with societal ills and that they were inspired—even if not directly by violent protest—by the fear of violent protest in the future.[69]

Between 1900 and 1949, sociologist Allen Grimshaw estimates that thirty-three "major disturbances" took place in the United States.[70] Reflecting on these "first decades of the new century," historian William M. Tuttle Jr. notes that the "North as well as the South saw a burgeoning of racial violence," and the fact that this was occurring in northern cities was especially disturbing to white policymakers.[71]

Sharing the anxieties of Carnegie Corporation trustee Newton Baker about the increased migration of Black Americans from southern states to northern urban areas in the early decades of the twentieth century, white policymakers in the early twentieth century appointed groups of elected officials and social scientists to analyze the causes of violence between white and Black people in northern communities.

Commissioned by public policymakers at varying levels of government in the United States, the three studies coordinated in response to massacres, terror, and rebellions in 1917 East St. Louis, 1919 Chicago, and 1935 Harlem not only would continue to focus on Black Americans as the locus of blame for peaked violence among white and Black Americans, but the three studies also would restrict any scope of public policy prescriptions to the local or state level.

To note, many Americans long have described these moments of public protest and violence between white and Black Americans as "riots" and, in the process, have associated Black Americans rather than white Americans as instigators of the violence.[72] That is, by calling these moments "riots" rather than "rebellions" or "revolts," Americans long have suggested that Black Americans have been unruly mobs unprovoked and unjustified in their actions, rather than acting in self-defense or in violent protest based on decades of built-up righteous resentment and anger towards white Americans' anti-Black discrimination, terrorization, and deadly violence.[73] Equally so, the use of the word "riot" also has served to deflect the central role of white Americans in executing state-sanctioned massacres of Black people, such as in the "East St. Louis riots of 1917."[74]

In describing the studies of Black Americans and "race relations" that policymakers commissioned in the first decades of the twentieth century, the following section both acknowledges historical actors' use of the word "riot" and tries to bring some greater clarity to these events by describing the "East St. Louis riots of 1917" as a massacre and the "Chicago riots of 1919" and "Harlem riots of 1935" as rebellions following white Americans' long-standing and heightened terrorization of Black Americans. By using the word "rebellion" rather than "riot," it becomes that much clearer how Black Americans had been "subject to oppression at the hands of the predominantly White power structure, and therefore held legitimate grievances against the system."[75]

## Studying the "East St. Louis Riots of 1917"

In 1917, the NAACP sent two staff members, Black scholar W. E. B. Du Bois and white investigator Martha Gruening, to examine the "recent outrages" in East St. Louis, Illinois, which the authors ultimately described as "the massacre of East St. Louis."[76] Gruening and Du Bois began their twenty-page report by noting that, on July 2 of that year "a mob of white men, women and children burned and destroyed at least $400,000 worth of property belonging to both whites and Negroes; drove 6,000 Negroes out of their homes; and deliberately [m]urdered, by shooting, burning and hanging, between one and two hundred human beings who were black."[77] Trying to make sense of white residents' heightened terrorization and violence toward fellow Black residents of East St. Louis, the authors pointed to the "jealousy of white labor unions and prejudice" after Black southerners who had moved to the city for industrial work then served as strikebreakers the previous summer.[78] As Gruening and Du Bois recounted, the white labor unions in East St. Louis played a critical role in fueling white residents' flames of prejudice and hatred toward Black Americans.

Complementing Du Bois and Gruening's account, sociologist Elliott Rudwick began his narrative of the 1917 massacre in East St. Louis with the broader context of Black Americans' increased migration from southern states to northern cities since 1915. He reasoned that the racial norms of white supremacy and Black subjection in East St. Louis were disrupted by the presence of greater numbers of newer Black residents and so too by older Black residents' increased embrace of "racial equality doctrine."[79] For months prior to July 1917, white residents violently resisted Black Americans' presence in the city, and at least since May of that year, white mobs had attacked and demolished businesses that Black residents patronized, beat and threatened with lynching Black residents, and set fire to Black homes.[80] White people's violence and terrorization of Black residents in East St. Louis only intensified over that summer of 1917, when Gruening and Du Bois traveled to the city on behalf of the NAACP.

Early in July that year, a group of white men had driven into a Black district of the city and opened fire from both sides of the car. In response, some Black residents ran for their guns, fired back at the white men, and some of the armed men followed the car on foot. In the process, the Black men killed two white policemen. For weeks before and weeks after, as historian Malcolm McLaughlin notes, white residents had "beaten and harassed African Americans on the streets" and yet the police had refused to intervene.[81]

In the wake of white people's terrorization of Black residents in East St. Louis, white and Black citizens across the country looked to the U.S. federal government for a response. To this point, Gruening and Du Bois ended their report by asking: "And what of the Federal Government?"[82]

While President Woodrow Wilson remained silent, the U.S. Congress took it upon itself to respond to the public outcry.[83] Propelled by Representative Leonidas C. Dyer from St. Louis, Missouri (across the Mississippi River from East St. Louis, Illinois), the House of Representatives authorized a committee of five representatives from California, Illinois, Wisconsin, and Kentucky to conduct hearings in East St. Louis and to produce its analysis of the community.[84] Justifying federal involvement, the committee reasoned that the massacre had obstructed interstate commerce.[85]

Later that fall, the five representatives traveled to East St. Louis. They collected records of testimony from state officials and heard testimony from city leaders and white and Black residents alike. "After a month of listening to accounts of graft, corruption, prostitution, murder, race prejudice, and community apathy, one legislator told the press, 'I had never dreamed that such a condition existed in this country—or on the face of the earth.'"[86] After collecting nearly five thousand pages of testimony, the five members of the U.S. House of Representatives returned to Washington, D.C., and produced their final report.[87] It amounted to "a stinging condemnation of the community's mores, clearly showing how the activities of employers, labor organizers, and politicians created a milieu which made the race riot possible."[88] That said, this investigation did not propel the U.S. Congress to enact new legislation.[89]

## Studying the "Chicago Riots of 1919"

When Black scholar James Weldon Johnson talked about "the Red Summer" of 1919, he was referring to the "race riots that bloodied the streets of twenty-five towns and cities in the six-month period from April to early October 1919," resulting in at least 120 deaths.[90] Political scientist Megan Ming Francis adds that "1919 marked the bloodiest summer in recent memory."[91]

Along with Black Americans' greater presence in northern cities, Tuttle includes a wartime backdrop to explain this peak in white violence against Black Americans. Particularly after a First World War that many Americans described as a war in defense of democracy, Tuttle writes that Black men and women "entered 1919 with aspirations for a larger share of both the nation's democracy and its wealth."[92] That year, white mobs lynched seventy-eight Black citizens, largely in the South, and half of the violent public clashes between white and Black Americans took place in northern cities, including Chicago, where thirty-eight people died and five hundred were injured.[93]

Observers such as white writer Carl Sandburg and Black sociologist Charles S. Johnson understood the white terror and Black rebellion in 1919 Chicago to be the culmination of several "clashes" among white and Black city residents.[94] Most immediately, a white man had stoned a Black teenager named Eugene Williams. On July 27, Williams and three friends had brought a raft onto Lake Michigan, and while they were playing on it, white onlookers at the white beach perceived that the four Black teenagers had trespassed onto a white-only area. In response, a white man repeatedly hurled rocks at the children, hitting Eugene on the forehead. Without aid from lifeguards, divers recovered Williams's body a half hour later.[95] As further disregard for Williams' life, the first police officer on the scene refused to take into custody the white man who had murdered Williams in broad daylight.[96]

For the next five days, Tuttle writes: "Day and night white toughs assaulted isolated blacks, and teenage black mobsters beat white peddlers and merchants in the black belt. As rumors of atrocities circulated throughout the city, members of both races craved vengeance."[97] Historian Timuel Black Jr., who moved to Chicago with his family in the summer of 1919, recounted that one reason the violence came to an end "was that a group of black veterans broke into an armory and armed themselves to protect their neighbors."[98] To put in greater perspective this moment of self-defense among Black Chicagoans, white residents had been bombing Black homes and terrorizing nonunion Black workers and strikebreakers for years, and the police force refused to protect Black citizens.[99]

Within days, the NAACP requested Illinois Governor Frank Lowden to appoint a commission to study "race relations" in the state, which was followed two days later by a comparable appeal to the governor from other leading Chicago residents.[100] Scholar Anthony Platt notes that the "Chicago Commission on Race Relations" resulted from these two separate appeals. Though backed by the governor's office, the Chicago Commission would remain financially vulnerable and dependent on the support of individual Chicagoans and, most prominently, white philanthropist and fellow Chicago resident Julius Rosenwald.[101] Aside from providing the commission with funding, Rosenwald also played a part in selecting the six Black men to serve alongside the six other white men on the committee.[102] Unlike the House committee that responded to the East St. Louis massacre of 1917 and consisted of congressional representatives from across the country, this one was made up of white and Black residents of Chicago.[103] Also unlike the previous congressional commission, the Illinois governor's commission expected to go beyond hearings to conduct its own fieldwork on Black life in the city.[104] With this in mind, the group created six subcommittees with particular foci: housing, industry, crime, "racial contacts," "racial clashes," and public opinion.[105]

Between March and November of 1920, the commission's two executive secretaries and their staff collected material on Black life in Chicago, selecting 274 Black homes within the geographic span of 238 city blocks and sending three Black female staff members "well equipped to deal intelligently and sympathetically with these families." With a five-page questionnaire in hand, these three researchers dedicated approximately two hours to each home.[106] The commission also sent questionnaires to thirty banking institutions in the city to learn more about their interactions with potential and current Black homeowners; twenty-three responded.[107]

One of the two leading investigators was Graham Romeyn Taylor, a white researcher with experience with citywide field investigations, who had written Satellite Cities, A Study of Industrial Suburbs (1915) and had been a member of Survey magazine's editorial staff. The other investigator, Black scholar Charles S. Johnson, had returned to the University of Chicago's Sociology Department to continue graduate work after the First World War and in fact drafted the majority of the Chicago Commission's final report.[108] Johnson and Taylor were assisted by approximately thirty-seven white and Black individuals, whom they described in their report as "well qualified by educational background and practical experience in social work."[109]

With respect to industry, the commission's team of researchers interviewed superintendents of 123 industrial plants "to ascertain the numbers of whites and Negroes employed in offices and in plants, transportation line used by workers, nature of work and its effect upon cleanliness of person and clothing, provision of baths, etc."[110] The investigators also made use of questionnaires distributed to employees in the city, along with questionnaires, interviews, and conferences with employers.[111]

The final report, entitled The Negro in Chicago, specified that information "concerning race relations in industry was received from employers through questionnaires returned by 137 establishments employing a total of 22,337 Negroes, through interviews at places of business with representatives of 101 employers, through industrial conferences held by the Commission, and through interviews with 865 Negro workers."[112] Based on its collection of data, the commission made fifty-nine policy recommendations for the "consideration and action of state and local authorities, and of the social agencies and citizens of Chicago."[113]

In moving beyond the traditional structure of a governmental commission to embrace fieldwork, the Chicago Commission differed from the one that investigated East St. Louis. However, like the East St. Louis report, *The Negro in Chicago* did not lead to public policy changes. Political scientist Lindsey Lupo points out that Frank Lowden, who had enlisted the report, was no longer Illinois governor by the time of the report's publication: "Ex-Governor Lowden, who had appointed the commission, could praise the commission's work in his forward to *The Negro in Chicago* because no one could later accuse him of not acting on it. At the same time, his successor, Lennington Small, was not at all accountable or beholden to this commission that he had not instituted. The result was that few, if any, recommendations were implemented."[114]

Irrespective of its policy impact, though, the Chicago Commission was an early instance of a U.S. government—in this case, the Illinois governor's office—relating cooperative research on Black Americans in the social sciences to public policymaking. So while Carnegie Corporation's national study of Black Americans would have a novel research structure and public policy purpose in the United States (both by being directed by a European statesman responsible for the final report and intended to guide national policies on Black Americans), policymakers in the country indeed already had been relating the potential utility of cooperative research on Black Americans in the social sciences to policymaking, if only at the city level.

Sixteen years later, another governmental commission convened to analyze Black Americans and "race relations," again, at the city level.[115]

## Studying the "Harlem Riots of 1935"

On March 19, 1935, a Black Puerto Rican teenager named Lino Rivera stole a pocketknife from a department store on 125th street in New York City's Harlem neighborhood. Historian Cheryl Lynn Greenberg writes: "A store employee caught him. The sixteen-year-old struggled to free himself and bit his captor, who summoned the manager. While the store called an ambulance for the bitten employee, a woman who had observed the scuffle began to scream that the boy had been hurt or killed. A crowd quickly gathered."[116] Apparently in an effort to avoid the crowds outside Kress's Store, policemen subsequently directed Rivera to leave through the back of the store via the basement. Seeing no trace of Rivera, however, the crowd assumed that the police had beaten and killed Rivera. "The rumor of Rivera's death and of police brutality spread like wildfire through Harlem and by nightfall the streets of Harlem were brimming with rioters. The riot lasted two days, resulted in four deaths, and property damage and looting was extensive."[117] The violence caused an "estimated $2 million worth of damage, mostly to white-owned property. By the end of the rioting, three black people were dead and over 200 wounded."[118] Scholars have described the event as "a spontaneous outpouring of anger and frustration at police brutality, worsening economic conditions, and ongoing racial discrimination in Harlem."[119]

New York City mayor Fiorello LaGuardia subsequently appointed a commission to investigate the causes of the public violence.[120] Like the Chicago Commission, the Harlem Mayor's Commission would include white and Black members, though with a slight majority of Black members. And like the Chicago Commission, the Harlem Commission had a Black sociologist trained at the University of Chicago as figurehead. In this case, it was E. Franklin Frazier, who by then was professor at Howard University and, as the committee recognized, an "authority on The Family." Particularly relevant to the commissioners, Frazier had been part of the Chicago Commission's research staff and had completed the "study for the Chicago Crime Commission following the riot in Chicago some years ago."[121] His role in shaping the research structure of the Harlem Commission, however, was relatively limited in that he was appointed "technical director."[122] And with this in mind, it is little surprise that the proceedings of the Harlem Commission were in line with the more traditional form of data collection most familiar to government officials: hearings rather than fieldwork. Lindsey Lupo notes that the "commission process took just under a year, had 25 hearings, and 160 witnesses. The hearings were public and well attended. Most hearings were held on Saturdays so that workers could attend."[123]

Published in 1935, *The Negro in Harlem: A Report on Social and Economic Conditions Responsible for the Outbreak of March 19, 1935,* reasoned that the March 19 episode had not been an isolated one, but rather reflected the pent up anger of Black people who during the economic depression of the previous five years had become ever more aware of "the injustices of discrimination in employment, the aggressions of the police, and racial segregation."[124] In its public policy recommendations, the commission pointed to specific ways that the city could—with the power of the purse and in its role as governor and employer—play a part in decreasing discrimination in employment, relief, housing, education and recreation, health and hospitalization, and police practices.[125]

Unlike *The Negro in Chicago*, the committee completed *The Negro in Harlem* while the main policymaker who had initiated the commission was still in office. However, for his part, New York City mayor LaGuardia was not sympathetic to the report and did not release it to the general audience. His biographer, Thomas Kessner, explains: "Precisely because the recommendations were so sweeping, LaGuardia did not want its prescriptions to establish the standard by which his good faith toward blacks would be judged."[126] Without support from the mayor's office, the report predictably failed to influence city policies.

THUS, BETWEEN EAST ST. LOUIS AND CHICAGO in the 1910s and Harlem in the 1930s, white policymakers across city, state, and federal governments in the United States responded to their various concerns about public violence between white and Black people by commissioning teams of government officials, private citizens, and social scientists to analyze the causes and solutions. Their reports differed in research structure and policy recommendations, and policymakers largely ignored their findings. But the existence of these social investigations suggests that, when Carnegie Corporation President Keppel introduced his U.S. analogue to Lord Hailey's ongoing African survey, some U.S. public policymakers had some experience with cooperative research studies on Black Americans that incorporated policy objectives.

For such U.S. policymakers, Carnegie Corporation's intention to fund a social scientific study on Black Americans with some public policy aspirations thus would not have been surprising or novel. However, the corporation's study was more than that. As an echo to Malcolm Hailey's *African Survey* both in research structure and public policy intent, it would be a cooperative study in the social sciences headed by a statesman entrusted alone to write the final report and, in the process, to provide policymakers across the country with means to harmonize their public policies on Black Americans at the national level. As this and the prior chapter have underscored, Keppel was entering uncharted territory in the United States by suggesting and financing such a project because in a U.S. context, it was unprecedented to have a single director responsible for authoring the entire final report for a cooperative study in the social sciences. Even more, many Americans at the time remained deeply hostile to the idea of coordinating public policies on Black Americans beyond the local or state levels. And Keppel was entering such uncharted territory at a time when funding for any research in the social sciences on Black Americans and "race relations" (not to mention financial support for large-scale cooperative studies on the topic) was minimal, if existent at all, in the United States. So Keppel was not just financing an experiment in national planning, but an expensive experiment that U.S. social scientists reasonably might have considered reckless considering the otherwise limited resources that these foundations then put at their disposal for the study of Black Americans and "race relations."

To underscore, in taking the gamble of funding a cooperative study on Black Americans modeled on Hailey's survey of Africa, Keppel had no intention of threatening the racial norms of white supremacy and Black subordination in the United States any more than he did in British Africa. In fact, he found these racial norms to be critical for national and international order. He saw value in financing and overseeing this national study—not because he intended to set in motion the liberation of Black Americans, but rather—because he intended for it to help white policymakers in the United States, as the ongoing African Survey already was doing among government officials in colonial Africa, to share knowledge among themselves about their common problems governing Black people. Because, again, Keppel viewed himself and white American colleagues in philanthropy and government akin to white European colonizers in Africa—and Black Americans akin to Black Africans. For Keppel, Black Americans, like Black Africans, were colonized people in the white Anglo-American world who needed to be governed and controlled effectively, or else the white Anglo-American order that he and colleagues worked hard to protect would fall apart.

During the next years, and as the next chapter makes clear, Keppel would find reason to feel more confident and less anxious about his decision to commission and fund this national study of Black Americans and, in the process, to introduce into a U.S. context a study with an unprecedented research structure and groundbreaking national aspirations to coordinate public policies on Black Americans across the country. To Keppel's satisfaction, several key colleagues in New York City, Washington, D.C., and throughout the United States would agree to collaborate with Myrdal and his team of researchers, making it that much easier for Keppel to imagine that this U.S. study would gain support across governments comparable to that of its London-based predecessor.

## CHAPTER 8

# The "Hailey Type" Study Gains Support in the United States

Just as Malcolm Hailey completed *An African Survey*, his U.S. analogue was stepping into his role. From London in August of 1938, Philip Kerr had written to Carnegie Corporation president Keppel saying that the African survey was "rapidly approaching completion," specifying that the "volume itself ought to be out in October or early in November."[1] By November, Keppel had in his possession a printed copy of Malcolm Hailey's *African Survey* (1938).[2] Though Keppel already had read drafts of Hailey's introduction and final chapters, he now had the final manuscript in hand. Keppel emphasized to Kerr how grateful Carnegie Corporation was for its "share in this enterprise and very grateful to you and your associates for making that share possible."[3]

Two months earlier, in September 1938, Gunnar Myrdal had arrived in New York City to direct the "Hailey type" study whose research structure and public policy goals Keppel had shaped, inspired by his discussions with Carnegie Corporation's Chatham House advisers in the 1930s.

Tracing Myrdal throughout his years as director of the project from 1938 to 1942, this chapter details how Myrdal built on Keppel's networks in the United States and obtained assistance from key figures in philanthropy, the social sciences, and government. As this chapter argues, Myrdal played his part to approximate Keppel's expectations that the U.S. director and his study on Black Americans, modeled on Malcolm Hailey and his *African Survey*, would be able to solicit the cooperation of key figures across regions in the United States and, in the process, produce a national policy program on Black Americans that key white Americans—resistant as they might be to such a national policymaking focus—would consider acknowledging and applying.

## 1. Carnegie Corporation's U.S. Study Gains Key Americans' Cooperation

In June of 1938, three months shy of Gunnar Myrdal's arrival in the United States, Carnegie Corporation president Keppel had asked Raymond Fosdick, president of the Rockefeller Foundation and Rockefellers' General Education Board (GEB), if he could lend him GEB associate director Jackson Davis. A graduate of Columbia College, where Keppel once served as dean, Davis had been state supervisor for Black rural schools in Virginia in the 1910s and then a field agent appointed by the GEB to coordinate supervisors' work across the region. In 1937, just a year before Keppel sought his help, Davis had moved his offices from Richmond, Virginia, to the GEB's central location in New York City.[4] Keppel would ask Davis to guide Myrdal throughout the South.

This decision to send Myrdal south, rather than pointing Myrdal to urban centers in the north such as Cleveland and New York City, might have seemed puzzling to Newton Baker, if Baker (who passed away some months earlier in December 1937) had lived to see the evolution of Keppel's study.[5] It would not have seemed obvious to Baker why a director of a national study of Black Americans—a project which presumably evolved from his own critique of Carnegie Corporation's focus on Black education in the South and his suggestion for the organization instead to focus on societal problems he associated with Black Americans in the North—should start with a tour of the South.

However, more than dutifully following Baker's criticism, Keppel had built upon this board member's critiques in order to coordinate a project he himself had in mind: a U.S. analogue to the ongoing African survey with nationwide implications.[6] And not only was the southern United States yet another region of the country worthy of investigation for a national study on Black Americans, but as the next chapter stresses in its analysis of Myrdal's final report, Keppel remained particularly anxious for Myrdal to appreciate white southerners' perspective on Black Americans. Because without these white Americans' support, Keppel saw little chance of securing a national public policy program on Black people in the United States.

Beyond the GEB, the Rockefellers' wealthier and broader philanthropy—the Rockefeller Foundation—increased its interest in the corporation's study once it realized that a former Rockefeller fellow (1929–1930) and star adviser on the social sciences in Europe, Gunnar Myrdal, was to direct it. To this point and throughout the 1930s, the Rockefeller organizations' staff long had discussed Gunnar Myrdal as one of its luminaries in Europe, with one foundation director writing to a fellow colleague: "Apparently, in granting Myrdal [a social science] fellowship, the Foundation placed its money on a winning horse! I wish we might register a larger proportion of such notable successes."[7] Historian Walter Jackson notes that "Rockefeller officials admired in Myrdal not merely his brilliance as an economist but his effectiveness in applying social science research to legislation and public policy."[8]

During the 1930s, the Rockefeller Foundation maintained Myrdal as a key contact in Europe and funded his research ventures at the Social Science Institute in Stockholm. Not only had Myrdal attained a chair of economics at Stockholm University, but he also had become a successful politician by applying his knowledge in the social sciences to propose a national policy program to address the societal problem of Swedes' decreasing fertility rates. Both developments pleased his Rockefeller networks in the 1930s who intended the Rockefeller fellowships to produce scholars precisely such as Myrdal who would both strengthen the social science fields in their home countries in Europe and apply these academic disciplines to contemporary societal problems on the continent.

Myrdal had achieved these professional goals with the constant collaboration of his wife, Alva Reimer Myrdal, also a former 1929–1930 Rockefeller fellow. And yet reflecting both Gunnar Myrdal's greater international reputation as a leading economist and the inequities that Alva Myrdal faced as a female scholar among peers in government and academia as well as foundation officials, the Rockefeller Foundation long had reached out more often to her husband for advice throughout the 1930s.

The couple pushed back against Alva Myrdal's devaluation, however. And partly due to the couple's efforts to be treated as a unit, both Gunnar and Alva Myrdal remained key contacts for the Rockefeller Foundation in the 1930s. In 1933, for example, when the Nazis came to power in Germany and dismissed Jewish and left-leaning social scientists from institutes and university departments that the Rockefeller Foundation was funding in Germany, the organization contacted both Alva and Gunnar Myrdal and asked them to survey the situation at the Institute für Seeverkehr und Weltwirtschaft at Kiel—one of the Rockefeller Foundation's most prized grantees in Germany. Already, the foundation was mobilizing to help place displaced German scholars through the creation of an "Emergency Committee."[9] That said, these U.S. funders wanted to know if the newly appointed members in the Institute, along with its continuing members, were capable of "free research" untainted by "political bias" under Nazi leadership.[10] The couple traveled to Germany and compiled a six-page summary of their impressions of the institute and of its members.

Thus, Gunnar and Alva Myrdal were well known to the Rockefeller organizations in 1930s. While in the United States to deliver the Godkin Lectures, for example, Gunnar had met with the Rockefeller's acting director and assistant directors in the social sciences. The Swedish economist then successfully recommended that a student of his at Stockholm University be considered for a Rockefeller fellowship to spend a year working in the Department of Agriculture in Washington.[11]

However, the Rockefeller groups' admiration for Gunnar Myrdal did not mean that they thought he was the best candidate to direct Carnegie Corporation's study on Black Americans. Remembering the Rockefeller groups' initial reactions to his selection as the project's director, Myrdal recalled some years later that "this idea of having a foreigner to direct the work on such a study was not popular in America. For instance, my old friends in the Rockefeller Foundation did not find that approach a wise one, and Donald Young, then chief of the Social Science Research Council, was also more than skeptical. But they and many others who shared their critical reaction, once I was on the spot and began work, did everything to help me."[12] And, indeed, Myrdal's colleagues at the Rockefeller organizations did want to see him succeed in this venture and went on to offer Myrdal their expertise and even loan him staff members. Furthermore, throughout the duration of the study, Rockefeller staff members and managers maintained an active interest in the development of the project and met routinely with both Myrdal and Keppel.[13]

And yet, the Rockefeller organizations' interest in Carnegie Corporation's study cannot simply be explained by an intention to help one of their own social science fellows achieve success as director of a cooperative study in the social sciences, financed by colleagues at an equally prestigious foundation. This is because the Rockefeller organizations were also at a crossroads in their funding practices for Black Americans and were curious to see if Carnegie Corporation's study produced new grantmaking ideas in the field. This is because Keppel's philanthropic peers were both experiencing financial strains and at a crossroads in their collective approach to addressing their perceived "problem of Black Americans" in the United States, which long had focused on financing the Tuskegee educational model.

During the Great Depression, the GEB, which then represented the Rockefellers' grantmaking focus on Black Americans, foresaw the liquidation of its endowment. As president of the Rockefeller Foundation and the GEB Raymond Fosdick later wrote, "The uninterrupted years of spending from capital, starting in 1920, had so reduced the Board's free funds that the acceptable ratio between overhead and appropriation was sharply disturbed. By 1937 the General Education Board had dipped into its capital account to the extent of $139 million, and the free and uncommitted balance of the funds remaining (exclusive of appropriations and earmarkings) was something like $8.7 million."[14] However, with the financial assistance of the Rockefeller Foundation, the GEB was able to continue operations until 1960.[15]

Like the GEB, the Julius Rosenwald Fund was confronting dire financial woes in the 1930s.[16] A partner of Sears, Roebuck, and Sears, Julius Rosenwald had given his foundation Sears's stock. By mid-1932, however, Sears's stock had lost most of its value and the Julius Rosenwald Fund subsequently suffered a 95 percent decline in wealth.[17] Historian Alfred Perkins explained that "technically, the philanthropy was bankrupt. Months of scrambling to keep the Rosenwald Fund afloat had proved insufficient."[18] In order to meet the fund's existing commitments, its president, Edwin R. Embree, solicited help from the Rockefeller Foundation, the GEB, and Carnegie Corporation. Although the latter two organizations offered $250,000 and $200,000, respectively, the Fund ceased to exist only a decade later, in 1948.[19]

That said, the financial strains of the dominant GEB and the smaller (though influential) Julius Rosenwald Fund do not fully explain why elite U.S. foundations in the 1930s were looking to move beyond their established funding practices for Black Americans. Another reason was that these foundations were turning over Black schools to local school districts in the South.

In 1932, the Julius Rosenwald Fund reasoned that any further support of Black schools would delay southern school districts from assuming responsibility for Black school children, with southern states delaying their "full responsibilities for the schools of this section of the population as a regular and integral part of the public provisions for the education of all the people."[20] The GEB had similar ideas and for decades had been financing the Southern Education Board (SEB). Sharing almost identical boards with the GEB, the SEB was the propaganda arm of the GEB and its principal aim was to "promote in the Southern states the idea of a tax-supported school system—particularly at the elementary level. Through a bureau of investigation and information it poured out an avalanche of statistics and arguments to the press and educational groups."[21] As with the foundations themselves, however, school districts suffered financial stress during the Depression, and so the GEB decided to continue making appropriations to southern school districts, though "on a somewhat reduced scale, to sixteen Southern states until the end of 1938, when public funds again became available."[22]

For various reasons, then, elite U.S. foundations' lockstep support for the Tuskegee educational model as their principal grantmaking focus on Black Americans was coming to an end in the mid-1930s. The lead actor in this funding practice—the GEB—was depleting its resources, and so were smaller foundations such as the Julius Rosenwald Fund. And in any case, these philanthropies had already been planning for local school districts to take over financial responsibility for Black schools that they helped fund in the South.

Thus, the cooperation of the Rockefeller boards with Carnegie Corporation and its grantee Gunnar Myrdal should be understood not simply as efforts to help a philanthropic colleague and a former Rockefeller fellow succeed, but rather, as a reflection of their own interests to see if Carnegie Corporation could produce a new grantmaking approach to Black Americans—or as they understood it, to Black Americans as a continuing societal problem.

In response to Keppel's request to borrow the GEB's Jackson Davis, Fosdick replied: "We are happy to cooperate, and I suggest that Mr. Davis remain on our payroll but adapt his plans to yours."[23] Once in New York City that September of 1938, Gunnar and Alva Myrdal, along with their children and nannies, settled into their family apartment near Columbia University on the far Upper West Side of Manhattan.[24] Within days, Gunnar Myrdal and his assistant, Richard Sterner, who had traveled with the Myrdals from Stockholm, joined Jackson Davis for a Carnegie-Corporation-sponsored trip to the southern states.

Keeping a diary of his trip throughout the South with Myrdal and Sterner, Davis detailed the various cities and communities that the three men visited. They drove through Richmond, Hampton, Norfolk, and Petersburg, Virginia. In North Carolina, they visited Raleigh and Chapel Hill, and in South Carolina, they traveled to Hartsville, Columbia, and Orangeburg. Farther south, they passed through Georgia and Alabama before ending their trip in Louisiana.[25] Once back in New York, Myrdal recounted to Keppel that he had been able to establish "contact with a great number of white and Negro leaders in various activities; visited universities, colleges, schools, churches, and various state and community agencies as well as factories and plantations, talked to police officers, teachers, preachers, politicians, journalists, agriculturists, workers, sharecroppers, and in fact, all sorts of people, colored and white."[26] Through his relationship with Davis, Myrdal was able to establish various contacts with leading white and Black southerners and, in the process, gain an introduction to the subject matter of his study: the so-called problem of Black Americans.

Back in New York, Myrdal settled into his office, rented by Carnegie Corporation and located just three blocks east from the organization's own offices on Fifth Avenue and Forty-Third Street.[27] This arrangement enabled Carnegie leadership and Myrdal to communicate easily throughout the span of the project. Writing from his office, Gunnar Myrdal could not help but brag to a colleague back in Stockholm: "I am writing to you from the 46th floor of the Chrysler Building where we have half of a tower apartment for the Negro study."[28] By underscoring the location of his offices in one of the world's tallest skyscrapers at the time, situated in the center of Manhattan, Myrdal conveyed to friends and colleagues in Stockholm the significance of his new posting and its proximity to white men of influence in the United States.

Over two years earlier, when Keppel was still planning the structure for the cooperative study, Donald Young of the Social Science Research Council (SSRC) had agreed to help Keppel to coordinate and staff the project's team of researchers. During the next years, Young would continue to play a central role in managing Carnegie Corporation's cooperative study on Black Americans. Most immediately that spring of 1939, Young helped Myrdal organize a three-day conference with a view toward staffing his team of researchers, among other things.

The conference, held in April of 1939 at an oceanfront hotel in New Jersey, brought together white sociologist Thomas Jackson Woofter of the Works Progress Administration, Black sociologist Charles S. Johnson of Fisk University; white sociologist Guy Benton Johnson of the University of North Carolina; Black political scientist Ralph J. Bunche of Howard University; and white sociologist Dorothy Thomas, with whom the Myrdals had collaborated on Rockefeller-funded research in Stockholm.[29] Together with these guests, Myrdal, Young, and Sterner came up with a list of social researchers who could "devote their whole time to the project and who [could] be located in New York."[30] They decided that the permanent staff members should include Sterner, Thomas, Guy Johnson, and Bunche, (who had just returned from a two-year fellowship abroad funded by the SSRC), along with education professor Doxey A. Wilkerson, also from Howard University.[31]

In his letter to Keppel at the end of the three-day conference, Myrdal described the tasks that each of his staff members would undertake. He regarded Sterner as an "expert in social statistics" who would be in charge of research "centered around the standard of living (amount and security of family income, actual family consumption, and [the] related problem of medical facilities, relief, etc.)."[32] Thomas, who was also a statistician, as well as a demographer, "will be in charge of problems relating to population (distribution, migration, fertility, mortality, etc.), mental and personality aptitudes and performance on the basis of tests and measurements, social attitudes, and patterns of segregation, discrimination and contact."[33] Johnson, a "recognised expert from the South," would be "in charge of a great variety of problems; recreation and use of leisure time, social structure within the Negro group, family life and sexual patterns, church, lodge and interracial organizations, crime and related problems."[34]

In this summary letter to Keppel, Myrdal noted that the final two of the five staff members, Bunche and Wilkerson, would analyze the presence of Black Americans in politics, education, and the press. As Myrdal explained to his funder, Bunche was an obvious choice as "one of the best of the younger

Negro social scientists" and Wilkerson's "close cooperation with other social scientists, as well as his high qualifications in his own field, convince me that he is a happy choice. Since he has also studied the Negro press, he can be put in charge of this problem too."[35]

During the next months, the five staff members collected data and drafted memoranda for Myrdal. Sterner, Myrdal, and Guy Johnson worked from the Chrysler Building office, while Bunche conducted his research from the Congressional Library in Washington, D.C.[36] Later in August, Wilkerson joined the staff in the New York Office. A month later, so did Dorothy Thomas.[37]

Aside from these five central staff members, Myrdal also asked for working memoranda from other U.S. social researchers. He received reports from Columbia anthropologist Ralph Linton; Chicago sociologist Louis Wirth; Fisk sociologist Charles S. Johnson; sociologist at Howard University, E. Franklin Frazier; and sociologist Horace Roscoe Cayton, who was then leading a "Works Projects Administration project that studied the social structure of the African-American family."[38] By the summer of 1939, Linton had written a memorandum "on the anthropological point of view," Wirth had begun his memorandum on "Race Mixture and Racial Hybridity among American Negroes," and Johnson had engaged three fieldworkers in his analysis of "Discrimination and Segregation" in the South.[39]

Along with these U.S. social scientists, Myrdal also told Keppel that he was asking "certain outsiders . . . to make major contributions in cooperation with the staff and under my direction."[40] Such outsiders included Woofter of the WPA; Howard University economist Abram Harris (who also served on the Consumers Advocacy Board of the National Recovery Administration); North Carolina sociologist and "prominent New Dealer" Arthur Raper; Howard University poet and editor on "Negro Affairs for the Federal Writers' Project," Sterling Brown; labor movement activists and historians Charles and Mary Beard; and historian Guion Griffis Johnson.[41]

Carnegie Corporation's prestige helped Myrdal attract these scholars' collaboration. After all, these elite networks of foundations in the United States already had a reputation among U.S. social scientists for being significant gatekeepers in the academe. Many of them had watched as the Rockefeller Foundation, for example, long had shaped the research agenda at the SSRC. And most recently, several of these U.S. social scientists had observed how the Rockefeller and Carnegie organizations' decreased interest in financing the "Encyclopedia of the Negro" led to the demise of the project. It furthermore helped Myrdal that he was requesting U.S. colleagues' assistance when the

Great Depression was straining organizations that potentially would otherwise have financed these scholars' work.

For all these reasons, a growing cadre of U.S. social scientists collaborated with Myrdal. However, some scholars remained skeptical of the potential success of the study. As noted earlier, some of Myrdal's closest collaborators and friends in the Rockefeller organizations questioned whether a non-American such as he could really direct a study of Black Americans. Even more specifically, some of these individuals questioned whether Myrdal could capture the perspective of white southerners, a group of Americans they assumed would be critically important for any successful policy coordination on Black Americans.

They had reason for concern. On returning from his trip throughout the South with Myrdal, Davis admitted to Keppel that the Swedish director had met with skepticism in the region. In particular, Davis related that there had been "some misgivings on the part of persons of both races which seemed to indicate that Myrdal's quick mind and remarkably successful work in Sweden made him jump to conclusions about southern problems, instead of keeping his mind open with a willingness to hear and appraise discussion by people most concerned with the several aspects of southern life."[42] Perhaps Davis was simply relaying southerners' observations of Myrdal, but he may well have also been conveying his own similar impressions of Myrdal. In addition, Davis also told Keppel that white southerners had found Myrdal's confidence as a social engineer particularly troublesome. That is, they feared that his success as a population expert back home in Sweden might set him up to become too optimistic about a policy solution to the problems that they associated with Black Americans.

Davis and his colleagues at the GEB had spent their careers navigating and appealing to white southerners' (and northerners') expectations for white supremacy and Black subjection in the United States. And here, for a national study of Black Americans, Carnegie Corporation had tasked a European economist and population expert with the responsibility of not only learning, within a two-year period, the nuanced ways that white northerners and southerners treated Black Americans as a societal problem, but also arriving at national public policy suggestions for solving the supposed societal problem of Black Americans. The corporation's expectations for the Swedish economist reasonably astonished and overwhelmed colleagues such as Davis.

And yet, even as Myrdal's Rockefeller contacts remained skeptical, they helped him along.[43] For the length of the project from 1938 to 1942, Myrdal had access to staff members at the Rockefeller organizations and the Rockefeller-funded SSRC. For its part Carnegie Corporation kept the Rockefeller Foundation and the GEB abreast of the study's progress. And the staffs of both foundations collaborated, as in the spring of 1939, for example, when they met with Myrdal to provide feedback on his first significant memorandum to Carnegie Corporation.[44] Even more, Davis checked in with Myrdal during the writing stage of the project, and Davis's colleague at the GEB, Fred Mc-Cuistion, did the same.[45] And though quite skeptical about Myrdal's potential value as a director for the corporation's study, Davis later would conclude that *An American Dilemma* had exceeded his "best expectations."[46]

Other organizations, such as the National Association for the Advancement of Colored People (NAACP), also collaborated with Myrdal.[47] Just when Myrdal started work on the study, the NAACP was managing lawsuits calling for the desegregation of public graduate and professional schools and others seeking to equalize Black and white teachers' salaries as well as the building facilities of white and Black grade schools.[48] Later, when Myrdal planned a second trip through the South, the NAACP's president, Walter White, provided Myrdal and his collaborator, Ralph Bunche, with letters of introduction in which White stated that both scholars were engaged in what "may be one of the most far-reaching studies which has been made."[49] Reflecting Carnegie Corporation's gratitude to the NAACP for its assistance throughout the study, the corporation, in 1942, would invite both White and Wilkins to a tea in New York City to celebrate the completion of the multiyear study.[50]

Beyond these figures in philanthropy and nonprofits across the United States, Myrdal also secured the assistance of key figures in government, as Keppel had expected him to do.

## 2. The U.S. Study Secures Government Officials' Collaboration

In the final manuscript of *An American Dilemma*, Myrdal acknowledged that throughout the previous years of investigation "several branches of the federal government, and state and municipal authorities in different parts of the country, and, in addition, a great number of individuals, have aided me and my collaborators to an extent which makes any detailed acknowledgement difficult."[51] Although he did not name these individuals, Myrdal and his research team's correspondence confirm that Eleanor Roosevelt agreed to an interview at the White House and so too did U.S. Supreme Court Justice Hugo L. Black and several U.S. senators from states such as Tennessee, South Carolina, North Carolina, Nevada, Texas, and Mississippi.[52]

Myrdal's team also had ongoing correspondence with senior officials at the Agriculture Adjustment Administration, the Farm Security Administration, the Federal Works Agency, the Bureau of Labor Statistics, and the Public Health Service.[53] These federal agencies and departments provided Myrdal and his team with government data and, at times, with more researchers. The surgeon general, for example, loaned to Myrdal a demographer on his staff, Harold F. Dorn, who wrote for Myrdal a memorandum on "The Health of the Negro."[54] For these parties in Washington, D.C., providing Myrdal and his staff with researchers, data, interviews, and the like was far less politically fraught than trying to convince the Democratic Party and a skittish President Roosevelt to push through legislation on Black Americans.

Beyond this increasing concern among mid-1930s policymakers that the federal government had a role to play in shaping Black Americans' status across the country, there were also other, more personal reasons that these Americans in the federal government cooperated with Myrdal.

As a Rockefeller fellow, for example, Myrdal already had nurtured some of these contacts and had maintained transatlantic correspondence with these Americans during the 1930s. To this point, U.S. senator Robert LaFollette, whom Myrdal had known since the 1920s, helped open up Myrdal's access to the U.S. Senate.[55] Even more, Myrdal moved with relative ease in the U.S. Congress, because these white Americans generally identified with this former member of the Swedish Parliament as a fellow colleague. On this point, Myrdal recalled years later: "In Washington I met also Congress members, particularly Senators. As I had just retired from the First Chamber of the Swedish Parliament I was granted 'the privilege of the floor,' which meant that I could wander around the Senate and talk to anybody I wanted." Myrdal's correspondence with the economist and chairman of the board of the National Bank of Nicaragua, C. E. McGuire, for example, suggests that he might have met Senator Henrik Shipstead with whom McGuire had "talked in considerable detail about [Myrdal]" and who promised to arrange for Myrdal "to meet colleagues of his in the Senate."[56]

Reflecting on his relationships with members of the U.S. Congress at the time, Myrdal later recalled: "I remember that a friendship developed between me and Harry S. Truman, who later was made Vice President by Roosevelt and would become President when Roosevelt died in 1945."[57] This friendship continued through the years, and during a trip to the United States in the summer of 1947, Myrdal met with President Truman in the Oval Office to present him with a copy of *An American Dilemma*. "Truman took the book and said: 'I hope there is an inscription!' And there certainly was. I had written: 'To Harry S. Truman, President of the United States and Defender of Human Rights.' Truman read it aloud, but then protested: 'No, no, I am not *The* Defender. You might be *The* defender. I am just a defender. I am an ordinary American but as an ordinary American I have a sense of decency.'"[58]

As director of Carnegie Corporation's study on Black Americans, Gunnar Myrdal also corresponded and lunched with Felix Frankfurter, a Harvard law professor who became a U.S. Supreme Court justice while the study was being completed.[59] Myrdal recollected that he had "intensive discussions on the Negro problem" with Frankfurter, who "gave me much detailed advice for my work outside the legal sphere, and brought me together with Harry Lloyd Hopkins, one of Roosevelt's trusted lieutenants."[60] Through Frankfurter, Myrdal also gained further access to key contacts in Washington, as well as entry to the U.S. Supreme Court.

Myrdal not only became friendly with Washington policymakers, but also gained their active cooperation. In January of 1939, for example, he reached out and requested that the Department of Agriculture's adviser to the secretary guide his assistant, Richard Sterner, who was traveling to Washington in order to conduct a preliminary survey of national data on Black Americans.[61] Two years later, an administrator at the Department reemphasized to Myrdal his group's willingness to collaborate, saying that Myrdal's researchers could "count on us for whatever cooperation we may be able to give."[62] Though not specific on the extent of the cooperation, Myrdal's correspondence at the time suggests that the Public Works Administration and the Department of Labor's Bureau of Labor Statistics assisted as well, likely by providing data to the study's staff.[63] And support came from the White House, too.

In the spring of 1940, Myrdal's then-research associate Ralph Bunche had written to Eleanor Roosevelt requesting an interview, explaining that "Carnegie Corporation of New York is conducting a comprehensive survey of the Negro in America. . . . The undertaking is strictly a scholarly one though in the very nature of things it will have a practical significance in a world in which racial theories and hatreds assume increasing prominence." He continued: "As a staff member of the Survey I would be deeply appreciative if you might find it convenient at some time within the reasonable future to grant me an interview during which I might obtain your broad impressions of this problem as based upon your extensive travel about the country, your wide contacts and your richly democratic social philosophy."[64]

Soon after, Ralph Bunche was driving to the White House from his office at nearby Howard University. The political scientist's memorandum of the White House visit suggested just how taken aback he had been by Roosevelt's lunch invitation. He noted to Roosevelt and her secretaries that he had told his family and several associates about the upcoming interview and that many had wondered if the first lady knew he was Black.[65]

For Bunche's colleagues and family, such personal information was relevant since some white Americans would find a white woman and Black man sharing a meal at the same table to be an act that necessarily transgressed norms in white supremacy and Black subjection in the United States that, particularly if done in the White House, many white Americans at the time would find especially objectionable. To this point, in 1901, when President Theodore Roosevelt invited Booker T. Washington to dine with his family at the White House, the event "provoked inflammatory newspaper articles, political cartoons, fire-and-brimstone speeches, even vulgar songs."[66]

As the first lady's secretary noted to Bunche, Eleanor Roosevelt had extended the invitation to Bunche without knowing his race. His letter "was credential enough and . . . no further investigation needed to be made."[67] As an associate of Myrdal's study, financed by Carnegie Corporation, Bunche had sufficient credentials to access the White House and interview the first lady.[68]

That same spring, when Myrdal was in the midst of collecting data for the study and had not yet written the final manuscript, Germany invaded Denmark and Norway, both of which bordered Sweden. Myrdal explained to Keppel that it was his duty to return to help his fellow countrymen fight a probable Third Reich invasion and to share their fate. The corporation subsequently made plans for Samuel Stouffer, a white U.S. sociologist in Chicago, to manage the team's reports submitted during Myrdal's absence.[69] Showing the importance that the U.S. federal government was then placing on Carnegie Corporation's study, the foundation received the assistance of under secretary of state Sumner Welles and British minister of economic warfare Hugh Dalton to ensure that the Swedish director and his family could safely traverse a warring European continent.[70]

Remaining fearful that Germany and Sweden soon would be engaged in war, the Swedish family ultimately chose not to fly over Germany en route to Stockholm. Instead, the couple and their three children boarded a Finnish ship that was sailing from New York to Petsamo in far northern Finland.[71] Years later, Myrdal remembered the voyage: "The boat was filled high above the deck with barrels containing explosives, certainly breaking all safety regulations. Also against the rules, it took us in a wide circle north of Iceland, avoiding the controls in Scotland. And as we neared our destination a Russian warship informed us that the ocean was full of mines, though nobody knew just where they were located. After the stormiest passage I have ever experienced we reached Petsamo."[72] They then left Petsamo by car with a

Swedish military delegation, which had been awaiting the ship in order to collect war materials. With the help of Carnegie Corporation and the U.S. and
British governments, which remained attentive to the family's travel plans, the
Myrdals found their way from the United States, through a warring Europe,
and back home to a still-neutral Sweden.

By the end of the year, and with his final report yet to be written, Gunnar
Myrdal took steps to ensure that he could travel back to the United States. In
January of 1941, Myrdal coordinated his travel with the Russian ambassador
to Stockholm, Alexandra Kollontai.[73] He journeyed to Moscow and then took
the Trans-Siberian Railway to Vladivostok, where he took a ship to Japan.[74]
Since Japan was then neutral, Myrdal was able to board a Japanese boat to San
Francisco. In March of 1941, three months after he had left Stockholm, Myrdal
made his way to Carnegie Corporation offices in New York City.[75]

Even before Myrdal returned to the United States in 1941 in order to collect
his research team's memoranda and write the study's final report, President
Keppel would have had reason to grow ever more confident that this cooperative
study on Black Americans—like *An African Survey* (1938) throughout colonial
Africa—would capture the imagination of policymakers across regions in the
United States. Because while Myrdal and his team had collected data between
1938 and 1940, the national study had gained the assistance of key policy figures
throughout the United States, from federal employees in Washington, D.C., to
their advisers and funders at the SSRC and the Rockefeller organizations.

During the research stage of the project, Keppel also most likely found
pleasing that Myrdal had secured the cooperation of the NAACP. Because
even if Keppel did not privilege Black people's dignity and equality—on the
contrary, he placed greater value in white supremacy and Black subjection as
key elements for international order along the color line—he valued Black
people's approval of his cooperative research studies aimed at further solidifying white domination. As noted earlier in this book, for example, this was
evident in Keppel's amused reception of Black South African D. D. T. Jabavu's
reading of *An African Survey*.

Moving from the research to the writing stage of Carnegie Corporation's
cooperative study of Black Americans, the next chapter demonstrates Keppel's
active role in that process. As Myrdal began drafting chapters of the final report, Keppel would routinely read and comment on the drafts, hoping to ensure that Myrdal would achieve the project's national policy objectives. And
Keppel would prove most concerned about Myrdal's portrayal of the white
South, whose collaboration Keppel thought to be critical for any national
policy program on Black Americans.

## CHAPTER 9

# In Sync with Carnegie Corporation

*Gunnar Myrdal Offers Blueprints for a New Dynamic
Equilibrium in White Anglo-American Domination*

Focusing on the writing stage of Carnegie Corporation's study on Black Americans, this chapter illustrates how President Keppel read and commented on
drafts of Myrdal's final report. The chapter argues that *An American Dilemma*
reflected Myrdal's intellectual influences and observations in 1930s and 1940s
Sweden and the United States and, equally so, largely met—and in some ways,
exceeded—Keppel's expectations for a national policy program that would
help stabilize white domination in the United States. This is because, in *An
American Dilemma*, Gunnar Myrdal provided a means for white Anglo-
Americans to fortify their supremacy within the United States, as Keppel expected, and also beyond the United States, a point which Keppel long had
valued.

In fact, the biggest difference of opinion between Keppel and Myrdal during
the writing stage of the study rested on their varying perspectives on the significance of white southerners for achieving Myrdal's national policy plan on
Black Americans. While Keppel thought that white southerners were critical
for such a national effort, Myrdal discounted their importance by pointing to
the political and economic power of white northerners and the New Deal federal government, as well as to intellectual divides among white southerners.

In this way, Myrdal felt confident in including peppered criticisms of the
white South in *An American Dilemma*, while Keppel viewed these scattered
phrases as liabilities that could potentially limit the project's national policy
goals. This difference of perspectives between Myrdal and Keppel helps explain why Keppel decided to play his part to court white southern readers in
his preface to *An American Dilemma*. In this introductory section of *An American Dilemma*, Keppel not only highlighted former Carnegie Corporation
trustee Newton Baker's southern roots but also emphasized that Myrdal was
a foreigner whose use of the English language was imperfect.

Describing the evolution of Carnegie Corporation's cooperative study on
Black Americans while Myrdal drafted its final report and how it largely met
and, in some ways, exceeded Keppel's expectations, the chapter begins by describing Myrdal's conversations about *An African Survey* with Keppel and

Keppel's assistant, Charles Dollard. After all, *An African Survey* inspired the research structure and public policy purpose of the corporation's U.S. study.

## 1. Gunnar Myrdal and *An African Survey*

After spending a year in Sweden during the Second World War, Myrdal returned to the United. States in 1941 to read over his U.S. researchers' memoranda and to write his final report. To this end, Myrdal, his wife, Alva Reimer Myrdal (who followed her husband a few months later through an equally harrowing voyage across the Atlantic), and two research associates, Richard Sterner and Arnold Rose, secluded themselves in Princeton, New Jersey.

An experienced Swedish social statistician, Sterner had worked with Myrdal on the study since its start in 1938. By contrast, Rose was a "young sociology graduate student from the University of Chicago whom Stouffer had brought on board while Myrdal had been in Sweden"; Rose joined the two men during this final writing stage of the study.[1] While relatively new to the team, Myrdal stressed to Carnegie Corporation that Rose was playing an active role in this final phase of the project.[2] In fact, Rose ultimately drafted several chapters of the final manuscript.[3] Eager to acknowledge the central roles played by Rose and Sterner on the project, Myrdal tweaked the corporation's initial intentions by arguing to Keppel and Dollard that he should list the two men as assistants in the book's title page.

Beyond these two white men whose inclusion on the book's title page Gunnar Myrdal justified to Carnegie Corporation by stressing the centrality of their roles on the project, neither he nor his funders ever considered the possibility of expanding such public recognition to Alva Myrdal or close staff members such as Ralph J. Bunche, Guy B. Johnson, Paul H. Norgren, Dorothy S. Thomas, and Doxey A. Wilkerson, let alone the numerous other social scientists commissioned to conduct fieldwork and produce memoranda for the study.[4]

Rather, as Keppel intended from the start, a single director would be front and center. In this spirit, the title page of *An American Dilemma* (1944) announces that it was written "by Gunnar Myrdal with the assistance of Richard Sterner and Arnold Rose."[5]

Located some fifty miles from each other, Gunnar Myrdal's writing team in Princeton and Carnegie Corporation leaders in New York City not only discussed names on the final report's title page, but exchanged correspondence and chapter drafts throughout 1941 and 1942. It was during this time that Keppel, his new assistant, Charles Dollard, and Myrdal made increasing mention of the U.S. study's antecedents and particularly its London-based predecessor.

In the summer of 1941, for example, Dollard promised to send Myrdal *The Poor White Problem in South Africa.*[6] And the following summer, while completing the manuscript, Myrdal noted to Dollard that he had structured the book along the lines of *An African Survey* (1938). Resisting Dollard's calls to shorten the manuscript, Myrdal argued that no one "will read it who is not something of a 'scholar' himself and who has special interests in the problems treated." In this way, Myrdal urged, neither Dollard nor any other reader should "think of it as a book which should be read from cover to cover, just as little as you assume that Hailey's book on Africa is ever used in that way. I have no reason why I shouldn't write general chapters as interestingly as possible and all have encouraged me in this."[7]

Compared to Keppel, Dollard had little firsthand knowledge with Carnegie Corporation's advisers at Chatham House and their evolving plans for an African survey during the 1930s.[8] With little awareness that the Chatham House project initially also had been envisioned as a shorter report, Dollard responded to Myrdal by acknowledging that Myrdal's "analogy to Lord Hailey's survey is fair enough, but I have always cherished the hope that your book would have something of a popular audience which Hailey's, of course, did not. Moreover, Hailey's work is essentially an encyclopedia from which other researchers can draw material rather than a real analysis of the African picture."[9] Downplaying the impact of *An African Survey* among imperial and colonial administrators in the British Empire, Dollard preferred to underscore its length and urged Myrdal to write a shorter manuscript, which, as Dollard imagined, would enjoy greater readership in the United States. Myrdal ultimately completed a two-volume study compared to *An African Survey*'s single volume, though, at 1,483 pages, *An American Dilemma* nearly reached the length of the 1,837-page *African Survey.*

Further noting the extent to which Myrdal inherited his funder's perspective of *An African Survey* as model for the U.S. study, Myrdal more publicly engaged with Hailey's study within the pages of *An American Dilemma.* Thus, for example, in his chapter on "Negro Popular Theories" and specifically a section titled "Back to Africa," Myrdal considered the possibility that white Americans' resentment of Black Americans could increase if the United States entered another period of unemployment. And in that case, Myrdal argued in *An American Dilemma* that it was "not beyond possibility that a large proportion of Southern whites might under certain circumstances come to demand the sending away of Negroes from America."[10] Looking to Africa as a geographic space where Black Americans presumably would settle in response to heightened hostility from white Americans and particularly from white southerners,

Myrdal added, "Lord Hailey, an Englishman, has already done some of the necessary spade work of scientific inquiry for such practical work" that would be needed for imperial powers to develop the region to the point that it ultimately could become an independent "Black Continent."[11]

And yet, Myrdal did not simply produce a manuscript to Carnegie Corporation president Keppel's liking simply by reading and citing *An African Survey*. Rather, and more deeply, Myrdal reached such a complementary goal by being the national policymaker from Sweden Keppel had found so very attractive to lead the U.S. analogue to *An African Survey*.[12] Of course, and contrary to Keppel's initial hopes for the U.S. director, Myrdal was not a white Briton with colonial administrative experience. But Keppel was accustomed to adapting his expectations depending on changing geographies and combinations of white advisers in the Anglo-American world. In this vein, Keppel had once relied on white Afrikaner researchers in a South African environment more hospitable to Afrikaner rather than British researchers, and in a similar spirit, he adapted this ideal for a U.S. context seemingly more comfortable with a Scandinavian, rather than a British colonial administrator, director for the U.S. study.

That said, Myrdal could have been a different person in a U.S. context than Keppel had expected when he first had offered him the directorship, or Myrdal simply could have changed his perspective on the value of a national policy program on Black Americans during the span of the project. So the question is just how Myrdal—positioned from the start, as Keppel hoped, to provide white policymakers across governments in the United States with a national policy program on Black people—produced a study complementary to his funder's expectations.

Analyzing just how and why Myrdal ultimately wrote a final report largely to Keppel's liking, the following sections explore key elements of Myrdal's thesis in *An American Dilemma* and place them in the context of his lived experiences and observations both in the United States and Sweden during the 1930s and 1940s, because it was during those years that Myrdal evolved and reinforced his views on the "nation," the "folk," and the urgency for white Anglo-American domination across the Atlantic.

## 2. Myrdal Flatters and Focuses on White Americans

Reading drafts of Gunnar Myrdal's first chapters in the fall of 1941, Keppel praised the author for "hanging the whole study on the peg which [he] describe[d] as the American dilemma, i.e., the conflict between the average American's faith in the democratic creed and his tacit acceptance of social and legal measures designed to repress a large segment of the population."[13]

For Keppel, Myrdal's positive portrayal of Americans—and particularly white Americans who Myrdal suggested experienced moral anxiety in their discriminatory treatment of Black Americans—could only help inspire other white Americans throughout the country to come together and coordinate their policies on Black Americans. Considering the preferred model of white rule embraced by Keppel, his board at Carnegie Corporation, and their Chatham House advisers, it expectedly pleased him that Myrdal imagined proposing a national policy program on Black Americans to be led by white Americans and designed to counteract Black Americans' absolute repression. Because this preferred model of white rule not only centered the needs and interests of white Anglo-Americans, but expressed a concern to help Black people under white rule, efforts which these white men imagined should not challenge, but rather reinforce, the legitimacy of white Anglo-American domination.

While Myrdal drafted his final manuscript, Keppel retired from Carnegie Corporation and, yet, Keppel retained an office at the organization and would continue overseeing the project. In this spirit, Keppel received numerous and evolving drafts of Myrdal's manuscript between 1941 and 1942, and continued to celebrate the project. In a confidential memorandum to his successor at Carnegie Corporation, Walter Jessup, Keppel called Myrdal's thesis "an original and challenging one, namely that the essence of the Negro problem lies in the heart of the white man."[14] Indeed, throughout *An American Dilemma*, Myrdal argued that white Americans harbored national ideals of equality and liberty, "the American Creed," which necessarily made them feel morally culpable for discriminating against fellow Black Americans, and this argument met with Keppel's approval. After all, and again, it was an image of white Americans as a particularly moral people, which would only help white Anglo-Americans justify their dominant roles in the United States and, as Myrdal noted in the book too, at the international level.

This aspect of Gunnar Myrdal's central thesis in *An American Dilemma*, which Keppel found so compelling, had roots in Myrdal's year-long sabbatical away from the U.S. project, when he and his family had returned to Sweden expecting to play critical wartime roles in their home country. This European context during the Second World War helps explain how Myrdal came to privilege and develop this central concept in *An American Dilemma*, a positive portrayal of white Americans' psychology which countered research memoranda

on white psychology that Myrdal's team had produced for him.[15] This wartime context also helps explain how and why Myrdal became particularly invested in white Anglo-American leadership, not only within the United
States, but also at a global level.

Particularly after he had returned to Sweden in 1940, for example, Gunnar
Myrdal had begun to view the U.S. project as wartime service on behalf of the
Allied Powers and especially the United States. With past leading roles in
Sweden's Social Democratic Party and Parliament, he and Alva Myrdal had
imagined that they would have had important government roles to play in
resisting a potential invasion from Nazi Germany. Contrary to these expectations, however, historian Yvonne Hirdman notes that upon arriving in Stockholm in 1940 the Myrdals "were not offered the heroic tasks they had hoped
for."[16] This predictably bruised their egos, but the couple quickly created
wartime work for themselves by drafting a three-hundred-page defense and
glowing description of the United States. Written in Swedish for a Swedish
audience, Alva and Gunnar Myrdal in *Kontakt med Amerika* (Contact with
America, 1941) developed their ideas about white Americans' allegiance to an
"American Creed" and, relatedly, the value of global U.S. leadership.[17]

As the Myrdals explained in *Kontakt*, the main inspiration for writing the
book came after they perceived their fellow countrymen were folding to the
pressures of the Third Reich. Alva had written to a U.S. friend that she even
saw some colleagues and friends turn into outright Nazis. In correspondence
with a Swedish friend, she had wondered how their country had transformed
from a modern, democratic, and forward-thinking Sweden to one that was conservative, traditional, and tolerant of the Third Reich.[18]

In writing *Kontakt*, the Myrdals thus aimed to mobilize fellow countrymen
against the Third Reich and, in the process, garner Swedish citizens' support
for the United States. By then, the United States was informally engaged in
the Second World War and, from the Myrdals' perspectives in 1940, soon
would likely become a formally belligerent country.[19] In this critical moment
of global allegiances, the couple wanted to make clear to Swedes that there was
an inherent difference between modern-day Germans and Americans, that the
United States was worthy of Swedes' allegiance during the war, and thus that
there was purpose in defending Sweden against a Third Reich invasion.

In the 1941 book, Alva and Gunnar Myrdal disproved two stereotypes about
the United States that fellow Swedish citizens seemed to hold. In particular, they
explained that the United States was not simply a heterogeneous group of
people who treated racial minorities and particularly Black Americans as

badly as Germans treated Jews. Rather, the Myrdals stressed that the United States was a common "folk"—a community of like-minded people united by their shared egalitarian ideals. That said, the authors acknowledged that "America is more heterogeneous" than other countries and that it "takes a long time and through lively studies before one discovers that which is shared and stable in America."[20] They noted that the "secret is that America, more than any other land in the Western world, large or small, has the most homogeneous, firmly and clearly formulated, vividly living system of expressed ideals for human social life, which is vividly living in the people's mind. . . . Each American has had them stamped in his mind." This, the Myrdals explained, was the "American creed" that brought the U.S. folk together.[21] The couple thus previewed for the first time the concept that was to frame the thesis in *An American Dilemma*: the American Creed.

All Americans, Gunnar and Alva reasoned in *Kontakt*, shared the belief that "all individuals have the same rights in relation to each other and before the state, independent of race, religion, and standing. Around each individual, in whatever condition he lives, stands therefore an aura of clear rights which even the state must respect."[22] These were shared egalitarian ideals, the Myrdals noted, which Swedes could relate to and which were lacking among the German people.

The Myrdals admitted that Americans, like Germans, treated racial minorities abominably. However, they noted that Americans, unlike Germans, wanted to correct their discriminatory behavior to meet their egalitarian ideals. To this point, they explained that "no people on earth are (or ever were) so passionately interested in finding and crying out their own deficiencies as Americans."[23] As an example, Gunnar mentioned that he had been asked to research Black Americans in the United States and that he very much doubted that Germany would ever have invited a foreign researcher to analyze "the country's most difficult race problem—the Jewish question."[24]

Gunnar Myrdal underscored that white Americans distinguished themselves from their counterparts in Germany, not only by commissioning and thus welcoming a critical analysis of their treatment of Black Americans, but also by expressing remorse in their discrimination and violence towards this group of Americans. Gunnar Myrdal wrote: "I often would ask [Americans] how they could criticize so much the treatment of Jews in Germany, while their own Negroes and so often many of their poor whites did not have it much better. The answer was: 'But we do not say that what happens is right! That is the difference between America and Germany, that here that goes against our ideals.'"[25] The Myrdals reasoned that, unlike Germans, white Americans held egalitarian ideals and acknowledged that their violent and discriminatory treatment of Black Americans contradicted their ideals.

Furthermore, Alva and Gunnar Myrdal noted that this gap between white Americans' actions and ideals caused Americans emotional distress: "The Negro problem, like all the other difficult social problems, is mainly a problem in Americans' own hearts."[26] In other words, white Americans' national character was bound together by egalitarian ideals. So when white Americans treated Black Americans unequally, the Myrdals explained, guilt overwhelmed these Americans. In this way, and as the Myrdals urged fellow Swedes to realize during the war, white Americans proved that they indeed aspired to be a more egalitarian people.

In comparing these two countries in *Kontakt*, Gunnar and Alva Myrdal hoped to convince Swedes that they had more in common with Americans than with Germans. In Gunnar Myrdal's words: "One of those who writes this has had, for the last two years, the assignment of becoming an expert exactly on America's social deficiencies and he knows more about those imperfections than maybe anyone else who writes in the Swedish language. He knows quite well how much more evil, injustice and shortcomings that still remain in America compared to Sweden. But he has also learned how much more there is of goodness, justice, and extraordinary power."[27] Despite white Americans' discriminatory and violent treatment of Black Americans, the Myrdals underscored that the United States was worthy of Sweden's support.

Just as this book went to press in Sweden in the first weeks of 1941, Gunnar Myrdal returned to the United States in order to complete Carnegie Corporation's study of Black Americans. As in *Kontakt med Amerika*, Gunnar Myrdal explained in *An American Dilemma* that the supposed problem of Black Americans was "a problem in the heart of the American. It is there that the interracial tension has its focus. It is there that the decisive struggle goes on."[28] Stressing the importance of understanding the supposed problem of Black Americans as a moral problem, Myrdal continued in *An American Dilemma*: "Though our study includes economic, social, and political race relations, at bottom our problem is the moral dilemma of the American—the conflict between his moral valuations on various levels of consciousness and generality."[29]

Throughout *An American Dilemma*, the American Creed is front and center. As Myrdal put it in the first chapter: "From the point of view of the American Creed the status accorded the Negro in America represents nothing more and nothing less than a century-long lag of public morals."[30] In both *Kontakt med America* and *An American Dilemma*, that is, Gunnar Myrdal observed that white Americans' treatment of Black Americans fell short of white Americans' egalitarian ideals. And in both books, the American Creed would give grounds for a positive image of white Americans. Particularly in *An American Dilemma*, he mobilized this concept to inspire white Americans toward a solution to their so-called "Negro problem," the very existence of which, Myrdal argued, jeopardized white Americans' national and global leadership.

Regarding that "problem," Myrdal wrote: "The Negro in America has not yet been given the elemental civil and political rights of formal democracy, including a fair opportunity to earn his living, upon which a general accord was already won when the American Creed was first taking form. And this anachronism constitutes the contemporary 'problem' both to Negroes and to whites. If those rights were respected . . . there would not longer be a *Negro* problem."[31] To U.S. readers, Gunnar Myrdal stressed that white Americans would cease viewing Black people as a societal problem once they lined up their behavior and policies toward Black Americans with their American Creed. In effect, Myrdal viewed white Americans as particularly moral beings willing and capable of treating Black Americans as they themselves would want to be treated, especially when confronted with their moral failings.

The author's positive portrayal of white Americans did not simply begin and end with his discussion of the American Creed. In *An American Dilemma*, Myrdal also extended this favorable image in his model of social change, a vision of national public policy reform placing white people—and particularly white northerners and white policymakers in the U.S. federal government—as principal catalysts improving the lived experiences of Black Americans. In a section of *An American Dilemma* titled "A White Man's Problem," he admitted that his analysis of Black Americans was intended "to give *primary* attention to what goes on in the minds of white Americans" because it was "the white majority group that naturally determines the Negro's 'place.'"[32]

In this vein, Myrdal's model of social change in *An American Dilemma*—or rather, to use Myrdal's terminology, his theory of "cumulative causation"—privileged the interests, views, and agency of white Americans.[33] Titled "A Methodological Note on the Principle of Cumulation," this second appendix to *An American Dilemma* begins by noting that "equilibrium" was a concept that the various branches of the social sciences had adopted from the natural sciences. To this point, Myrdal argued that social scientists long had analyzed the social world in an effort to return to a stable equilibrium: "It is this equilibrium notion which is implicit in the sociological constructions of 'maladjustment' and 'adjustment' and all their several synonyms or near-synonyms, where equilibrium is thought of as having a virtual reality in determining the direction of change."[34] Myrdal thus clarified in *An American Dilemma* that social scientists who looked at the social world and categorized people and events either as maladjustments or adjustments had in mind an ideal—or rather, a static—equilibrium from which social reality deviated.

In *An American Dilemma*, Myrdal argued that social scientists should abandon this definition of equilibrium for a more dynamic one. Rather than hearkening back to an original and static state of balance, for example, Myrdal stressed that a more dynamic equilibrium model would consider the "cumulation of forces" affecting social change and thus seek stability within this ever-changing, forward-moving motion.[35] Relating the relevance of this alternative equilibrium model, Myrdal noted in this concluding section of *An American Dilemma* that he had applied this concept in an earlier work on economic theory, citing the 1939 English-language translation of his 1931 text, *Monetary Equilibrium* (*Om penningteoretisk jämvikt*).[36]

Transplanting in *An American Dilemma* elements of his "model of cumulative economic causation," Myrdal characterized the various factors impacting relations between white and Black Americans as "the 'principle of cumulation,' also commonly called the 'vicious circle.'"[37] Before discussing the vicious circle theory, though, Myrdal first defined the "hypothetically balanced state" between Black and white Americans from which he and his team had worked, writing: "There is—under these static conditions—just enough prejudice on the part of the whites to keep down the Negro plane of living to that level which maintains the specific degree of prejudice, or the other way around."[38] In this "hypothetically balanced state," Myrdal clarified that white Americans' prejudice toward Black Americans created a lowered living standard for Black Americans which then reinforced white Americans' prejudice toward Black Americans. As far as the genesis of white Americans' prejudice, Myrdal thus explained that Black people's lower "plane of living" partly explained white Americans' initial "reason for discrimination." Here, Myrdal wrote that Black Americans' "poverty, ignorance, superstition, slum dwellings, health deficiencies, dirty appearance, disorderly conduct, bad odor and criminality stimulate and feed the antipathy of the whites for them."[39]

In *An American Dilemma*, Myrdal furthermore detailed that this balanced state between white and Black Americans actually was never static, because any change "will, by the aggregate weight of the cumulative effects running back and forth between them all, start the whole system moving in one direction or the other."[40] Noting that various factors caused shifts in this equilibrium, Myrdal together termed these various elements "the principle of cumulation," "the vicious circle," or rather, "a model of dynamic social causation."[41] The focus of social scientists, Myrdal stressed, should not be on trying to achieve an imagined, prior "stable equilibrium" but, rather, trying to "analyze the causal interrelation within the system itself as it works under the influence of outside pushes and the momentum of on-going processes within."[42]

With a focus on white Americans as leading change agents in the country, Myrdal hypothesized that white people in the United States would be decreasing their own prejudice toward Black people in the United States by improving Black people's status in society. In the process of ameliorating the lives of Black Americans, Myrdal thus argued that white Americans increasingly would regard Black Americans as equals.[43] However, realizing that this was likely too complimentary of an image of white Americans, he admitted later in the appendix that a rise in Black Americans' status would be met by an increase of prejudice among some—though, as he perceived it, not the majority of—white Americans.[44]

Assuming his targeted white readers were intent on improving Black Americans' social condition and decreasing their own anti-Black prejudice, Myrdal proposed a means for putting into motion his model of "cumulative causation." Detailing "the white man's rank order of discriminations," or rather, a hierarchy of white Americans' relative sensitivity to various forms of anti-Black discrimination, Myrdal suggested that white Americans' public policy actions should begin with those forms of discrimination that were *least* important to white Americans.[45]

In *An American Dilemma*, Myrdal thus advised that white Americans, inspired by the American Creed and following a "white man's rank order of discriminations," should begin by addressing discriminations "in securing land, credit, jobs, or other means of earning a living, and discriminations in public relief and other social welfare activities."[46] Then they could focus on tackling "discriminations in law courts, by the police, and by other public services" followed by Black Americans' "political disfranchisement."[47] Inching closer to forms of discriminatory behaviors and public policies to which white Americans were increasingly committed, Myrdal then suggested confronting "segregation and discrimination in use of public facilities such as schools, churches and means of conveyance" along with "several etiquettes and discriminations, which specifically concern behavior in personal relations," with the last focus being "the bar against intermarriage and sexual intercourse involving white women."[48]

Inspired by the American Creed and following the "white man's rank order of discriminations," Myrdal thus expected that his targeted group of white Americans first would attack public policies and behavior discriminatory of

Black Americans that were least important to them. And Myrdal encouraged white Americans to make these "pushes" to the current equilibrium in the "Negro problem." As Myrdal imagined it, these "pushes"—these ameliorative changes to anti-Black public policies and behavior—would lead to improvements in Black Americans' "plane of living." To Myrdal, such policy improvements necessarily meant opening up the way for Black Americans to achieve "white levels" in all aspects of life in the United States.[49] Furthermore, he reasoned that Black Americans' achievement of such "white levels" would help decrease white Americans' prejudice of Black people because white Americans' prejudice, at least in part, as he suggested, was a reaction to societal problems that many white Americans associated with Black Americans: "In other words, we assume that a movement in any of the Negro variables in the direction toward the corresponding white levels will tend to decrease white prejudice."[50] As its ultimate outcome, Myrdal's dynamic model of social causation aimed to provide further proof of white Americans' moral leadership in the United States and, in the process, increase Black Americans' "plane of living" to "white levels" at a speed and level comfortable to white Americans. Over time, and again at a speed that was suitable for white Americans, Myrdal imagined that this should lead to the full assimilation of Black Americans into white life in the United States, as a people invited to reflect (and ultimately reflecting) white Americans' values.

In this theory of social change, Myrdal thus proposed that Black Americans not only would attain "white levels" in various aspects of life in the United States and thus increasingly reflect white Americans' values, but relatedly, white Americans would decrease their anti-Black prejudice and begin to view Black Americans as an assimilable people, worthy of miscegenation with white Americans. Following Myrdal's logic in *An American Dilemma*, white Americans thus would ultimately treat Black Americans much like "all the Northern European stocks, but also the people from Eastern and Southern Europe, the Near East and Mexico" whose ultimate fate in the United States was to shed their various ethnic identities, marry white Anglo-Americans and, in the process, assimilate into "a homogenous nation" defined by Anglo American whiteness.[51] If given such an opportunity by white Americans to assimilate fully into whiteness, Myrdal reasoned that Black Americans would embrace it. Because while there was a "strong practical reason for the Negro's preaching 'race pride' in his own group," Myrdal explained that "it is almost certainly not based on any fundamental feeling condemning miscegenation on racial or biological groups."[52] For Myrdal, any contemporary resistance from Black Americans to assimilation into the white "homogenous nation" of the United States was simply a response to white Americans' long-standing assumption that Black Americans were "unassimilable."[53]

Myrdal furthermore argued in *An American Dilemma* that, by expediting this assimilationist national policy program on Black Americans, white Americans would be justifying their moral leadership, not only within the United States, but also abroad. Focusing on the final chapter of *An American Dilemma*, which Myrdal titled "America Again at the Crossroads in the Negro Problem," scholar Nikhil Pal Singh observes that, for Myrdal, solving the "Negro problem" in the United States "would both affirm the underlying theory of American nationhood and also prove that the United States was the world's greatest democracy, whose ability to harmonize the needs of a heterogeneous population fitted it to be the broker of the world's security concerns and aspirations for social progress."[54]

Alluding to the evolving international significance of the study, Myrdal wrote in these final pages of *An American Dilemma* that: "What has actually happened within the last few years is not only that the Negro problem has become national in scope after having been mainly a Southern worry. It has also acquired tremendous international implications."[55] Further specifying the international significance of white Americans' resolve to solve the so-called "Negro problem" by incorporating Black Americans into white life, he also stressed that "America, for its international prestige, power, and future security, needs to demonstrate to the world that American Negroes can be satisfactorily integrated into its democracy."[56]

Making it even clearer to his white U.S. readers how he imagined that a national approach to Black Americans would help serve to solidify white Anglo-American rule both within and beyond the United States, Myrdal further predicted that "the coming difficult decades will be America's turn in the endless sequence of main actors on the world stage. . . . For perhaps several decades, the whites will still hold the lead, and America will be the most powerful white nation."[57] For such a "white nation" to maintain global domination, Myrdal calculated that it would need to prove its moral superiority, and ideally by treating Black Americans as white Americans would treat each other and, in the process, by assimilating Black Americans into white Anglo-American whiteness. To this point, Myrdal reasoned that *"America is free to choose whether the Negro shall remain her liability or become her opportunity."*[58] Myrdal called upon white Americans to demonstrate their moral sensibilities to a national and global audience, with a definition of racial equality leaving intact white

Anglo-American domination. In the process, he hoped to be offering white Anglo-Americans blueprints for further solidifying, rather than challenging, their leadership within and beyond the continental United States.

Considering his expectations for Myrdal's study, Keppel predictably celebrated Myrdal for centering white Americans and for arguing in favor of the global significance of the national study on Black Americans. Thus, in his preface to *An American Dilemma*, Keppel echoed Myrdal's own explanation of how the study had gained international importance during the span of the previous few years, noting that this was a time "when the eyes of men of all races the world over are turned upon us to see how the people of the most powerful of the United Nations are dealing *at home* with a major problem of race relations."[59] By addressing this "major problem" within the United States, both Keppel and Myrdal hoped to preserve the central place of the United States and its white allies on the global stage. Again, while Myrdal felt this sense of urgency particularly during the Second World War, Keppel long had harbored this anxiety about the frailty of white Anglo-American domination—and so too, international order along the color line—at least since the First World War.

By contrast to its effort to flatter and center white Americans, Gunnar Myrdal's *An American Dilemma* remained consistent in its negative portrayal of Black life, even beyond its theory of dynamic social causation and within Myrdal's definition of racial equality. Because his assimilationist vision of racial equality clearly required Black Americans to strip themselves of Blackness—that is, of anything that distinguished them from the habits, tastes, culture, and linguistic preferences of white Americans. To this point, Myrdal stressed in *An American Dilemma* that he and his team "assume that it is to the advantage of American Negroes as individuals and as a group to become assimilated into American culture, to acquire the traits held in esteem by the dominant white Americans."[60] By calling Black Americans to divorce themselves from Black identities, Myrdal proposed a national policy program on Black Americans that not only would be spearheaded by white Americans, but also would serve to reinforce the supremacy of whiteness and call for the disappearance of Blackness.

This was, indeed, Myrdal's long-term goal with his national policy program. Because as he reasoned in *An American Dilemma*, he was simply helping white Americans achieve, through means that they found morally acceptable, what they actually wanted to accomplish with Black Americans: their full eradication. Myrdal wrote in *An American Dilemma*: "If the Negroes could be eliminated from America or greatly decreased in numbers, this would meet the whites' approval—*provided that it could be accomplished by means which are also approved.*"[61] One such approved means, Myrdal explained, was the full as-similation of Black Americans into white U.S. life, to the point that Blackness ceased to exist: "Therefore, the dominant American valuation is that the Ne-gro should be eliminated from the American scene, but *slowly.*"[62]

As the following section highlights, this vision of white and Black Ameri-cans' coexistence in a white-dominated United States—and its assumption that racial equality in the United States would require Black Americans' full assimilation into a white "homogenous nation" and, relatedly, the erasure of Black identities—not only reflected Gunnar Myrdal's reading of white Ameri-cans' valuations, but also his and Alva Myrdal's earlier analysis of population quantity, quality, and nation-building in *Kris i befolkningsfrågan* (Crisis in the Population Question, 1934).[63]

## 3. White Domination and Black Subjection in Myrdal's Definition of Racial Equality

Engaging with debates on population quantity, quality, and nation-building in continental Europe in the 1930s, Alva and Gunnar Myrdal's *Kris i befolknings-frågan* begins with a description of economic theory. And in this section au-thored by Gunnar Myrdal, the Myrdals made clear that they situated their theory on ideal population sizes against that of the English scholar, Thomas Robert Malthus.

In the late eighteenth and early nineteenth centuries, Gunnar Myrdal ex-plained in *Kris*, Malthus had argued that there were limited resources on the earth, meaning that population growth threatened the existing public's qual-ity of life. While Malthus had been hesitant to suggest contraception, the En-glishman had recommended that people should marry later and try to have fewer children than they were having.[64] In a similar vein, Gunnar Myrdal re-counted in *Kris* that a subsequent generation of Malthusian scholars then warned fellow citizens that populations were becoming too numerous for the limited resources that humans could produce. However, unlike Malthus, Myrdal noted that contemporary Malthusians were much more vocal about condoning and promoting the use of contraception in an effort to limit fertil-ity rates. Among these proponents of contraception was, in fact, the famous American, Margaret Sanger, whose work spread across both continents.[65]

By contrast to Malthusians, who believed that humans needed to decrease fertility rates to maintain their quality of life, Gunnar Myrdal asserted that a balanced population size was more beneficial for these same purposes.[66] In *Kris*, Gunnar and Alva Myrdal argued that crafting a balanced population with sufficient numbers of productive citizens to support the unproductive citizens, such as children and the elderly, was more important than limiting the total population numbers.

In the case of Sweden, the Myrdals explained that Malthusians had been so successful in promoting delayed marriages and contraception that, as a consequence, the country suffered alarmingly low fertility rates. This low reproduction rate, the Myrdals argued, not only threatened the country's ability to support the future aging population, but also its existence as a cultural entity: as a "folk." With such low population numbers, the authors explained that other groups could immigrate into Sweden and overwhelm and threaten the dwindling Swedish population's ethnic identity.[67] Such immigrants, the couple wrote, "would signify the race's degeneration and mean 'racial suicide.' If the population size is reduced, the land would be flooded by immigrants of alien groups with high fertility rates. With their stronger reproduction rates, they could take over and transform our precious cultural heritage."[68] Because such migration would threaten the identity of their own population, Alva and Gunnar Myrdal argued that fellow Swedes could not rely on immigration to increase their population size. Instead, they suggested that Swedish citizens should expand the population by increasing their own fertility rates.

The authors were aware that young Swedish couples would not easily respond to this message. During the previous decade, many young Swedes had moved from the countryside to urban centers and did not necessarily want to give up the modern lives that they had established for themselves. Swedish women still wanted to work and when they married; they, like their husbands, were unwilling to make the financial sacrifices that having children represented. Put simply, the Myrdals in *Kris* noted that many young citizens chose not to have children because they represented significant financial burdens and lifestyle changes, especially in modern urban settings. If Sweden wanted to increase its fertility rates, the Myrdals argued that it would need to keep this kind of young couple in mind and create policies that limited the burdens of childrearing.

In the process of suggesting a national public policy initiative to increase fertility rates in Sweden, Alva and Gunnar Myrdal in *Kris* directly distinguished themselves from other contemporary population experts in Germany, Italy and France who they thought were merely interested in growing the population size irrespective of how childbearing and childrearing affected couples' quality of life. In *Kris*, the Myrdals thus explained that they were not only interested in expanding the *quantity* of the population, but also its *quality*. And in contemplating quality, they considered how childrearing affected parents.

To this point, the Myrdals asserted that potential young parents should neither be forced into parenthood nor should they be burdened with new financial responsibilities that decreased their quality of life. In this vein, the couple suggested that the state should promote the free exchange and use of contraception, ensure mothers' ability to retain their employment outside their homes, and provide services that covered the main costs associated with parenting. Specifically, they concluded that the Swedish state could cover living subsidies for families with children; free public nurseries, baby cribs, and kindergartens; free health services and free school lunch for all children; price reductions for necessary food items for children living at home; all costs for school materials (free school books and free school material, school transportation and school houses were needed); and, education stipends.[69]

Beyond parents' quality of life, the Myrdals acknowledged that the quality of the children they brought to the world mattered as well. These state benefits would ensure that Sweden's future children would be more educated and more physically healthy than previous generations. In other words, the couple argued in *Kris* that the way to improve the quality and quantity of the future generations of Swedes was to create public policies offering more robust public resources to parents and children alike. The Myrdals' policy proposals came to be, for many Swedes, the genesis of their modern welfare state.[70]

In providing their analyses of the best means for increasing the size and quality of the Swedish population, Alva and Gunnar Myrdal moreover were responding to contemporaneous discussions on the relative importance of hereditary characteristics and genetics for improving population quality, which famously defined Nazi Germany's population program at the time. In response to such conversations in continental Europe, the Myrdals thus argued that the "quality problem can be tackled thus, with studying individual differences in the population and finding to which degree those differences are hereditary or conditioned by the environment. . . . In the case of differences conditioned by the environment, one can of course change the population's quality by (in different ways) changing the environmental conditions for certain individuals."[71] Most differences among individuals, the Myrdals noted, were caused by the environment. And because of that, the couple argued in *Kris* that such distinctions could be remedied by changing the population's surroundings, such as improving living, health, and education standards.

In this section of *Kris* focusing on population quality, the Myrdals then paused to discuss the case of the mentally ill and mentally deficient, noting that "race biologists" and "social pedagogues" each had different reasons for sterilizing these individuals.

The Myrdals explained that race biologists asserted that the mentally ill and deficient should be sterilized because these traits could be passed on to their offspring, while social pedagogues argued that these mental characteristics limited these individuals' ability to parent. In reference to race biologists, the couple noted that "hereditary biologists have already made interesting and practically meaningful contributions and one has reason to expect more in the future."[72] However, the Myrdals were not ready to say that mental illnesses and deficiencies were necessarily passed on from parent to child. Instead, the authors of *Kris* concluded that individuals with such characteristics should be sterilized for the reasons social pedagogues listed. Gunnar and Alva Myrdal wrote: "More and more we come to meet for example, large broods of children with unmarried imbecile mothers, where the whole troop must be supported by the public and where their frequent associability and criminality in the future come to cause additional worry. That a number of those sorts of individuals are prevented from coming into the world leads to an important social relief, quite apart from the results these restrictions can bring about in the future population's quality."[73] Because the Myrdals assumed that these individuals' abilities to parent were limited, they concluded that the state should take the extra measure of sterilizing them. Similarly, other Swedes at the time supported sterilization on "eugenic, social, humanitarian and criminal" grounds, with the social grounds entailing "'first and foremost the situation where persons are psychologically or physically inferior to such a degree that they cannot, or are not suited to care for their children.'"[74] The Myrdals were thus part and parcel of conversations on eugenics in 1920s and 1930s Europe and, like some of the "social pedagogues" they described in *Kris*, supported the sterilization of the "mentally ill and deficient" on "social grounds."[75]

In fact, the Myrdals' engagement with discussions on eugenics would showcase itself in *An American Dilemma*. For example, and again under the assumption that the solution to the problem of Black Americans in the United States ultimately called for the erasure of Blackness, Gunnar Myrdal included a section in *An American Dilemma* titled, "The Case for Controlling the Negro Birth Rate."[76] Here, Myrdal analogized Black Americans to the "mentally ill and deficient" by arguing that many Black Americans are "so ignorant and so poor that they are not desirable parents and cannot offer their children a reasonably good home."[77] Taking for granted that no social policy "would be able to lift the standards of these people immediately," Myrdal supported "the argument for sterilization of destitute Negroes."[78] In this way, Myrdal in *An American Dilemma*—like the couple in *Kris*—justified eugenics on the grounds that certain people or certain groups of people were incapable of parenting well.

In *An American Dilemma*, however, Myrdal ultimately would push away from recommending sterilization as part of his proposed national program to solve the "Negro problem," if only because "such proposals, if they are made at all, are almost repugnant to the average white American in the South and the North as to the Negro."[79] Keeping in mind the values and perspectives of white Americans, while offering a national policy program that would align with white Americans' interest to decrease the visibility and presence of Blackness in the United States, Myrdal suggested instead greater access to birth control among Black Americans. "Until these reforms [passed by white Americans following their 'rank order of discriminations'] are carried out," Myrdal reasoned, "an extreme birth control program is warranted by reasons of individual and social welfare."[80] Myrdal in *An American Dilemma* thus embraced greater birth control access among Black Americans as one way to decrease population numbers among Black Americans and, thus, to erase the problem of Black Americans for white Americans; the problem being white Americans' moral dilemma in discriminating against and victimizing a population that they considered to be culturally, if not biologically, inferior.

And yet, *An American Dilemma* would focus even more heavily on Black Americans' assimilation into white U.S. life as principal means of erasing Blackness and, relatedly, Black Americans as a moral dilemma for white Americans. This dominant thread in *An American Dilemma*'s theory of social change also had roots in the Myrdals' analysis of population quality in *Kris*.

Later in their discussion of population quality in *Kris*, for example, Alva and Gunnar Myrdal suggested that the state should go about improving the quality and quantity of the population by ameliorating and equalizing Swedes' environments. To this point, they made clear that "social group differences" were irrelevant in discussions of population quality. And to illustrate this point, the Myrdals discussed class distinctions in Sweden and how the differences between these groups were caused by social rather than hereditary or genetic factors. In the case of intelligence, for example, the couple referred to a contemporary study of schoolchildren in England and noted that children of academics, doctors, lawyers, and writers scored higher than children of factory workers on intelligence tests. However, they explained these conclusions by noting that children of different social classes generally grew up differently.[81] They wrote: "Those children of intellectual workers have, from their very early ages, more intellectual training at home than is often granted the children of heavy work or wholesale traders."[82] This intelligence gap between poorer and more affluent children in England or in Sweden, the Myrdals reasoned, could be bridged if children were offered similar childhood benefits.

In the case of the higher classes' multi-generational affluence and success, Gunnar and Alva Myrdal noted that "the higher classes' children receive better upbringing, better education, they are accustomed to significant social security and know how to make use of personal connections."[83] That is, environmental factors such as childrearing, education, and friendships led the more affluent classes to perform better on intelligence exams and to be more successful and prosperous than the less affluent classes. There were no hereditary or genetic characteristics that made the lower socio-economic classes less intelligent, affluent, or successful.

In fact, Alva and Gunnar Myrdal in *Kris* explained that social group differences like these had no hereditary or genetic roots, explaining that "researchers do not support the hypothesis of the existence of socially significant character differences between social classes that are of hereditary quality."[84] Instead, as the Myrdals stressed, society created these distinctions. To this point, the authors wrote: "A social group is actually not (like an individual) a naturally given biological unit; but rather, created by social and institutional factors established and accumulated by highly different individuals."[85] If policymakers erased the social and institutional factors that maintained poor and lower class Swedes' inferiority, *Kris* emphasized, then these Swedes could achieve the same health and intelligence standards as the rest of the population.

In *Kris*, Alva and Gunnar Myrdal underscored that their claims about the root causes of social group differences reflected the findings of leading scholars across the globe.[86] And in this way, they furthermore noted that their examination of social group differences in Sweden applied in other corners of the world. The Myrdals wrote: "If blacks in America or Jews in Poland display certain average racial characteristics in their actions, by that it should be explained, that since childhood they had been branded, treated and had to react just as blacks in America or Jews in Poland."[87] Just as social and institutional environments were to blame for creating differences between more and less affluent Swedes, they reasoned in *Kris* that environmental factors largely were responsible for creating Black Americans' and Jews' own distinctions in their respective national societies. If Black Americans and "Jews in Poland" were not raised and treated as Black Americans or Jews, the Myrdals asserted, they could assimilate and achieve the same standards of their nations' dominant groups.

In *Kris*, Alva and Gunnar Myrdal mentioned Black Americans within the context of social group differences among Swedish citizens rather than in their discussion of immigrants. In other words, they viewed Black Americans to be Americans who had a rightful place in the U.S. folk in a way that "immigrants of alien groups," existing outside the Swedish national body, did not belong within the Swedish folk. And in this vein, they argued that the differences between white and Black Americans, like the differences between richer and poorer Swedes and Jews and non-Jews in Poland, could be erased in order to help these groups become part of the dominant national community.

From *Kris* to *An American Dilemma*, Gunnar Myrdal would remain consistent in his urgency that social group differences between Black and white Americans could be erased, and that this would mean ridding Black Americans of Blackness, much as it would mean ridding Jews of Jewishness in Poland and poorer Swedes of traits that the Myrdals associated with poverty in Sweden. Granted, much as in *Kris*, which discussed the possibility of eugenics among the "mentally ill and deficient," *An American Dilemma* would entertain the possibility of eugenics programs targeted at Black Americans, though only as a temporary measure for expediting the ultimate goal of decreasing the presence of Blackness and the societal ills Myrdal associated with Black people. Much like its discussion of Black Americans in *Kris*, *An American Dilemma* emphasized more strongly Black Americans' assimilation into white American life as the dominant key towards solving white Americans' moral dilemma in treating with violence and discrimination a group of Americans whom they perceived to be less desirable members of the white homogenous national body.

In embodying white Americans' sensibilities, Gunnar Myrdal furthermore incorporated in *An American Dilemma* his and Alva Myrdal's inclination in *Kris* to tailor their public policy recommendations to the values and interests of the demographic groups that they believed were key to realizing their policy goals. In *Kris*, he and Alva Myrdal had been sensitive to the preferences and values of young urban Swedish couples because it was this group of Swedes whom they had hoped to motivate to procreate at higher rates and, thus, to solve their country's declining population numbers. Similarly, in *An American Dilemma*, for example, Gunnar Myrdal would shy away from suggesting sterilization as an immediate means for addressing the problem of Black Americans' very existence in the United States, because it was counter to the values of white Americans, relying instead on Black Americans' gradual assimilation into white U.S. life as the principal solution to the problem.

Throughout *An American Dilemma*, and as this next section further highlights, Myrdal emphasized that he had taken into consideration the values of white Americans, and particularly those in the northern states and those working in the U.S. federal government, in shaping his analysis in the book. Because it was this group of white Americans who he thought could expedite his national policy program on Black Americans in the United States.

## 4. The Main White U.S. Audiences for *An American Dilemma*

Throughout *An American Dilemma*, Myrdal clarified that he was "motivated by an ambition to be realistic about the actual power relations in American society."[88] So while Myrdal acknowledged that he was writing a book *on* Black Americans in the United States, he did not write a book *for* Black Americans. Writing this final report between 1941 and 1942, he stressed that his target audience would be white Americans, and particularly those with the most political and economic power in the country: white northerners and New Dealers in Washington, D.C. Not only were they more sympathetic to Black Americans than other groups of white Americans, as Myrdal had deduced during his years in the United States, and thus more likely to respond to his moralistic means for seducing white people into action in *An American Dilemma*, but this "dominant white majority" held "practically all the economic, social, and political power" in the country.[89]

By underscoring the particular relevance of white Anglo-Americans in the northern United States and those working within the U.S. federal government, Myrdal was far from being a disinterested observer of existing power dynamics in the United States. Rather, at a personal level, he looked at these white Americans' increased national power with some satisfaction. As director of Carnegie Corporation's study between 1938 and 1942, Myrdal had witnessed how public control in the United States had been moving from local governments to state governments and from states to the federal government. And this centralization of government was a positive thing, Myrdal explained in *An American Dilemma*, because "a capable and uncorrupted bureaucracy, independent in its work except for the laws and regulations passed by the legislatures and the continuous control by legislators and executives, is as important for the efficient working of a modern democracy as is the voter's final word on the general direction of this administration."[90] Not only was a central government more efficient, capable, and less corrupt than local and state governments, according to Myrdal, but their employees were thus fairer to Black Americans.[91]

During this era of economic depression and increasing centralization of state power in the United States, Myrdal also detected that the federal government controlled the South. This was an observable fact during the depression when the South had accepted the federal government's New Deal legislation and federally-led social reform, including the Farm Security Administration and its local health programs.[92] Myrdal noted: "Apart from the fact of party allegiance, the South was actually too poor to scorn systematically the gifts of national charity, even if the price to be paid was the acceptance of social legislation and organized social reform."[93] Myrdal acknowledged that New Deal legislation and reform still discriminated against Black Americans, but he also reasoned that these initiatives undermined to some extent the more hard-line forms of white supremacy and Black subjection supported by white southerners. To this point, he argued that the federal presence in the South already was undermining practices of white domination in the region, by providing services both to white and Black Americans. As examples of such New Deal agents in the southern United States, Myrdal included "the relief administrator, the county farm agent, the Farm Security supervisor, the home demonstration agent, and the doctors and nurses of local health programs."[94]

Observing power dynamics between the North and South and between the New Deal government and the South, Myrdal predicted in *An American Dilemma* that white northerners and the U.S. federal government would be able to push forward more egalitarian national policies on Black Americans than white southerners might want to embrace, and that much as it did during the Depression, the South would have no other choice but to accept the federal government's policies. For starters, Myrdal noted that the South was poor and in need of federal assistance.[95] To this point, Myrdal wrote in *An American Dilemma*: "If, in the main, the New Deal has to deal tactfully with Southern congressmen, the latter cannot afford to break off entirely from the New Deal either. . . . In this way Southern political conservatism as a whole, and even on the race point, has to retreat and compromise."[96] As Myrdal saw it, this poor and depressed region of the United States would not risk losing the federal government's assistance.

During the span of the project, that is, Myrdal retained his focus on white Americans as key change agents in the country. Specifically, he became convinced that a national coordination of public policies on Black Americans would incorporate the active participation of northern whites and the U.S. federal government. Keppel seemed to agree, if not with Myrdal's emphasis on white northerners, with Myrdal's insistence that the U.S. federal government had a critical role to play in incorporating a national program on Black Americans. To this point, Keppel had cautioned Myrdal to remain attentive to the 1940 national election before drafting policy recommendations on Black Americans. For both Keppel and Myrdal, a national coordination of public policies on Black Americans would not simply call for white policymakers across governments in the United States to learn from each other and harmonize their respective local, state, and regional policies, but also beckon the participation and guidance of the U.S. federal government.

And yet, during the writing stage of the project, Myrdal and Keppel did maintain one major disagreement: it concerned Myrdal's insistence in the final report that white southerners were not crucial for realizing a national policy program on Black people.

## 5. Keppel's Concerns about Myrdal's Centering of White Northerners and New Dealers at the Expense of the White South

During the first two years of the study, from 1938 to 1940, Frederick Keppel had remained mindful of GEB associate director Jackson Davis's criticism that Myrdal had proven to be, throughout his trip to the South in the fall of 1938, rather insensitive to white southerners' particular commitments to white supremacy and Black subordination.[97] As Keppel perceived at the time, no national policy program on Black Americans was then possible without the support of white southerners, who dominated the U.S. Congress. But Davis and Keppel found comfort from the fact that Myrdal himself realized that "he knew nothing about the situation and that he wanted now to read and study and think through his own plans before taking any further steps in the field." Thus, they agreed that it would "be best to say nothing further about" Myrdal's lack of understanding of the white South.[98]

Then in 1939, Myrdal did another tour of the South, this time with Black political scientist and fellow research staff member, Ralph Bunche. And once again, Myrdal would find himself brushing up against white southern sensibilities, with such news reaching Carnegie Corporation's office in New York City. Keppel's assistant, Charles Dollard, noted in his records that in 1939 Myrdal and Bunche had "left Georgia rather hurriedly after being advised that an Atlanta woman, with whom he had had a conference, had gotten out a warrant for [Myrdal]."[99] Historian Walter Jackson notes that, in Georgia, Myrdal had visited the home of a "fanatical white supremacist, Mrs. Andrews . . . after listening to a long tirade about the evils of miscegenation and the lust of Negro men, he asked her if she was aware of psychological theories that people with such sexual phobias secretly desired that which they professed to abhor."[100] Once the woman became aware of Myrdal's suggestion, she ushered him out of her house and subsequently "called the police and had a warrant sworn out against Myrdal for indecent language."[101]

When this news reached Keppel, he decided to meet with Myrdal over lunch in New York City, hoping to assess the director's general grasp of white southerners' perspectives on Black Americans and "race relations."[102] Keppel recorded in his notes that he had been comforted by Myrdal's analysis of the situation, with the director showing a "real grasp of the mentality and attitude of the southern white in connection with the Negro."[103]

Keppel's level of deference to and patience with Myrdal's analysis of white southerners, however, would change during the writing stage of the study. Then both Keppel and Dollard would play more active roles as critical advisers on the project. From Princeton, New Jersey, Myrdal would mail draft chapters to the two men in New York City, and both Keppel and Dollard routinely and continuously would respond with their joint comments.[104] At first, Keppel and Dollard eased into their roles as editors by suggesting, rather than commanding, changes in the manuscript. Writing to Myrdal in November of 1941, for example, Dollard was rather circumspect about his and Keppel's reactions to his latest chapter drafts: "Many of your statements inevitably tend to alienate some of the good people on both sides of the Mason and Dixon line who were helpful to you in the course of the study, it might be well for you to say plainly in your introduction that in a job of this kind complete honesty involved the author in the risk of losing friends. This won't heal all the wounds, but it may reduce the bleeding."[105] Subsequently, however, Keppel's anxiety persisted, and by the summer of 1942, his instructions became all the more direct. Rather than using Dollard as messenger, and reflecting the importance he placed on this message, Keppel ultimately decided to write directly to Myrdal.

Thus, in July 1942, Keppel followed up on a letter Dollard had written to Myrdal, stressing to Myrdal: "You and [Dollard] can fight it out as to most of his suggestions without help from me, though I will make one exception, and that is to back Dollard about the inherent dangers of over-emphasizing the Woman-Negro analogy in Chapter 4, and I would also suggest that you give special consideration to his comments and suggestions on Chapter 20."[106] The fourth chapter's analysis on the "Woman-Negro analogy" was a segment of the book that Gunnar and Alva Myrdal seemed to have written in greater collaboration, with its final citation referring to a chapter of Alva's then-recently published *Nation and Family* (1941), the U.S. adaptation of *Kris i befolknings-frågan* (1934).[107] Complying with Keppel's concerns, Gunnar Myrdal ejected the "Woman-Negro analogy" from the chapter draft and relegated it to a fifth appendix of the manuscript.

In this "Appendix 5: A Parallel to the Negro Problem," Myrdal's *An American Dilemma* includes negative descriptions of white southerners which clearly did not please Keppel. But if this had been the extent of the problem for Keppel with the "Woman-Negro analogy," he likely would have suggested for

Myrdal simply to rethink his description of the antebellum South as "conservative and increasingly antiquarian," or his decision to include a quotation from former first lady of the United States Dolley Madison that the "the Southern wife was 'the chief slave of the harem.'"[108] But as Keppel realized while reading chapter drafts in 1942, such editorial decisions would do little to save Myrdal's central take-away from the analogy—that "an especially close relation in the South [existed] between the subordination of women and that of Negroes"—which would directly challenge white southerners' image of "southern white ladyhood" as particularly "pure," and thus, antithetical to the status of Black people.[109]

When faced with his funder's disapproval, Myrdal moved the analysis of the race-sex analogy to an appendix, rather than simply deleting it. But by placing it well in the depths of the second volume starting on page 1,073, he also acquiesced to Keppel's demand that it remain outside the body of his central manuscript, and thus, increase the chances that white southern readers might miss these slights in the manuscript.[110]

Keppel and Dollard also found fault with Myrdal's draft of chapter twenty. In his letter to Myrdal, Dollard suggested to Myrdal that he "should be careful not to overplay [his] first-hand acquaintance with the South with Southerners—and especially not [to] use [his] own limited experience as the basis for broad generalizations."[111] Without access to this earlier draft of chapter twenty, it remains unclear the extent to which Myrdal responded to his funders' criticisms. What is clear is that in its final form, Myrdal did not shy away from a critical view of the South. Thus, he began that chapter of *An American Dilemma* by noting that he would "concentrate on the South, not only because this region contains the great majority of the Negro people, but because the South is the only region where Negro suffrage is a problem."[112] From there, he went on to describe "Southern conservative illegality" in their long-standing and violent efforts to disenfranchise Black southerners and, more generally, their "opportunistic disrespect for law, order and public morals."[113]

Years later, Myrdal recalled Keppel's two main anxieties about his final report as he drafted it between 1941 and 1942, echoing the very tensions they shared in correspondence during the project's writing stage: "I remember two things where he was eager. One was that he was very disturbed that I called the direction in the South—that it was illegal; that they were illegalists. And he said those were very harsh words . . . The other point was this, I had a section where I made a parallel to the Negro problem from the woman's problem. And that made him, I remember he was very sad about that . . . That section I reworked and now it was an Appendix 5."[114] For those readers of *An*

*American Dilemma* simply reading the main sections of the book and gleaning from it the book's main argument, as Keppel likely hoped they would, these sections critical of white southerners might remain unread. These portions of the text were tucked away in the depths of the two-volume manuscript.

## 6. Keppel Channels His Lingering Anxiety in *An American Dilemma*'s Foreword

In the summer of 1942, just as Gunnar Myrdal was preparing to return to Sweden, leaving behind his final report, Keppel shared with his successor at Carnegie Corporation, Walter Jessup, his reservations about Myrdal's portrayal of white southerners and wondered whether the foundation should request that a leading white southerner review the manuscript before publication.

Communicating his own goals and expectations for the study, Keppel reasoned to Jessup: "A phrase here and there could rouse men who might otherwise be of help to such fury that they would become incapable of finding any good whatever in the report, and would work actively to prevent its exerting any influence in the south."[115] If white southerners took offence to the study, Keppel calculated that his expectations that it would arouse a national policy program on Black Americans would be undermined. Underscoring the significance of his comments, Keppel admitted to Jessup that he and Dollard had already "been on alert to catch instances where this has happened, and Myrdal has been very generous in adopting the changes we have suggested. But we are none of us Southerners, and the question arises whether, as a measure of insurance to the Corporation no less than in the interest of the report itself, it might not be wise to have someone of southern birth and background read the ms. with this question of southern susceptibilities constantly in mind."[116] No longer president of the foundation, Keppel only went so far as to advise his successor, concluding his letter with the suggestion that he was "rather incline[d] toward our taking" the decision to commission a white southern reader.[117] In the end, though, Jessup thought that the corporation should refrain from taking this extra step, because it would undermine Keppel's own initial idea of commissioning a "fresh mind" to analyze Black Americans in the United States.[118]

And yet, as Jessup likely knew, Keppel had been less invested in some opaque concept of a "fresh mind" when selecting the U.S. director than he had been in ensuring that such an individual could provide a viable national policy plan on Black Americans. Remaining anxious about the white South's perception of the project, Keppel chose to use the foreword that he was drafting for

*An American Dilemma* to appeal to this group of Americans, and thus, to increase the chances that the project would achieve his policy goal.

Completed in December 1942, Keppel began this foreword to *An American Dilemma* by describing the role of foundations in the United States. Though Americans usually associated these organizations with "gifts for endowment and buildings to universities, colleges and other cultural and scientific institutions, and to a lesser degree with the financial support of fundamental research," Keppel underscored that they did from time to time finance comprehensive studies.[119] The difficulty here was explaining why Carnegie Corporation would sponsor such a project as Myrdal's without there having been any particular demand for it in the United States. Part of Keppel's strategy was to generalize. Thus, he pointed out that, sometimes there were "problems which face the American people, and sometimes mankind in general, which call for studies upon a scale too broad for any single institution or association to undertake."[120]

He also deflected his own role in the project by focusing on Newton Baker as the originator of the study and, in doing so, emphasized Baker's southern roots. Baker, he wrote, had been the "son of a Confederate officer, attended the Episcopal Academy in Virginia and the Law School of Washington and Lee University, and spent the greater part of his early years in the Border states of West Virginia and Maryland."[121] In effect, Keppel was trying to portray Baker to white southerners as one of their own and characterize the report as having southern roots. From this, such readers presumably would conclude that they should read the book with an open mind.

In this foreword to *An American Dilemma*, Keppel also explained why Gunnar Myrdal had been selected to lead the project. Omitting mention of Gunnar and Alva Myrdal's prior work in "crime and disorder" and national public policy planning in response to the population problem in Sweden—which was in fact what had attracted Keppel and his board—Keppel described Gunnar Myrdal as someone who had "achieved an international reputation as a social economist, a professor in the University of Stockholm, economic adviser to the Swedish Government, and a member of the Swedish Senate."[122] After describing Myrdal's task as director of the U.S. project, Keppel stopped once again to appeal to white southern readers rather directly.

In view of those sections of *An American Dilemma* that remained critical of the white South, Keppel underscored the global significance of the project during the Second World War. He also noted that any "freshness" and "piquancy" in the manuscript's prose was due to the fact that Myrdal did not have full command of the English language. Keppel thus suggested to white southern readers of *An American Dilemma* that they should focus on Myrdal's general arguments in the book. And indeed, Myrdal's general message in *An American Dilemma*—which pleased Keppel—was that white Americans were a moral and egalitarian people who would come together to craft a national program on Black Americans: a national program promoting Black Americans' assimilation into white American life following white Americans' rank order of priorities in white domination and Black subordination. It was a policy program completely in the hands of white Americans, with a seemingly empathetic lens on improving the lived conditions of Black Americans to standards enjoyed by white Americans. As Myrdal stressed in the book, this assimilationist national policy program on Black Americans would only help strengthen, rather than challenge, the United States as a "powerful white nation."[123] Relatedly, and as Myrdal further underscored in the book, this national effort would help fortify and justify white Anglo-American domination on the global stage.[124]

Since Frederick Keppel passed away just two years after his retirement and before the publication of *An American Dilemma* (1944), he never had the chance to see whether the project achieved these goals. The next chapter explores the extent to which it did so.

## CHAPTER 10

# A Bound English-Speaking White World
## Solidifying International Order along the Color Line

When *An American Dilemma* came out in print in 1944, Gunnar Myrdal already had settled back in Stockholm. Reelected to the Swedish Senate and appointed to chair a commission on postwar economic planning, created in anticipation of a postwar Europe, he had moved on to other policy topics in Sweden and remained relatively divorced from U.S. conversations on Black Americans which he himself had helped inspire.

In the United States *An American Dilemma* would have considerable impact, and not least among key policy figures in Washington, D.C., who had cooperated with Myrdal and his research team. These included First Lady Eleanor Roosevelt, Supreme Court Justice Felix Frankfurter, and President Harry S. Truman. Within this network of national policymakers, others too played a part in promoting *An American Dilemma*. Beyond such national public policy circles, *An American Dilemma* also gained popularity among a broader U.S. public. Building upon the endorsement of former collaborators and Carnegie Corporation staff and board members, along with the visibility privileged to such a high-profile study financed over the span of several years by one of the wealthiest philanthropic organizations in the world, newspapers and magazine across the country promoted, discussed, and reviewed Gunnar Myrdal's two-volume book.

While the introduction to this book includes an overview of the general U.S. reception of *An American Dilemma*, this concluding chapter specifically analyzes the national and international impact of *An American Dilemma* through the lens of former Carnegie Corporation president Keppel's expectations for the study. It argues that *An American Dilemma* moderately achieved Keppel's immediate goal of inspiring white American policymakers across regions of the United States to come together and follow Myrdal's proposed national policy program on Black Americans: the "white man's rank order of discriminations." Inspired by their commitment to the American Creed, Myrdal suggested that white Americans could tackle this list, which prioritized the forms of white supremacy least critical for white Americans and, thus, start the work of assimilating Black Americans into all aspects of white U.S. life.

That said, *An American Dilemma* largely failed to achieved Keppel's ultimate expectation that it would help to bring greater stability to white Anglo-
American rule within (and outside) the United States. This was not simply, as
this chapter explains, because white southerners ultimately resisted Myrdal's
policy blueprint (as they did) but, more deeply, because Keppel's idea for national and international order along the color line aimed to hold off the unavoidable: Black people's direct resistance to white rule and Black oppression.
In the latter half of the twentieth century, such Black resistance movements
would come to the fore—from Black Power in the United States and Black
Consciousness in South Africa to anticolonialism throughout Africa—and
they would underscore President Keppel's naivete in the 1920s and 1930s that
white policymakers, assisted by social science studies, could free white
Anglo-American rule across the Atlantic from its inherent fragility as a model
of international order based on the privileging of white Anglo-Americans and
the suppression of Black people.

The chapter begins with a description of *An American Dilemma*'s reception
in U.S. policy circles.


## 1. Moderately Achieving Keppel's Immediate National Policy Goals

In 1944, the Public Affairs Committee in the United States produced a thirty-
two-page pamphlet of *An American Dilemma*, authored by Maxwell S. Stewart.
Launched in 1937, the Public Affairs Pamphlets—a collaborative project between the Public Affairs Committee, the U.S. Office of Education, and the
American Library Association—circulated summaries of works confronting
"major present day economic and social problem[s]," thus presenting "millions of dollars of research in only 32 pages, illustrated with drawings, picto-
graphs and charts."[1] By 1945, the *Journal of Education* underscored that "over
nine million Public Affairs Pamphlets [had] been distributed since the Public
Affairs Committee was formed in 1935. During the first seven months of 1945
the Committee received orders for almost two million of these bright-colored
pamphlets, issued monthly."[2] The committee's chair was Ordway Tead, president of the Board of Higher Education in New York City, and its vice-chair,
Harry Gideonse, economist and president of Brooklyn College.

An early reviewer of Maxwell S. Stewart's summary, titled *The Negro in
America* (1944), urged fellow Americans to access this synthesis: "Where
[Myrdal's] volumes are not accessible, the present summary deserves careful

reading, if only to sharpen the sensibilities of a nation which now makes high professions among the peoples of the earth against the doctrine of a superior race while it practices at home a consonant form of behavior with respect to the negro tenth of its population."[3] Similarly, over sixty-five glowing reviews of Gunnar Myrdal's *An American Dilemma* were published in U.S. newspapers and magazines during its first year in press, and the lengthy study went through four editions in just its first year. It is from this broader cultural context too that the study's impact in 1940s and 1950s Washington, D.C., should be understood.

In 1946, President Truman issued an executive order creating the President's Committee on Civil Rights, and, in 1947, the committee published its report, *To Secure These Rights.*[4] Like Gunnar Myrdal, Truman's Committee on Civil Rights noted the important role that the federal government could play in expediting Myrdal's call for white Americans to bridge their egalitarian values with their behavior and public policies on Black Americans, writing that the "National Government of the United States must take the lead in safeguarding the civil rights of all Americans."[5] The committee members had faith that the federal apparatus, including the United States Supreme Court, could expedite social change.[6] And throughout its report, the committee echoed Myrdal's characterization of Black Americans' status in the United States as a moral dilemma. To this point, the committee described U.S. ideals of freedom and equality and, within the context of civil rights, explained "how far short [Americans] have fallen in living up to the ideals" of the country.[7]

Leaning on various elements of Gunnar Myrdal's thesis in *An American Dilemma*, Truman's civil rights committee posited that white Americans confronted a moral tension in their treatment of minority groups, and particularly in relation to Black Americans. In this vein, the committee argued that white Americans wanted to correct the gulf between their ideals and their practices and that they should feel empowered and emboldened to use the federal government as a means of bringing national policies in line with these ideals.[8]

Providing a list of national policy recommendations, U.S. president Truman's civil rights committee further imitated *An American Dilemma*. It matched, for example, Gunnar Myrdal's "white man's rank order of discriminations," which he had created with an eye toward first addressing the forms of discrimination that white Americans found least threatening to white supremacy. On this point, Truman's committee members first proposed that the federal government should rectify discrimination within the judicial system and governmental agencies, and then in the franchise. Quite tellingly, the committee's list of public policy recommendations omitted the very last category of key forms of white supremacy in the United States that Myrdal had

mentioned in his rank order of discriminations, and thus the most threatening to white Americans: "the bar against intermarriage and sexual intercourse
involving white women."[9] Cautioned by the Swedish author's research of
white American preferences, Truman's civil rights committee presented to
the U.S. public what it likely perceived to be a reasonable and realistic list of
federal reform recommendations on civil rights that white Americans would
embrace.

That said, Truman's report—and its digestion of *An American Dilemma*—
did not lead to immediate national public policy changes in the U.S. Congress. As historian Steven F. Lawson writes: "The problem was not so much
that conservative Republicans were in control of the Eightieth Congress, but
that powerful southern Democrats could block attempts to pass legislation
by undertaking a filibuster in the Senate, the graveyard of civil rights bills."[10]
Rather, Myrdal's book would have its most visible and concrete national policy impact some years later when the U.S. Supreme Court cited it in its school
desegregation case, *Brown v. Board of Education* (1954).

In *Brown*, the U.S. Supreme Court cited Myrdal's study as a means of justifying its decision to sidestep binding legal precedent established in *Plessy v.
Ferguson* (1896), which held that "separate-but-equal" public schools for Black
and white children satisfied the Constitution's Equal Protection Clause. Citing social science studies (with a "see generally" to Myrdal's *An American Dilemma*), the U.S. Supreme Court argued that recent scientific knowledge
illustrated how racially separate schooling was inherently unequal and, thus,
that state laws mandating or enforcing racial segregation in public education
were necessarily unconstitutional. This was indeed a pathbreaking Supreme
Court decision and, years later, both Carnegie Corporation and Americans at
large would signal the importance of *An American Dilemma* by referencing its
citation in *Brown*.

And yet, as much as these two moments in national political life illustrate
the political significance of *An American Dilemma*, the study failed to achieve
Keppel's goal of bringing white Americans together across the country to
pass a holistic national policy program on Black Americans. And indeed,
Myrdal had illustrated to white American readers how they could achieve
Keppel's goals: by correcting their behavior and public policies on Black
Americans to meet their national egalitarian ideals. And they could start this
process by engaging the U.S. federal government to follow the "white man's
rank order of discriminations," thus beginning with those forms of anti-Black
behaviors and public policies in which white Americans felt least invested
and threatened. To this point, Myrdal had relayed in *An American Dilemma*

that white Americans were more wedded to maintaining a "bar against inter-marriage and sexual intercourse involving white women," for example, than in preserving anti-Black discrimination in "land, credit, jobs, or other means of earning a living."[11] In practice, though, *An American Dilemma* most directly inspired the U.S. government—and specifically the U.S. Supreme Court—to address racial segregation in public schools, which Myrdal ranked third in his list of six forms of discriminatory public policies with which white Americans would find most difficult to part.

At one level, the inability of *An American Dilemma* to inspire the necessary cohesion among white U.S. policymakers to execute its list of proposed na-tional public policy reforms could be rationalized by the fact that white Americans did not dutifully follow Myrdal's "white man's rank order of dis-criminations," which he had tailored to ease white Americans into Black Americans' full assimilation into white U.S. life. Beyond that, it also could be rationalized by white southerners' own resistance to Myrdal's text, a resis-tance that materialized much later than Keppel had expected for the project and for reasons beyond Myrdal's decision to include in *An American Dilemma* peppered criticisms of the white South. In fact, it would have much to do with the project's impact in Washington, D.C., and specifically in *Brown v. Board of Education*: a case that, as historian Mary Dudziak explains, the U.S. Supreme Court decided against the backdrop of a Cold War, which by 1947, "came to dominate the American political scene."[12]

During these Cold War years pitting the United States against the Soviet Union, Dudziak writes: "'McCarthyism' took hold in domestic politics. If communism was such a serious threat world-wide, the existence of commu-nists within the United States seemed particularly frightening. As the nation closed ranks, critics of American society often found themselves labeled as 'subversive.'"[13] In this vein, some leading U.S. policymakers, most promi-nently U.S. senator Joseph McCarthy, worked towards ridding the domestic United States of communist influences, with socialism considered by such Americans to be a close cousin of communism. In this spirit, foundations and their support for the social sciences came under scrutiny in the U.S. Congress in the 1950s, if only for their international reach and ties with social reform.

In 1954, for example, and following up on the U.S. House of Representa-tives Select Committee to Investigate Foundations and Other Organizations (the "Cox Committee"), which concluded with little fanfare the prior year, Congress commenced yet another investigation of foundation practices. Re publican representative B. Carroll Reece argued that the previous committee had not had enough time to conduct a thorough investigation of subversive activities at these organizations, and their use of funds for political purposes, propaganda, or attempts to influence legislation.[14] Reflecting the "paranoia about the internal Communist threat" in the United States, a paranoia then inflamed by U.S. senator Joe McCarthy, who had launched a series of "highly publicized probes into alleged Communist penetration of the State Department" between 1950 and 1954," the Reece Committee scrutinized private foundations' funding of the social sciences. From Reece's perspective, empirical social science was ungodly in its obedience to data collection and, more broadly, any of the social sciences that went beyond condoning the status quo was suspect and, thus, possibly sympathetic to communism, and by extension the Soviet Union.[15] Equally so, according to the committee's logic, the funders of such social science research also were suspect, especially since they financed projects in these fields with "foreigners" and through institutions based outside of the United States.

The Reece Committee thus called foundation leaders to defend their grant-making practices in the social sciences and international relations: all topics that for the Reece Committee might suggest sympathy with internationalism, social reform and, thus, with communism. In response to these accusations, leaders at the Rockefeller, Carnegie, and Ford Foundations wrote defenses of their funding practices.[16] For example, the current Carnegie Corporation president Charles Dollard (former assistant to Keppel who took the helm at the Corporation between 1948 and 1955, succeeding most immediately Devereux C. Josephs and Walter Jessup) declared in a statement to the Reece Committee that Americans long had found value in the social sciences and that their interest in these fields likely would not subside.[17] Far from funding "un-American" research, Carnegie Corporation argued that it was funding research that Americans respected.

Beyond these broad accusations, the Reece Committee also had specific charges against certain projects that the foundations had taken on throughout the years, and Gunnar Myrdal's *An American Dilemma* was prominently mentioned among them.[18] Earlier that year, the *Brown* Court had cited *An American Dilemma*, and critics of school desegregation then took particular notice of the book. And they subsequently attacked Gunnar Myrdal and the social sciences more generally for being foreign and, thus, suspect as intellectual influences in the United States.[19] These U.S. commentators, like those on the Reece Committee, largely blamed the U.S. Supreme Court justices for relying on the social sciences rather than, as they argued, legal precedent such as the "separate-but-equal" doctrine established in *Plessy* to decide the constitutionality of racially segregated public schools in the United States.

After *Brown*, Gunnar Myrdal's study became a flashpoint for white segregationists and radical conservatives in the South. Historian David Southern explains that these white southerners paid little attention to *An American Dilemma* before *Brown*. But after the Supreme Court decision, and playing into Cold War politics at the time, they promoted an image of Myrdal as a "diabolical foreigner who worked inside the international communist conspiracy to subvert Anglo-Saxon America."[20] Likewise, the Reece Committee regarded *An American Dilemma* as being overly critical of the United States and accused its author of being a socialist. The Reece Committee also questioned Carnegie Corporation's intentions for undertaking the study and for selecting a "foreigner" for the project.[21]

At the invitation of the Reece Committee, Carnegie Corporation president Charles Dollard and Russell Leffingwell, chair of Carnegie Corporation's board, prepared written testimony; "a sixty-eight-page document [that] reviewed the history of the foundation."[22] After the material was sent to the committee, scholar Patricia Rosenfield writes that "the Corporation was soon informed that there would be no public hearings; Dollard and the trustees were never called to testify."[23] In fact, Rosenfield explains that the "commission never formally published its report, the recommendations were never adopted, and there was no follow-up legislation."[24]

For his part, Dollard published Carnegie Corporation's testimony, if only as means to ensure that the U.S. public had access to the organization's response to allegations from the Reece Committee. In this published public statement, Dollard first confronted the committee's accusation that Myrdal had been "consistently and bitterly critical of everything American."[25] Without mentioning Gunnar Myrdal's dispersed criticisms of white southerners in the manuscript, which he and Keppel had tried to tame, Dollard focused on the committee's criticism that Myrdal had embraced Charles Beard's *An Economic Interpretation of the Constitution of the United States* (1913). Leaning on this text, Dollard admitted that Myrdal had described the Declaration of Independence as a document crafted by "property consciousness and designed as a defense against the democratic spirit let loose during the Revolution."[26] However, Dollard continued reading from *An American Dilemma*, emphasizing that Myrdal had complimented the U.S. Constitution as a document which "provided for the most democratic state structure in existence anywhere in the world at that time."[27] With a series of quotations directly from *An American Dilemma*, Dollard argued to the Reece Committee, and equally to all other Americans reading the published statement, that Gunnar Myrdal in fact had a "profound respect for America and Americans."[28]

In response to claims that Myrdal was a "foreigner" and "socialist," Dollard admitted that Myrdal indeed was born in Sweden and remained a Swedish citizen, so his foreign identity could not be denied. That said, Dollard also urged the committee to question whether those making such accusations "would similarly dismiss Lord Bryce and de Tocqueville, two other foreign-born scholars, who helped America to see its problems in new perspectives and to understand and appreciate its own greatness."[29]

As far as Myrdal's membership with the Social Democratic Party in Sweden, Dollard explained that socialism meant different things in the two countries. While the Swedish state indeed provided social services beyond those of the U.S. state, Dollard noted that as in the United States "production and distribution of goods are still almost entirely in private hands. Sweden's economy remains a private enterprise economy."[30] Much like the United States and unlike the Soviet Union, Dollard made clear that Sweden had a robust private sector and, thus, was a capitalist society.

Dismissing any problem with Myrdal's identity as a Social Democrat and a foreigner, Dollard then explained why former Carnegie Corporation president Frederick Keppel had, in the words of the committee, sought a "foreign scholar" and why Keppel ultimately decided on "a Swedish scholar." To answer this question, Dollard quoted from Keppel's foreword to *An American Dilemma*. As already noted, Keppel here sidestepped his own central role as architect of the study and simply echoed his own letter of invitation to Gunnar Myrdal, where he emphasized the need for a fresh mind to analyze Black Americans in the United States.[31]

In the Reece Committee's final report, director of research Norman Dodd continued to chastise Carnegie Corporation for funding *An American Dilemma* and put blame on the organization for the author's thesis. Condemning the organization, Dodd wrote: "While this refers to but one project out of many, it becomes significant when it is realized that the project to which these books relate involves some $250,000, and led to the publication of statements which were most critical of our Constitution."[32] Referring to the two-volume study written by Myrdal and financed by Carnegie Corporation, Dodd was thus suggesting that Myrdal was not the only one recommending the acceleration of racial desegregation; so was the organization that had commissioned and expended so much money for the project.

However, little did these critics of school desegregation and *An American Dilemma* know, Keppel had commissioned the study precisely in order to bring stability to, rather than to challenge, white domination in the United States. Even more, Myrdal had written a final report complementary to Keppel's goals. This is to say that, in ways difficult for Keppel to have foreseen, *An American Dilemma* would be forever associated with a U.S. Supreme Court decision pitting white Americans in the federal government against white southern resisters.

By the mid-to-late 1950s, it would have become clear to anyone privy to Keppel's hopes for *An American Dilemma* that the project was falling short of this former foundation president's immediate hopes that it would help bring together white American policymakers across regions to achieve a holistic national public policy program on Black Americans. Relatedly, *An American Dilemma* also largely would fall short of Keppel's expectations that it would help white U.S. policymakers stabilize white domination in the country or help solidify white Anglo-American domination at the global level.

Beginning with *An American Dilemma*'s role at the international level, the next section describes its critical reception in 1960s United States and how these critics were writing against the backdrop of the Black Power movement in the United States, the Black Consciousness movement in South Africa, and anticolonialism throughout Africa. As this next section underscores, *An American Dilemma* failed to achieve Keppel's ultimate national and international expectations for it, not simply or largely because white U.S. policymakers failed to embrace fully the study's list of public policy goals under the "white man's rank order of discriminations" but, more deeply, because it was a project whose definition of racial equality assumed white Anglo-American domination and Black subjection, and was thus destined to meet resistance from Black people. Ultimately too, and for similar reasons, Keppel's two other cooperative studies on the social sciences would fail to achieve their intended regional and international goals.

## 2. Keppel's Vision for National and International Order Confronts Inherent Limitations

Beyond the Reece Committee members, and much like the U.S. Supreme Court justices in *Brown*, some U.S. policymakers in the 1950s maintaining an eye towards the global image of the United States generally embraced *An American Dilemma* as a potentially useful tool for fostering a more positive image of white Americans at the international level.[33] "Public relations exigencies of the Cold War," historian Carol Anderson writes, "called for sanitizing and camouflaging the reality of America's Jim Crow democracy."[34] With its positive portrayal of white Americans as a people eager to confront their discriminatory treatment of Black Americans, such U.S. policymakers reasoned that *An American Dilemma* could play a part in convincing people around the world that the United States was a racially egalitarian country and, thus, that the United States could counter the Soviet Union's prominent use of the "race issue" in "anti-American propaganda."[35]

To this point, historian Penny M. Von Eschen writes that the United States Information Service (USIS), located in the Gold Coast, Nigeria, Kenya, and South Africa, "attempted to project positive images of black American life. Drawing on the economist Gunnar Myrdal's *An American Dilemma*, the State Department developed a clear strategy that acknowledged that discrimination existed but hastened to add that racism was a fast disappearing aberration, capable of being overcome by a talented and motivated individual."[36]

Guided by *An American Dilemma*'s emphasis on the power of behavioral changes at the individual level to effect societal change and Myrdal's emphasis on white Americans as a particularly moral people who would urgently address the gap between their national egalitarian ideals and anti-Black discrimination, the U.S. government in the 1950s was earnest in its efforts to present to foreign audiences both a positive image of white Americans and proof of Black Americans' advancement towards freedom in the country. Though as far as reception of this Cold War propaganda abroad, Von Eschen equally writes that "while attempting to defend American racial practices and foreign policy, the USIS itself sometimes became the object of biting criticism and wit."[37]

White Americans' belief that *An American Dilemma* could help serve—whether simply within the United States or more globally—as an effective and subtle tool to justify white American domination would be short-lived. By the 1960s, there were greater numbers of writers publicly criticizing *An American Dilemma*'s limitations as a blueprint for racial equality, and white Americans could barely fail to take notice.

Before the 1960s, of course, there were comparable critics of the book, including figures such as Oliver C. Cox, Herbert Aptheker, C. L. R. James, and Doxey A. Wilkerson, who had served as a research associate on Myrdal's study. In the introduction to Aptheker's booklet-length critical review of *An American Dilemma* published in 1946, for example, Wilkerson had said that he hoped that Americans "would not be misled by *An American Dilemma*'s distorted interpretation of the Negro question as a 'moral problem.'"[38] A white U.S. historian who served as Du Bois's literary executor, Aptheker followed up by arguing that "Myrdal's values are those of a pleader of moderation, of a bourgeois liberal reformer."[39]

Similarly, in 1948, C. L. R. James characterized Myrdal's book as a project of the U.S. bourgeoisie.[40] And in his *Caste, Class and Race* (1948), Cox called

*An American Dilemma* "a powerful piece of propaganda in favor of the status quo."[41] Reasoning through Myrdal's suggestion that the so-called "Negro problem" must be resolved by appealing morally to the ruling class of white Americans, Cox argued that this "conclusion is precisely the social illusion which the ruling political class has constantly sought to produce."[42] Rooted in Marxist analyses on the importance of challenging rather than appealing to the ruling class, these early critics of *An American Dilemma* saw through to the book's role as an intended tool for continued white domination.

This was a critique of *An American Dilemma* with which, as historian David Levering Lewis notes, W. E. B. Du Bois privately sympathized even while, as noted earlier in this book, he publicly celebrated *An American Dilemma* most directly in a 1944 review of Myrdal's study in his journal *Phylon*.[43] In his 1944 review of *An American Dilemma*, for example, Du Bois praised the book, by stating: "Never before in American history has a scholar so completely covered this field. The work is monumental."[44] In his published review, Du Bois equally celebrated Myrdal for focusing on "the Negro problem as basically a moral problem."[45] In public, if not in private, Du Bois would simply praise *An American Dilemma*. That said, he did provide in his publications at the time some sense of how he diverged in perspective from Myrdal.

In *Color and Democracy: Colonies and Peace* (1945)—published just a year after *An American Dilemma*—Du Bois distinguished himself from Myrdal by placing the African American experience within a global context of "brown, yellow, and black races" subjugated by "white peoples," whose authority rested on prejudicial judgments about these varying groups' superiorities, inferiorities, and varying capabilities for "civilization" and "self-government."[46] Even more, and again distinct from Myrdal, Du Bois reasoned in *Color and Democracy* that the principal means for Black Americans' freedom in the United States was—not as Myrdal suggested, to appeal to white Americans' moral sensibilities and to encourage these white Americans to change their anti-Black behavior and public policies, but rather—to join with other oppressed racialized people across geographies to challenge global white rule. Only then, when white rule ceased to exist at a global level, Du Bois reasoned, could there be sincere freedom for Black people and peace between peoples across races, including between white and Black Americans.[47]

But for Americans in the 1940s to have read *Color and Democracy* as Du Bois's own (albeit indirect) response to *An American Dilemma* would have required some knowledge at the time that Du Bois was unsatisfied with Myrdal's text. And at the time, Du Bois preferred to keep his direct criticisms of *An American Dilemma* within private company.[48] To this point, historian

Walter Jackson notes that: "To most observers in the 1940s, Myrdal's critics appeared to be only a few discordant voices amid a general chorus of approbation."[49]

By the 1960s, however, the number and visibility of such critical voices acknowledging *An American Dilemma*'s complicity in white domination would increase and gain attention. Jackson highlights that it "was not just Myrdal's moral dilemma thesis that was in jeopardy by the mid-1960s. His whole strategy of appealing to the conscience of whites, which had been brilliantly executed by Martin Luther King, was giving way to an emphasis upon black political power."[50]

Critics of *An American Dilemma* in the 1960s wrote during, and at times as part of, a broader Black Power movement then directly challenging white domination in the United States. As historian Peniel E. Joseph writes, "Black Power scandalized America in the 1960s, but its apparent novelty masked a deeper history."[51] Thus, Joseph notes that efforts "to secure political self-determination, cultural and racial self-definition, and social and political justice in the United States and the larger Third World united Marcus Garvey-era iterations of Black Power with the age of Stokely Carmichael and the Black Panthers."[52] Though part of a longer history, Joseph underscores that the Black Power movement in the United States achieved "full national prominence in the subsequent decade, 1966–1975, a period best described as Black Power's *classical* era."[53]

Stokely Carmichael and the Black Panther Party were among leading figures and organizations of the Black Power movement, along with Malcolm X and the Nation of Islam. Founded in 1966 Oakland, California, by Black freedom activists Huey P. Newton and Bobby Seale, sociologist Alondra Nelson writes that the Black Panther organization sought "to afford protection for poor blacks from police brutality and to offer varied other services to the same communities," including healthcare clinics.[54] By 1971, Nelson furthermore underscores that this Oakland-based organization had established a national network of chapters and health clinics. "In this and other ways," Nelson writes, "the Party encouraged the poor and predominantly African American communities on whose behalf it advocated to take some measure of control over their healthcare."[55]

Stokely Carmichael was a former leader in the Student Non-Violent Coordinating Committee (SNCC) who transformed from a nonviolent civil rights actor to a Black Power activist in the 1960s—a transformation made quite public in a June 1966 speech in which Carmichael popularized the term "Black Power." Two years later, in 1968, Peniel E. Joseph writes, the "Black

Panther Party named Stokely Carmichael the party's honorary prime minister. The title aptly described his new identity: he imagined himself, like Malcolm X, able to unite disparate strands of the black community into a cohesive political force."[56]

Three years earlier, Malcolm X was assassinated while delivering a speech in Washington Heights, a neighborhood in northern Manhattan. Malcolm X had risen to national attention in the early 1960s as leader figure of the Nation of Islam (NOI), which historian Gerald Horne writes "had been founded decades earlier but only gained traction in the 1960s."[57] More stridently critical of white rule than more mainstream civil rights activists such as the NAACP, the NOI led by Elijah Muhammad and Malcolm X argued that "Euro-Americans were 'devils.'"[58]

Malcolm X subsequently left the NOI and established his own group, Muslim Mosque, Inc, though as historian Manning Marable writes, he "continued to make highly controversial statements. 'There will be more violence than ever this year,' he predicted to a *New York Times* reporter in March 1964, for instance. 'The whites had better understand this while there is still time. The negroes at the mass level are ready to act.'"[59]

That same year as this *New York Times* interview with Malcolm X, Ralph Ellison felt sufficiently confident to publish his criticism of *An American Dilemma*. It was against this backdrop of a rising Black Power movement in 1960s United States—a movement quite directly disapproving of white domination in the United States—that Black critics of *An American Dilemma* gained greater strength and visibility.

Included in his collection of essays *Shadow and Act* (1964), Ellison shared his 1944 review of Gunnar Myrdal's two-volume study precisely two decades after penning it. In 1944 and against largely unequivocal praise in the United States for *An American Dilemma*, the literary magazine *The Antioch Review* had commissioned Ellison to review Myrdal's text. Ellison, who had survived the Great Depression by working in the Federal Writers' Project and most recently had joined the merchant marines as a cook was, in 1944, still a year away from starting work on *Invisible Man* (1952).

Ralph Ellison's biographer Arnold Rampersad notes that the novelist and editor at *The Antioch Review* ultimately decided not to publish his critique of *An American Dilemma* in 1944 because both author and editor agreed that it was "a mess of loose ends and shallow thinking."[60] Another reason for this decision could have been, as already suggested, that many (especially white) Americans in the 1940s treated *An American Dilemma* as *the* very blueprint for racial equality, even if they did not fully apply its national policy recommendations. Such white Americans preferred instead to focus on Myrdal's positive description of white Americans as a particularly moral people who felt guilty for their anti-Black behavior and public policies. By the 1960s and against the backdrop of a Black Power movement, though, *An American Dilemma* was losing its preeminent role among white Americans as "the most important study of the race issue" in the United States.[61] So in 1964, Ellison was on safer grounds to publicize his criticisms of *An American Dilemma*, no less too because he was then the celebrated author of *Invisible Man* (1952).[62]

Like other admirers of *An American Dilemma*, Ellison found much to praise. Its "main virtue," he wrote, "lies in its demonstration of how the mechanism of prejudice operates to disguise the moral conflict in the minds of whites produced by the clash on the social level between the American Creed and anti-Negro practices."[63] By showing white American readers that their behavior and policies towards fellow Black Americans ran against their national egalitarian ideals, Ellison noted that *An American Dilemma* was set to play an important social role in the United States.

Like some of the study's few early critics, though, Ellison also found some weaknesses in the text and he expounded on these shortcomings. Ellison doubted, for example, whether white Americans indeed experienced this pang of moral angst when discriminating against and terrorizing Black Americans. But more broadly, Ellison questioned Myrdal's vision of racial equality, which required Black Americans to patiently wait for white Americans' moral awakening and subsequent mobilization; for white people to relinquish their anti-Black discriminatory behavior in a timeline that was comfortable for them; and so too for Black people to accept that their equal treatment as U.S. citizens hinged on their ability and willingness to appropriate, as much as possible, white people's social, political, economic, and cultural values. Ellison argued that full egalitarian democracy should promise more: "For the solution of the problem of the American Negro and democracy lies partially in the white man's free will. Its full solution will lie in the creation of a democracy in which the Negro will be free to define himself for what he is and, within the large frame-work of that democracy, for what he desires to be." Ellison thus explained that *An American Dilemma* presented an egalitarian dream for Black Americans that was still layered with white supremacy and Black subordination. The limitations of Myrdal's vision for U.S. democracy, Ellison noted in this review, "do not lie vague and misty beyond the horizon of history They can be easily discerned through the Negro perspective."

One white U.S. reporter in the 1960s found it difficult to see what Ralph Ellison meant by a Black U.S. culture worth preserving. The Black novelist

elaborated for him that this dominant vision of racial equality in the 1960s—
which reflected Gunnar Myrdal's own argument in *An American Dilemma*
calling for the erasure of Blackness—"ignores the fact that we love our Harlems, love to be with other Negroes, marry mostly Negroes, and would consider the loss of such churches as Harlem's Abyssinia[n] a national calamity,
just as we consider the destruction of the Savoy Ballroom a cultural disaster of
international dimensions."[64] Specifically mentioning the Savoy Ballroom and
the Abyssinian Baptist Church in Harlem, Ellison referred to two central cultural institutions in New York City at the center of Black U.S. life. If Black
Americans embraced Myrdal's definition of equality which assumed that it
was in the interest of Black Americans "to become assimilated into American
culture, to acquire the traits held in esteem by the dominant white Americans,"
Ellison suggested that Black cultural institutions such as Abyssinian Baptist
Church and the Savoy Ballroom would necessarily cease to exist.[65] And as Ellison underscored, no definition of racial equality should call for such a sacrifice.

Opened in 1926, the Savoy Ballroom was a dance hall occupying the second floor of a building spanning an entire city block in Harlem, long attracting Black and white Americans alike every night of the week. For example,
"*Ebony* reported in 1946 that the Savoy cost about half a million dollars a year
to operate, that it took in around a million dollars a year, and that in the twenty
years of its existence '28 million feet stomped' there."[66] As Ralph Ellison lamented in this 1967 interview, the Savoy closed in 1958.[67]

Beyond the Savoy, Ellison also praised Harlem's Abyssinian Baptist Church.
In the early decades of the century, the New York City church had moved to
this northern neighborhood in Manhattan and became the largest and
wealthiest Black Baptist congregation in the world.[68] Commenting on a visit
to Abyssinian Baptist Church in the 1920s, for example, one white journalist
remembered that the "pastor, a tall, colored man, with a thunderous voice
and big curly head of hair, looks very much like the picture of Alexandre
Dumas . . . I am yet to listen to a better choir . . . I am yet to listen to a better
church organist."[69] Abyssinian was a point of pride for Harlemites, and the
respect was mutual with Abyssinian Church pastor Adam Clayton Powell
Sr. who noted that the neighborhood had become "the symbol of liberty and
the Promised Land to Negroes everywhere."[70]

By celebrating Harlem and two of its key institutions, Ralph Ellison resisted white Americans' negative lens on Black cultural life in the United States.
While white Americans might excuse their own shortcomings and exaggerate
a negative perspective on Black Americans, Ellison argued that both white
and Black Americans were flawed and beautiful and that a more egalitarian

country less committed to white supremacy and Black subordination would be capable of seeing that. As he emphasized in his critique of *An American Dilemma*: "Much of Negro culture might be negative, but there is also much of great value, of richness, which, because it has been secreted by living and has made their lives more meaningful, Negroes will not willingly disregard."[71]

In this review of *An American Dilemma*, Ellison quoted directly from Gunnar Myrdal's text to further emphasize Myrdal's negative portrayal of Black life. As Ellison related, Myrdal had written: The "Negro's entire life and, consequently, also his opinions on the Negro problem are, in the main, to be considered as secondary reactions to more primary pressures from the side of the dominant white majority."[72] Ellison thus underscored how Myrdal had interpreted Black culture to be merely a consequence of white people's exclusion of Black people from white society. With this assumption, Ellison explained that *An American Dilemma* thus had presumed that Black Americans would and should be willing to sacrifice Black culture, communities, and societies and appropriate whiteness as much as possible, in order to be treated by fellow white Americans as equal human beings.[73]

Looking at a definition of racial equality broadcast by Gunnar Myrdal, which called Black Americans to strip themselves of Blackness—of anything, for example, that distinguished the Harlems of the United States from their neighboring white communities—to the best of Black Americans' ability and to the extent that white Americans allowed, Ellison pointed out in his review that Black Americans needed to understand, defend, and promote the value of Black culture for the United States as a whole: "What is needed in our country is not an exchange of pathologies, but a change of the basis of society. This is a job which both Negroes and whites must perform together. In Negro culture there is much of value for America as a whole. What is needed are Negroes to take it and create of it 'the uncreated consciousness of their race.' In doing so they will do far more, they'll help create a more human American."[74] By resisting white America's insistence that white people and whiteness were superior to Black people and Blackness, Ellison argued in his 1944 review of *An American Dilemma* that it was critical to challenge these elements of white supremacy and Black subordination in Gunnar Myrdal's—and more broadly, many white Americans'—definition of equality in order to create a far more democratic society in the United States.

Beyond criticizing Myrdal's substantive definition of equality in *An American Dilemma*, Ellison equally asserted that white Americans could not, as Myrdal maintained in the two volumes, be the gatekeepers to Black Americans' equality.[75] In an egalitarian democracy respecting citizens equally, Ellison stressed that no group should have should have the power to define the speed and extent of others' freedom.

Like Ellison, other Black critics of *An American Dilemma* in the 1960s would criticize Myrdal's insistence that Black Americans' equality required their acceptance of assimilation into whiteness, or rather the implicit acceptance of white superiority and Black subjection. They were also critical of Myrdal's suggestion that white Americans were a particularly moral people who, when confronted with the gap between their national egalitarian values and anti-Black discrimination, would begin to treat Black Americans with greater dignity and equality. Because again, as these critics underscored, white Americans' own perceived sense of superiority not only colored their definition of racial equality and insistence on determining the speed and scope of Black Americans' equality, but it also led them to stall any sincere attempts to eradicate anti-Black discrimination in the United States.[76]

Also in 1964, for example, Black political scientist Samuel DuBois Cook wrote in the pages of the *Journal of Negro History* that he was "not entirely convinced of the validity of Myrdal's thesis." Cook continued, "Only the whites of the most sensitive consciences have been, in the least, troubled by the degradation, suppression, and humiliation of the Negro. On the whole, white Americans have had an easy and complacent conscience about slavery and its progeny, the caste system of segregation and discrimination."[77] As Cook explained, there was little in reality to support Myrdal's claim that white Americans experienced a moral dilemma in their treatment of fellow Black Americans that they would rectify on their own.

Similarly in 1965, Black writer John Oliver Killens wrote in *Black Man's Burden* (1965) that white Americans had a distorted perspective of their past, which hindered any ability to move towards a more racial egalitarian future. "There is much inhumanity, violence, and brutality in our country's history," Killens explained. "White Americans have been sheltered from their history. History is a people's memory, and a people have a habit of remembering the very best about themselves. It is an all too human trait. But in the final analysis, a people must face its history squarely in order to transcend it."[78]

Writing against the backdrop of the Black Power movement increasingly critical of white Americans as a particularly moral people, a movement increasingly and directly critical of white supremacy and, relatedly, increasingly and directly championing the value of Blackness and Black freedom, these 1960s critics of *An American Dilemma* pinpointed key elements of *An American Dilemma* with roots in white rule and Black subjection: The book's emphasis on white Americans as a particularly moral people; its stress on white Americans as key decisionmakers on the speed and content of Black Americans' assimilation into white American life; and its assumption that Black Americans should feel little pride in retaining Black U.S. culture.

In a special conference on Black Americans held by the American Academy of Arts and Sciences in May of 1965, Ralph Ellison reinforced his criticism of *An American Dilemma* by asking attendants: "One thing that is not quite clear to me is the implication that Negroes have come together and decided that we want to lose our identity as quickly as possible. Where does that idea come from?"[79] Exposing a key assumption in Myrdal's definition of racial equality, an assumption and expectation that Myrdal shared with many white Americans, Ellison questioned how and why calling white Americans to bridge their egalitarian values with their anti-Black behavior and public policies should result in a simultaneous call for Black Americans to rid themselves of Black identities.

Complementing Ellison, Cook, and Killens, white journalist I. F. Stone reviewed a book resulting from this 1965 gathering in the *New York Review of Books*, and reasoned that the "non-violent oppressed cannot twinge the conscience of the oppressor unless he has one."[80] And contrary to Myrdal's claims in *An American Dilemma*, Stone did not believe that white Americans had such a conscience. Moreover, and again contrary to Myrdal, Stone reasoned that "there is no reason why [greater racial equality] must change the Negro merely into a darker version of the white man. The new emphasis on 'blackness' in the civil rights movement reflects a healthy instinct. The Negro has two basic needs. One is more jobs and the other is the restoration of self-respect."[81]

Similarly unwilling to indulge a favorable image of white Americans, Black scholar Harold Cruse wrote in *The Crisis of the Negro Intellectual* (1967) that "America is a nation that lies to itself about who and what it is. It is a nation of minorities ruled by a minority of one—it thinks and acts as if it were a nation of white Anglo-Saxon Protestants." In this spirit, for example, Cruse argued that the role of the Black intellectual was to "tell this brainwashed white America, this 'nation of sheep,' this overfed, over-developed, overprivileged (but culturally pauperized) federation of unassimilated European remnants that their days of grace are numbered."[82]

That same year, Black Power activist Stokely Carmichael and political scientist Charles V. Hamilton argued in *Black Power: The Politics of Liberation in America* (1967) that the "tragedy of race relations in the United States is that there is no American Dilemma. White Americans are not torn and tortured by the conflict between their devotion to the American creed and their actual behavior."[83] Rather than viewing the United States as a country led by egalitarian white Americans eager to correct their discriminatory treatment of Black

Americans, as Myrdal favored in *An American Dilemma*, Carmichael and Hamilton stressed comparisons between white supremacy and Black subjection abroad: "To put it another way, there is no 'American dilemma' because black people in this country form a colony, and it is not in the interest of the colonial power to liberate them."[84]

As an antidote to an existing "colonial white power structure" in the United States, Carmichael and Hamilton proposed "Black Power," calling for "black people in this country to unite, to recognize their heritage, to build a sense of community. It is a call for black people to begin to define their own goals, to lead their own organizations and to support those organizations."[85] Proposing a positive image of Black Americans as key players in their own freedom and a critical image of white Americans as immoral oppressors, the coauthors distinguished themselves quite clearly from Myrdal's presentations of white and Black Americans. Further underscoring the value and beauty of Black life— and, again, writing against *An American Dilemma*—Carmichael and Hamilton underscored that the "racial and cultural personality of the black community must be preserved and that community must win its freedom while preserving its cultural integrity."[86] With Black Americans rather than white Americans at the helm of Black freedom in the United States, the authors imagined an alternative form of racial integration in the United States—alternative to the one proposed in *An American Dilemma*—where Black Americans would retain pride in Black identities.

Also in 1967, Martin Luther King Jr.— long accustomed to appealing to white Americans' moral compass in his role as a leading figure of the U.S. civil rights movement—quoted *An American Dilemma* in his own critical reading of white Americans.[87] In *Where Do We Go from Here: Chaos or Community?* (1967), King described white Americans as "oppressors," noting that during the past decade as Black Americans and white allies engaged in peaceful protests such as bus boycotts, sit-ins, and marches, and met with violent white resistance from imprisonment to physical torture and death, white Americans' moral conscience "burned only dimly, and when atrocious behavior was curbed, the spirit settled easily into well-padded pockets of complacency."[88]

Less convinced than Myrdal of white Americans' moral fabric, Martin Luther King Jr. still stressed that white Americans indeed needed—as Myrdal suggested—to bridge the gap between their egalitarian ideals and discriminatory treatment of Black Americans. Though like contemporary Black Power leaders, King in 1967 had little expectation that white Americans would mobilize toward more egalitarian behavior on their own. Rather, King reasoned that white Americans would make such behavioral and policy changes because

Black Americans would continue, as they had, to stand up in nonviolent protest and confront their oppressor. "In this decade of change," King wrote, "the
Negro stood up and confronted his oppressor—he faced the bullies and the
guns, the dogs and the tear gas, he put himself squarely before the vicious mobs
and moved with strength and dignity toward them and decisively defeated
them."[89] Contrary to Myrdal, King stressed that Black Americans, rather than
white Americans, were the moral compass in the United States.

These 1960s critics of *An American Dilemma* were writing not only against
the backdrop of the Black Power movement in the United States, but also in
the context of complementary movements across the Atlantic such as the
Black Consciousness movement in South Africa and anticolonialism throughout Africa. Like the Black Power movement in the United States, these antico-
lonial and anti-apartheid projects in Africa were calling into direct question
the validity of white rule across oceans. Even more specifically, these Black
freedom movements in the 1960s called into question the very white domination that Carnegie Corporation president Keppel's three cooperative studies
on white and Black people had intended to help fortify and justify in the
United States, South Africa, and throughout colonial Africa during the 1920s,
1930s, and early 1940s.

"At midnight on March 6, 1957," political scientist Adom Getachew writes,
"Kwame Nkrumah took the stage in Accra to announce the independence of
the Gold Coast, renamed Ghana in homage to the ancient West African empire. In his speech, Nkrumah declared that 1957 marked the birth of a new
Africa 'ready to fight its own battles and show that after all the black man is
capable of managing his own affairs.'"[90] Four years later, Ghanaian president
Nkrumah celebrated the movement for independence throughout Africa, observing that there were then twenty-eight independent states in Africa. And
this independence, Nkrumah underscored in *I Speak of Freedom* (1961), was
from white Europeans who had dominated the African continent for decades:
"The white man arrogated to himself the right to rule and to be obeyed by the
non-white; his mission, he claimed was to 'civilise' Africa. Under this cloak,
the Europeans robbed the continent of vast riches and inflicted unimaginable
suffering on the African people."[91]

Criticizing white domination in ways and tones with which Black Power
activists in the United States would recognize and sympathize, Nkrumah
called for greater unity across Africa. Because it was only through such unity
among Africans, he argued, that African countries could defend each other
from becoming "weak and dependent" countries reliant on European aid and,
thus, vulnerable to continued white domination in Africa.

In this spirit, and throughout his leadership of Ghana from 1957 to 1966, Nkrumah would convene numerous pan-African congresses in his efforts to promote greater African independence and unity—the very unity among Black people in Africa that the white men at the center of this book tried to forestall.[92] Nkrumah's pan-Africanism also caught the attention of many Black Americans who applauded his leadership. Political scientist Robert Vitalis, for example, relays that when Nkrumah "traveled to the United States in July 1958 as leader of the new independent state of Ghana, 10,000 African Americans lined the long motorcade's route to New York's 369th Coast Artillery Armory on 143rd street and 5th Avenue. The *New York Times* headline the next day read, 'Harlem Hails Ghanaian Leader as Returning Hero.'"[93]

Complementing the rising Black Power movement and anticolonialism throughout Africa, a Black Consciousness movement (BCM) in South Africa was directly challenging white rule in yet another region of the world where Carnegie Corporation had attempted to preserve white rule as key element for international order along the color line. Led by Black South African Steve Biko—who years later, in 1977, was stripped "naked in the back of a police van" and "died between Port Elizabeth and Pretoria from police-inflicted head injuries"—the BCM of the 1960s and 1970s "was seen as a way of preparing people for equal participation in a transformed society that reflected the outlook of the [Black] majority. Psychological liberation was sought through a return to African values of communalism, shared decision-making, and more personal communication styles, in contrast to the individualism of white consumer society."[94] Underscoring the importance of the BCM in South Africa, even after Biko's death and through years of government suppression, intimidation, and violence, sociologist Kogila Moodley writes that "Black Consciousness laid the ground for the self-confident challenge of the *apartheid* state whether through refusals of co-optation or astute negotiations."[95]

Credited with moving the pendulum decisively toward more expansive Black freedom from white rule, these movements of Black resistance across the pan-African diaspora in the 1960s and 1970s—from Black Power in the United States and Black Consciousness in South Africa to anticolonialism throughout Africa—predictably met with the resistance of white people. In 1963, Nkrumah already described this white opposition as "neo-colonialism." In 1967, Martin Luther King called it "white backlash." On both sides of the Atlantic, white oppressors would prove obstinate in retaining white rule and Black subjection in the face of Black people's resistance.[96]

And yet, the very existence and social traction of these three Black freedom movements successfully underscored just how naive Carnegie Corporation president Frederick Keppel, his colleagues, and advisers, and Andrew Carnegie before them, had been to believe that either the Tuskegee educational model for Black people or social scientific research on white and Black people could be critical tools to help solidify white Anglo-American domination and preclude the inevitable: a people's ability to rise up against their oppressors. While these Black freedom movements did not fully displace white Anglo-American rule across oceans—indeed, as Martin Luther King Jr. and Kwame Nkrumah observed, these decades would be marked by white backlash in the United States and neocolonialism in Africa—they succeeded in underscoring the vulnerability of a world order based on racial domination.

But W. E. B. Du Bois could have told them this. In fact, he had. In his critical reviews of Thomas Jesse Jones's *Negro Education* (1917) and Malcolm Hailey's *An African Survey* (1938), Du Bois had warned Keppel and his peers in U.S. philanthropy about the weaknesses of their efforts to help fortify the making of a white Anglo-American world order. Throughout the 1930s, Du Bois also had made direct appeals to Keppel to steer the organization away from this global project, most prominently by requesting financial support for a pan-African encyclopedia and for the opportunity to visit the British dominion of South Africa.[97] In response, Keppel described "the idea of a specialized Negro Encyclopedia" as a "mistake" and stressed that his white advisers in South Africa, who long had restricted these Carnegie-Corporation-funded travel grants between South Africa and the United States to white scholars, doubted "the desirability of your making a visit to the Union [of South Africa] just now."[98]

As Keppel underscored for Du Bois in the 1930s, "We have done pretty well in the past fifteen years by seeking and following [our South African advisers'] advice and I hesitate to break away from the policy."[99] Keppel rejected both proposals from Du Bois, in line with his longstanding efforts as Carnegie Corporation president to promote white solidarity—while discouraging comparable Black unity—across the Atlantic. In *Color and Democracy* (1945), published a year after Myrdal's *An American Dilemma* (1944) and two years after Keppel's passing, Du Bois further crystalized his critique of the white Anglo-American world order whose solidification he had seen U.S. philanthropy aid. Underscoring the very fragility of these white men's global project and foreseeing its eventual demise, Du Bois both observed and predicted: "The hope of the world lay in the union of Britain and the United States to dominate mankind. Yet up from the throats of these peoples—the colonials, the minorities, and the depressed classes—one increasing cry for freedom, democracy, and social progress continually wells."[100]

# Epilogue

Carnegie Corporation's Frederick Keppel never wrote a manifesto on international order along the color line. Rather, the research at the heart of this book illustrating his perspective on the need for a white Anglo-American world order is based on years reading through his papers at Carnegie Corporation, the archives of the corporation more broadly, and the personal papers of advisers and social scientists in Keppel's network at the time. In Carnegie Corporation's and Keppel's papers, it furthermore required moving beyond files on the organization's grantmaking practices in the United States and to its grantmaking practices abroad.

As a first step, for example, and reading simply through Carnegie Corporation material on the organization's work in the United States, it could easily seem that Keppel, if not fellow Carnegie Corporation trustee Newton Baker, might have been a relatively closeted advocate of Black Americans' absolute equality in the United States. To this point, Carnegie Corporation material illustrates that Keppel chose a Swedish economist to direct the U.S. study of Black Americans, and Gunnar Myrdal indeed wrote a manuscript emphasizing the importance for white Americans to correct anti-Black discrimination to match their national egalitarian ideals. And far from criticizing this argument, Keppel celebrated this part of the book in correspondence with colleagues at the organization.

And even when Keppel agonized over the project's dismissal of white southerners as a critical group of white Americans for shaping a national policy program on Black Americans, his anxieties—if placed only in a U.S. context—would seem to suggest that the foundation president was simply being a "realistic" advocate of Black Americans' equality who remained aware of power dynamics in the United States and, thus, eager to recruit support from white southerners. To this point and anxious about Myrdal's portrayal of these white Americans, Keppel had admitted to a colleague: "I feel that the blow is coming to them, in fact it is long overdue, but I feel also that we must be particularly careful as to the manner in which the blow is delivered."[1] And so, simply reading Keppel's commentary on the white South along with his support of Gunnar Myrdal's general thesis in *An American Dilemma*, one reasonably could assume that Keppel simply had been, as the Swedish director concluded years later, "a liberal of that period."[2]

Maintaining a focus on Keppel's work in the United States, there are other archival examples suggesting Keppel's potential empathy for Black Americans' subjection under white rule in the country. For example, secretary of war Newton Baker's special adviser on Black affairs Emmett Jay Scott recounted that his colleague, third assistant secretary of war Keppel, had been "especially charged with the duty of looking after many complaints and matters of vital concern to colored Americans generally, and not only did he manifest a keen interest in their welfare but, in many cases, was successful in translating that interest into remedial action."[3] Then as Carnegie Corporation president, Keppel too had asked Myrdal to include distinguished Black scholars W. E. B. Du Bois and Alain Locke as collaborators in the study. And when Myrdal failed to find tasks for the two men, Keppel had suggested that Myrdal "write them each a nice letter, telling them that I was now in a preliminary stage of fact collection and that I have selected a staff to do the fact collection job, but that I should later have to turn to them for advice when the study was in the critical stage of fixing the broad view points."[4] Keppel thus seemingly respected the renowned Black historian and philosopher sufficiently to suggest to Myrdal that he send them each a "nice letter."[5]

However, once Keppel's actions are analyzed within a broader transnational lens—within Carnegie Corporation's funding practices in the British Empire during his tenure, as this book has done—his reasons for financing *An American Dilemma* become that much clearer and yet also that much more complicated.

Some six years before giving thought to the study of Black Americans, for example, Keppel had written to his principal adviser in South Africa, Charles Loram, and related impressions of former South African prime minister Jan Smuts's recent visit to the United States. Keppel wrote: "Smuts has been here and made, as you can imagine, a most favorable impression, though he stirred up feeling among the Negroes by referring to the patience of the ass."[6] Visiting New York City within weeks of delivering the Rhodes Lectures at Oxford, Smuts had spoken with an audience of white and Black Americans. If Jan Smuts said anything in New York City close to what he had shared during his Rhodes Lectures (lectures that had inspired J. H. Oldham to criticize Smuts's complete assumption of the inferiority of Black people), one could imagine that Keppel (assuming he had great empathy for Black people), would have found the former South African prime minister to have been off-putting. But Keppel did not seem as impassioned as Oldham. And to be clear, as this book has shown, Oldham was barely a supporter of Black people's freedom from white oppression.

Most strikingly, communications between Keppel and his contacts in British Africa in the 1920s and 1930s illustrate how this network of white men discussed anxieties about white Anglo-American rule from a transnational perspective. Not only did they conflate white Americans, Britons, and Afrikaners as potential white allies in the making of a white Anglo-American world (and relatedly conflated Black Americans and Africans as comparable subject groups in the Anglo-American world), but as archival material on Carnegie Corporation's work outside of the United States exposes, Keppel developed a vision for international order along the color line during the span of his tenure at the corporation.

President Keppel's transatlantic perspective on white Anglo-American rule makes it possible to piece together both his vision for white rule and Black subordination on both sides of the Atlantic and thus too his specific intentions for *An American Dilemma*. To this point, as this book clarifies, Keppel had found convincing J. H. Oldham's 1925 memorandum stressing the threat of Black consciousness in Africa and the need for scientific research to aid white policymakers in stabilizing control on the continent.[7] He was not taken aback by Oldham's suggestion that white people should work toward stamping out Black people's attempts toward a shared consciousness as Black people. On the contrary, Keppel had interpreted the memorandum to be sufficiently important to circulate among fellow trustees at Carnegie Corporation and to use it as a basis for developing a grantmaking program in Africa that, in line with the corporation's priorities, would privilege the interests of white Anglo-Americans there. Even more, Keppel maintained Oldham as a key contact in years to come, suggesting sympathy in their views on the importance of white Anglo-American rule across the Atlantic and the need to address rising Black consciousness as a serious threat to it.

That said, Keppel and Oldham were not unique in their views. Rather, Keppel's and Oldham's efforts to promote and finance cooperative studies in the social sciences as means of helping white policymakers fortify white rule were in harmony with a network of advisers and colleagues who championed the need for stable white governance in colonial Africa and the United States, and the critical role that the social sciences could play towards this end. Keppel and Oldham, like many others in this transatlantic network, furthermore assumed that white Anglo-Americans would govern Black people and that Black people would remain in a subordinate position to white Anglo-Americans and their white allies for the foreseeable future.

And yet, their vision of white domination was relatively nuanced. This is because, at times, it incorporated some public declaration (even if half-hearted, patronizing, and insincere) for ameliorating the condition of Black people, though without threatening the validity of continued white domination. This was a viewpoint that Andrew Carnegie and James Bertram had embraced; that the British Colonial Office increasingly held in the 1920s; and that Carnegie Corporation's advisers at Chatham House in the 1930s, including Oldham, shared in their search for a director of the African survey. Keppel was never quite as adamant on this point; though if his decision to make routine trips to London throughout the 1930s is any indication, he seemed more at ease with this set of advisers who privileged this vision of white rule than he had been with his South African network, who more publicly demonized Black people. Granted, Keppel remained in contact with South African advisers such as Charles Loram, Ernst Malherbe, and Jan Smuts, but he returned most often to his Chatham House contacts—and especially Oldham—and even reached out to them for advice when he started making plans for a study of Black Americans.

This book takes readers through this global context to Carnegie Corporation's grantmaking practices and networks of advisers and grantees in the 1920s and 1930s in order to present Keppel's reasons for commissioning, funding, and overseeing a national study of Black Americans in the mid-1930s, and what he saw favorable and thus worthy of celebration in Gunnar Myrdal's final report. As this book explains, Keppel was part of a network of white Anglo-Americans and their white allies in South Africa who increasingly believed that the social sciences could be an important tool in helping white policymakers placate Black people's challenges to white rule in British Africa and the United States and, in the process, avoid a global conflict along the color line. And they were rather up-front about what they meant by international order: white Anglo-American domination.

For this network of white men, it was possible to admire individual Black intellectuals such as Booker T. Washington, W. E. B. Du Bois, Alain Locke, D. D. T. Jabavu, and Ralph Bunche, for example, and yet still fear Black consciousness and, thus, Black people as a group. For this network of white Anglo-American men, it also was possible to be critical of particularly egregious forms of white supremacy and Black subordination—from repressive labor laws in Kenya to the public demonization of Africans in South Africa and Jim Crow laws in the southern United States—without throwing out the very value of white supremacy and Black subordination. This is because, again, their ideal form of national and international order required white governance and Black subordination, though, for them, it also preferably included a form of white rule whose public face showed some effort (whether sincere, insincere, or simply patronizing) to improve the status of Black people. In line with this vision of white governance, reflected most closely in *An African Survey* and *An American Dilemma*, white people would retain control over the content and speed of ameliorative changes in Black people's subordinate status across the Atlantic.

This was the global intellectual and political context that bore *An American Dilemma*, a text that for too long has been wrongly understood by too many Americans to be an exclusively U.S. project advocating foremost Black Americans' equality. As some critics of *An American Dilemma* well knew, even though they did not have the archival records to prove it, Myrdal's text was part of a complicated and global history peopled with cross-Atlantic networks of white philanthropic managers, advisers, social researchers, and policymakers. And though Myrdal himself was not part of this transatlantic network, he wrote a book in dialogue with and complementing the transatlantic intentions of these white Anglo-American men.

Now, in the twenty-first century, when we all can see *An American Dilemma* through this global and imperial lens, it seems time for all Americans to find inspiration in *An American Dilemma*'s critics—from W. E. B. Du Bois, Ralph Ellison, and Oliver Cox to Harold Cruse, Stokely Carmichael, Charles V. Hamilton, Samuel DuBois Cook, John Oliver Killens, and Martin Luther King Jr.—and embrace definitions and means toward racial equality that are free of white domination and, thus, will actually move us toward a truly free and peaceful United States and world.

# Acknowledgments

It was in college when I first realized that "scholars" existed and that perhaps I could become one. From my undergraduate days, I thus thank Eileen Hunt Botting for, quite honestly, showing me how intellectual brilliance and absolute joy could coexist. I will never forget reading through books at Hesburgh Library and running over to your office to share what I had just learned, and your own generosity in meeting my own enthusiasm as an undergraduate. For that, I absolutely thank you. In a similar spirit, I thank Christina Wolbrecht, Alvin B. Tillery, and Catherine Perry, who also served as academic role models during those undergraduate years at Notre Dame.

At New York University Law School, I am indebted to the faithful mentorship of William E. Nelson and Carol Gilligan. I also thank Derrick Bell, posthumously, for his generous and thoughtful correspondence. At Princeton, I am indebted to Hendrik Hartog, Stanley N. Katz, and Anson Rabinbach, who modeled scholarly rigor and encouraged me to produce work of great significance. I also thank Melissa Harris-Perry for being a beacon of brilliance, kindness, and truth in the quite intimidating space of Princeton University. From my trips to Sweden during the past decade, I also thank Rob Hannah, Niclas Fogelström, Vanessa Barker, and Lars Trägårdh, who became family away from home. More recently, I thank Michael McEachrane, Jason Diakité, and Madubuko Diakité for their friendship and long-standing work to make Sweden and the global community more comprehensible and breathable for the Global Majority.

Beyond universities and to the archives, I owe great thanks to the Rockefeller Archive Center's Tom Rosenbaum and Michele Hiltzik Beckerman; the Swedish Labour Movement Archives and Library's Stellan Andersson; and Carnegie Corporation curators and archivists Jane Gorjevsky and Jennifer S. Comins at Columbia University. Thank you for your engaged interest in this project and, even more, for being highlights of my trips to the archives. And Tom, I thank you posthumously: You were sunshine at the Rockefeller Archive Center.

I also thank the librarians at Columbia University's Butler Library—both past and present—who have created the vast collection from which I deeply benefited in the process of researching and writing this book. Because of this robust library collection, I was able to access various and difficult-to-find published sources so critical for the research in this book.

For financial support, I thank especially Carnegie Corporation's Andrew Carnegie Fellowship Program, which facilitated research travel and a two-year research sabbatical from teaching at Clemson University between 2016 and 2018. During this time, the irony of writing a book that critically engages with the history of Carnegie Corporation and that in many ways has been financed by Carnegie Corporation was not lost on me. In fact, this two-year fellowship led me to self-reflect on the role that I want to play in the academe and, subsequently, to the founding of the Miami Institute for the Social Sciences. A year-long sabbatical at Ersta Sköndal Bräcke Högskola's Center on Civil Society Research in Stockholm,

Sweden, during the 2019–2020 academic year also facilitated the writing of this book, even as the COVID-19 pandemic led us to Miami earlier than expected.

I thank Elizabeth Mahan, Athena Tan, and the team at Westchester Publishing Services, especially production editor Kirsten Elmer, for their proofreading, indexing, and copyediting work on this manuscript. I thank, too, the University of North Carolina Press—particularly editorial, design, and production editor Iris Levesque and acquisitions editor Lucas Church—and the two reviewers who believed in this project and helped me to see ways to improve it. Reviewer Two changed my life by leading me to write *this* book, and more broadly through the readings she suggested to propel me further into an analysis of the role I want to play in the academe. Thank you deeply, Tiffany Willoughby-Herard. Without you, we both know that this book would still remain unpublished. And thank you too, Inderjeet Parmar and Claude A. Clegg III, for playing critical roles in bringing this book to publication at the University of North Carolina Press. Even more, Tiffany and Inderjeet, thank you for bringing me into your rich communities of scholars. I will be forever grateful for your warmth, generosity, and purpose as human beings and scholars.

I also thank Megan Ming Francis who has witnessed the long journey this project has taken. Thank you for your moral support throughout these years, Megan. Karida Brown, thank you too for your wise counsel to reach out to the University of North Carolina Press when this project was meeting dead ends towards publication. And thank you, Takiyah Harper-Shipman, for guiding me toward your trusted proofreader. For their general encouragement, many thanks as well to Alondra Nelson, Khalil Muhammad, Patricia Rosenfield, Mary Dudziak, Daniel Sharfstein, Rob Reich, Tomiko Brown-Nagin, Sven Eliaeson, Alden Young, Fadzilah Yahaya, Kenneth Mack, Sam Moyn, Nils Gilman, Noliwe Rooks, and, posthumously, Vartan Gregorian, Tony Judt and Walter Jackson. You all have played critical roles in encouraging the work in this book.

Of course, all errors and omissions are my own.

Closer to home, I thank my family and especially my parents, Daysi and Jorge Morey, who have modeled courage in life and long have encouraged me to take my own path, even if it has meant eternally burying myself in books and traveling to archives. And thank you, Jason and Frankie, for being my center wherever we are in the world. *Los quiero mucho.* Frankie, I will always love you "more than one million."

# Notes

## Introduction

1. Morris, *The Scholar Denied*, 198.
2. Steinberg, "An American Dilemma," 64.
3. Murakawa, *The First Civil Right*, 15; Scott, *Contempt & Pity*, 54.
4. Sugrue, "Hearts and Minds."
5. Myrdal, *An American Dilemma*, xliii. Unless otherwise noted, all references are to the 1944 edition of this work.
6. Myrdal, 60–61, 437, 1066.
7. Myrdal, 1015–1024.
8. Myrdal, 929.
9. See, for example, Stewart, *The Negro in America*.
10. Garlington, "Newsettes"; Hansen, "First Reader"; newspaper clipping, *Call*, March 10, 1945; "Documents from Gunnar Myrdal's Work," vol. 4.2.05:004, folder "An American Dilemma 1945," Gunnar and Alva Myrdal Archive (hereafter GAMA).
11. Norman, "World to Live In"; "Documents from Gunnar Myrdal's Work," GAMA.
12. Committee of 100 Dinner Invitation, "Documents from Gunnar Myrdal's Work," June 2, 1948, vol. 4.2.05:003, folder "Klipp," GAMA. For a discussion of the Committee of 100, see Tushnet, *Making Civil Rights Law*, 34–35.
13. Committee of 100 Dinner Invitation, "Documents from Gunnar Myrdal's Work."
14. Southern, *Gunnar Myrdal and Black-White Relations*.
15. Baker, *From Savage to Negro*, 194–95.
16. O'Connor, *Poverty Knowledge*, 76.
17. O'Connor, 76.
18. Gordon, *From Power to Prejudice*, 36.
19. Gordon, 38.
20. Lawson, *To Secure These Rights*, 14.
21. Mack, *Representing the Race*, 244.
22. John Gunther, *Inside U.S.A.* (New York: New Press, 1947), 683, 926, quoted in Southern, *Gunnar Myrdal and Black-White Relations*, 129.
23. Theodore G. Bilbo, *Take Your Choice*, 150.
24. Eastland, *The Supreme Court's "Modern Scientific Authorities,"* 10.
25. Ellison, *Shadow and Act*, 303.
26. Myrdal, *An American Dilemma*, 929.
27. Myrdal, 929.
28. Cox, *Caste, Class and Race*; Aptheker, *The Negro People in America*; Wilkerson, introduction; Carmichael and Hamilton, *Black Power*; James, "The Revolutionary Answer to the Negro Problem."
29. Cox, *Caste, Class and Race*.

30. Jackson, *Gunnar Myrdal and America's Conscience*, 308.

31. Cox, *Caste, Class and Race*; Carmichael and Hamilton, *Black Power*; Cook, review; Cruse, *Crisis of the Negro Intellectual*.

32. Cruse, *Crisis of the Negro Intellectual*, 494.

33. Southern, *Gunnar Myrdal and Black-White Relations*, 290.

34. Lewis, *W. E. B. Du Bois*, 453.

35. "Memorandum of Conversations with Colonel Arthur S. Woods and Dr. Ruml of the Laura Spelman Foundation, October 26, 28 and November 5, 1925," box 281, folder 281.2, Grant Files, Carnegie Corporation of New York Records (hereafter CCNYR); Newton Baker to Robert Lester, December 26, 1934, folder "Carnegie Corporation, 1934," Newton D. Baker Papers (hereafter NBP).

36. Jackson, *Gunnar Myrdal and America's Conscience*, 33.

37. Dubow, *A Commonwealth of Knowledge*, 7–8.

38. Tilley, *Africa as a Living Laboratory*, 71.

39. Ellison, *Shadow and Act*; Cox, *Caste, Class and Race*; James, "The Revolutionary Answer to the Negro Problem"; Scott, *Contempt & Pity*; Singh, *Black Is a Country*; Melamed, *Represent and Destroy*; Morris, *The Scholar Denied*; Lewis, *W. E. B. Du Bois*; Stewart, *The New Negro*.

40. See, for example, Mack, *Representing the Race*; Klarman, *Brown v. Board and the Civil Rights Movement*; Klarman, *From Jim Crow to Civil Rights*, 169; Tushnet, *Making Constitutional Law*; Tushnet, *Brown v. Board of Education*; Tushnet, *The Warren Court in Historical Perspective*; Tushnet, *NAACP's Legal Strategy against Segregated Education, 1925–1950*; Dudziak, *Cold War Civil Rights*; Whitman, *Brown v. Board of Education*; Southern, *Gunnar Myrdal and Black-White Relations*; Jackson, *Gunnar Myrdal and America's Conscience*; Cottrol, "Justice Advanced," 841.

41. Jackson, *Gunnar Myrdal and America's Conscience*; Gordon, *From Power to Prejudice*; Murakawa, *The First Civil Right*; Scott, *Contempt & Pity*; Baker, *From Savage to Negro*; Melamed, *Represent and Destroy*.

42. Lagemann, *The Politics of Knowledge*, 486.

43. See, for example, Lagemann, *The Politics of Knowledge*; O'Connor, *Poverty Knowledge*; Zunz, *Philanthropy in America*, 184.

44. For historical research on the making of a white Anglo-American world order and Black resistance to global white supremacy, early prominent examples include Du Bois, "The Souls of White Folk"; Du Bois, *Color and Democracy*; Frantz Fanon, *Black Skin, White Masks*; Fanon, *The Wretched of the Earth*. More contemporary historical analyses include Willoughby-Herard, *Waste of a White Skin*; Vitalis, *White World Order, Black Power Politics*; Wallerstein, *Africa, the Politics of Unity*; Mazower, *No Enchanted Palace*; Lake and Reynolds, *Drawing the Global Colour Line*; Zimmerman, *Alabama in Africa*; Bell, *The Idea of Greater Britain*; Matera, *Black London*; Makalani, *In the Cause of Freedom*; Eschen, *Race against Empire*; Horne, *Black Revolutionary*; Ewing, *The Age of Garvey*; Robinson, *Black Marxism*; Edwards, *The Practice of Diaspora*; Blain, *Set the World on Fire*; Getachew, *Worldmaking after Empire*; Parmar, *Think Tanks and Power in Foreign Policy*; Vucetic, *The Anglosphere*; Ledwidge and Parmar, "Clash of Pans"; Mitcham, *Race and Imperial Defence in the British World, 1870–1914*; Füredi, *The Silent War*.

45. See, for example, Morris, *The Scholar Denied*; Horne, *Black Revolutionary*; Robinson, *Black Marxism*.

46. Keppel, foreword, vi.

47. Keppel, vi.

48. Keppel, vi.

49. Keppel, vi.

50. Charles Dollard, interviewed by Isabel Grossner, February 15, 1966, Interview No. 1, Reminiscences of Charles Dollard: 1966, Carnegie Corporation Oral History Project (hereafter CCOHP).

51. Donald Young, interviewed by Isabel S. Grossner, March 16, 1967, CCOHP.

52. Myrdal, *An American Dilemma* (1964).

53. Keppel, foreword, vi.

54. Myrdal, *An American Dilemma*, ix, ix–xi.

## Chapter 1

1. James Bertram to Frederick Keppel, March 30, 1931, Administrative Records, Policy & Program, box 5, folder 5.4, Carnegie Corporation of New York Records (hereafter CCNYR).

2. Rosenfield, *World of Giving*, chap. 2.

3. Ellen Condliffe Lagemann notes that Francis Keppel was the youngest of Frederick P. Keppel's five sons. Francis Keppel was born in 1916, which means that the Keppels had their five sons prior to the war. Lagemann, *Politics of Knowledge*, 162.

4. Rosenthal, *Nicholas Miraculous*, 357.

5. Rosenfield, *World of Giving*, 93.

6. Stackpole, *Carnegie Corporation Commonwealth Program*.

7. "Report of the President & of the Treasurer," 1931, CCNYR.

8. Nasaw, *Andrew Carnegie*, 768.

9. Annual Report, 1921, CCNYR.

10. Carnegie Corporation, *Charter, Constitution, and Bylaws*.

11. Root, Clark, Buckner & Howland to Frederick Keppel, February 11, 1936, legal files, box 4, folder 2, CCNYR,; Elihu Root Jr. to Henry S. Pritchett, December 2, 1922, legal files, box 3, folder 34, CCNYR; Elihu Root to Frederick Keppel, October 19, 1923, legal files, box 3, folder 38, CCNYR.

12. Root, Clark, Buckner & Howland to Frederick Keppel, April 25, 1924, Legal Files, box 3, folder 32, CCNYR; Root, Clark, Buckner & Howland to Henry S. Pritchett, January 18, 1922, Administrative Records, Secretary's Office Records, box 4, folder 1, CCNYR; Bertram to Keppel, March 30, 1931.

13. Nasaw, *Andrew Carnegie*, 14.

14. Nasaw, 33.

15. Wall, "Carnegie, Andrew."

16. Nasaw, *Andrew Carnegie*, 209.

17. Nasaw, 580.

18. Nasaw, 585; Edge, *Andrew Carnegie*, 99; Morris, *The Tycoons*, 262.

19. Carnegie, "Wealth."

20. Nasaw, *Andrew Carnegie*, 716.

21. White, *Republic for Which It Stands*, 656.

22. Nasaw, *Andrew Carnegie*, 498.

23. Nasaw; White, *Republic for Which It Stands*.

24. Carnegie, "Gospel of Wealth" and "Best Fields of Philanthropy."

25. Carnegie, *Gospel of Wealth and Other Writings*, 2.

26. Carnegie, 6.

27. Carnegie, 1.

28. Carnegie, 12.

29. Carnegie, 2.

30. Carnegie, 7.

31. Carnegie, 8.

32. Carnegie, 8.

33. Carnegie, 10.

34. Carnegie, 11.

35. Carnegie, 11.

36. Carnegie, 12.

37. Gladstone, "Mr. Carnegie's Gospel of Wealth," 677; Nasaw, *Andrew Carnegie*, 350.

38. Carnegie, *Gospel of Wealth and Other Writings*, 14.

39. See, for example, "Spreading Gospels of Wealth"; Strom, "Pledge to Give Away Fortunes Stirs Debate"; Walker, "Towards a New Gospel of Wealth."

40. Henderson, "Industrial Insurance," 589; Tolman, *Social Engineering*, 162–164.

41. Nasaw, *Andrew Carnegie*, 597–98; Levy, "Accounting for Profit and the History of Capital," 192. For a broader lens on the history on the devolving public purposes of private corporations and the evolution of private philanthropies serving the "public good," see, for example, Hartog, *Public Property and Private Power*; and Levy, "Altruism and the Origins of Nonprofit Philanthropy."

42. Nielsen, *Big Foundations*, 34.

43. Nasaw, *Andrew Carnegie*, 642.

44. Nasaw, 665–66.

45. Carnegie Corporation, "History of the Carnegie Hero Fund Commission"; Carnegie Corporation, "Other Carnegie Organizations."

46. Nasaw, *Andrew Carnegie*, 671.

47. Nasaw, 672.

48. Rosenfield, *World of Giving*, 18.

49. Nielsen, *Big Foundations*, 50–54.

50. Nasaw, *Andrew Carnegie*, 767.

51. Carnegie Corporation, *Charter, Constitution, and Bylaws*.

52. Board Minutes, January 12, 1923, CCNYR.

53. "Records History," James Bertram Collection (hereafter JBC).

54. Nasaw, *Andrew Carnegie*, 537.

55. Nasaw, 605.

56. Nasaw, 602.

57. Nasaw, 585.

58. Nasaw, 606.

59. Board Minutes, November 28, 1919, CCNYR.
60. Board Minutes, January 12, 1923, CCNYR.
61. Board Minutes.
62. Board Minutes.
63. Board Minutes.
64. Bertram to Keppel, March 30, 1931.
65. Bertram to Keppel.
66. Bertram to Keppel.
67. Bertram to Keppel.
68. Carnegie, *Triumphant Democracy*, 520; Carnegie, "Look Ahead," 685–710.
69. Carnegie, *Triumphant Democracy*, 520.
70. Carnegie, 520.
71. Carnegie, 520.
72. Carnegie, 520, 539.
73. Carnegie, 520.
74. Carnegie, 538–539.
75. Carnegie, 539.
76. Bell, *Idea of Greater Britain*, 1, 254.
77. Bell, 114.
78. James Russell, 1968, Interviewed by Isabel S. Grossner, Carnegie Corporation Oral History Project (hereafter CCOHP).
79. "Report of the President & the Secretary as to an Educational Program in Africa," December 1, 1927, VIIII.A.3 CCNY publications, miscellany volumes, no. 12 Africa, CCNYR.
80. Memorandum of Interview, January 25, 1927, III.A. Grant Files, ca. 1911–1988, box 281, folder 281.2, CCNYR.
81. Carnegie Corporation, *Charter, Constitution, and Bylaws.*
82. Carnegie Corporation. And yet, some decades earlier, the trustees and staff at Carnegie Corporation seemed relatively comfortable with these two coexisting means of interpreting the geographic scope of their organization's charter. See generally, Rosenfield, *A World of Giving*, 96; Stackpole, *Carnegie Corporation Commonwealth Program*; and, Lester, *Forty Years of Carnegie Giving.*
83. Bertram to Keppel, March 30, 1931.

## Chapter 2

1. James Bertram to Frederick Keppel, March 30, 1931, I.D. CCNY Administrative Records, Policy & Program, box 5, folder 5.4, Carnegie Corporation of New York Records (hereafter CCNYR).
2. Frederick Keppel to Thomas Jesse Jones, April 7, 1925, III.A. Grant Files, box 188A, folder 188A.5, CCNYR.
3. James Bertram to Frederick Keppel, March 30, 1931.
4. For a discussion of John D. Rockefeller Sr. and his son, see, for example, Chernow, *Titan*, 481–483.
5. Carnegie, *The Negro in America.*
6. Carnegie, 4–5.

7. Carnegie, 4.

8. Carnegie, 5.

9. Carnegie, 30.

10. Carnegie, 5.

11. Carnegie, 30.

12. Carnegie, 5.

13. Carnegie, 5.

14. Carnegie, 32.

15. Carnegie, 32.

16. Chernow, *Titan*, 483.

17. Hunter, *To 'Joy My Freedom*, 40.

18. Anderson, *The Education of Blacks in the South, 1860–1935*, 4.

19. Hunter, *To 'Joy My Freedom*, 41; Chernow, *Titan*, 483.

20. Marable, "Booker T. Washington and African Nationalism," 400; Dagbovie, "Exploring a Century of Historical Scholarship on Booker T. Washington," 257–259.

21. Thornbrough, "Booker T. Washington as Seen by His White Contemporaries," 166–167.

22. Beilke, "Peabody Education Fund," 553.

23. Anderson, "Northern Foundations," 373. See also Anderson, *The Education of Blacks in the South*.

24. Beilke, "John F. Slater Fund," 291–292; Fultz, "Teacher Training."

25. Anderson, "Northern Foundations," 378.

26. Brundage, *"Up from Slavery" by Booker T. Washington*, chap. 14.

27. See, for example, Foner, *Reconstruction*.

28. Hunter, *To 'Joy My Freedom*, 99.

29. Washington, *Up from Slavery*, 142.

30. Washington, 142.

31. Washington, 142–143.

32. Washington, 143.

33. Painter, *Standing at Armageddon*, 113.

34. Painter, 114.

35. Washington, *Up from Slavery*, 143.

36. Washington, 142.

37. Washington, 143.

38. Chernow, *Titan*, 239–242, 482.

39. Anderson, "Northern Foundations," 378.

40. Anderson, 379.

41. "The General Education Board." For more information on the smaller Peabody, Slater, and Jeanes Funds, see, for example, Alexander, *Slater and Jeanes Funds*, 2; "Administrative History," Phelps Stokes Fund Records (hereafter PSFR). ; West, "The Peabody Education Fund and Negro Education, 1867–1880."

42. "$600,000 for Tuskegee and B. T. Washington."

43. "$600,000 for Tuskegee and B. T. Washington."

44. It is also worth noting that John D. Rockefeller founded the Rockefeller Foundation two years later, in 1913, with a $100 million endowment. See "Finding a Footing."

45. Beilke, "General Education Board," 242–243.

46. Beilke, "Negro Rural School Fund," 507–508.

47. Beilke, "Peabody Education Fund," 553.

48. Jones, *Negro Education*, 1:xi.

49. Booker T. Washington to Phelps Stokes, May 15, 1911, quoted in King, *Pan-Africanism and Education*, 31.

50. Jones, *Negro Education*, 1:xi.

51. Anson Phelps Stokes to Booker T. Washington, November 12, 1912, in Harlan and Smock, *The Booker T. Washington Papers*.

52. Commissioner P. P. Claxton to Anson Phelps Stokes, January 21, 1913, box 44, folder 1, PSFR.

53. Jones, *Negro Education*, 1:xii.

54. Jones, 1: 1.

55. Jones, 1:22.

56. Jones, 1:10–11.

57. Jones, 1:12.

58. Jones, 1:12.

59. Jones, 1:12.

60. Jones, 1:12.

61. Thomas Jesse Jones to Anson Phelps Stokes, May 3, 1917, box 44, folder 5, PSFR. By the summer of 1919, Jones was using Phelps Stokes Fund letterhead. Compare the letterhead in Thomas Jesse Jones's correspondence to Anson Phelps Stokes Fund up until February 24, 1919, and then after August 13, 1919, box 44, folder 6 "U.S. Government Agencies, Bureau of Education, 1918–1919," PSFR.

62. Act of Congress (Act of March 3, 1917; 39 Stat. L., 1070, 1106; 5 U.S.C. 66).

63. Jones to Phelps Stokes, May 3, 1917.

64. Anderson, "Northern Foundations," 383.

65. Johnson, "W. E. B. Du Bois, Thomas Jesse Jones."

66. Du Bois, "Negro Education."

67. Du Bois.

68. Du Bois.

69. Du Bois.

70. Du Bois.

71. Carter G. Woodson to "Gentlemen," June 26, 1936, 1.1. projects, series 200 United States, box 9, folder 81, Rockefeller Foundation Records. See also, for example, Holmes "Twenty-Five Years of Thomas Jesse Jones." For discussion of the conference, see, for example, Thomas Jesse Jones to Wallace Buttrick, July 7, 1917 (with attached memorandum "Tentative Plans for a Conference on Negro Education"), series 1, subseries 2, box 264, folder 2728, General Education Board Records.

72. Woodson to "Gentlemen," June 26, 1936.

73. Woodson to "Gentlemen."

74. Woodson, "Thomas Jesse Jones."

75. Board of Trustees Minutes, November 20, 1918, box 2, folder 1, PSFR.

76. Memorandum, "Future Work of the Phelps Stokes Fund," February 3, 1919, enclosed in Thomas Jesse Jones to Anson Phelps Stokes, February 3, 1919, box 44, folder 6, PSFR.

77. Oldham, "Christian Missions."
78. Memorandum, "Future Work of the Phelps Stokes Fund."
79. Jones, *Education in Africa*; Jones, *Education in East Africa.*
80. Jones, *Education in Africa*; Clements, *Faith on the Frontier*, 220.
81. Jacobs, "James Emman Kwegyir Aggrey," 47, 54.
82. Jacobs, 55.
83. Jones, *Education in Africa*, 6.
84. Jones, 6.
85. Jones, 6.
86. Jones, 6.
87. Jones, 12.
88. Jones, 13, 15.
89. Berman, "American Influence on African Education," 135.
90. Berman, 135–136.
91. Wilson, "End of the 'Great Dark Continent.'"
92. Wilson.
93. Norman Leys to J. H. Oldham, November 14, 1921, in Cell, *By Kenya Possessed.*
94. Saville, "Britain," 572. Leys's perspective on Africa was well known presumably on both sides of the Atlantic. At least since 1921, for example, W. E. B. Du Bois had been in correspondence with Leys about attending the next Pan-African Congress. See W. E. B. Du Bois to Norman Leys, May 27, 1921, W. E. B. Du Bois Papers.
95. Leys to Oldham, November 14, 1921.
96. Leys to Oldham.
97. Clements, *Faith on the Frontier*, 221.
98. Clements, 221.
99. Clements, 221; "Education Mission Going to Africa."
100. Clements, *Faith on the Frontier*, 221.
101. Jones, *Education in East Africa*, 3.
102. Jones, 7.
103. Thomas Jesse Jones to Anson Phelps Stokes, March 20, 1925, box 16, folder 11, PSFR.
104. Lowe, "Sadler, Sir Michael Ernest (1861–1943)."
105. Whitehead, "Education Policy in British Tropical Africa."
106. Oldham, "Educational Policy of the British Government in Africa," 424.
107. Wilson, "Africa, the Continent of Misunderstandings."
108. Frederick P. Keppel to Thomas Jesse Jones, May 27, 1925, box 188A, folder 188A.5, CCNYR; CCNY Memorandum of Interview "MAC, Thomas Jesse Jones, and Mr. Dougall—Kenya Colony," box 188A, folder 188A.5, CCNYR.
109. Carnegie Corporation of New York Report of the President, 1931, CCNYR; Phelps Stokes Fund to Frederick P. Keppel, January 20, 1932, III.A. Grant Files, ca. 1911–1988, box 188A, folder 188A.6 "Jeanes Schools—Miscellaneous," CCNYR; Frederick P. Keppel to J. H. Oldham, March 11, 1929, III.A. Grant Files, ca. 1911–1988, box 188A, folder "Jeanes Schools—Ny[a]saland."
110. Carnegie Corporation of New York Report of the President, 1931, CCNYR.
111. J. H. Oldham to Frederick P. Keppel, April 30, 1925, grant files, box 188A, folder 188A-5, CCNYR.

*Chapter 3*

1. J. H. Oldham to Frederick P. Keppel, "Memorandum of Conversations with Colonel Arthur S. Woods and Dr Ruml of the Laura Spelman Foundation, October 26, 28 and November 5, 1925," III.A. grant files, box 281, folder 281.2, 5, Carnegie Corporation of New York Records (hereafter CCNYR).

2. Oldham to Keppel, "Memorandum of Conversations," 2–3; Rose, *Survey of Sources*, 5.

3. "Cross Reference Sheet, FA 1977," III.A. Grant Files, box 196, folder 196.6, CCNYR.

4. Oldham to Keppel, "Memorandum of Conversations," 1.

5. Oldham to Keppel, 2–3.

6. Oldham to Keppel, 2.

7. Vitalis, *White World Order, Black Power Politics*, 57.

8. Painter, *History of White People*, 341; Willoughby-Herard, *Waste of a White Skin*; Bell, *Idea of Greater Britain*; Mazower, *No Enchanted Palace*; Magubane, *Making of a Racist State*; Zimmerman, *Alabama in Africa*; Padmore, *Africa*; Bunche, *World View of Race*; Du Bois, "The Souls of White Folk"; Fanon, *Wretched of the Earth*; Fanon, *Black Skin, White Masks*.

9. Lake and Reynolds, *Drawing the Global Colour Line*, 4.

10. Lake and Reynolds; Vitalis, *White World Order, Black Power Politics*; Robinson, *Black Marxism*; Getachew, *Worldmaking after Empire*; Blain, *Set the World on Fire*; Matera, *Black London*; Makalani, *In the Cause of Freedom*; Moses, *Golden Age of Black Nationalism, 1850–1925*; Edwards, *Practice of Diaspora*; Ewing, *Age of Garvey*.

11. Blain, *Set the World on Fire*, 2.

12. Blain, 12.

13. Blain, 6.

14. Moses, *Creative Conflict in African American Thought*, 249.

15. Stein, *World of Marcus Garvey*.

16. See Ewing, *Age of Garvey*.

17. Ewing; Blain, *Set the World on Fire*.

18. Pamphlet describing M1440, "Correspondence of the Military Intelligence Division Relating to 'Negro Subversion,' 1917–1941," 2–3, 5 (hereafter CMI); Ellis, *Race, War, and Surveillance*, 82.

19. Ellis, *Race, War, and Surveillance*, xix–xx.

20. Ellis, 53.

21. Ellis, 53.

22. Ellis, 82.

23. Pamphlet describing M1440, 4.

24. Pamphlet, 4.

25. Pamphlet, 5.

26. Robinson, *Black Marxism*, 217; Blain, *Set the World on Fire*; Stewart, *New Negro*.

27. W. E. B. Du Bois, "The Conservation of Races," American Negro Academy Address, 1896, quoted in Moses, *Creative Conflict in African American Thought*, 207.

28. Van Deburg, *Modern Black Nationalism*, 40.

29. "Mr Keppel Accepts New Call."

30. Füredi, *The Silent War*, 38.

31. Füredi, 78.

32. Füredi, 59, 88.

33. Walters, "Pan-Africanism."

34. W. E. B. Du Bois to George S. Oettlé, October 22, 1934, W. E. B. Du Bois Records (hereafter DBR).

35. Du Bois to Oettlé.

36. Du Bois to "The Carnegie Fund," October 6, 1937, DBR; Du Bois to Mr. Russell, November 12, 1937, DBR.

37. Du Bois to Frederick Keppel, May 30, 1939, DBR.

38. Keppel to Du Bois, August 29, 1939, DBR.

39. Keppel to Du Bois.

40. Vitalis, *White World Order, Black Power Politics*, ix.

41. J. H. Oldham to Lionel Curtis, February 11, 1921, cited in King, "Africa and the Southern States of the U.S.A.," 665.

42. J. H. Oldham to Lionel Curtis, February 11, 1921, cited in Clements, *Faith on the Frontier*, 176.

43. Cell, *Hailey*, 62.

44. Oldham to Curtis, February 11, 1921, cited in Clements, *Faith on the Frontier*, 176; King, "African Students in Negro American Colleges," 19.

45. King, *Pan-Africanism and Education*, 215.

46. Little, "Higher Education," 562; Nkomo, *How I Found Christ in the Jungles of Africa*, 10.

47. Nkomo, *How I Found Christ in the Jungles of Africa*, 2–3.

48. Nkomo, 5.

49. Nkomo, 10.

50. Nkomo, 10.

51. King, *Pan-Africanism and Education*, 215.

52. Little, "Higher Education," 562.

53. King, *Pan-Africanism and Education*, 215.

54. King, 221.

55. Oldham to Curtis, February 11, 1921, cited in Clements, *Faith on the Frontier*, 176; King, "African Students in Negro American Colleges," 19–20.

56. Oldham to Curtis, 176.

57. Oldham to Keppel, "Memorandum of Conversations," 3.

58. Bennett, "Paramountcy to Partnership," 357.

59. "Education Policy in British Tropical Africa: Memorandum Submitted to the Secretary of State for the Colonies by the Advisory Committee on Native Education in the British Tropical African Dependencies," March 1925, III.A. grant files, box 196, folder 196.6, CCNYR.

60. Ormsby-Gore, *East Africa*.

61. Bennett, "Paramountcy to Partnership," 357–358.

62. Bennett, 358.

63. Oldham to Keppel, "Memorandum of Conversations," 5.

64. Oldham to Keppel, 5.

65. Oldham to Keppel, 5.

66. Oldham to Keppel, 5.

67. Oldham, *Christianity and the Race Problem*, 23.

68. In promoting this research methodology, Oldham and the British Colonial Office were far from unique at the time. Rather, they were reflecting growing trends in these fields. See Bulmer and Bulmer, "Philanthropy and Social Sciences in the 1920s," 369.

69. Anson Phelps Stokes to Raymond Fosdick, undated, box 31, folder 2, Phelps Stokes Fund Records (hereafter PSFR); Beardsley Ruml to Anson Phelps Stokes, June 2, 1927, box 31, folder 2, PSFR. Several letters between Stokes, J. H. Oldham, Charles Loram, and Thomas Jesse Jones highlight the Rockefellers' (and particularly the Laura Spelman Rockefeller Memorial's) preference for the "research approach." See, for example, J. H. Oldham to Thomas Jesse Jones, April 27, 1927, box 31, folder 2, PSFR; Thomas Jesse Jones to Charles Loram, June 3, 1927, box 31, folder 2, PSFR.

70. Beardsley Ruml to Anson Phelps Stokes, April 9, 1926, box 31, folder 1, PSFR; Ruml to Stokes, July 2, 1926: "The Memorial would appreciate it if no public announcement of this appropriation were made other than that which you make in your regular report," box 31, folder 1, PSFR.

71. S. H. Church to Frederick Keppel, November 5, 1925, box 281, folder 281.1, CCNYR; J. H. Oldham to Carnegie Corporation, December 10, 1925, box 281, folder 281.1, CCNYR.

72. Donald Young, interview by Isabel S. Grossner, March 16, 1967, transcript, Carnegie Corporation Oral History Project (hereafter CCOHP).

73. Quoted in Lewis, *W. E. B. Du Bois*, 448.

74. Jones, *Education in Africa*; Glotzer, "Long Shadow," 636–637.

75. Oldham to Keppel, "Memorandum of Conversations," 5–6.

76. James Bertram Finding Aid, Special Collecting Initiative, James Bertram Collection; Glotzer, "Long Shadow," 644.

77. Oldham, "Christian Missions and the Education of the Negro." See also Heyman, "C. T. Loram," 41–50.

78. Jones, *Education in Africa*, xxii.

79. Davie, *Poverty Knowledge in South Africa*, 9.

80. Thompson, *History of South Africa*, 143.

81. Thompson, 141–153.

82. Davie, *Poverty Knowledge in South Africa*, 30.

83. Davie, 30.

84. Davie, 33.

85. Davie, 59.

86. Thompson, *History of South Africa*, 158; Marks, "Smuts, Jan Christiaan (1870–1950)."

87. For more on Russell's trip, see, for example, E. G. Malherbe, "The Carnegie Poor White Investigation: Its Origin and Sequels" (1973), box 295, folder 295.7, CCNYR.

88. Thompson, *History of South Africa*, 159.

89. Seekings, "'Not a Single White Person Should Be Allowed to Go Under.'"

90. Seekings, 380; Davie, *Poverty Knowledge*, 50–51.

91. Seekings, "'Not a Single White Person,'" 380. See also Fleisch, "Social Scientists as Policy Makers."

92. Tayler, "'Our Poor,'" 40.

93. Glotzer, "Long Shadow," 636–637.

94. Malherbe, *Education in South Africa*.

95. Fleisch, "Social Scientists as Policy Makers," 349–372, 353.

96. Fleisch, 349–372, 353.

97. Fleisch, 353.

98. "Report of the President & the Secretary as to an Educational Program in Africa, Printed for the Information of the Board of Trustees," December 1, 1927, Carnegie Corporation of New York Publications vol. 55, "Miscellany 12 Africa 1951," CCNYR; Glotzer, "Career of Mable Carney," 325.

99. John Russell, interview by Isabel S. Grossner, 1968, CCOHP.

100. James Bertram Finding Aid; and, Glotzer, "Long Shadow," 644.

101. Jones to Loram, June 3, 1927.

102. "Report of the President & The Secretary as to An Educational Program in Africa."

103. Fleisch, "Social Scientists as Policymakers," 355.

104. E. G. Malherbe, "The Carnegie Poor White Investigation: Its Origin and Sequels," 1973, box 295, folder 295.7, CCNYR. Fleisch, "Social Scientists as Policy Makers," 355.

105. Magubane, "The American Construction of the Poor White Problem in South Africa," 696.

106. "Report of the President & the Secretary as to an Educational Program in Africa."

107. "Report of the President & the Secretary as to an Educational Program in Africa."

108. "Report of the President & the Secretary as to an Educational Program in Africa."

109. "Report of the President & the Secretary as to an Educational Program in Africa."

110. "Report of the President & the Secretary as to an Educational Program in Africa."

111. "Report of the President & the Secretary as to an Educational Program in Africa."

112. Fleisch, "Social Scientists as Policy Makers," 352.

113. Driver, *Patrick Duncan*, 22; Crawford, "Sir Carruthers Beattie"; Fantham, "Outdshoorn Meeting of the South African Association for the Advancement of Science."

114. "Report of the President & the Secretary as to an Educational Program in Africa."

115. Füredi, *The Silent War*, 66.

116. "Report of the President & the Secretary as to an Educational Program in Africa."

117. J. H. Oldham to Frederick Keppel, December 1, 1927, grant files, box 196, folder 196.6, CCNYR.

118. Frederick Keppel to Godfrey Thompson, December 2, 1927, grant files, box 196, folder 196.6, CCNYR.

119. Oldham to Keppel, December 1, 1927.

120. Oliver, *General Intelligence Test for Africans*; "Final Report to Carnegie Corporation on Educational Research in East Africa," grant files, box 196, folder 196.6, CCNYR.

121. See, generally, grant files, box 196, folder 196.6, CCNYR.

122. "Report of the President & the Secretary as to an Educational Program in Africa."

## Chapter 4

1. "Report of the President & the Secretary as to an Educational Program in Africa," December 1, 1927, Carnegie Corporation of New York Records (hereafter CCNYR); Frederick Keppel to Charles Loram, September 14, 1927, Carnegie Corporation Administrative Records, box 5, folder "P&P Commonwealth, Africa, 1927–1955, FPK-Loram correspondence," CCNYR.

2. "Report of the President & the Secretary as to an Educational Program in Africa," December 1, 1927, CCNYR.

3. F. S. Malan to Frederick Keppel, September 14, 1927, Grant Files, box 295, folder 295.5, CCNYR.

4. See, for example, Davie, *Poverty Knowledge in South Africa*, 42.

5. Reverends F. X. Roome, F. S. Malan, and Charles Murray to Carnegie Corporation, December 1, 1927, Carnegie Corporation Records, Grant Files, box 295, folder 295.5, CCNYR.

6. Reverends F. X. Roome, F. S. Malan, and Charles Murray to Carnegie Corporation, December 1, 1927, Grant Files, box 295, folder 295.5, CCNYR.

7. E. G. Malherbe, "The Carnegie Poor White Investigation: Its Origin and Sequels," 1973, box 295, folder 295.7, CCNYR.

8. "Report of the President & the Secretary as to an Educational Program in Africa"; Keppel to Loram, September 14, 1927.

9. Bulmer and Bulmer, "Philanthropy and Social Science in the 1920s," 384; Merriam, "Annual Report of the Social Sciences Research Council."

10. Ross, *Origins of American Social Science*, 401.

11. Lyons, *Uneasy Partnership*, 44–45. See, generally, SSRC, accession 1, series 5, Hanover Conferences, boxes 329–330.

12. "General Memorandum by the Director," series 2, box 2, folder 31, quoted in Bulmer and Bulmer, "Philanthropy and Social Science in the 1920s," 361.

13. "General Memorandum by the Director," series 2, box 2, folder 31, quoted in Bulmer and Bulmer, "Philanthropy and Social Science in the 1920s," 361.

14. See, for example, Maribel Morey, "Rockefeller, Carnegie, and the SSRC's Focus."

15. Donald Fisher, *Fundamental Development of the Social Sciences*; Worcester, "Social Science Research Council," 19.

16. "Friday Evening Session," accession 1, series 5, Hanover Conference, box 330, folder 1895 "Hanover Conference 1930," SSRC Papers, 23.

17. Frederick Keppel to Charles E. Merriam, June 8, 1926, Social Science Research Council (SSRC) Committee on P&P Minutes, accession 1, series 2.1, Minute, box 307, Social Science Research Council Records (hereafter SSRCR); SSRC Minutes, Hanover, September 1, 1928, SSRCR; SSRC, accession 1, series 9, Council (SSRC Minutes), box 352, folder 2086; SSRC, accession 1, series 2.1, Minutes, box 309, folder 1769, SSRRCR.

18. Keppel, "The Arts in Social Life."

19. Charles T. Loram to Frederick Keppel, April 11, 1928, Grant Files, series 1, box 295, folder 295.5, CCNYR.

20. Loram to Keppel, April 11, 1928, and accompanying "Report on Sociological Aspect of Poor White Question," Grant Files, box 295, folder 295.5, CCNYR.

21. Malherbe, *Education Report*, foreword; Stephen H. Stackpole, "CC Funds in South Africa for Social Research," April 17, 1953, box 333, folder 333.5, CCNYR.

22. Alan Pifer to Fred van Wyk, "Memo on Poor White Study," May 8, 1973, box 295, folder 295.7, CCNYR.

23. Malherbe, Foreword, in Malherbe, *Educational Report*.

24. Loram to Keppel, April 11, 1928, and accompanying "Report on Sociological Aspect of Poor White Question."

25. Charles Loram to Frederick Keppel, February 10, 1929, Grant Files, series 1, box 102, folder "Poor White Study—Keppel-Loram Correspondence."

26. Loram to Keppel, April 11, 1928.

27. "Report of the President & the Secretary as to an Educational Program in Africa," VIII.A.3 CCNY publications, Miscellany Volumes, no. 12 Africa, CCNYR.

28. Wickliffe Rose to Frederick Keppel, December 29, 1927, Grant Files, box 295, folder 295.5, CCNYR; Frederick Keppel to Wickliffe Rose, December 28, 1927, Grant Files, box 295, folder 295.5, CCNYR.

29. Keppel to Rose.

30. Frederick Keppel to R. W. Wilcocks, March 28, 1929, Grant Files, box 295, folder 295.5, CCNYR; Driberg to Keppel, March 28, 1928, Grant Files, box 295, folder 295.5, CCNYR.

31. Charles Loram to Frederick Keppel, April 15, 1928, Grant Files, box 295, folder 295.5, CCNYR.

32. Loram to Keppel, April 15, 1928.

33. Loram to Keppel, April 15, 1928.

34. Charles Loram to Frederick Keppel, July 31, 1928, Grant Files, box 295, folder 295.4, CCNYR.

35. "Background on Kenyon Leech Butterfield," Kenyon L. Butterfield Papers (hereafter KLBP); Ring, *The Problem South*, 158 256; Charles Loram to Frederick Keppel, December 7, 1929, Grant Files, box 126, folder "Coulter, Charles W. 1928–1934," CCNYR

36. See, for example, Keppel, foreword, v.

37. Malherbe served as the educational researcher; Stellenbosch University professor J. F. Grosskopf as the economist; Stellenbosch University professor R. W. Wilcocks as the psychologist; the Department of Health's W. A. Murray as the health researcher. The journalist M. E. Rothman (the only woman researcher on the team) provided the "gender component."

38. Keppel, "The Arts in Social Life."

39. Malherbe, *Education Report*, 6.

40. Malherbe, 8–12; Bulmer, *The Chicago School of Sociology*, 108.

41. Malherbe, *Education Report*, 8.

42. Malherbe, 8.

43. Malherbe, 9.

44. Malherbe, 8.

45. Malherbe, 8.

46. Malherbe, 9.

47. Quoted in Willoughby-Herard, *Waste of a White Skin*, 157.

48. Willoughby-Herard, *Waste of a White Skin*, 155.

49. Carnegie Commission, "Joint Findings and Recommendations of the Commission," *The Poor White Problem in South Africa*, xix.

50. Wilcocks, *Psychological Report*, chap. 12; Malherbe, *Education Report*, chap. 8.

51. Two years later, for example, Gunnar and Alva Myrdal would make a similar argument about white Swedes of different social classes in *Kris i befolkningsfrågan*.

52. Carnegie Commission, "Joint Findings," viii.

53. Carnegie Commission, viii.

54. Carnegie Commission, ix–x.

55. Carnegie Commission, x.

56. Carnegie Commission, x.

57. Carnegie Commission, xi.

58. Carnegie Commission, xviii–xix.

59. Carnegie Commission, xxi.

60. Carnegie Commission, xx–xxi.

61. Seekings, "Carnegie Commission," 517.

62. Davis, "Charles T. Loram and the American Model," 90.

63. Carnegie Commission, "Joint Findings," xx.

64. Carnegie Commission, xx.

65. Carnegie Commission, xxi.

66. Carnegie Commission, xviii, xxi–xxii.

67. Carnegie Commission, xxiii.

68. Carnegie Commission, xxvi–xxvii.

69. Carnegie Commission, xxviii.

70. Carnegie Commission, xxxii, xxxiii.

71. Stephen H. Stackpole, "Carnegie Corporation Commonwealth Program 1911–1961," 1963, CCNYR; Dubow, *A Commonwealth of Knowledge*, 227; Fleisch, "Social Scientists as Policy Makers," 350.

72. Malherbe, "The Carnegie Poor White Investigation."

73. Tayler, "'Our Poor,'" 49; Stultz, *Afrikaner Politics in South Africa*, 178; Davis, "Charles T. Loram and the American Model," 110.

74. Tayler, "'Our Poor,'" 41n4.

75. Tayler, 51.

76. Tayler, 44; Pick, Rispel, and Naidoo, "Poverty, Health and Policy," 169. See also Bell, "American Philanthropy, Carnegie Corporation and Poverty in South Africa," 482.

77. James Bertram to Frederick Keppel, February 18, 1930, Grant Files, box 206, folder 206.1, CCNYR.

78. Bertram to Keppel.

79. Davis, "Charles T. Loram and the American Model," 90; Charles Loram to Frederick Keppel, January 6, 1930, Grant Files, box 206, folder 206.1, CCNY.

80. Bertram to Keppel.

81. Bertram to Keppel.

82. Myrdal, *An American Dilemma*.

83. Office of the President, Record of Interview, March 16, 1939, Grant Files, box 295, folder 295.6, CCNYR.

84. Carnegie Corporation Executive Committee Meeting, March 28, 1929, series I.A.4, Bound Agendas and Minutes, vol. 7, CCNYR.

85. Frederick Keppel to Col. O.F. Watkins, February 10, 1928, Carnegie Corporation Records, Grant Files, box 6, folder 6.1.

86. Frederick Keppel to Charles Loram, November 9, 1927, Grant Files, box 295, folder 295.9, CCNYR.

87. Clements, *Faith on the Frontier*, 238–240.

88. 1931 Report to the Trustees, I.D. Administrative Records, Policy & Program, box 6, folder 6.2, CCNYR.

*Chapter 5*

1. "Luncheon for Dr. Keppel, Summary of Discussion," June 13, 1933, Administrative Records, I.D., Policy & Program, box 6, folder 6.3, Carnegie Corporation of New York Records (hereafter CCNYR).

2. Report to the Trustees, 1931, Administrative Records, I.D., Policy & Program, box 6, folder 6.2, CCNYR; Murphy, *Carnegie Corporation and Africa*, 24.

3. Bertram to Keppel.

4. Bertram to Keppel.

5. "Luncheon for Dr. Keppel"; "Office of the Secretary Memorandum from RML to JMR," August 10, 1939, Legal Files, box 4, folder 17, CCNYR.

6. Executive Committee Meeting, March 27, 1931, CCNYR.

7. Keppel to Oldham, February 28, 1931, Administrative Records, I.D., box 6, folder 6.2, CCNYR

8. See Chatham House, "Our History"; May, "Curtis, Lionel George."

9. Parmar, *Think Tanks and Power in Foreign Policy*, 80.

10. Executive Committee Meeting, October 5, 1933, CCNYR.

11. "Memorandum of Conversations with Colonel Arthur S. Woods and Dr. Ruml of the Laura Spelman Foundation, October 26, 28 and November 5, 1925," grant files, box 281, folder 281.2, CCNYR.

12. See, generally, Administrative Records, I.D. Policy & Program, box 6, folder 6.2–6.5, CCNYR.

13. See, for example, Ivison Macadam to Frederick Keppel, April 28, 1933, III.A. grant files, ca. 1911–1988, box 797, folder 797.5, CCNYR.

14. Lugard, *Dual Mandate in British Tropical Africa*.

15. Smuts, *Africa and Some World Problems*.

16. "June 23, 1931, Notes, Special Fund Conference, London Notes, Chatham House Conference, May 21, 1931," Administrative Records, I.D., Policy & Program, box 6, folder 6.2, CCNYR.

17. "June 23, 1931, Notes."

18. "June 23, 1931, Notes."

19. "June 23, 1931, Notes."

20. "June 23, 1931, Notes"; and Peter Gosden, "Heath, Sir (Henry) Frank."

21. "London Conference, Report to the Trustees (1931)," Administrative Records, I.D., Policy & Program, box 6, folder 6.2, CCNYR.

22. "London Conference."

23. "London Conference."

24. "London Conference."

25. Executive Committee Meeting, May, 17, 1934, CCNYR.

26. Lionel Curtis to Frederick Keppel, July 20, 1931, III.A. grant files, box 797, folder 797.5, CCNYR.

27. Curtis to Keppel.

28. Curtis to Keppel.

29. Curtis to Keppel.

30. Keppel to Curtis, July 29, 1931, III.A. grant files, box 797, folder 797.5, CCNYR.

31. Curtis to Keppel.
32. "Luncheon for Dr. Keppel."
33. "Luncheon for Dr. Keppel."
34. "Luncheon for Dr. Keppel."
35. Lothian, foreword.
36. Tilley, *Africa as a Living Laboratory*, 76.
37. See, for example, Coupland, "The Hailey Survey," 1; Hetherington, *British Paternalism and Africa*, 7; Rich, *Race and Empire in British Politics*, 146–147; Brown, "Godfrey Wilson and the Rhodes-Livingston Institute," 176; Cell, *Hailey*; Tilley, *Africa as a Living Laboratory*; Hailey, Foreword, in Hailey, *An African Survey*.
38. Tilley, *Africa as a Living Laboratory*, 78–79, n40.
39. Lothian, foreword, i.
40. Tilley, *Africa as a Living Laboratory*, 86.
41. Philip Kerr to Frank Aydelotte, November 14, 1929, Rhodes House Archive (RHA), File 2792.
42. Frederick Keppel to Charles Loram, December 26, 1929, grant files, box 295, folder 295.7, CCNYR.
43. "Memorandum of Conversations with Colonel Arthur S. Woods and Dr. Ruml of the Laura Spelman Foundation, October 26, 28, and November 5, 1925," grant files, box 281, folder 281.2, CCNYR.
44. Lugard, *Dual Mandate*; Tilley, *Africa as a Living Laboratory*, 70.
45. Kuper, *Anthropologists and Anthropology*, 130–133; Tilley, *Africa as a Living Laboratory*, 70.
46. See, for example, Wala, *Council on Foreign Relations*.
47. May, "Milner's Kindergarten."
48. See, generally, Administrative Records, I.D., Policy & Program, box 6, folders 6.2–6.6, CCNYR.
49. Tilley, *Africa as a Living Laboratory* 70.
50. Parmar, *Think Tanks and Power in Foreign Policy*, 58; Louis, introduction, 14.
51. Rich, *Race and Empire in British Politics*, 54–55.
52. May, "Coupland, Sir Reginald."
53. May, "Coupland."
54. May, "Curtis, Lionel George."
55. May, "Kerr, Philip Henry, Eleventh Marquess of Lothian."
56. May, "Milner's Kindergarten."
57. Oldham, *White and Black in Africa*; Maxon, "Devonshire Declaration"; Okia, "The Northey Forced Labor Crisis, 1920–1921."
58. Oldham, *White and Black in Africa*, 70.
59. Oldham.
60. Füredi, *The Silent War*, 80.
61. "June 23, 1931, Notes."
62. "June 23, 1931, Notes."
63. Report of the President, 1931, CCNYR.
64. Report of the President.
65. Tilley, *Africa as a Living Laboratory*, 100.

66. Füredi, *Silent War*, 58–59.

67. Kuper, *Anthropologists and Anthropology*, 130–33.

68. See, for example, Rivière, "The Formative Years"; Davis, "How All Souls Got Its Anthropologist."

69. Malinowski, "Practical Anthropology."

70. Malinowski.

71. Kuper, *Anthropologists and Anthropology*, 125. See also James, "Anthropologist as Reluctant Imperialist."

72. James, "Anthropologist as Reluctant Imperialist," 53–54.

73. Malinowski, "Practical Anthropology."

74. James, "Anthropologist as Reluctant Imperialist," 51.

75. Tilley, *Africa as a Living Laboratory*, 100.

76. See, for example, Lugard, *Dual Mandate in British Tropical Africa*, 18; "Memorandum from British Colonial Secretary," 260.

77. Curtis to Keppel, July 20, 1931; Keppel to Curtis, July 29, 1931; Honoré, "Feetham, Richard"; Lavin, "Duncan, Sir Patrick."

78. Lionel Curtis to Frederick Keppel, August 11, 1932, III.A. grant files, box 797, folder 797.5, CCNYR.

79. Keppel to Curtis, July 29, 1931, III.A. grant files, box 797, folder 797.5, CCNYR.

80. "Notes, August 10, 1931," Administrative Records, I.D., Policy & Program, box 6, folder 6.2, CCNYR.

81. Frederick Keppel to Ivison Macadam, October 17, 1931, III.A. grant files, box 797, folder 797.5, CCNYR.

82. Ivison Macadam to Frederick Keppel, June 23, 1933, III.A. grant files, box 797, folder 797.5, CCNYR.

83. "Luncheon for Dr. Keppel"; Cell, *Hailey*, 215, 220–221.

84. Cell, *Hailey*, 222.

85. Cell, 222–223.

86. Cell, 224, 227.

87. Cell, 224, 227.

88. Cell, 224.

89. Cell, 229.

90. Cell, 233.

91. Cell, 229.

92. Lord Lothian (Philip Kerr) to Frederick Keppel, December 16, 1936, III.A. grant files, box 797, folder 797.6, CCNYR; Keppel to Lothian, January 11, 1937, III.A. grant files, box 797, folder 797.6, CCNYR; Keppel to John Russell, April 15, 1937, III.A. grant files, box 797, folder 797.6; Russell to Lothian, May 14, 1937, III.A. grant files, box 797, folder 797.6, CCNYR.

93. Cell, *Hailey*, 230–231.

94. Cell, 231.

95. Cell, 232; Stockwell, "Pedler, Sir Frederick Johnson."

96. Cell, *Hailey*, 232, 233.

97. Lord Lothian (Philip Kerr) to Frederick Keppel, August 2, 1938, III.A. grant files, box 797, folder 797.6, CCNYR.

98. "Aug. 28–29, 1941, Office of the President Record of Interview, CD and Dr. Myrdal," "Negro Study" General Correspondence, Roll #1, CCNYR.

99. "Aug. 28–29, 1941, Office of the President Record of Interview."

100. Gunnar Myrdal to Frederick Keppel, July 7, 1941, "Negro Study" General Correspondence, Roll #1, CCNYR.

101. Jackson, *Gunnar Myrdal and America's Conscience*, 161.

102. Myrdal, *An American Dilemma*, xvi.

103. Hailey, *An African Survey*.

104. Hailey, xxi.

105. Hailey, xxi.

106. Hailey, xxi.

107. Hailey, xxi.

108. Hailey, xxv.

109. Hailey, ix–xvii.

110. Hailey.

111. Cell, *Hailey*, 231, 236.

112. Hailey, *An African Survey*, xxii.

113. Hailey, xxiii.

114. Hailey, xxiv–xxv.

115. "[London Conference of Advisers], April 14, 1937, Summary of Discussion," Administrative Records, I.D., Policy & Program, box 6, folder 6.5, CCNYR.

116. Frederick Keppel to Lord Lothian (Philip Kerr), November 29, 1938, III.A. grant files, box 797, folder 797.6, CCNYR.

117. "[London Conference of Advisers], April 14, 1937."

118. "[London Conference of Advisers], April 14, 1937."

119. "[London Conference of Advisers], April 14, 1937"; Jewkes and Jewkes, "Clay, Sir Henry (1883–1954).

120. Frederick Keppel to Malcolm Hailey, September 20, 1939, grant files, box 797, folder 797.6, CCNYR. For more on Jabavu, see Higgs, *Ghost of Equality*.

121. Keppel to Hailey.

122. Davie, *Poverty Knowledge in South Africa*, 46–47.

123. Mkhize, "'To See Us as We See Ourselves.'"

124. Higgs, "Jabavu, Davidson Don Tengo (1885–1959)."

125. Higgs.

126. Saunders, "Biography of a Political Activist."

127. "Memo," February 3, 1939, III.A. grant files, box 797, folder 797.6, CCNYR.

128. Hetherington, *British Paternalism and Africa*, 4–5, 7.

129. Pedler, "Lord Hailey," 486.

130. Keppel to Matheson, August 16, 1939, grant files, box 797, folder 797.6, CCNYR; Royal Scottish Geographical Society, "Livingstone Medal."

131. Cell, *Hailey*, 217.

132. Hetherington, *British Paternalism and Africa*, 110; Brown, "Godfrey Wilson and the Rhodes-Livingstone Institute," 176; Kuper, *Anthropologists and Anthropology*, 134; "Tribute to Lord Hailey," 94–96.

133. Cell, *Hailey*, 235.

134. Hailey, *An African Survey*, xxiv–xxv.

135. Hailey, xxi.

136. Plant, "An African Survey," 205.

137. Worthington, "Lord Hailey on the African Survey," 582.

138. Worthington, 582.

139. Hailey, *An African Survey*, xxv.

140. Hailey, *An African Survey*, xxiv.

141. Matera, *Black London*, 89–90; Robinson, *Black Marxism*.

142. McLemee and Le Blanc, *C. L. R. James and Revolutionary Marxism*, 132.

143. Matera, *Black London*, 89.

144. Matera, 90–91.

145. Du Bois, review, 121. See also, Du Bois, *Color and Democracy*, 257.

146. Lewis, *W. E. B. Du Bois*, 453.

147. Du Bois, review," 123.

148. Du Bois, 121.

## Chapter 6

1. Jackson, *Gunnar Myrdal and America's Conscience*, 33.

2. Frederick Keppel and J. H. Oldham, Record of Interview, November 23, 1936, box 281, folder 281.1, Carnegie Corporation of New York Records (hereafter CCNYR).

3. John Russell, interview by Isabel S. Grossner, 1968, Carnegie Corporation Oral History Project (hereafter CCOHP).

4. Russell interview.

5. Russell interview.

6. Russell interview.

7. Russell interview.

8. Russell interview.

9. Russell interview.

10. Russel interview.

11. Ellis, *Race, War, and Surveillance*, 53.

12. W. E. B. Du Bois, *Dusk of Dawn*, quoted in Ellis, 251.

13. Board of Trustees Meeting, October 24, 1935, CCNYR. Carnegie Corporation listed "Negro education" as a grantmaking category as recently as its previous meeting on March 21, 1935.

14. Frederick P. Keppel and Henry James, Memorandum of Interview, June 18, 1930, folder 24.5, CCNYR.

15. Leffingwell to Keppel, February 14, 1929, I.E.5. Trustee Files, box 24, folder 24.10, CCNYR; Russel interview.

16. Leffingwell to Keppel.

17. Russell interview.

18. Russell interview.

19. Leffingwell to Keppel.

20. Russell interview.

21. Russell interview.

22. Rosenthal, *Nicholas Miraculous*, 357.

23. Rosenthal, 357.

24. Rosenthal, 358.

25. Russell interview. Keppel expressed his frustrations with his board in another context, including an SSRC meeting that year. See, "Friday Evening Session," accession 1, series 5, Hanover Conference, box 330, folder 1895, Social Science Research Council Records (hereafter SSRCR).

26. "2 Carnegie Aides Die on Same Day:; "R. A. Franks, 73, Carnegie Aid, Dies in Jersey."

27. Russell interview.

28. Russell interview; Board of Trustees Meeting, October 24, 1935.

29. Cleveland Foundation, Centennial Website, "An Idea Whose Time Had Come."

30. Bulmer, "Social Survey Movement," 16.

31. Bulmer, 16; Anderson and Greenwald, introduction, 8.

32. Bulmer, "Social Survey Movement," 16. For more context to the social survey movement in Great Britain and the United States, see, for example, O'Connor, *Poverty Knowledge*, 26–44; Greenwald and Anderson, *Pittsburgh Surveyed*.

33. Russell interview.

34. Russell interview.

35. Russell interview; Alan Pifer to John Russell, March 12, 1974, I. E. Staff and Trustees Files, 1913–1996, box 18, CCNYR. For more on the Cleveland Foundation, see Tittle, *Rebuilding Cleveland*.

36. Newton Baker to Robert Lester, December 26, 1934, folder "Carnegie Corporation, 1934," Newton D. Baker Papers (hereafter NBP).

37. Newton Baker to Frederick Keppel, April 22, 1936, folder "Carnegie Corporation, 1936," NBP.

38. Lumpkins, *American Pogrom*, 1.

39. Rudwick, *Race Riot at East St. Louis*, chap. 11; Lumpkins, *American Pogrom*, 207.

40. Lumpkins, *American Pogrom*, 3.

41. Russell interview.

42. Platt, *Politics of Riot Commissions*, 161.

43. Platt, 161.

44. "Background Note," Frederick Henry Osborn Papers (hereafter FHOP).

45. Lorimer and Osborn, *Dynamics of Population*.

46. Lach, "Coffman, Lotus Delta."

47. Frederick Keppel and Henry James, Memorandum of Interview, June 18, 1930, I. E. Staff and Trustee Files, box 24, folder 24.5, CCNYR.

48. Frederick Keppel and Newton Baker, Record of Interview, September 30, 1936, I. E. Staff and Trustee Files, box 22, folder 22.9, CCNYR.

49. Keppel and Baker, Record of Interview.

50. Keppel and Baker, Record of Interview.

51. J. Th. Moll to Frederick Keppel, November 2, 1936, "Negro Study" General Correspondence, roll 1, CCNYR

52. Moll to Keppel.

53. Frederick Keppel and J. H. Oldham, Record of Interview, November 23, 1936, box 281, folder 281.1, CCNYR.

54. Moll to Keppel.

55. Schrieke, *Alien Americans*, vii.

56. Schrieke, viii.

57. Schrieke, 191.

58. Lindgren, "Bertram Johannes Otto Schrieke," 131.

59. "Negro Study, Personnel Suggestions through July 15, 1937," "Negro Study," roll 1, CCNYR; Jackson, *Gunnar Myrdal and America's Conscience*, 29.

60. Kennedy, *Freedom from Fear*, chap. 1.

61. Keppel, "Arts in Social Life," 958–1008.

62. Robert M. Lester, interview by Isabel S. Grossner, 1968, vol.1, CCOHP.

63. For more on Herskovits, see, for example, Gershenhorn, *Melville J. Herskovits*.

64. Melville Herskovits to Frederick Keppel, April 8, 1936, Series 35/6, box 5, folder 10, Melville J. Herskovits Papers (hereafter MHP).

65. For developing correspondence between Herskovits and Keppel, see Series 35/6, box 5, folder 10, MHP.

66. Melville Herskovits to Donald Young, January 2, 1936, Series 35/6, box 14, folder 1, MHP.

67. Herskovits to Young.

68. Donald Young to Frederick Keppel, January 30, 1937, "Negro Study" General Correspondence, roll 1, CCNYR.

69. Young to Keppel.

70. Donald Young, 1967, CCOHP.

71. Young to Keppel.

72. Young to Keppel.

73. "[FPK Log—London visit], April 1937," Administrative Records, I.D., Policy & Program, box 6, folder 6.5, CCNYR.

74. "[FPK Log—London visit], April 1937."

75. "[FPK Log—London visit], April 1937."

76. Grayson, "Layton, Walter Thomas, first Baron Layton."

77. "[FPK Log—London visit], April 1937."

78. "[FPK Log—London visit], April 1937."

79. Rickett, "Salter, (James) Arthur, Baron Salter"; "Negro Study Personnel," n.d., "Negro Study" General Correspondence, roll 1, CCNYR.

80. "[FPK Log—London visit], April 1937."

81. "[FPK Log—London visit], April 1937."

82. "[FPK Log—London visit], April 1937."

83. "[FPK Log—London visit], April 1937."

84. Cell, *Hailey*, 222.

85. "[FPK Log—London visit], April 1937."

86. Frederick Keppel to Robert Lester, June 24, 1933, III.A. grant files, box 797, folder 797.5, CCNYR.

87. Young to Keppel.

88. Young to Keppel.

89. "Negro Study, Personnel Suggestions through July 15, 1937."

90. Jackson, *Gunnar Myrdal and America's Conscience*, 33.

91. Fleck, *Transatlantic History of the Social Sciences*, 41–43; See, generally, Fisher, *Fundamental Development of the Social Sciences*.

92. Carlson, *Swedish Experiment in Family Politics*, 45.

93. Hirdman, *Alva Myrdal*, 201; Carlson, *Swedish Experiment*, 50; Rappaport, *Encyclopedia of Women Social Reformers*, 1:472; Hirdman, *Alva Myrdal*, 158.

94. Myrdal, *Nation and Family*, vii.

95. Myrdal and Myrdal, *Kris i befolkningsfrågan*, chap. 2.

96. For further discussion on the "social corpus," see Rabinbach, *Human Motor*, chaps. 8 and 10.

97. See Mazower, *Dark Continent*, chap. 3; Connelly, *Fatal Misconception*, chap. 2.

98. See, for example, Bock and Thane, *Maternity & Gender Policies*.

99. Mazower, *Dark Continent*, chap. 3; Connelly, *Fatal Misconception*, chap. 3.

100. Spektorowski and Mizrachi, "Eugenics and the Welfare State in Sweden," 345.

101. Hirdman, *Alva Myrdal*, 203.

102. Frederick Keppel to Gunnar Myrdal, August 18, 1937, "Negro Study" General Correspondence, roll 1, CCNYR.

103. Keppel and Duffus, *Arts in American Life*.

104. Keppel and Duffus, 2.

105. Keppel and Duffus, vi.

106. Keppel to Myrdal, 2.

107. Keppel to Myrdal, 2.

108. Myrdal to Boström, Feb. 9, 1939, Gunnar Myrdal Correspondence, vol. 3.2.1:1, file "Boström, Wollmar," Gunnar and Alva Myrdal Archives (hereafter GAMA); Myrdal to Kinberg, June 8, 1939, Gunnar Myrdal Correspondence, vol. 3.2.1:6, GAMA; Myrdal, *An American Dilemma*, ix–xx.

109. Myrdal, *An American Dilemma* (1964), xxv.

110. MeasuringWorth, "Seven Ways to Compute the Relative Value."

111. Myrdal, *An American Dilemma*, xvii.

112. James B. Conant to Gunnar Myrdal, June 9, 1937, Papers of President James B. Conant, UAI 5.168, box 83, folder "Godkin Lecture, 1936–1937," James B. Conant Papers (hereafter cited as JBCP); O. E. Baker (United States Department of Agriculture) to Gunnar Myrdal, December 17, 1937, Korrespondens: Gunnar Myrdal 1920–1929, vol. 3.2.1:1, folder "1930-t Ba," GAMA; H. D. White (Director of Monetary Research, Treasury Department) to Gunnar Myrdal, June 24, 1938, Korrespondens: Gunnar Myrdal 1930–1939, vol. 3.2.1: 11, GAMA; T. J. Woofter Jr. (Coordinator of Rural Research, Works Progress Administration) to Gunnar Myrdal, May 23, 1938, Korrespondens: Gunnar Myrdal 1930–1939, vol. 3.2.1: 11, GAMA; Nathan Straus (Administrator, Department of the Interior United States Housing Authority) to Gunnar Myrdal, June 24, 1938, Brevsamling 1930–1939 S, vol. 9, GAMA.

113. Gunnar Myrdal, interview by Isabel A. Grossner, November 27, 1967, Interview 1, CCOIIP.

114. Moynihan, "Foreword to the Paperback Edition," v.

*Chapter 7*

1. "GM conference with Dr. Keppel, May 2, on the plan contained in letter of April 28, 1939," "Negro Study" General Correspondence, roll. 1, Carnegie Corporation of New York Records (hereafter CCNYR).

2. Frederick Keppel to Gunnar Myrdal, September 4, 1942, "Documents from Gunnar Myrdal's Work: An American Dilemma, 1937–1947," folder 1942, Gunnar and Alva Myrdal Archives (hereafter GAMA).

3. Dollard interview.

4. Charles Dollard, interviewed by Isabel Grossner, 1969, Carnegie Corporation Oral History Project (hereafter CCOHP).

5. Lagemann, "Keppel, Frederick Paul."

6. For broader context for these historical actors' conflation of the study of race relations and Black Americans, see, for example, Walton, Miller, and McCormick, "Race and Political Science"; Steinberg, *Race Relations*; Bhambra, "A Sociological Dilemma."

7. "May 8, 1930 Memo," RG 1.1 Projects, series 200 U.S., box 9, folder 80, Rockefeller Foundation Records (hereafter RFR).

8. "Ruml—Pers. Memoranda 1929," series II, correspondence, box 5, folder 3, Beardsley Ruml Papers (hereafter BRP).

9. "Ruml—Pers. Memoranda 1929."

10. Katz and Sugrue, *W. E. B. Du Bois, Race, and the City*, 13–14; O'Connor, *Poverty Knowledge*, 34.

11. Katz and Sugrue, *W. E. B. Du Bois, Race, and the City*, 13–14.

12. Katz, *American Negro*, iii; Moss, *American Negro Academy*; Young and Deskins, "Early Traditions of African-American Sociological Thought."

13. "Memorandum: The Executive Committee and Director to the Board of Trustees (The Laura Spelman Rockefeller Memorial for the year October 1, 1924 through September 30, 1925)," series 2, box 2, folder 15, Laura Spelman Rockefeller Memorial Records (hereafter LSRMR).

14. "Race Relations and Negro Work, 1926–1927," III. Appropriations, subseries 8, box 98, folder 996, LSRMR; "Excerpt 'Race Relations' from Memorandum: The Executive Committee and Directors to the Board of Trustees."

15. "Race Relations and Negro Work"; "Excerpt 'Race Relations' from Memorandum."

16. "Race Relations and Negro Work"; "Excerpt 'Race Relations' from Memorandum."

17. "Race Relations and Negro Work."

18. "Race Relations and Negro Work."

19. "Race Relations and Negro Work."

20. "Race Relations and Negro Work."

21. Correspondence between Carter G. Woodson and Rockefeller Foundation Managers (March 1930–April 1932), RG 1.1 Projects, series 200, box 9, folders 80 and 81, RFR; Jones, *Negro Education*.

22. "Excerpt—Trustees' Confidential Report," June 1951, Minutes of SSRC general program, folder 4738, box 554, subseries 100S, RG 1.2, RFR.

23. "Race Relations and Negro Work"; "Excerpt 'Race Relations' from Memorandum."

24. "P&P A Nov 24 1928 Committee Personnel," accession 1, series 1, committee projects, subseries 19, miscellaneous projects, box 174, folder 998, Social Science Research Council Records (hereafter SSRCR).

25. "Advisory Committee on Interracial Relations, 1925–30," SSRC Annual Reports (1925–1933), 51, SSRCR.

26. Jackson, "Herskovits, Melville Jean"; Manning, "Just, Ernest Everett." The Sub-Committee on Tests for Race Differences, 1928–1930, included M. J. Herskovits, Ernest E. Just, Joseph Peterson, M. S. Viteles, and T. J. Woofter. The Sub-Committee on Governmental and Political Aspects of Interracial Relations, 1928–1930, included H. F. Gosnell, Joseph P. Harris, Kirk H. Porter, Frank Stewart, and E. J. Woodhouse.

27. Gilmore, "How Anne Scott and Pauli Murray Found Each Other."

28. "Advisory Committee on Interracial Relations," 52–53.

29. "Advisory Committee on Interracial Relations," 52–53.

30. "Advisory Committee on Interracial Relations," 52–53.

31. "Conference on Racial Differences," accession 1, series 1, committee projects, subseries 10, miscellaneous projects, box 173, folder 997, SSRCR.

32. "P&P December 14–15, 1930 'Joint Committee on Racial Problems,'" accession 1, series 1, committee projects, subseries 10, miscellaneous projects, box 174, folder 998, 339–340, SSRCR.

33. "Appendix VII. Report of Interracial Committee, May 24, 1930," accession 1, series 1, committee projects, subseries 10, miscellaneous projects, box 174, folder 998, 38–39, SSRCR.

34. Correspondence between Carter G. Woodson and Rockefeller Foundation Managers.

35. Woofter, "Status of Racial and Ethnic Groups"; "Advisory Committee on Interracial Relations," 51. Woofter had been a member of the SSRC's Advisory Committee on Interracial Relations.

36. Young, *Research Memorandum*.

37. "Encyclopedia of the Negro Memorandum," September 15, 1938, series 35:6, box 7, folder 19, folder "Encyclopedia of the Negro, 1935–1940," Melvin Herskovits Papers (hereafter MHP).

38. C. G. Woodson to the Rockefeller Foundation, June 29, 1936, 1.1. projects, series 200 U.S., box 9, folder 81, RFR; "Memorandum Regarding Encyclopedia of the Negro," April 27, 1931, box 17, folder 2, Phelps Stokes Fund Records (hereafter PSFR).

39. Woodson to Rockefeller Foundation.

40. Woodson to Rockefeller Foundation.

41. Woodson to Rockefeller Foundation.

42. Anson Phelps Stokes to Jackson Davis, March 31, 1932, box 39, folder 2, PSFR.

43. Phelps Stokes to Davis.

44. SSRC Minutes of the Committee on Problems and Policy, March 17, 1934, accession 1, series 2, Committee on P&P, subseries 1, Minutes, box 313, folder 1781, SSRCR; "Memorandum on the Negro Encyclopedia," III.A. grant files, ca. 1911–1988, box 139, folder 139.11, CCNYR.

45. "Encyclopedia of the Negro Memorandum," August 2, 1938, series 35:6, box 7, folder 19, MHP.

46. Donald Young to Melville Herskovits, April 7, 1936, series 35.6, box 22, folder 3, MHP; Herskovits to Young, April 13, 1936, series 35:6, box 22, folder 3, MHP.

278 *Notes to Chapter 7*

47. Young to Herskovits; Herskovits to Young.

48. Young to Herskovits; Herskovits to Young.

49. Frederick Keppel to Anson Phelps Stokes, November 17, 1938, III.A. grant files, box 139, folder 139.11, CCNYR.

50. Karl, *Uneasy State*; Leuchtenburg, "New Deal and the Analogue of War."

51. Karl and Katz, "American Private Philanthropic Foundation," 242.

52. Sitkoff, *New Deal for Blacks*, chap. 3.

53. White, *Man Called White*, 169–170.

54. Kennedy, *Freedom from Fear*, 341–343.

55. Kennedy, 341–343.

56. Sitkoff, 342.

57. Brown, *Strain of Violence*, appendix; Rushdy, *End of American Lynching*, 94.

58. Wright Rigueur, *The Loneliness of the Black Republican*, 15, 18.

59. Wright Rigueur, 13–14.

60. Sitkoff, *A New Deal for Blacks*, 64.

61. Sitkoff, 65–66.

62. Sitkoff, 65–66.

63. Sitkoff, 79.

64. Sitkoff, 79.

65. "Negro in Industry," 345.

66. "Negro in Industry," 345–346.

67. Drake and Cayton, *Black Metropolis*.

68. Drake and Cayton, xiii; Washington, "Horace Cayton," 56.

69. Peretz, "Making of *Black Metropolis*."

70. Grimshaw, "A Study in Social Violence," PhD diss., University of Pennsylvania, 1959, cited in Rudwick, *Race Riot*, 3.

71. Tuttle, *Race Riot*, 11.

72. Blain and Zoellner, "'Riots,' 'Mobs,' 'Chaos.'"

73. Harris, "Logic of Black Urban Rebellions."

74. Gruening and Du Bois, "Massacre of East St. Louis."

75. Herman, "Ten Years After."

76. Gruening and Du Bois, "Massacre of East St. Louis," 219.

77. Gruening and Du Bois, 219.

78. Gruening and Du Bois, 219.

79. Rudwick, *Race Riot*, 6.

80. Rudwick, 27–33.

81. McLaughlin, "Ghetto Formation and Armed Resistance."

82. Gruening and Du Bois, "Massacre of East St. Louis," 238.

83. Rudwick, *Race Riot*, chap. 10.

84. Rudwick, 138.

85. Rudwick, 139.

86. Rudwick, 140.

87. Rudwick, chap. 10; Platt, *Politics of Riot Commissions*.

88. Rudwick, *Race Riot*, 140–141.

89. Rudwick, 140–141.

90. Tuttle, *Race Riot*, 14.
91. Francis, *Civil Rights and the Making of the Modern American State*, 57.
92. Tuttle, *Race Riot*, 21.
93. Tuttle, 22, 23.
94. Platt, *Politics of Riot Commissions*, 95.
95. Tuttle, *Race Riot*, 6–7.
96. "Summary of the 1919 Chicago Race Riots."
97. Tuttle, *Race Riot*, 9–10.
98. Daley, "To Remember the Chicago Race Riot."
99. Tuttle, *Race Riot*, 32.
100. Platt, *Politics of Riot Commissions*, 120; Farber, "Charles S. Johnson's 'The Negro in Chicago,'" 79.
101. Lupo, *Flak-Catchers*, chap. 4.
102. Lupo, chap. 4.
103. Chicago Commission on Race Relations, *Negro in Chicago*, 652–653.
104. Chicago Commission, xvii.
105. Chicago Commission, xvii.
106. Chicago Commission, 152.
107. Chicago Commission, 221.
108. Lewis, foreword, ix–x.
109. Chicago Commission, *Negro in Chicago*, 221.
110. Chicago Commission, 300.
111. Chicago Commission, 362.
112. Chicago Commission, 393, 494.
113. Chicago Commission, 640–651.
114. Lupo, *Flak-Catchers*, chap. 4.
115. Lupo, chap. 5.
116. Greenberg, *"Or Does it Explode?,"* 3.
117. Lupo, *Flak-Catchers*, chap. 5.
118. Fay, "Harlem Riot of 1935."
119. Johnson, "Generation of Women Activists," 225.
120. Platt, *Politics of Riot Commissions*, 161–162.
121. Mayor's Commission on Conditions in Harlem, *Negro in Harlem*.
122. Mayor's Commission.
123. Lupo, *Flak-Catchers*, chap. 5.
124. Mayor's Commission, *Negro in Harlem*, chap. 9.
125. Mayor's Commission, chap. 9.
126. Kessner, *Fiorello H. LaGuardia*, quoted in Lupo, *Flak-Catchers*, chap. 5.

## Chapter 8

1. Lord Lothian (Philip Kerr) to Frederick Keppel, August 2, 1938, III.A. grant files, box 797, folder 797.6, Carnegie Corporation of New York Records (hereafter CCNYR); Frederick Keppel to Lord Lothian, November 29, 1938, III A. grant files, box 797, folder 797.6, CCNYR.

2. Lothian to Keppel; Keppel to Lothian.

3. Keppel to Lothian.

4. Anderson, "Northern Foundations and the Shaping of Southern Black Rural Education"; Link, "Jackson Davis and the Lost World of Jim Crow Education."

5. Beaver, "Baker, Newton Diehl."

6. Frederick Keppel to Raymond Fosdick, June 8, 1938, "Negro Study" General Correspondence, reel 1, CCNYR; Fosdick to Keppel, June 15, 1938, "Negro Study" General Correspondence, reel 1, CCNYR.

7. Day to Gunn, June 21, 1932, box 111, 1.1 Projects 800, folder 800S, Rockefeller Foundation Records (hereafter RFR).

8. Jackson, *Gunnar Myrdal and America's Conscience*, 32.

9. Diary entries, May 12, 1933, and October 5, 1933, Officers Diaries, Max Mason, reel 1, RFR.

10. Alva and Gunnar Myrdal to Van Sickle, July 20, 1933, 1.1 Projects, 717S, box 20, folder 181, RFR.

11. Myrdal to Kittredge, June 8, 1938, Gunnar Myrdal Correspondence, vol. 3.2.1:8, Gunnar and Alva Myrdal Archives (hereafter GAMA); Kittredge to Myrdal, July 6, 1938, Gunnar Myrdal Correspondence, vol. 3.2.1:8, GAMA; Rockefeller Foundation, *Directory of Fellowships and Scholarships*.

12. "Chapter 1: The Old Study" (1983 Draft), Documents from Gunnar Myrdal's Work, vol. 4.2.11:6, GAMA.

13. See, generally, "Negro Study" General Correspondence, roll 1, CCNYR.

14. Fosdick, *Adventure in Giving*, 266.

15. Fosdick, vii.

16. Perkins, *Edwin Rogers Embree.*

17. Perkins, 110.

18. Perkins, 110.

19. Perkins, 110.

20. Embree, *Julius Rosenwald*, 13–15.

21. Fosdick, *Adventure in Giving*, 20.

22. Fosdick, 125.

23. Fosdick to Keppel, June 15, 1938, series 1, subseries 1.2, box 270, folder 2789, General Education Board Records (hereafter GEBR); Myrdal to Keppel, January 28, 1939, series 1, subseries 1.2, box 270, folder 2789, GEBR; Memorandum from Davis to Keppel ("Trip with Gunnar Myrdal and Richard Sterner, October 3–20, 1938"), series 1, subseries 1.2, box 270, folder 2787, GEBP.

24. Goodrich to Myrdal, August 5, 1939, vol. 3.2.1:3, folder "130-t- C," GAMA.

25. Fosdick to Keppel; Myrdal to Keppel, January 28, 1939; Memorandum from Davis to Keppel.

26. Myrdal to Keppel, January 28, 1939.

27. Myrdal to Boström, February 9, 1939, Gunnar Myrdal Correspondence, vol. 3.2.1:1, folder "Boström, Wollmar," GAMA; Myrdal to Kinberg, June 8, 1939, Gunnar Myrdal Correspondence, vol. 3.2.1:6, GAMA.

28. Myrdal to Kinberg, June 8, 1939.

29. "Office of the President, Record of Interview, Subject: Negro Study, CD and Myrdal," March 21, 1939, "Negro Study" General Correspondence roll 1, CCNYR; Myrdal to Keppel, April 28, 1939, "Negro Study" General Correspondence roll 1, CCNYR; "Thomas, W. Jr. (Dissertation) Proposal for the Study of the Relation of Behavior to Social Structure in Scandinavia," Accession 1, Series 1, Committee Projects, Subseries 22, box 248, folder 1474, "Social Sciences Research Council Records (hereafter SSRCR); "Social Sciences Research Aid, No. 4; Recipient: Karl Gunnar Myrdal," June 16, 1932, 1.1. Projects, Record Group 800, box 10, folder 1010, RFR; Myrdal to Kittredge, March 28, 1935, 1.1. Projects, Record Group 800, box 10, folder 1010, RFR; Thomas to Walker, March 2, 1940, 1.1. Projects, Record Group 800, box 11, folder 106, RFR. See, for example, Myrdal and Bouvin, *Cost of Living in Sweden 1830–1930*; Myrdal, "Industrialization and Population"; Thomas, *Social and Economic Aspects*.

30. Myrdal to Keppel, April 28, 1939.

31. "Biographical/Historical Information," Doxey A. Wilkerson Papers (hereafter DWP); Clarkin, "Bunche, Ralph Johnson."

32. Myrdal to Keppel, April 28, 1939.

33. Myrdal to Keppel.

34. Myrdal to Keppel.

35. Myrdal to Keppel.

36. Myrdal to Keppel.

37. Myrdal to Keppel.

38. Myrdal to Keppel.

39. Myrdal to Keppel, "Report of Progress," July 25, 1939, "Negro Study" General Correspondence roll 1, CCNYR.

40. Myrdal to Keppel, April 28, 1939.

41. Nepa, "Harris, Abram Lincoln, Jr."; Mazzari, "Arthur Raper and Documentary Realism"; Stepto, "Brown, Sterling Allen"; Bender, "Beard, Charles Austin"; Cott, "Beard, Mary Ritter"; and "Collection Overview," Guion Griffis Johnson Papers.

42. "Carnegie Corporation Interview with Jackson Davis," November 28, 1938, series 1, subseries 1.2, box 270, folder 2787, GEBR.

43. "Chapter 1: The Old Study."

44. "Interviews with Myrdal and Sterner," March 6, 1939, series 12, Davis, subseries (Jackson Davis), box 8, folder 1939, GEBR.

45. Keppel to Davis, May 13, 1940, "Negro Study" General Correspondence, reel 1, CCNYR; "GEB Interview with Myrdal," April 8, 1941, "Negro Study" General Correspondence, reel 1, CCNYR; "GEB Interview with Myrdal," May 12, 1941, "Negro Study" General Correspondence, reel 1, CCNYR.

46. Davis to Flexner, May 2, 1944, "Negro Study" General Correspondence, reel 1, CCNYR.

47. "The Committee of 100 Dinner Invitation," June 2, 1948, "Documents from Gunnar Myrdal's Work," vol. 4.2.05:003, folder "Kipp," GAMA. For a discussion of the NAACP's Committee of 100, see Tushnet, *Making Civil Rights Law*, 34–35.

48. Tushnet, *NAACP's Legal Strategy against Segregated Education*, 2, 34. For greater context for the NAACP's shifting priorities in the mid- to late 1930s, see Francis, *Civil Rights and the Making of the Modern American State*; Tushnet, *NAACP's Legal Strategy*.

49. Walter White to "Whom It May Concern," September 19, 1939, box 10B, folder "General Correspondence, Walter White 1939–42," Ralph Bunche Papers (hereafter RBP).

50. "Guests at the Tea for Dr. Myrdal—September 10, 1942," box 77, folder "Mu (205)," Frederick P. Keppel Papers.

51. Myrdal, *An American Dilemma*, xiv.

52. See, for example, box 29, folder 2 "Carnegie-Myrdal Correspondence, 1939–40," RBP.

53. See, for example, box 29, folders 1 and 2, RBP; Gunnar Myrdal Correspondence, vol. 3.2.1:13, vol. 3.2.1:14, and vol. 3.2.1:16, GAMA. Specifically about Dorn, see Myrdal to Parran, April 29, 1940, vol. 3.2.1:16, GAMA.

54. "Harold F. Dorn (1906–1963)"; Myrdal, *An American Dilemma*, xiii.

55. Myrdal to LaFollette, September 10, 1937, Gunnar Myrdal Correspondence, vol. 3.2.1:6, GAMA; LaFollette to Myrdal, February 7, 1939, March 13, 1939, March 22, 1939, Gunnar Myrdal Correspondence, vol. 3.2.1:6, GAMA.

56. McGuire to Myrdal, May 17, 1938, Gunnar Myrdal Correspondence, vol. 3.2.1: 3, GAMA.

57. "January 1986 Gunnar Myrdal's manuscript of *An American Dilemma Revisited*," Documents from Gunnar Myrdal's Work, vol. 4.3.11:08b, 57, GAMA.

58. "January 1986 Gunnar Myrdal's manuscript," 208–209.

59. See, for example, Frankfurter to Myrdal, June 19, 1938, Gunnar Myrdal Correspondence, vol. 3.2.1:3, GAMA; Myrdal to Frankfurter, January 12, 1939, Gunnar Myrdal Correspondence, vol. 3.2.1:3, GAMA.

60. *An American Dilemma Revisited* (January 1986 draft), documents from Gunnar Myrdal's work, vol. 4.2.11:08b, 57, GAMA. See also Myrdal, *Historien om "An American Dilemma."*

61. Myrdal to Ezekiel, January 5, 1939, Gunnar Myrdal's Correspondence, vol. 3.2.1: 3, GAMA.

62. Myrdal to Ezekiel; Myrdal to Alexander, April 29, 1940, Gunnar Myrdal's Correspondence, vol. 3.2.1:13, GAMA.

63. Foreman to Myrdal, April 29, 1940, Gunnar Myrdal's Correspondence, vol. 3.2.1:14, GAMA; Hinrichs to Myrdal, January 7, 1944, Gunnar Myrdal's Correspondence, vol. 3.2.1:14, GAMA.

64. Bunche to Roosevelt, May 3, 1940, box 33, folder 20, RBP.

65. "Memorandum of the Interview," 13, box 33, folder 20, RBP.

66. Davis, *Guest of Honor*.

67. "Memorandum of the Interview," 14.

68. After the interview, Bunche provided Myrdal with a twenty-page summary of the White House with detailed descriptions of the meals, of his interactions with White House staff, and, of his conversations on Black Americans with First Lady Eleanor Roosevelt and her two secretaries.

69. Keppel to Myrdal's Staff, May 13, 1940, series 1, subseries 1.2, box 270, folder 2788, GEBR.

70. "January 1986 Gunnar Myrdal's manuscript."

71. "Notes on journey U.S. 1940–43," Alva Myrdal's Personal Documents, vol. 1.1:008, GAMA; "January 1986 Gunnar Myrdal's manuscript," 19.

72. "January 1986 Gunnar Myrdal's manuscript," 19.

73. "Notes on journey."

74. "January 1986 Gunnar Myrdal's manuscript," 22.

75. "Record of Interviews," February 28, 1941, and March 12, 1941, roll 1, CCNYR.

*Chapter 9*

1. Jackson, *Gunnar Myrdal and America's Conscience*, 161.

2. Myrdal to Dollard, July 22, 1942, "Negro Study" General Correspondence, roll 1, Carnegie Corporation of New York Records (hereafter CCNYR).

3. Myrdal, *An American Dilemma*, xv–xvi.

4. Myrdal, xi.

5. Myrdal, title page. Also worth noting: along with Gunnar Myrdal's central manuscript, Harper & Brothers also published four companion texts that members of his research team had initially had as memoranda. During Myrdal's absence in Sweden a year earlier, Carnegie Corporation and University of Chicago sociologist Samuel A. Stouffer agreed to publish these monographs in case Myrdal was not able to return from Europe to complete the U.S. project. See Herskovits, *Myth of the Negro Past*; Johnson, *Patterns of Negro Segregation*; Sterner, *Negro's Share*; Klineberg, *Characteristics of the American Negro*; Myrdal, *An American Dilemma*, xii.

6. Office of the President, Record of Interview, August 28–29, 1941, "Negro Study" General Correspondence, roll 1, CCNYR.

7. Gunnar Myrdal to Charles Dollard, July 22, 1942, "Negro Study" General Correspondence, roll 1, CCNYR.

8. Cell, *Hailey*, 229.

9. Dollard to Myrdal, July 24, 1942, "Negro Study" General Correspondence, roll 1, CCNYR.

10. Myrdal, *An American Dilemma*, 806.

11. Myrdal, 806–807.

12. See chapter 6 of this book.

13. Dollard to Myrdal, November 28, 1941, "Negro Study" General Correspondence, roll 1, CCNYR.

14. Record of Interview, July 27, 1942, "Negro Study" General Correspondence, roll 1, CCNYR.

15. Jackson, *Gunnar Myrdal and America's Conscience*, 200. See also, Myrdal, *An American Dilemma*, app. 10.

16. Hirdman, *Alva Myrdal*, 223.

17. Myrdal and Myrdal, *Kontakt med Amerika*.

18. Hirdman, *Alva Myrdal*.

19. Myrdal and Myrdal, *Kontakt*.

20. Myrdal and Myrdal, 32–33.

21. Myrdal and Myrdal, 33.

22. Myrdal and Myrdal, 34.

23. Myrdal and Myrdal, 51

24. Myrdal and Myrdal, 52.

25. Myrdal and Myrdal, 52.

26. Myrdal and Myrdal, 52.

27. Myrdal and Myrdal, 56.

28. Myrdal, *An American Dilemma*, xliii.

29. Myrdal, xliii.

30. Myrdal, 24.

31. Myrdal, 24.

32. Myrdal, xlvii.

33. Myrdal, 1065.

34. Myrdal, 1065.

35. Myrdal, 1065.

36. Myrdal, 1065. The author refers to his English-language text, *Monetary Equilibrium*. An earlier version was published in Swedish in 1931. See Myrdal, "Om penningteoretisk jämvikt."

37. Myrdal, *An American Dilemma*, 75, 1069.

38. Myrdal, 1066.

39. Myrdal, 1066.

40. Myrdal, 1067.

41. Myrdal, 1065–1066.

42. Myrdal, 1068.

43. Myrdal, 1067–1068.

44. Myrdal, 1068.

45. Myrdal, 60, 61.

46. Myrdal, 61.

47. Myrdal, 61.

48. Myrdal, 60–61.

49. Myrdal, 1066.

50. Myrdal, 1066.

51. Myrdal, 53.

52. Myrdal, 57.

53. Myrdal, 53, 57.

54. Singh, *Black Is a Country*.

55. Myrdal, *An American Dilemma*, 1015.

56. Myrdal, 1016.

57. Myrdal, 1019.

58. Myrdal, 1022.

59. Keppel, foreword, viii.

60. Myrdal, *An American Dilemma*, 929.

61. Myrdal, 167.

62. Myrdal, 168.

63. For more on the Myrdals in 1930s Sweden and the public policy significance of their coauthored text *Kris befolkningsfrågan*, see, for example, Ekerwald, "To Build a Nation"; Ekerwald, "Modernist Manifesto of Alva and Gunnar Myrdal"; Wisselgren, "Reforming the Science-Policy Boundary." For symposia on the Myrdals, see Lyman and Ellaeson, "Alva and Gunnar Myrdal"; Morey and Martin, "Gunnar Myrdal Symposium."

64. Myrdal and Myrdal, *Kris*, chap. 1.

65. Myrdal and Myrdal. See also Baker, *Margaret Sanger*, 91.

66. Myrdal and Myrdal, chap. 2, "Nativitet och inkomststandard."

67. Myrdal and Myrdal, 9.

68. Myrdal and Myrdal, 9.

69. Myrdal and Myrdal, chap. 6, "Utjämning av barnförsörjningskostnaden genom socialpolitik."

70. See, for example, Eliaeson, "Gunnar Myrdal"; Hirdman, *Alva Myrdal*; Carlson, *Swedish Experiment in Family Politics*.

71. Myrdal and Myrdal, *Kris*, 66.

72. Myrdal and Myrdal, 67.

73. Myrdal and Myrdal, 223.

74. Spektorowski and Mizrachi, "Eugenics and the Welfare State in Sweden," 347.

75. Spektorowski and Mizrachi, 347. See also Connelly, *Fatal Misconception*; Bashford and Levine, *Oxford Handbook of the History of Eugenics*.

76. Myrdal, *An American Dilemma*, 175–178.

77. Myrdal, 175–176.

78. Myrdal, 176.

79. Myrdal, 176.

80. Myrdal, 178.

81. Myrdal and Myrdal, *Kris*, 69.

82. Myrdal and Myrdal, 71.

83. Myrdal and Myrdal, 74.

84. Myrdal and Myrdal, 72.

85. Myrdal and Myrdal, 67.

86. Myrdal and Myrdal, 76, 224.

87. Myrdal and Myrdal, 76.

88. Myrdal, *An American Dilemma*, xlviii.

89. Myrdal, xlvii–xlviii, 462–466, 792–494.

90. Myrdal, 437.

91. Myrdal, 545.

92. Myrdal, 463, 545–546.

93. Myrdal, 463.

94. Myrdal, 546.

95. Myrdal, 1015.

96. Myrdal, 464–465.

97. "Interview Memorandum," November 17, 1938, series 1, subseries 1.2, box 270, folder 2787, General Education Board Records (hereafter GEBR).

98. "Interview Memorandum."

99. "Office of the President Record of Interview," November 20, 1939, "Negro Study" General Correspondence, roll 1, CCNYR.

100. Jackson, *Gunnar Myrdal and America's Conscience*, 124.

101. Jackson, 124.

102. "Office of the President Record of Interview."

103. "Record of Interview," November 27, 1939, "Negro Study" General Correspondence, roll 1, CCNYR.

104. See, for example, Dollard to Myrdal, November 28, 1941, "Negro Study" General Correspondence, roll 1, CCNYR.

105. Dollard to Myrdal.

106. Keppel to Myrdal, July 13, 1942, "Negro Study" General Correspondence, roll 1, CCNYR.

107. Myrdal, *Nation and Family* (1941), chap. 22, cited in Myrdal, *An American Dilemma*, 1078.

108. Myrdal, *An American Dilemma*, 1073.

109. Myrdal, 1075; Gilmore, *Gender & Jim Crow*, 23, 47, 72–73.

110. French philosopher Simone de Beauvoir would pick up on Myrdal's appendix and credit this section of *An American Dilemma* for inspiring her to write *Le Deuxieme Sexe* (*The Second Sex*, 1949). Morey, "A Displaced American Feminist in Paris."

111. Dollard to Myrdal, July 10, 1942, "Negro Study" General Correspondence, roll 1, CCNYR.

112. Myrdal, *An American Dilemma*, 429.

113. Myrdal, 449, 451.

114. Gunnar Myrdal, interview by Walter Jackson, August 8, 1980, Gunnar and Alva Myrdal Archives.

115. Keppel to Jessup, "Office of the President, Record of Interview, Confidential Memorandum to WAJ from FPK," July 27, 1942, "Negro Study" General Correspondence, roll 1, CCNYR.

116. Keppel to Jessup, "Office of the President."

117. Record of interview, July 27, 1942, "Negro Study" General Correspondence, roll 1, CCNYR.

118. Jessup to Keppel, July 30, 1942, "Negro Study" General Correspondence, roll 1, CCNYR.

119. Myrdal, *An American Dilemma*, v.

120. Myrdal, v.

121. Myrdal, vi.

122. Myrdal, vi–vii.

123. Myrdal, 1019.

124. Myrdal, vii.

*Chapter 10*

1. "Public Affairs Pamphlets are Best Sellers," 210.

2. "Public Affairs Pamphlets are Best Sellers," 210.

3. M. B., review, 332.

4. Lawson, *To Secure These Rights*, 126.

5. Lawson, 126.

6. Lawson, 138–139.

7. Lawson, 49.

8. Lawson, 54.

9. Myrdal, *An American Dilemma*, 60–61.

10. Lawson, "Introduction," 32.

11. Myrdal, *An American Dilemma*, 61.

12. Dudziak, *Cold War Civil Rights*, 6.

13. Dudziak, 11.

14. Solovey, *Shaky Foundations*, 123.

15. "Official Reports"; "McCarthyism and the Red Scare."

16. "Foundations Defend Freedom of Inquiry."

17. "Statements of Carnegie Corporation of New York submitted to Special Committee to Investigate Tax Exempt Foundations," July 1954, Documents from Gunnar Myrdal's Work, vol. 4.2.11:19, 15, 22, Gunnar and Alva Myrdal Archives.

18. "Statements of Carnegie Corporation of New York," 28; Orlans, "Social Science Research Policies in the United States."

19. Southern, *Gunnar Myrdal and Black-White Relations*, 157, 174–177.

20. Southern, 157, 174–177.

21. "Statements of Carnegie Corporation of New York," 28.

22. Rosenfield, *A World of Giving*, 153.

23. Rosenfield, 153.

24. Rosenfield, 153.

25. "Statements of Carnegie Corporation of New York," 30.

26. "Statements of Carnegie Corporation of New York," 30.

27. "Statements of Carnegie Corporation of New York," 30.

28. "Statements of Carnegie Corporation of New York," 30.

29. "Statements of Carnegie Corporation of New York," 31.

30. "Statements of Carnegie Corporation of New York," 32.

31. Myrdal, *An American Dilemma*, vi.

32. Dodd, *Dodd Report to the Reece Committee*. See also Solovey, *Shaky Foundations*, 126.

33. See, for example, Von Eschen, *Race against Empire*; Dudziak, *Cold War Civil Rights*; Bell, "Brown v. Board of Education."

34. Anderson, *Eyes off the Prize*, 3.

35. Dudziak, *Cold War Civil Rights*, 12.

36. Von Eschen, *Race against Empire*, 128.

37. Von Eschen, 129.

38. Wilkerson, introduction, 9.

39. Aptheker, *Negro People in America*, 54; Lehmann-Haupt, "Herbert Aptheker."

40. McLemee and Le Blanc, *C. L. R. James and Revolutionary Marxism*, 179.

41. Cox, *Caste, Class and Race*, 538.

42. Cox, 538.

43. Du Bois, review; Lewis, *W. E. B. Du Bois*, 453.

44. Du Bois, review, 121.

45. Du Bois, 123.

46. Du Bois, *Color and Democracy*, 274–275.

47. Du Bois, 311.

48. Lewis, *W. E. B. Du Bois*, 453.

49. Jackson, *Gunnar Myrdal and America's Conscience*, 261.

50. Jackson, 302.

51. Joseph, "Rethinking the Black Power Era," 707–708.

52. Joseph, 709.

53. Joseph, 711.

54. Nelson, *Body and Soul*, 5–6.

55. Nelson, 114.

56. Joseph, *Stokely*, 15, 268.

57. Horne, *Black Revolutionary*, 189.

58. Horne, 189.

59. Marable, *Malcolm X*, 3.

60. Rampersad, *Ralph Ellison*, 181–182.

61. Jackson, *Gunnar Myrdal and America's Conscience*, xi.

62. Ellison, *Invisible Man*.

63. Ellison, *Shadow and Act*.

64. Tuttle, *Race Riot*, v–vi.

65. Myrdal, *An American Dilemma*, 929.

66. Anderson, *This Was Harlem*, 307.

67. Anderson, 314.

68. Anderson, 23.

69. Anderson, 256.

70. Wall, *Harlem Renaissance*, 50.

71. Ellison, "*An American Dilemma*: A Review."

72. Ellison.

73. Myrdal, *An American Dilemma*, 929.

74. Ellison, "*An American Dilemma*: A Review."

75. Ellison.

76. Jackson, *Gunnar Myrdal and America's Conscience*, 302–311.

77. Cook, review, 207–209.

78. Killens, *Black Man's Burden*, 58.

79. Transcript of the Academy discussion, May 14–15, 1965, quoted in Southern, *Gunnar Myrdal and Black-White Relations*.

80. Stone, "People without a Country," 8–9, 11.

81. Stone, 8–9, 11.

82. Cruse, *The Crisis of the Negro Intellectual*, 455–56.

83. Carmichael and Hamilton, *Black Power*, 9–10, 5.

84. Carmichael and Hamilton, 5.

85. Carmichael and Hamilton, 22–23, 44.

86. Carmichael and Hamilton, 55.

87. King, *Where Do We Go from Here*, 84–85.

88. King, 9.

89. King, 15.

90. Getachew, *Worldmaking after Empire*, 1.

91. Nkrumah, *I Speak of Freedom*, xi, xiii.

92. For more on Nkruma's pan-African congresses, see, for example, Nkrumah, *Africa Must Unite*; Getachew, *Worldmaking after Empire*, chap. 3.

93. Vitalis, *White World Order, Black Power Politics*, 121.

94. Moodley, "Continued Impact of Black Consciousness in South Africa," 243–244; Davie, *Poverty Knowledge in South Africa*, 197–198.

95. Moodley, "Continued Impact of Black Consciousness in South Africa," 250–251.

96. See, for example, King, *Where Do We Go From Here*, chap. 3; Nkrumah, *Africa Must Unite*, 139.

97. Frederick Keppel to Anson Phelps Stokes, November 17, 1938, III.A. grant files, box 139, folder 139.11, Carnegie Corporation of New York Record; Frederick Keppel to W. E. B. Du Bois, August 29, 1939, W. E. B. Du Bois Papers.

98. Keppel to Phelps Stokes; Keppel to Du Bois.

99. Keppel to Du Bois.

100. Du Bois, *Color and Democracy*, 286.

## Epilogue

1. "Record of Interview," July 27, 1942, "Negro Study" General Correspondence, roll 1, Carnegie Corporation of New York Records (hereafter CCNYR).

2. Gunnar Myrdal, interview by Walter Jackson, August 18, 1980, Gunnar and Alva Myrdal Archives (hereafter GAMA).

3. Scott, *Scott's Official History*, 454.

4. "Conference, Myrdal and Keppel," May 2, 1939, "Negro Study" General Correspondence, roll 1, CCNYR.

5. Harris, "Locke, Alain Leroy."

6. Keppel to Loram, January 21, 1930, Administrative Records, I.D., Policy & Program, box 206, folder 206.1, CCNYR.

7. "Memorandum of Interview," 1925, box 281, folder 281.2, CCNYR.

# Bibliography

*Archival Collections*

Baker, Newton D., Papers. Library of Congress, Washington, DC. (NBP)

Bertram, James, Collection. Carnegie Mellon University Libraries and Collections, Pittsburgh, Pennsylvania. (JBC)

Bunche, Ralph Papers. Charles E. Young Research Library, University of California, Los Angeles. (RBP)

Butterfield, Kenyon L., Papers. University of Massachusetts Amherst Special Collections and University Archives. (KLBP)

Carnegie Corporation of New York Records. Columbia University Rare Book and Manuscript Library, New York. (CCNYR)

Carnegie Corporation Oral History Project. Columbia University Libraries Oral History Research Office, New York. (CCOHP)

Conant, James B., Papers. Harvard University Archives, Pusey Library, Harvard University, Cambridge, Massachusetts. (JBCP)

"Correspondence of the Military Intelligence Division Relating to 'Negro Subversion,' 1917–1941." National Archives Microfilm Publications, Washington, DC. (CMI)

Du Bois, W. E. B., Papers. University of Massachusetts Amherst Libraries, Special Collections and University Archives, USA. (DBP)

General Education Board Records. Rockefeller Archive Center, USA. (GEBR)

Herskovits, Melville, Papers. Northwestern University, Archival and Manuscript Collections, USA. (MHP)

Johnson, Guion Griffis, Papers. University of North Carolina, Southern Historical Collection, Louis Round Wilson Special Collections Library. (GGJP)

Keppel, Frederick P., Papers. Columbia University Rare Book & Manuscript Library, New York. (FKP)

Myrdal, Gunnar and Alva, Archives. Arbetarrörelsens Arkiv och Bibliotek, Stockholm, Sweden. (GAMA)

Osborne, Frederick Henry, Papers, American Philosophical Society, Philadelphia, Pennsylvania. (FHOP)

Phelps Stokes Fund Records. Schomburg Center for Research in Black Culture, New York Public Library. (PSFR)

Rhodes House Archive. Oxford, United Kingdom. (RHA)

Rockefeller Foundation Records. Rockefeller Archive Center, USA. (RFR)

Ruml, Beardsley, Papers. University of Chicago, Special Collections Research Center, USA. (BRP)

Social Science Research Council Records. Rockefeller Archive Center, USA. (SSRCR)

Spelman, Laura, Rockefeller Memorial Records, Rockefeller Archive Center, USA. (LSRMR)

Wilkerson, Doxey A., Papers. Schomburg Center for Research in Black Culture, New York Public Library. (DWP)

*Published Sources*

"2 Carnegie Aides Die on Same Day: Pneumonia Is Fatal to John A. Poynton and James Bertram Is Stricken at Table." *New York Times*, October 24, 1934.

"$600,000 for Tuskegee and B. T. Washington." *New York Times*, April 24, 1903.

Anderson, James D. *The Education of Blacks in the South, 1860–1935*. Chapel Hill: University of North Carolina Press, 1988.

———. "Northern Foundations and the Shaping of Southern Black Rural Education, 1902–1935." *History of Education Quarterly* 18, no. 4 (1978): 371–396.

Anderson, Margo, and Maurine W. Greenwald. Introduction to *Pittsburgh Surveyed: Social Science and Social Reform in the Early Twentieth Century*, edited by Maurine W. Greenwald and Margo Anderson, 1–14. Pittsburgh, PA: University of Pittsburgh Press, 1996.

Alexander, Will W. *The Slater and Jeanes Funds: An Educator's Approach to a Difficult Social Problem*. The Trustees of the John F. Slater Fund, Occasional Paper, no. 28. Washington, DC: n.p., 1934.

Anderson, Carol. *Eyes off the Prize: The United Nations and the African American Struggle for Human Rights, 1944–1955*. New York: Cambridge University Press, 2003.

Anderson, Jervis. *This Was Harlem: A Cultural Portrait, 1900–1950*. New York: Farrar Straus Giroux, 1982.

Aptheker, Herbert. *The Negro People in America: A Critique of Gunnar Myrdal's "An American Dilemma."* New York: International Publishers, 1946.

Baker, Jean H. *Margaret Sanger: A Life of Passion*. New York: Macmillan, 2011.

Baker, Lee D. *From Savage to Negro: Anthropology and the Construction of Race, 1896–1954*. Chapel Hill: University of North Carolina Press, 1998.

Bashford, Alison, and Philippa Levine, eds. *The Oxford Handbook of the History of Eugenics*. New York: Oxford University Press, 2010.

Bell, Derrick. "Brown v. Board of Education and the Interest-Convergence Dilemma." *Harvard Law Review* 93, no. 3 (1980): 518–533.

Bell, Duncan. *The Idea of Greater Britain: Empire and the Future of World Order, 1860–1900*. Princeton, NJ: Princeton University Press, 2007.

Bell, Morag. "American Philanthropy, Carnegie Corporation and Poverty in South Africa." *Journal of Southern African Studies* 26, no. 3 (2000): 481–504.

Bennett, George. "Paramountcy to Partnership: J. H. Oldham and Africa." *Africa: Journal of the International African Institute* 30, no. 4 (1960): 356–361.

Berman, Edward H. "American Influence on African Education: The Role of the Phelps-Stokes Fund's Education Commission." *Comparative Education Review* 15, no. 2 (1971): 132–145.

Bhambra, Gurminder K. "A Sociological Dilemma: Race, Segregation, and US Sociology." *Current Sociology* 62, no. 4 (2014): 472–492.

Bilbo, Theodore G. *Take Your Choice: Separation or Mongrelization*. Poplarville, MS: Dream House, 1947.

Blain, Keisha N. *Set the World on Fire: Black Nationalist Women and the Global Struggle for Freedom*. Philadelphia: University of Pennsylvania Press, 2018.

Blain, Keisha, and Tom Zoellner. "'Riots,' 'Mobs,' 'Chaos,': The Establishment Always Frames Change as Dangerous." *The Guardian*, June 2020.

Bock, Gisela, and Pat Thane, eds. *Maternity & Gender Policies: Women and the Rise of the European Welfare States, 1880s–1950s.* London: Routledge, 1991.

Brown, Richard. "Godfrey Wilson and the Rhodes-Livingstone Institute." In *Anthropology and the Colonial Encounter*, edited by Talal Asad, 173–197. London: Ithaca Press, 1973.

Brown, Richard Maxwell. *Strain of Violence: Historical Studies of American Violence and Vigilantism.* New York: Oxford University Press, 1975.

Brundage, W. Fitzhugh, ed. *Up from Slavery by Booker T. Washington with Related Documents.* Boston: Bedford/St. Martin's, 2003.

Bulmer, Martin. *The Chicago School of Sociology: Institutionalization, Diversity, and the Rise of Sociological Research.* Chicago: University of Chicago Press, 1984.

———. "The Social Survey Movement and Early Twentieth-Century Sociological Methodology." In Greenwald and Anderson, *Pittsburgh Surveyed*, 15–34.

Bulmer, Martin, and Joan Bulmer. "Philanthropy and Social Science in the 1920s: Beardsley Ruml and the Laura Spelman Rockefeller Memorial, 1922–29." *Minerva* 19, no. 3 (1981): 347–407.

Bunche, Ralph. *A World View of Race.* Washington, DC: Associates in Negro Folk Education, 1936.

Carlson, Allan. *Swedish Experiment in Family Politics: The Myrdals and the Interwar Population Crisis.* New Brunswick, NJ: Transaction Publishers, 1990.

Carmichael, Stokely, and Charles V. Hamilton, *Black Power: The Politics of Liberation in America.* New York: Random House, 1967.

Carnegie, Andrew. "The Best Fields of Philanthropy" (1889). In Carnegie, *The Gospel of Wealth and Other Writings*, 13–30.

———. "Gospel of Wealth" (1889). In Carnegie, *The Gospel of Wealth and Other Writings*, 1–12.

———. *The Gospel of Wealth and Other Writings*, edited by David Nasaw. New York: Penguin, 2006.

———. "A Look Ahead." *North American Review* 156, no. 439 (1893): 685–710.

———. *The Negro in America.* Cheyney, PA: Committee of Twelve for the Advancement of the Interests of the Negro Race, 1907.

———. *Triumphant Democracy: Sixty Years' March of the Republic.* 2nd ed. New York: Charles Scribner's Sons, 1893.

———. "Wealth" (1889). In Carnegie, *The Gospel of Wealth and Other Writings*, 1–12.

Carnegie Commission. *The Poor White Problem in South Africa: Report of the Carnegie Commission*, 5 vols. Stellenbosch: Pro ecclesia-drukkery, 1932.

Carnegie Corporation of New York. *Charter, Constitution, and Bylaws.* Accessed October 26, 2020. https://www.carnegie.org/publications/carnegie-corporation-of -new-york-charter-constitution-and-bylaws/.

———. "History of the Carnegie Hero Fund Commission." Accessed October 26, 2020 https://www.carnegiehero.org/about/history/.

———. "Other Carnegie Organizations." Accessed October 26, 2020. https://www .carnegie.org/about/our-history/other-carnegie-organizations/.

Cell, John W. *Hailey: A Study of British Imperialism, 1872–1969*. New York: Cambridge University Press, 1992.

———, ed. *By Kenya Possessed: The Correspondence of Norman Leys and J. H. Oldham 1918–1926*. Chicago: University of Chicago Press, 1976.

Chatham House. "Our History." Accessed October 28, 2020. https://www.chathamhouse .org/about-us/our-history.

Chernow, Ron. *Titan: The Life of John D. Rockefeller, Sr.* New York: Vintage Books, 1998.

The Chicago Commission on Race Relations. *The Negro in Chicago: A Study of Race Relations and a Race Riot*. Chicago: University of Chicago Press, 1922.

Clements, Keith. *Faith on the Frontier: A Life of J. H. Oldham*. Edinburgh: T & T Clark Ltd., 1999.

The Cleveland Foundation, Centennial Website. "An Idea Whose Time Had Come." Accessed April 23, 2020. http://www.clevelandfoundation100.org/foundation-of -change/invention/introduction/.

Connelly, Matthew. *Fatal Misconception: The Struggle to Control World Population*. Cambridge, MA: Harvard University Press, 2008.

Cook, Samuel DuBois. Review of *The Negro in America: The Condensed Version of Gunnar Myrdal's An American Dilemma*, by Arnold Rose. *Journal of Negro History* 49, no. 3 (1964): 207–209.

Cottrol, Robert J. "Justice Advanced: Comments on William Nelson's *Brown v. Board of Education* and the Jurisprudence of Legal Realism." *Saint Louis University Law Journal* 48 (Spring 2004): 839–850.

Coupland, R. "The Hailey Survey." *Africa: Journal of the International Institute of African Languages and Cultures* 12, no. 1 (1939): 1–11.

Cox, Oliver C. *Caste, Class and Race: A Study in Social Dynamics*. Garden City, NY: Doubleday, 1948.

Crawford, Lawrence. "Sir Carruthers Beattie, D.Sc.F.R.S.E., and His Scientific Work." *Transactions of the Royal Society of South Africa* 31, no. 5 (1948): 503–508.

Cruse, Harold. *The Crisis of the Negro Intellectual: A Historical Analysis of the Failure of Black Leadership*. 1967. New York: New York Review Book, 2005.

Dagbovie, Pero Gaglo. "Exploring a Century of Historical Scholarship on Booker T. Washington." *Journal of African American History* 92, no. 2 (2007): 239–264.

Daley, Jason. "To Remember the Chicago Race Riot of 1919, Commemoration Project Looks to Public Art." *Smithsonian Magazine*, July 30, 2019.

Davie, Grace. *Poverty Knowledge in South Africa: A Social History of Human Science, 1855–2005*. New York: Cambridge University Press, 2015.

Davis, Deborah. *Guest of Honor: Booker T. Washington, Theodore Roosevelt, and the White House Dinner That Shocked a Nation*. New York: Atria Books, 2012.

Davis, John. "How All Souls Got Its Anthropologist." In *A History of Oxford Anthropology*, edited by Peter Rivière, 62–82. New York: Berghahn Books, 2007.

Davis, R. Hunt, Jr. "Charles T. Loram and the American Model for African Education in South Africa." *African Studies Review* 19, no. 2 (September 1976): 87–99.

Dodd, Norman. *The Dodd Report to the Reece Committee on Foundations*. New York: The Long House, 1954.

Drake, St. Clair, and Horace R. Cayton. *Black Metropolis: A Study of Negro Life in a Northern City.* New York: Harcourt Brace, 1945.

Driver, C. J. *Patrick Duncan: South African and Pan-African.* Oxford: James Currey, 1980.

Du Bois, W. E. B. Review of *An American Dilemma: The Negro Problem and Modern Democracy* by Gunnar Myrdal, Richard Sterner; Arnold Rose. *Phylon* 5, no. 2 (1944): 118–124.

———. *Color and Democracy: Colonies and Peace.* 1945. In *The Oxford W. E. B. Du Bois,* edited by Henry Louis Gates Jr., 235–330. New York: Oxford University Press, 2007.

———. "Negro Education." *The Crisis,* February 1918, 173–178.

———. *The Souls of Black Folk.* Chicago: A. C. McClurg, 1903.

———. "The Souls of White Folk." In *Darkwater: Voices from within the Veil,* by W. E. B. Du Bois. 1920. Mineola, NY: Dover, 1999.

Dubow, Saul. *A Commonwealth of Knowledge: Science, Sensibility, and White South Africa 1820–2000.* New York: Oxford University Press, 2006.

Dudziak, Mary. *Cold War Civil Rights: Race and the Image of American Democracy.* Princeton, NJ: Princeton University Press, 2000.

Eastland, James O. *The Supreme Court's "Modern Scientific Authorities" in the Segregation Cases.* Washington, DC: Government Printing Office, 1955.

Edge, Laura Bufano. *Andrew Carnegie: Industrial Philanthropist.* Minneapolis: Lerner Publications, 2004.

"Education Mission Going to Africa: Dr. T. J. Jones of Phelps Stokes Fund Heads Expedition for Hygienic and Economic Survey." *New York Times,* December 27, 1923.

Edwards, Brent Hayes. *The Practice of Diaspora: Literature, Translation, and the Rise of Black Internationalism.* Cambridge, MA: Harvard University Press, 2003.

Ekerwald, Hedvig. "The Modernist Manifesto of Alva and Gunnar Myrdal: Modernization of Sweden in the Thirties and the Question of Sterilization." *International Journal of Politics, Culture, and Society* 14, no. 3 (2001): 539–561.

———. "To Build a Nation: Alva Myrdal and the Role of Family Politics in the Transformation of Sweden in the 1930s." In *After the Soviet Empire: Legacies and Pathways,* edited by Sven Eliaeson, Lyudmila Harutyunyan, and Larrissa Titarenko, 108–132. Leiden: Brill, 2015.

Eliaeson, Sven. "Gunnar Myrdal: A Theorist of Modernity." *Acta Sociologica* 43, no. 4 (2000): 331–341.

Ellis, Mark. *Race, War, and Surveillance: African Americans and the United States Government during World War I.* Bloomington: Indiana University Press, 2001.

Ellison, Ralph. "*An American Dilemma*: A Review." In Ellison, *The Shadow and Act,* 303–317.

———. *Invisible Man.* New York: Random House, 1952.

———. *The Shadow and Act.* New York: Random House, 1964.

Embree, Edwin R. *Julius Rosenwald: Review of Two Decades, 1917–1936.* Chicago: Julius Rosenwald Fund, 1936.

Ewing, Adam. *The Age of Garvey: How a Jamaican Activist Created a Mass Movement and Changed Global Black Politics.* Princeton, NJ: Princeton University Press, 2014.

Fanon, Frantz. *Black Skin, White Masks.* 1952. Translated by Richard Philcox. New York: Grove Press, 2008.

———. *The Wretched of the Earth.* 1961. Translated by Richard Philcox. New York: Grove Press, 2004.

Fantham, H. B. "The Oudtshoorn Meeting of the South African Association for the Advancement of Science." *Nature* 116 (December 19, 1925): 916–918.

Farber, Naomi. "Charles S. Johnson's 'The Negro in Chicago.'" *American Sociologist* 26, no. 3 (1995): 78–88.

"Finding a Footing." In *100 Years Later: The Rockefeller Foundation.* The Rockefeller Archive Center. Accessed October 27, 2020. https://rockfound.rockarch.org/finding-a-footing.

Fisher, Donald. *Fundamental Development of the Social Sciences: Rockefeller Philanthropy and the United States Social Science Research Council.* Ann Arbor: University of Michigan Press, 1993.

Fleck, Christian. *A Transatlantic History of the Social Sciences: Robber Barons, the Third Reich and the Invention of Empirical Social Research.* London: Bloomsbury Academic, 2011.

Fleisch, Brahm David. "Social Scientists as Policy Makers: E. G. Malherbe and the National Bureau for Educational and Social Research, 1929–1943." *Journal of Southern African Studies* 21, no. 3 (1995): 349–372.

Foner, Eric. *Reconstruction: America's Unfinished Revolution, 1863–1877.* New York: Harper & Row, 1988.

Fosdick, Raymond B. *Adventure in Giving: The Story of the General Education Board, a Foundation Established by John D. Rockefeller,* based on an unfinished manuscript prepared by the late Henry F. Pringle and Katharine Douglas Pringle). New York: Harper & Row, 1962.

"The Foundations Defend Freedom of Inquiry." *Social Service Review* 29, no. 1 (1955): 76–77.

Francis, Megan Ming. *Civil Rights and the Making of the Modern American State.* New York: Cambridge University Press, 2014.

Fultz, Michael. "Teacher Training and African American Education in the South, 1900–1940." *Journal of Negro Education* 64, no. 2 (1995): 196–210.

Füredi, Frank. *The Silent War: Imperialism and the Changing Perception of Race.* New Brunswick, NJ: Rutgers University Press, 1998.

Garlington, S. W. "Newsettes." *Amsterdam Star News,* December 1944.

"The General Education Board." In *100 Years Later: The Rockefeller Foundation.* The Rockefeller Archive Center. Accessed October 27, 2020. https://rockfound.rockarch.org/general_education_board.

Gershenhorn, Jerry. *Melville J. Herskovits and the Racial Politics of Knowledge.* Lincoln: University of Nebraska Press, 2004.

Getachew, Adom. *Worldmaking after Empire: The Rise and Fall of Self-Determination.* Princeton, NJ: Princeton University Press, 2019.

Gilmore, Glenda Elizabeth. *Gender & Jim Crow: Women and the Politics of White Supremacy in North Carolina, 1896–1920.* Chapel Hill: University of North Carolina Press, 1996.

———. "How Anne Scott and Pauli Murray Found Each Other." In *Writing Women's History: A Tribute to Anne Firor Scott,* edited by Elizabeth Anne Payne, 142–171. Jackson: University Press of Mississippi, 2011.

Gladstone, W. E. "Mr. Carnegie's Gospel of Wealth: A Review and a Recommendation." *North American Review* 38 (1890): 677–694.

Glotzer, Richard. "The Career of Mable Carney: The Study of Race and Rural Development in the United States and South Africa." *International Journal of African Historical Studies* 29, no. 2 (1996): 309–336.

———. "A Long Shadow: Frederick P. Keppel, Carnegie Corporation and the Dominions and Colonies Fund Area Experts 1923–1943." *History of Education*, 38, no. 5 (2009): 621–648.

Gordon, Leah. *From Power to Prejudice: The Rise of Racial Individualism in Midcentury America.* Chicago: University of Chicago Press, 2015.

Greenberg, Cheryl Lynn. *"Or Does it Explode?": Black Harlem in the Great Depression.* New York: Oxford University Press, 1991.

Greenwald, Maurine W., and Margo Anderson, eds. *Pittsburgh Surveyed: Social Science and Social Reform in the Early Twentieth Century.* Pittsburgh, PA: University of Pittsburgh Press, 1996.

Gruening, Martha, and W. E. B. Du Bois. "The Massacre of East St. Louis." *The Crisis,* September 1917, 219–238.

Hailey, Malcolm (Lord Hailey). *An African Survey: A Study of Problems Arising in Africa South of the Sahara.* London: Oxford University Press, 1938.

Hansen, Harry. "First Reader." *Virginian Pilot,* December 27, 1944.

Harlan, Louis R., and Raymond W. Smock, eds. *The Booker T. Washington Papers: Vol. 12, 1912–14.* Urbana: University of Illinois Press, 1982.

"Harold F. Dorn (1906–1963)." *Population Index* 29, no. 3 (1963): 237–242.

Harris, Daryl B. "The Logic of Black Urban Rebellions." *Journal of Black Studies* 28, no. 3 (1998): 368–385.

Hartog, Hendrik. *Public Property and Private Power: The Corporation of the City of New York in American Law, 1730–1870.* Chapel Hill: University of North Carolina Press, 1983.

Henderson, Charles Richmond. "Industrial Insurance. VIII. Insurance Plans of Railroad Corporations." *American Journal of Sociology* 13, no. 5 (1908): 584–616.

Herman, Max. "Ten Years After: A Critical Review of Scholarship on the 1992 Los Angeles Riot." *Race, Gender & Class* 11, no. 1 (2004): 116–135.

Herskovits, Melville J. *The Myth of the Negro Past.* New York: Harper & Brothers, 1941.

Hetherington, Penelope. *British Paternalism and Africa, 1920–1940.* London: Frank Cass, 1978.

Heyman, Richard D. "C. T. Loram: A South African Liberal in Race Relations." *International Journal of African Historical Studies* 5, no. 1 (1972): 41–50.

Higgs, Catherine. *The Ghost of Equality: The Public Lives of D. D. T. Jabavu of South Africa, 1885–1959.* Athens: Ohio University Press, 1997.

Hirdman, Yvonne. *Alva Myrdal: The Passionate Mind.* Translated by Linda Schenck. Bloomington: Indiana University Press, 2008.

Holmes, D. O. W. "Twenty-Five Years of Thomas Jesse Jones and the Phelps Stokes Fund." *Journal of Negro Education* 7, no. 4 (1938): 475–485.

Horne, Gerald. *Black Revolutionary: William Patterson and the Globalization of the African-American Freedom Struggle.* Urbana: University of Illinois Press, 2013.

Hunter, Tera. *To 'Joy My Freedom: Southern Black Women's Lives and Labors after the Civil War.* Cambridge, MA: Harvard University Press, 1997.

Jackson, Walter. *Gunnar Myrdal and America's Conscience: Social Engineering and Racial Liberalism, 1938–1987.* Chapel Hill: University of North Carolina Press, 1990.

Jacobs, Sylvia M. "James Emman Kwegyir Aggrey: An African Intellectual in the United States." *Journal of Negro History* 81, no. 1/4 (Winter/Autumn 1996): 47–61.

James, C. L. R. "The Revolutionary Answer to the Negro Problem in the United States." In McLemee and Le Blanc, *C. L. R. James and Revolutionary Marxism*, 179–187.

James, Wendy. "The Anthropologist as Reluctant Imperialist." In *Anthropology and the Colonial Encounter*, edited by Talal Asad, 41–69. London: Ithaca Press, 1973.

Johnson, Charles S. *Patterns of Negro Segregation*. New York: Harper & Brothers, 1943.

Johnson, Donald. "W. E. B. Du Bois, Thomas Jesse Jones and the Struggle for Social Education, 1900–1930." *Journal of Negro History* 85, no. 3 (2000): 71–95.

Johnson, Lauri. "A Generation of Women Activists: African American Female Educators in Harlem, 1930–1950." *Journal of African American History* (2004): 223–240.

Jones, Thomas Jesse. *Education in Africa: A Study of West, South, and Equatorial Africa by the African Education Commission, under The auspices of the Phelps-Stokes Fund and Foreign Mission Societies of North America and Europe*. New York: Phelps Stokes Fund, 1922.

———. *Education in East Africa: A Study of East, Central and South Africa*. New York: Phelps Stokes Fund, 1925.

———. *Negro Education: A Study of the Private and Higher Schools for Colored People in the United States*. 2 vols. Washington, DC: Government Printing Office, 1917.

Joseph, Peniel E. "Rethinking the Black Power Era." *Journal of Southern History* 75, no. 3 (2009): 707–716.

———. *Stokely: A Life*. New York: Basic Civitas, Perseus Books Group, 2014.

Karl, Barry. *The Uneasy State: The United States from 1915 to 1945*. Chicago: University of Chicago Press, 1983.

Karl, Barry, and Stanley N. Katz, "The American Private Philanthropic Foundation and the Public Sphere, 1890–1930." *Minerva* 19, no. 2 (1981): 236–270.

Katz, Michael B., and Thomas J. Sugrue. *W. E. B. Du Bois, Race, and the City: "The Philadelphia Negro" and Its Legacy*. Philadelphia: University of Pennsylvania Press, 1998.

Katz, William Loren, ed. *The American Negro: His History and Literature*. New York: Arno Press, 1969.

Kennedy, David M. *Freedom from Fear: The American People in Depression and War, 1929–1945*. New York: Oxford University Press, 1999.

Keppel, Frederick P. "The Arts in Social Life." In President's Research Committee on Social Trends, *Recent Social Trends in the United States*, 958–1008.

———. Foreword to *An American Dilemma*, by Gunnar Myrdal, v–viii. New York: Harper & Brothers, 1944.

Keppel, Frederick P., and R. L. Duffus. *The Arts in American Life*. New York: McGaw-Hill, 1933.

Kessner, Thomas. *Fiorello H. LaGuardia and the Making of Modern New York*. New York: McGraw-Hill, 1989.

Killens, John Oliver. *Black Man's Burden*. New York: Trident Press, 1965.

King, Kenneth J. "Africa and the Southern States of the U.S.A.: Notes on J. H. Oldham and the American Negro Education for Africans." *Journal of African History* 10, no. 4 (1969): 659–677.

———. "African Students in Negro American Colleges: Notes on the Good African." *Phylon* 31, no. 1 (1970): 16–30.

———. *Pan-Africanism and Education*. 1971. New York: Diasporic Africa Press, 2016.

King, Martin Luther, Jr. *Where Do We Go from Here: Chaos or Community?* New York: Harper & Row, 1967.

Klarman, Michael. *Brown v. Board and the Civil Rights Movement*. New York: Oxford University Press, 2007.

———. *From Jim Crow to Civil Rights: The Supreme Court and the Struggle for Racial Equality*. New York: Oxford University Press, 2004.

Klineberg, Otto, ed. *Characteristics of the American Negro*. New York: Harper & Brothers, 1944.

Kuper, Adam. *Anthropologists and Anthropology: The British School, 1922–1972*. Harmondsworth, UK: Penguin, 1973.

Lagemann, Ellen Condliffe. *The Politics of Knowledge: Carnegie Corporation, Philanthropy, and Public Policy*. Chicago: University of Chicago Press, 1989.

Lake, Marilyn, and Henry Reynolds. *Drawing the Global Colour Line: White Men's Countries and the International Challenge of Racial Equality*. Cambridge: Cambridge University Press, 2008.

Lawson, Steven F. "Introduction: Setting the Agenda of the Civil Rights Movement." In Lawson, *To Secure These Rights*, 1–41.

———, ed. *To Secure These Rights: The Report of President Harry S. Truman's Committee on Civil Rights*. Boston: Bedford/St. Martin's, 2004.

Ledwidge, Mark, and Inderjeet Parmar. "Clash of Pans: Pan-Africanism and Pan-Anglo-Saxonism and the Global Colour Line, 1919–1945." *International Politics* 55, no. 6 (2018): 765–781.

Lehmann-Haupt, Christopher. "Herbert Aptheker, 87, Dies; Prolific Marxist Historian." *New York Times*, March 20, 2003.

Lester, Robert M. *Forty Years of Carnegie Giving, 1901–1941*. New York: Charles Scribner's Sons, 1941.

Leuchtenburg, William E. "The New Deal and the Analogue of War." In *Change and Continuity in Twentieth-Century America*, edited by John Braeman, Robert Hamlett Bremner, and Everett Walters, 81–143. Columbus: Ohio State University Press, 1964.

Lewis, David Levering. Foreword to *Charles S. Johnson: Leadership beyond the Veil in the Age of Jim Crow*, by Patrick J. Gilpin and Marybeth Gasman, ix–xii. Albany: State University of New York Press, 2003.

———. *W. E. B. Du Bois: The Fight for Equality and the American Century, 1919–1963*. New York: Henry Holt, 2000.

Levy, Jonathan. "Accounting for Profit and the History of Capital." *Critical Historical Studies* 1, no. 2 (2014): 171–214.

———. "Altruism and the Origins of Nonprofit Philanthropy." In *Philanthropy in Democratic Societies: History, Institutions, Values*, edited by Rob Reich, Chiara Cordelli, and Lucy Bernholz, 19–43. Chicago: University of Chicago Press, 2016.

Lindgren, E. J. "Bertram Johannes Otto Schrieke: 1890–1945." *Man* 48 (October 1948): 113–117.

Link, William A. "Jackson Davis and the Lost World of Jim Crow Education." University of Virginia Albert and Shirley Small Special Collections Library. Accessed October 28, 2020. https://small.library.virginia.edu/collections/featured/jackson-davis-collection

-of-african-american-educational-photographs/related-resources/jackson-davis-and
-the-lost-world-of-jim-crow-education/.

Lorimer, Frank, and Frederick Henry Osborn. *Dynamics of Population: Social and Biological Significance of Changing Birth Rates in the United States.* New York: Macmillan, 1934.

Lothian, Philip Kerr (Lord Lothian). Foreword to *An African Survey,* by Malcolm Hailey. London: Oxford University Press, 1938.

Louis, Wm. Roger. Introduction to *The Oxford History of the British Empire,* vol. 5, *Historiography,* edited by Robin W. Winks, 1–42. Oxford: Oxford University Press, 1999).

Lugard, Frederick. *The Dual Mandate in British Tropical Africa.* London: W. Blackwood & Sons, 1923.

Lumpkins, Charles L. *American Pogrom: The East St. Louis Race Riot and Black Politics.* Athens: Ohio University Press, 2008.

Lupo, Lindsey. *Flak-Catchers: One Hundred Years of Riot Commission Politics in America.* Lanham, MD: Lexington Books, 2011.

Lyman, Stanford, and Sven Eliaeson, eds. "Alva and Gunnar Myrdal: A Symposium on Their Lives and Works." *International Journal of Politics, Culture, and Society* 14, no. 3 (2001): 439–441.

Lyons, Gene M. *The Uneasy Partnership: Social Science and the Federal Government in the Twentieth Century.* New York: Russell Sage, 1969.

Mack, Kenneth. *Representing the Race: The Creation of the Civil Rights Lawyer.* Cambridge: Harvard University Press, 2012.

Magubane, Bernard. *The Making of a Racist State: British Imperialism and the Union of South Africa, 1875–1910.* Trenton, NJ: Africa World Press, 1996.

Magubane, Zine. "The American Construction of the Poor White Problem in South Africa." *South Atlantic Quarterly* 107, no. 4 (2008): 691–713.

Makalani, Minkah. *In the Cause of Freedom: Radical Black Internationalism from Harlem to London, 1917–1939.* Chapel Hill: University of North Carolina Press, 2011.

Malherbe, E. G. *Education in South Africa (1652–1922): A Critical Survey of the Development of Educational Administration in the Cape, Natal, Transvaal and the Orange Free State.* Cape Town: Juta, 1925.

———. *Education Report: Education and the Poor White.* Vol. 3 of *The Poor White Problem in South Africa: Report of the Carnegie Commission.* Stellenbosch: Pro ecclesia-drukkery, 1932.

Malinowski, Bronislaw. "Practical Anthropology." *Africa: Journal of the International African Institute* 2, no. 1 (1929): 22–38.

Marable, Manning. "Booker T. Washington and African Nationalism." *Phylon* 35, no. 4 (1974): 398–406.

———. *Malcolm X: A Life of Reinvention.* New York: Penguin Group, 2011.

Matera, Marc. *Black London: The Imperial Metropolis and Decolonization in the Twentieth Century.* Oakland: University of California Press, 2015.

Maxon, Robert M. "The Devonshire Declaration: The Myth of Missionary Intervention." *History in Africa* 18 (1991): 259–270.

The Mayor's Commission on Conditions in Harlem. *The Negro in Harlem: A Report on Social and Economic Conditions Responsible for the Outbreak of March 19, 1935.* New York: Archived at Columbia University Butler Library, 1935.

Mazower, Mark. *Dark Continent: Europe's Twentieth Century.* 1998. New York: Vintage Books, 2000.

——. *No Enchanted Palace: The End of Empire and the Ideological Origins of the United Nations.* Princeton, NJ: Princeton University Press, 2009.

Mazzari, Louis. "Arthur Raper and Documentary Realism in Greene County, Georgia." *Georgia Historical Quarterly* 87, no. 3/4 (2003): 389–407.

M. B. Review of *The Negro in America,* by Maxwell S. Stewart. *American Journal of Psychology* 59, no. 2 (April 1946): 332.

"McCarthyism and the Red Scare." Miller Center. University of Virginia. Accessed May 2, 2021. https://millercenter.org/the-presidency/educational-resources/age-of -eisenhower/mcarthyism-red-scare.

McLaughlin, Malcolm. "Ghetto Formation and Armed Resistance in East St. Louis, Illinois." *Journal of American Studies* 41, no. 2 (2007): 435–467.

McLemee, Scott, and Paul Le Blanc, eds. *C. L. R. James and Revolutionary Marxism: Selected Writings of C. L. R. James, 1939–1949.* Chicago: Haymarket Books, 1994.

MeasuringWorth. "Seven Ways to Compute the Relative Value of a U.S. Dollar Amount—1790 to Present." Accessed April 23, 2021. https://www.measuringworth.com /calculators/uscompare/.

Melamed, Jodi. *Represent and Destroy: Rationalizing Violence in the New Racial Capitalism.* Minneapolis: University of Minnesota Press, 2011.

"Memorandum from British Colonial Secretary." In Samson, *The British Empire,* 260.

Merriam, Charles E. "Annual Report of the Social Science Research Council." *American Political Science Review* 20, no. 1 (1926): 185–189.

Mitcham, John C. *Race and Imperial Defence in the British World, 1870–1914.* New York: Cambridge University Press, 2019.

Mkhize, Khwezi. "'To See Us as We See Ourselves': John Tengo Jabavu and the Politics of the Black Periodical." *Journal of Southern African Studies* 44, no. 3 (2018): 413–430.

Moodley, Kogila. "The Continued Impact of Black Consciousness in South Africa," *Journal of Modern African Studies* 29, no. 2 (1991): 237–251.

Morey, Maribel. "Rockefeller, Carnegie, and the SSRC's Focus on Race in the 1920s and 1930s." *Items: Insights from the Social Sciences,* January 8, 2019.

——. "A Displaced American Feminist: Simone de Beauvoir's Race/Gender Analogy from Myrdal to Women's Lib." Unpublished manuscript, 2005.

Morey, Maribel, and Jamie Martin, eds. "Gunnar Myrdal Symposium." *Humanity Journal* 8, no. 1 (2017): 127–226.

Morris, Aldon D. *The Scholar Denied: W. E. B. Du Bois and the Birth of Modern Sociology.* Oakland: University of California Press, 2015.

Morris, Charles R. *The Tycoons: How Andrew Carnegie, John D. Rockefeller, Jay Gould, and J.P. Morgan Invented the American Supereconomy.* New York: Henry Holt, 2005.

Moses, Wilson Jeremiah. *Creative Conflict in African American Thought: Frederick Douglass, Alexander Crummell, Booker T. Washington, W. E. B. Du Bois, and Marcus Garvey.* New York: Cambridge University Press, 2004.

——. *The Golden Age of Black Nationalism, 1850–1925.* New York. Oxford University Press, 1978.

Moss, Alfred A., Jr. *The American Negro Academy: Voice of the Talented Tenth*. Baton Rouge: Louisiana State University Press, 1981.

Moynihan, Daniel P. "Foreword to the Paperback Edition." In *National and Family: The Swedish Experiment in Democratic Family and Population Policy* by Alva Myrdal, v–xvii. Cambridge: MIT Press, 1968.

"Mr. Keppel Accepts New Call." *Red Cross Bulletin*, October 18, 1920, 4.

Murakawa, Naomi. *The First Civil Right: How Liberals Built Prison America*. New York: Oxford University Press, 2014.

Murphy, E. Jefferson. *Carnegie Corporation and Africa: 1953–1973*. New York: Carnegie Corporation of New York, 1976.

Myrdal, Alva. *Nation and Family: The Swedish Experiment in Democratic Family and Population Policy*. New York: Harper & Brothers, 1941.

Myrdal, Alva, and Gunnar Myrdal. *Kris i befolkningsfrågan*. Stockholm: Bonniers, 1934.

———. *Kontakt med Amerika*. Stockholm: A. Bonnier, 1941.

Myrdal, Gunnar. *An American Dilemma: The Complete Twentieth Anniversary Edition*. New York: McGraw-Hill, 1964.

———. *An American Dilemma: The Negro Problem and Modern Democracy*. New York: Harper & Brothers, 1944.

———. *Historien om "An American Dilemma."* Stockholm: SNS Förlag, 1987.

———. "Industrialization and Population." In *Economic Essays in Honour of Gustav Cassell, October 20th, 1933*, by Gustav Cassel, 435–458. London: G. Allen & Unwin, 1933.

———. *Monetary Equilibrium*. London: William Hodge, 1939.

———. "Om penningteoretisk jämvikt: En studie över den 'normala räntan' I Wicksells penninglära." *Ekonomisk Tidskrift* 33, no. 5/6 (1931): 191–302.

Myrdal, Gunnar, and Sven Bouvin. *The Cost of Living in Sweden 1830–1930*. London: P. S. King & Son, 1933.

Nasaw, David. *Andrew Carnegie*. New York: Penguin, 2006.

"The Negro in Industry." *Monthly Labor Review* 44, no. 2 (1937): 345–348.

Nelson, Alondra. *Body and Soul: The Black Panther Party and the Fight against Medical Discrimination*. Minneapolis: University of Minnesota Press, 2011.

Nielsen, Waldemar. *The Big Foundations: A Twentieth Century Fund Study*. New York: Columbia University Press, 1972.

Nkomo, S. M. *How I Found Christ in the Jungles of Africa*. Chicago: Committee on Friendly Relations among Foreign Students, 1917.

Nkrumah, Kwame. *Africa Must Unite*. New York: Frederick A. Praeger, 1963.

———. *I Speak of Freedom: A Statement of African Ideology*. London: Heinemann, 1961.

Norman, Dorothy. "A World to Live In: Recent Books on Race Relations." *New York Post*, September 17, 1945.

O'Connor, Alice. *Poverty Knowledge: Social Science, Social Policy, and the Poor in Twentieth-Century U.S. History*. Princeton, NJ: Princeton University Press, 2001.

"Official Reports." *Social Problems* 3, no. 3 (1956): 200–208.

Okia, Opolot. "The Northey Forced Labor Crisis, 1920–1921: A Symptomatic Reading." *International Journal of African Historical Studies* 41, no. 2 (2008): 263–293.

Oliver, R. A. C. *General Intelligence Test for Africans: Manual of Directions*. Nairobi, Kenya Colony: Government Printer, 1932.

Oldham, J. H. *Christianity and the Race Problem*. London: Student Christian Movement, 1924.

———. "Christian Missions and the Education of the Negro." *International Review of Missions* 7 (1918): 242–247.

———. "Educational Policy of the British Government in Africa." *International Review of Missions* 14 (1925): 421–427.

———. *White and Black in Africa: A Critical Examination of the Rhodes Lectures of General Smuts*. London: Longmans, Green, 1930.

Orlans, Harold. "Social Science Research Policies in the United States." *Minerva* 9, no. 1 (1971): 7–31.

Ormsby-Gore, William George Arthur. *East Africa: Report of the East Africa Commission, Presented by the Secretary of State for the Colonies to Parliament by Command of His Majesty, April 1925*. London: H. M. Stationery Office, 1925.

Padmore, George. *Africa: Britain's Third Empire*. London: Dennis Dobson, 1949.

Painter, Nell Irvin. *The History of White People*. New York: W. W. Norton, 2010.

———. *Standing at Armageddon: The United States, 1877–1919*. New York: W. W. Norton, 1987.

Parmar, Inderjeet. *Think Tanks and Power in Foreign Policy: A Comparative Study of the Role and Influence of the Council on Foreign Relations and the Royal Institute of International Affairs, 1939–1945*. New York: Palgrave, 2004.

Pedler, Frederick. "Lord Hailey: His Contribution to Africa." *Journal of the Royal Society of Arts* 118, no. 5168 (1970): 484–492.

Peretz, Henri. "The Making of *Black Metropolis*." *Annals of the American Academy of Political and Social Science* 595 (September 2004): 168–175.

Perkins, Alfred. *Edwin Rogers Embree: The Julius Rosenwald Fund, Foundation Philanthropy and American Race Relations*. Bloomington: Indiana University Press, 2011.

Pick, William, Laetitia Rispel, and Shan Naidoo. "Poverty, Health and Policy: A Historical Look at the South African Experience." *Journal of Public Health* 29, no. 2 (2008): 165–178.

Plant, Arnold. "An African Survey." *Economica* 6, no. 22 (May 1939): 205–212.

Platt, Anthony, ed. *The Politics of Riot Commissions, 1917–1970: A Collection of Official Reports and Critical Essays*. New York: Macmillan, 1971.

President's Research Committee on Social Trends. *Recent Social Trends in the United States: Report of the President's Research Committee on Social Trends*. New York: McGraw-Hill, 1933.

"Public Affairs Pamphlets are Best Sellers." *Journal of Education* 128, no. 5 (September 1945): 210–211.

Rabinbach, Anson. *The Human Motor: Energy, Fatigue, and the Origins of Modernity*. Berkeley: University of California Press, 1990.

"R. A. Franks, 73, Carnegie Aid, Dies in Jersey: Financial Secretary of Steel Manufacturer Passes at Llewellyn Park Home." *New York Herald Tribune*, September 2, 1935.

Rampersad, Arnold. *Ralph Ellison: A Biography*. New York: Random House, 2007.

Rana, Aziz. "Race and the American Creed: Recovering Black Radicalism." *N+1* 24 (Winter 2016): 13–21.

Rappaport, Helen. *Encyclopedia of Women Social Reformers*, 2 vols. Santa Barbara: ABC-CLIO, 2001.

Reuter, E. B. Review of *An American Dilemma: The Negro Problem and Modern Democracy* by Gunnar Myrdal, Richard Sterner, and Arnold Rose. *Phylon* 5, no. 2 (1944): 118–124.

Rich, Paul B. *Race and Empire in British Politics*, 2nd ed. Cambridge: Cambridge University Press, 1990.

Ring, Natalie J. *The Problem South: Region, Empire, and the New Liberal State, 1880–1930*. Athens: University of Georgia Press, 2012.

Rivière, Peter. "The Formative Years: The Committee for Anthropology, 1905–38." In *A History of Oxford Anthropology*, edited by Peter Rivière, 43–61. New York: Berghahn Books, 2007.

Robinson, Cedric J. *Black Marxism: The Making of the Black Radical Tradition*. 1983. Chapel Hill: University of North Carolina Press, 2000.

Royal Scottish Geographical Society. "Livingstone Medal." Accessed April 22, 2021. https://www.rsgs.org/livingstone-medal#:~:text=Livingstone%20Medal%3A%20 for%20outstanding%20service,Neil%20Armstrong%2C%20and%20Michael%20Palin.

Rockefeller Foundation. *Directory of Fellowships and Scholarships: 1917–1970*. New York: Rockefeller Foundation, 1972.

Rose, Kenneth W. *A Survey of Sources at the Rockefeller Archive Center for the Study of Twentieth Century Africa*. Tarrytown, NY: Rockefeller Archive Center, 1996.

Rosenfield, Patricia. *A World of Giving: Carnegie Corporation of New York, a Century of International Philanthropy*. New York: Public Affairs, 2014.

Rosenthal, Michael. *Nicholas Miraculous: The Amazing Career of the Redoubtable Dr. Nicholas Murray Butler*. New York: Farrar, Straus, and Giroux, 2006.

Ross, Dorothy. *The Origins of American Social Science*. Cambridge: Cambridge University Press, 1991.

Rudwick, Elliott M. *Race Riot at East St. Louis, July 2, 1917*. Carbondale: Southern Illinois University Press, 1964.

Rushdy, Ashraf H. A. *The End of American Lynching*. New Brunswick, NJ: Rutgers University Press, 2012.

Samson, Jane, ed. *The British Empire: Oxford Readers*. New York: Oxford University Press, 2001.

Saunders, Christopher. "Biography of a Political Activist." *Journal of African History* 39, no. 3 (1998): 499–500.

Saville, John. "Britain: Internationalism and the Labour Movement between the Wars." In *Internationalism in the Labour Movement, 1830–1940*, edited by Frits van Holthoon and Marcel van der Linden, 565–582. Leiden: E. J. Brill, 1988.

Schrieke, Bertram. *Alien Americans: A Study of Race Relations*. New York: Viking Press, 1936.

Scott, Daryl Michael. *Contempt & Pity: Social Policy and the Image of the Damaged Black Psyche*. Chapel Hill: University of North Carolina Press, 1997.

Scott, Emmett Jay. *Scott's Official History of the American Negro in the World War*. Chicago: Homewood Press, 1919.

Seekings, Jeremy. "'Not a Single White Person Should Be Allowed to Go Under': Swartgevaar and the Origins of South Africa's Welfare State, 1924–1929." *Journal of African History* 48, no. 3 (2007): 375–394.

———. "The Carnegie Commission and the Backlash against Welfare State-Building in South Africa, 1931–1937." *Journal of Southern African Studies* 34, no. 3 (September 2008): 515–537.

Singh, Nikhil Pal. *Black Is a Country: Race and the Unfinished Struggle for Democracy.* Cambridge, MA: Harvard University Press, 2004.

Sitkoff, Harvard. *A New Deal for Blacks: The Emergence of Civil Rights as a National Issue.* Volume 1: *The Depression Decade.* New York: Oxford University Press, 1978.

Smuts, J. C. *Africa and Some World Problems: Including The Rhodes Memorial Lectures Delivered in Michaelmas Term, 1929.* London: Oxford University Press, 1930.

"South Africa: The General Election." *Round Table* 38, no. 151 (1948): 719–722.

Southern, David W. *Gunnar Myrdal and Black-White Relations: The Use and Abuse of "An American Dilemma."* Baton Rouge: Louisiana State University Press, 1994.

Solovey, Mark. *Shaky Foundations: The Politics–Patronage–Social Science Nexus in Cold War America.* New Brunswick, NJ: Rutgers University Press, 2013.

Spektorowski, Alberto, and Elisabet Mizrachi. "Eugenics and the Welfare State in Sweden: The Politics of Social Margins and the Idea of a Productive Society." *Journal of Contemporary History* 39, no. 3 (2004): 333–352.

"Spreading Gospels of Wealth." *Economist,* May 19, 2012.

Stackpole, Stephen. *Carnegie Corporation Commonwealth Program, 1911–1961.* New York: Carnegie Corporation of New York, 1963.

Stein, Judith. *The World of Marcus Garvey: Race and Class in Modern Society.* Baton Rouge: Louisiana State University Press, 1986.

Steinberg, Stephen. "An American Dilemma: The Collapse of the Racial Orthodoxy of Gunnar Myrdal." *Journal of Blacks in Higher Education* 10 (Winter 1995–1996): 64–70.

———. *Race Relations: A Critique.* Stanford, CA: Stanford University Press, 2007.

Sterner, Richard. *The Negro's Share.* New York: Harper & Brothers, 1943.

Stewart, Jeffrey C. *The New Negro: The Life of Alain Locke.* New York: Oxford University Press, 2018.

Stewart, Maxwell. *The Negro in America: Public Affairs Pamphlet no. 95.* New York: Public Affairs Committee, 1944.

Stone, I. F. "People without a Country." Review of *The Negro American,* edited by Talcott Parsons and Kenneth B. Clark. *New York Review of Books* 7, no. 2 (August 18, 1966): 8–12.

Strom, Stephanie. "Pledge to Give Away Fortunes Stirs Debate." *New York Times,* November 10, 2010.

Stultz, Newell Maynard. *Afrikaner Politics in South Africa, 1934–1948.* Oakland: University of California Press, 1974.

Sugrue, Thomas J. "Hearts and Minds." Review of Richard Thompson Ford, *The Race Card*; Randall Kennedy, *Sellout*; Bill Cosby and Alan Poussaint, *Come on People*; and Stephen Steinberg, *Race Relations: A Critique. The Nation,* April 24, 2008.

"Summary of the 1919 Chicago Race Riots." *Chicago 1919: Confronting the Race Riots,* February 10, 2021. https://www.chicago1919.org/resources.

Tayler, Judith. "'Our Poor': The Politicisation of the Poor White Problem, 1932–1942." *Kleio* 24, no. 1 (1992): 40–65.

Thomas, Dorothy. *Social and Economic Aspects of Swedish Population Movements, 1750–1933.* New York: Macmillan, 1941.

Thompson, Leonard. *A History of South Africa.* 3rd ed. New Haven, CT: Yale University Press, 2001.

Thornbrough, Emma L. "Booker T. Washington as Seen by His White Contemporaries." *Journal of Negro History* 53, no. 2 (1968): 161–182.

Tilley, Helen. *Africa as a Living Laboratory: Empire, Development, and the Problem of Scientific Knowledge, 1870–1950.* Chicago: University of Chicago Press, 2011.

Tittle, Diana. *Rebuilding Cleveland: The Cleveland Foundation and Its Evolving Urban Strategy.* Columbus: Ohio State University Press, 1992.

Tolman, William H. *Social Engineering: A Record of Things Done by American Industrialists Employing Upwards of One and One-Half Million of People.* New York: McGraw, 1909.

Townsend, Robert B. "The AHA in the Second World War: Trying to Win the Peace with Wartime Pamphlets." *Perspectives on History*, April 1, 2009. https://www.historians.org /publications-and-directories/perspectives-on-history/april-2009/the-aha-in-the -second-world-war-trying-to-win-the-peace-with-wartime-pamphlets.

"Tribute to Lord Hailey." *African Affairs* 61, no. 243 (April 1962): 94–96.

Tushnet, Mark. *Brown v. Board of Education: A Documentary History.* New York: Franklin Watts 1995.

———. *Making Civil Rights Law: Thurgood Marshall and the Supreme Court, 1936–1961.* New York: Oxford University Press, 1994.

———. *Making Constitutional Law: Thurgood Marshall and the Supreme Court.* New York: Oxford University Press, 1997.

———. *NAACP's Legal Strategy against Segregated Education, 1925–1950.* Chapel Hill: University of North Carolina Press, 1987.

———, ed. *The Warren Court in Historical Perspective.* Charlottesville: University Press of Virginia, 1993.

Tuttle, William M., Jr. *Race Riot: Chicago in the Red Summer of 1919.* New York: Atheneum, 1970.

Van Deburg, William L. *Modern Black Nationalism: From Marcus Garvey to Louis Farrakkan.* New York: New York University Press, 1997.

Vitalis, Robert. *Africa, the Politics of Unity: An Analysis of a Contemporary Social Movement.* New York: Random House, 1969.

———. *White World Order, Black Power Politics: The Birth of American International Relations.* Ithaca, NY: Cornell University Press, 2015.

Von Eschen, Penny. *Race against Empire: Black Americans and Anticolonialism, 1937–1957.* Ithaca, NY: Cornell University Press, 1997.

Vucetic, Srdjan. *The Anglosphere: A Genealogy of a Racialized Identity in International Relations.* Stanford, CA: Stanford University Press, 2011.

Wala, Michael. *The Council on Foreign Relations and American Foreign Policy in the Early Cold War.* Providence, RI: Berghahn Books, 1990.

Walker, Darren. "Towards a New Gospel of Wealth." Ford Foundation, October 1, 2015. https://www.fordfoundation.org/equals-change/post/toward-a-new-gospel-of-wealth.

Wall, Cheryl A. *The Harlem Renaissance: A Very Short Introduction.* New York: Oxford University Press, 2016.

Wallerstein, Immanuel. *Africa, the Politics of Unity: An Analysis of a Contemporary Social Movement.* New York: Random House, 1967.

Walton, Hanes, Jr., Cheryl M. Miller, and Joseph M. Cormick II "Race and Political Science: The Dual Traditions of Race Relations Politics and African American Politics."

In *Political Science in History: Research Programs and Political Traditions*, edited by James Farr, John S. Dryzek, and Stephen T. Leonard, 145–174. New York: Cambridge University Press, 1995.

Washington, Robert. "Horace Cayton: Reflections on an Unfulfilled Sociological Career." *American Sociologist* 28, no. 1 (1997): 55–74.

West, Earl H. "The Peabody Education Fund and Negro Education, 1867–1880." *History of Education Quarterly* 6, no. 2 (1996): 3–21.

White, Richard. *The Republic for Which It Stands: The United States during Reconstruction and the Gilded Age, 1865–1896*. New York: Oxford University Press, 2017.

White, Walter. *A Man Called White: The Autobiography of Walter White*. New York: Viking Press, 1948.

Whitehead, Clive. "Education Policy in British Tropical Africa: The 1925 White Paper in Retrospect." *History of Education* 10, no. 3 (1981): 195–203.

Whitman, Mark. *Brown v. Board of Education: A Documentary History*. Princeton, NJ: Markus Weiner, 1993.

Wilcocks, R. W. *Psychological Report: The Poor White*. Vol. 2 of *The Poor White Problem in South Africa: Report of the Carnegie Commission*. Stellenbosch: Pro ecclesia-drukkery, 1932.

Wilkerson, Doxey A. Introduction to *The Negro People in America: A Critique of Gunnar Myrdal's "An American Dilemma,"* edited by Herbert Aptheker, 7–16. New York: International Publishers, 1946.

Willoughby-Herard, Tiffany. *Waste of a White Skin: Carnegie Corporation and the Racial Logic of White Vulnerability*. Oakland: University of California Press, 2015.

Wilson, P. W. "Africa, the Continent of Misunderstandings *Report of an Education Mission Revises Current Notions*: Review of *Education in East Africa*." *New York Times*, May 24, 1925.

———. "End of the 'Great Dark Continent': Review of *Education in Africa*." *New York Times*, December 24, 1922.

Wisselgren, Per. "Reforming the Science-Policy Boundary: The Myrdals and the Swedish Tradition of Governmental Commissions." In *Academics as Public Intellectuals*, edited by Sven Eliaeson and Ragnvald Kalleberg, 173–195. Newcastle: Cambridge Scholars, 2008.

Worcester, Kenton W. *Social Science Research Council, 1923–1998*. New York: Social Science Research Council, 2001.

Woofter, T. J., Jr. "The Status of Racial and Ethnic Groups." In President's Research Committee on Social Trends, *Recent Social Trends in the United States*, 553–601.

Woodson, C. G. "Thomas Jesse Jones." *Journal of Negro History* 35, no. 1 (1950): 107–109.

Worthington, E. Barton. "Lord Hailey on the African Survey: Some Comments." *African Affairs* 89, no. 357 (October 1990): 579–583.

Wright Rigueur, Leah. *The Loneliness of the Black Republican: Pragmatic Politics and the Pursuit of Power*. Princeton, NJ: Princeton University Press, 2015.

Young, Alford A., Jr., and Donald R. Deskins Jr. "Early Traditions of African-American Sociological Thought." *Annual Review of Sociology* 27 (2001): 445–477.

Young, Donald. *Research Memorandum on Minority Peoples in the Depression*. New York: Social Science Research Council, 1937.

Zimmerman, Andrew. *Alabama in Africa: Booker T Washington, the German Empire, and the Globalization of the New South*. Princeton, NJ: Princeton University Press, 2010.

Zunz, Olivier. *Philanthropy in America: A History.* Princeton, NJ: Princeton University Press, 2012.

ENCYCLOPEDIA ENTRIES

Beaver, Daniel R. "Baker, Newton Diehl." In *American National Biography Online,* February 2020.

Beilke, Jayne R. "General Education Board." In *Organizing Black America: An Encyclopedia of African American Associations,* edited by Nina Mjagkij. New York: Garland, 2001.

———. "John F. Slater Fund." In *Organizing Black America: An Encyclopedia of African American Associations,* edited by Nina Mjagkij. New York: Garland, 2001.

———. "Negro Rural School Fund." In *Organizing Black America: An Encyclopedia of African American Associations,* edited by Nina Mjagkij. New York: Garland, 2001

———. "Peabody Education Fund." In *Organizing Black America: An Encyclopedia of African American Associations,* edited by Nina Mjagkij. New York: Garland, 2001.

Bender, Thomas. "Beard, Charles Austin." In *American National Biography Online,* February 2000.

Clarkin, Thomas. "Bunche, Ralph Johnson." In *American National Biography Online,* February 2000.

Cott, Nancy F. "Beard, Mary Ritter." In *American National Biography Online,* February 2000.

Gosden, Peter. "Heath, Sir (Henry) Frank (1863–1946)." In *Oxford Dictionary of National Biography.* London: Oxford University Press, 2008.

Grayson, Richard S. "Layton, Walter Thomas, first Baron Layton." In *Oxford Dictionary of National Biography.* London: Oxford University Press, 2021.

Higgs, Catherine. "Jabavu, Davidson Don Tengo (1885–1959)." In *Dictionary of African Biography,* edited by Emmanuel K. Akyeampong and Henry Louis Gates Jr. New York: Oxford University Press, 2012.

Honoré, Tony. "Feetham, Richard." In *Oxford Dictionary of National Biography Online,* February 2000.

Jackson, John P. "Herskovits, Melville Jean." In *Oxford Dictionary of National Biography Online,* February 2000.

Lach, Edward L., Jr. "Coffman, Lotus Delta." In *Oxford Dictionary of National Biography Online,* February 2000.

Lagemann, Ellen Condliffe. "Keppel, Frederick Paul." *Oxford Dictionary of National Biography Online,* February 2000.

Lavin, Deborah. "Duncan, Sir Patrick." In *Oxford Dictionary of National Biography.* London: Oxford University Press, 2004.

Little, Monroe. "Higher Education." In *Encyclopedia of the Harlem Renaissance,* edited by Cary D. Wintz and Paul Finkelman. New York: Routledge, 2004.

Lowe, Roy. "Sadler, Sir Michael Ernest (1861–1943)." In *Oxford Dictionary of National Biography.* London: Oxford University Press, 2004.

Manning, Kenneth R. "Just, Ernest Everett." In *American National Biography.* New York: Oxford University Press, 1999.

Marks, Shula. "Smuts, Jan Christiaan (1870–1950)." In *Oxford Dictionary of National Biography.* London: Oxford University Press, 2004.

May, Alex. "Coupland, Sir Reginald." In *Oxford Dictionary of National Biography*. London: Oxford University Press, 2004.

———. "Curtis, Lionel George." In *Oxford Dictionary of National Biography*. London: Oxford University Press, 2004.

———. "Kerr, Philip Henry, Eleventh Marquess of Lothian." In *Oxford Dictionary of National Biography*. London: Oxford University Press, 2004.

———. "Milner's Kindergarten." In *Oxford Dictionary of National Biography*. London: Oxford University Press, 2005.

Nepa, Francesco L. "Harris, Abram Lincoln, Jr." In *American National Biography Online*, February 2000.

Rickett, Denis. "Salter, (James) Arthur, Baron Salter (1881–1975)." In *Oxford Dictionary of National Biography*. London: Oxford University Press, 2004.

Stepto, Robert. "Brown, Sterling Allen." In *American National Biography Online*, February 2000.

Stockwell, Sarah. "Pedler, Sir Frederick Johnson." In *Oxford Dictionary of National Biography*. London: Oxford University Press, 2008.

Wall, Joseph Frazier. "Carnegie, Andrew." In *American National Biography Online*, February 2000.

Walters, Ronald. "Pan-Africanism." In *Encyclopedia of African American History, 1896 to the Present: From the Age of Segregation to the Twenty-First Century*, edited by Paul Finkelman. New York: Oxford University Press, 2006.

# Index

CPSIA information can be obtained
at www.ICGtesting.com
Printed in the USA
LVHW092307011121
702185LV00006B/313

9 781469 664743